Irish American Ancestors: Using U.S. Strategies and Records to Identify Irish Origins

By Dwight A. Radford

Getting Them Over the Water—An Irish Immigration Strategies Series, Vol.3

Published by Family Roots Publishing Co., LLC
P.O. Box 1682
Orting, Washington 98360-1682
www.FamilyRootsPublishing.com

Library of Congress Control Number: 2021930062

Softbound: 978-1-62859-297-9
eBook: 978-1-62859-298-6
Item #: FR0153

Printed in the United States of America

Recommended Citation:
Radford, Dwight A. *Irish American Ancestors: Using U.S. Strategies and Records to Identify Irish Origins.* Orting, Washington: Family Roots Publishing Co., LLC, 2022.

Other volumes currently in this series:

Vol. 1: Radford, Dwight A. *American Scots-Irish Research: Strategies and Sources in the Quest for Ulster-Scots Origins.* Orting, Washington: Family Roots Publishing Co., LLC, 2020. Item #: FR0151

Vol. 2: Radford, Dwight A. *Discovering Irish Origins Using the Records of Ireland.* Orting, Washington: Family Roots Publishing Co., LLC, 2021. Item #: FR0152

All maps and charts were commissioned from and are used by permission and courtesy of E. Wade Hone unless otherwise noted. All rights reserved.

Front Cover: Manhattan Bridge and Empire State Building seen from Washington Street in the DUMBO neighborhood, Brooklyn, New York. *Shutterstock 11699608.*

Dedication

Once again, I dedicate this book to two of my good friends whose devoted assistance and donated time made this work possible. First, to Karen Meyn of Pennsylvania, who spent countless hours with the manuscript and questioning me so that the text would emerge as comprehensible as possible. Writing about and explaining genealogy is difficult, and she was on my left side throughout it all despite other commitments. Second, to Wade Hone of Utah, whose friendship over the last 30 years resulted in his creation of an amazing layout of graphics for the book. He was on my right side while withstanding daily interferences.

Both Karen and Wade are my inspiration for never allowing any circumstance to be a hindrance to friendship and love. They are indeed the best friends one could have. It has been my honor to be part of their lives.

Dwight Radford
West Valley City, Utah
U.S.A

Maps, Images, Charts, Photographs, Reference Aids

Photographs/Illustrations

Ecclesiastical/Spiritualist/Religious Orders

Access/Reference Aids

Abbreviations Referenced in Maps and Text

ASPR = American Society for Psychical Research
BLM = Bureau of Land Management
FHL = Family History Library
GLO = General Land Office
INS = Immigration and Naturalization Services
NEHGS = New England Historic Genealogical Society
NESCA = The New England Spiritualist Campmeeting Association
NSAC = National Spiritualist Association of Churches
PerSI = Periodical Source Index
PRONI = Public Record Office of Northern Ireland
TNSA = The National Spiritualist Alliance

Table of Contents

Foreword

By Ann Eccles

One of the first lessons a competent family historian appreciates is to start with the known and move backward by generation, verifying facts to discover an Irish place of origin for an ancestor. In doing so, we look for the best help we can find.

This is the third in a series of guides to researching Irish ancestors that Dwight Radford has developed. In this volume, he reviews American sources that can be used to push Irish ancestral investigations to successful conclusions, offering strategies to assist family historians and genealogists in their quests.

While the author covers basic resources, many of which are contained in other guides to genealogical study, what gives this book distinction is the inclusion of sources that are sometimes overlooked or less frequently explained. And Radford explains their value. He links both general and unique American documents through examples and sage advice about scrutinizing them.

In the chapter on church records, he describes the registers of the major religions (Catholic, Baptist, and Episcopal) as well as those of smaller religious denominations, such as Congregational, Religious Society of Friends (Quakers), United Society of Believers in Christ's Second Appearing (Shakers), and the Stone Campbell Movement.

Throughout the book, record types and strategies that enable the tracing of an ancestor's life are outlined. Radford goes beyond the popular websites to investigate lesser-known resources, describing how to use them to supplement other ones. His examples are based on experience as a professional genealogist. In each chapter, he includes mainline and minor repositories, describing both and often adding "the exceptions to the rule." Incorporated are lists of older published works of early newspapers and directories that provide additional background and facts for lineages.

He emphasizes techniques for locating potential immigration evidence as well as additional methods for digging deeper for more information. Such clues may be found among material from the investigations of other family members.

Researchers who have trouble finding facts about an Irish ancestor will appreciate this book's extra points. The final chapters delineate specific strategies for four unique inquiries: early colonial convicts, indentured servants, runaways, and the "Spirited Away"; African American descendants of an Irish slave holder; family background of Catholics in religious life; and connections with American Spiritualism.

Radford highlights United States records and sources that are most useful or sought when a brick wall presents itself in the path to discovery. This book is a great addition to any Irish family historian's personal library.

Ann Eccles, President
Irish Genealogical Society International
Mendota Heights, Minnesota, USA

Introduction

By Dwight A. Radford

As a professional genealogist for over thirty years, I have scrutinized lineages from innumerable perspectives. Just when I conclude that no other angle could lead to identifying a birthplace in Ireland, another one presents itself. This is the nature of Irish immigration: convoluted, contradictory, frustrating, and from a genealogist's standpoint, brutal. In fact, some professionals simply refuse to undertake an Irish immigrant research case. Although I understand their unwillingness, I have found that once a few principles are understood, the study becomes practicable. It does not mean that I always discover where someone was born in Ireland, but throughout the decades, the process of objectively reinvestigating and reinterpreting records and procedures has helped me perceive evidence that otherwise can be overlooked.

Irish American Ancestors: Using U.S. Strategies and Records to Identify Origins (Orting, Washington: Family Roots Publishing Company, LLC, 2022) is the third in my series addressing Irish immigration research. It is aimed at assisting both Americans and Canadians with their difficult investigations. With so much migration back and forth across the border, Canadians with American ancestries, or, more specifically, Irish-American ancestries, are plentiful. The first and second volumes in my collection are:

American Scots-Irish Research: Strategies and Sources in the Quest for Ulster-Scots Origins (Orting, Washington: Family Roots Publishing Co., LLC, 2020).

Discovering Irish Origins Using the Records of Ireland (Orting, Washington: Family Roots Publishing Co., LLC, 2021).

The books, with this being only the third, have expanded chapters without too much duplication between them. Some repetition of concepts is expected and intentional because certain ideas and research tactics are so important that they need to be stressed. Thus, if the researcher misses them in one chapter or book, the concepts are in another. All in my series are intended to be utilized together to provide a more holistic framework from which to explore proven strategies or to design new ones. The goal is to identify immigrants' birthplaces in Ireland.

In the present book, several chapters are longer than others. Some topics are straightforward, saying what I mean and meaning what I say, without belaboring them. Other subjects are extensive because not much is published about them from an immigration standpoint or, as presented in "Church Records," from even a denominational one. These chapters are intended to reduce the gaps.

General Strategies and Sources

Genealogy instruction books appropriately list primary and secondary sources for investigating families, and that information is contained in this volume as well. Most guides, however, lack strategies to accompany the listings of records. The omissions are usually because every family research problem is different. There is no universal answer, especially for identifying immigrants' origins in Ireland.

A birthplace in Ireland noted in an American record is exceptional. If happened upon, though, sometimes it yet is not enough to benefit fully from the Irish records. If a birthplace is not found in the American records and all the primary and secondary sources have been exhausted, research customarily must take an unusual approach. Often, these same documents have to be revisited for inferences. This plan may indirectly yield a birthplace. For example, who were the godparents at the christenings of the immigrant's children? Obviously, they were trusted family or friends. Maybe they were from the same place in Ireland as the ancestor was, and so following them can potentially identify birthplaces.

Knowing who the siblings are is also mandatory in tracing an Irish ancestor. Although the parents' names are not known, it was common, for instance, for a family member to join another who was already in America. Treating the siblings with equal research skill increases the chance that the birthplace in Ireland or the names of parents are in one of their records. Logically, they were all from the same place in Ireland. Under no circumstances in Irish immigrant research can the effort be limited to only the direct line. Doing so is a barrier to successful results.

Who went where is another investigative aspect. Tracking and documenting either a cousin or a sibling of the direct line anywhere they migrated is important. If Irish origins are not found through the American branch, concentrate on the sibling who went to Canada or Australia. The answer may lie there. If Uncle Joe homesteaded in Colorado, look for his homestead case file, which did require birthplaces and naturalization information. If Aunt Mary joined a convent, search for her records. Her birthplace may be within the documents of the motherhouse of her order.

General United States Reference Books

Over the decades, countless books have been written about American research in general or a specific topic, such as land records or cemetery records. In today's technological world, any reference book is nearly outdated the moment it is published. However, a reliable one will have information about how to use a record source, and what to expect from it will not change. The discussions vary only about where records are located and, of course, the never-ending appearances of databases. Strategies remain the same regardless of the date the book was published. Recommended works on United States research that can supplement the material presented in this book or reveal new sources include:

Eichholz, Alice. *Redbook: American State, County, and Town Sources*. Provo, Utah: Ancestry Publishing, 2004.

Greenwood, Val D. *The Researcher's Guide to American Genealogy*. 4th ed., Baltimore, Maryland: Genealogical Publishing Company, 2017.

The Handybook for Genealogists: United States of America. 10th ed., Draper, Utah: Everton Publishers, 2002.

Radford, Dwight. *American Scots-Irish Research: Strategies and Sources in the Quest for Ulster-Scots Origins*. Orting, Washington: Family Roots Publishing, 2020.

Szucs, Loretto Dennis and Sandra Hargreaves Luebking. *The Source: A Guidebook to American Genealogy*. 3rd ed., Provo, Utah: Ancestry, 2006.

Research Libraries

Through the years, a few archives and libraries—aside from the well-known National Archives, Library of Congress, and state archives—have become pilgrimage places for family historians. Among them are:

- Allen County Public Library, Fort Wayne, Indiana
- BYU Family History Center, Provo, Utah
- Clayton Library of the Houston Public Library System, Houston, Texas
- Dallas Public Library, Dallas, Texas
- Family History Library, Salt Lake City, Utah
- Midwest Genealogy Center of Mid-Continent Public Library, Independence, Missouri
- New England Historic Genealogical Society, Boston, Massachusetts
- Newberry Library, Chicago, Illinois
- St. Louis County Library, St. Louis, Missouri
- Sutro Library, San Francisco, California
- Wisconsin Historical Society, Madison, Wisconsin

The most eminent library related to genealogy is the Family History Library in Salt Lake City, which houses the largest collection of books, microfilm, digitized images, and periodicals in the world. To digitize materials, it has working relationships with libraries across the country as well as those belonging to the National Archives, state archives, and church libraries. Furthermore, its reach is worldwide, multiplying its holdings to a scope that is staggering to comprehend. Its free website, FamilySearch.org, hosts digitized images in the public domain or where contracts permit.

Special Strategy Chapters

Included in this book are four "Special Strategy" chapters. Each is focused on a subject that requires more space than a standard chapter allows.

The first Special Strategy chapter is "Convicts, Indentured Servants, and the 'Spirited Away' (1615 to 1776)." It explains the repulsive industry of human trafficking. Under this institutionalized system, the poor, criminal, and unwanted under English rule or conquest were taken to the colonies and sold on the auction blocks to work on the plantations. These were whites: convicts, indentured servants, and even the kidnapped ("spirited away"). The Irish were an integral part of this trade. It was an unsettling period in American history, and almost everyone who has colonial roots has an ancestor who was in some sort of bondage. Also, part of the topic is the tri-racial isolates: the bi-racial, tri-racial, or quadroons who can be traced to these same white servants arriving in bondage. An enslaved African man having children with an Irish indentured woman was not uncommon.

The second Special Strategy is "African Americans and the Irish Slave Holder," which describes another disreputable facet of American history, the African slave trade. So many African Americans have Irish ancestors that identifying the slave owners becomes the main goal. The methods for finding them are significantly different than they are for traditional Irish-American strategies, where the initial effort is finding the Irish origins.

"Catholic Religious (Priests, Brothers, and Nuns)" is the third Special Strategy, about respected family members who can be overlooked in research. Men and women who joined orders were educated, dedicated to service, and often, well-traveled. The possibility of finding a paper trail for their lives is increased because of their activities. Perhaps most important is the candidates' processes of joining orders because their backgrounds were detailed, and frequently, birthplaces and parents' names were among those questions. In fact, their records may be the only ones with birthplaces more exact than just Ireland for immigrant families.

The fourth Special Strategy is "The Irish and American Spiritualism," a primer to a little-known area in American religious history. While it does examine some of the records left behind, it also attempts an instruction for recognizing an ancestor who might have been involved in Spiritualism. For many readers, this unfamiliar field is associated with the occult. However, the word *occult* was used in the nineteenth century to mean "hidden" as opposed to *apocalypse,* which meant "revealed." It had nothing to do with evil. Only later did the word evolve into something more sinister, which process did little to help researchers understand it today. There is no doubt that it is a quirky and colorful matter by any standard.

Conclusions

My objective in writing this book is to share the many surprising and exciting possibilities I have encountered as a professional genealogist. I realize some of this material is new and even strange. Nonetheless, the present work and the others I have written on Irish immigration are meant to demonstrate the point that Irish heritage is much more complicated and fascinating than most people realize. It is certainly deeper than the green leprechauns and shamrocks surrounding us on Saint Patrick's Day. It encompasses all racial lines, religious groups, and ethnic backgrounds. It is the story of being human, with its mixture of beauty and ugliness. I do not shy away from the repellent and the trauma in this presentation.

Irish-American research is difficult. This is not the final word on it but only the introduction to strategies of looking beyond the obvious in sources. My hope is that family historians in both the United States and Canada will continue the exploration.

Dwight A. Radford
West Valley City, Utah, USA

Figure 1: Irish graves at the Oakland Cemetery in Oakland, California, USA. (Image courtesy of the Historic Oakland Foundation. Permissions received.)

Chapter One

Cemeteries and Tombstones

Tombstones and cemetery records are a major part of a strategy for Irish immigration research. The two categories are not necessarily the same. Among Irish Catholics of all classes, birthplaces were often engraved on tombstones. With less frequency, they can be found on Protestant stones as well, especially among the moneyed class. Birthplaces can also be preserved in the records maintained by cemetery staffs.

Cemeteries are an exceptionally popular topic among family historians, and books have been published about how to properly approach this area of research. Some are centered on the tombstones and cemetery records, and others are concentrated on the symbols on the tombstones. Excellent works on this topic include:

Bartley, Scott Andrew. *Researching American Cemetery Records*. Toronto, Ontario: Heritage Productions, 2005.

Carmack, Sharon DeBartolo. *Your Guide to Cemetery Research*. Cincinnati, Ohio: Betterway Books, 2002.

Greenwood, Val D. "Cemetery and Burial Records," *The Researcher's Guide to American Genealogy*. 4th ed., Baltimore, Maryland: Genealogical Publishing Company, 2017, pp. 727-738.

Snider, Tui. *Understanding Cemetery Symbols: A Field Guide for Historic Graveyards*. [Place of publication not identified]: Castle Azle Press, 2017.

Szucs, Loretto Dennis and Sandra Hargreaves Luebking. *The Source: A Guidebook to American Genealogy*. 3rd ed., Provo, Utah: Ancestry, 2006., pp. 634-646, 861-862.

Where People Are Buried

When searching for records, remember that Irish Catholics might or might not have been interred in the graveyards of their own churches, and sometimes, a cemetery was predominantly for one ethnicity. Therefore, the Germans, Italians, Slovaks, and Irish Catholics were not inevitably buried in the same Catholic cemetery. What is certain is that because the ground is consecrated by the Church, only Catholics are to be buried there.

Protestants could be buried anywhere, which does bring some challenges to Irish Protestant cemetery research. Often, it is best to find a compilation of all tombstones in a cemetery or in a county to assure nothing has been missed. The natural assumption is that before embalming became customary, people were interred close to home, and so a Presbyterian might have been buried in the cemetery attached to the Methodist church if it was the closest community cemetery.

Rural cases present an immigration research strategy so straightforward that it is stunning. One such instance is the Catholic graveyard on Irish Mountain, Raleigh County, West Virginia. It sits above the New River and was settled beginning in 1855 by Irish immigrants. Its consecrated ground is around the old chapel building; however, the community was surrounded by a sea of Protestants. For this reason, Catholic and Protestant names may be the same in the area, but none of the people are related. Concentrating on the Irish Mountain Catholic graveyard limits the search to Catholics in the county. The process of sorting through common names can be used in any locality as long as the Catholics were buried in the consecrated cemetery and all others, elsewhere. It can also be done in reverse, with Protestants encircled by a sea of Catholics.

In the case of Irish Mountain, an overabundance of tombstones provides places of birth. Most are from County Clare and County Kerry, which border each other, more or less confirming a migration pattern from that area of Ireland.

The Tombstone Marker

Exactly what may or may not be engraved on a tombstone cannot be certain until a photograph or a transcript of it is studied. Even with that, some care has to be taken. Were birthplaces on the stone included in a published transcript? It is becoming customary for individuals or genealogical societies to transcribe, index, and publish all the information from cemeteries in their counties. A painstakingly compiled transcription includes additional details, such as "wife of" or "born Westmeath, Ireland," and is an appropriate point to consider in tombstone research.

The same questions arise with websites such as Findagrave.com or Billiongraves.com. It is difficult to rely on anything researchers add to hosted pictures of tombstones. This extra information is not on the tombstones, and while it may be beneficial, countless errors are attached. When someone inserts an obituary with the source, it is an amazing contribution. Sites such as Findagrave.com are as helpful as they can be, but they sometimes have photographs of only a side of each of the larger, erect tombstones, leaving the other three sides to the imagination. Therefore, continue asking questions about what is being viewed.

Keep in mind that in urban areas, the interments of many people are in one family's lot because space is at a premium. Consequently, a tombstone seldom reflects everyone buried at the site, and so cemetery records (sexton records) are valuable.

Three examples demonstrate that tombstone research has to be tailored according to circumstances of their locations. The first: two urban Calvary Cemeteries in Queens, New York; the second:

Figure 2: Calvary Cemetery in Queens Borough, Woodside, New York. This burial ground is divided into four large sections, one of which is referred to as "First" or "Old Cavalry." Currently, more than 1.75 million interments have occurred in Calvary, the largest cemetery in the United States. (Photograph courtesy of PlowboyLifestyle, 2006.)

surveys conducted before the grave removals by the Tennessee Valley Authority when the valley was flooded; and the third: removals and transfers of the San Francisco graveyards to mass gravesites in Colma, California. Records generated from all three were based upon the circumstances and the times, and they also explain what happened to tombstones in the process.

The first example is from the two-volume work by Rosemary Muscarella Ardolina, *Old Calvary Cemetery: New Yorkers Carved in Stone* (Bowie, Maryland: Heritage Books, Inc., 1996), and her *Second Calvary Cemetery: New Yorkers Carved in Stone* (Floral Park, New York: Delia Publications, 2000). However, to grasp the scope of these books, the introduction has to be read. In these massive, urban cemeteries in Queens, the stones were in danger of eroding, eradicating the inscriptions forever. A project was undertaken to transcribe and publish all the inscriptions with birthplaces listed on them, which means not all stones were transcribed, an understanding about the scope of this venture that is vital.

These two Queens' graveyards are Roman Catholic, but burials were from all over New York City. The source can be studied with the understanding that if an ancestor's tombstone is not found, it is because no birthplace was on the marker or a tombstone does not exist.

In New York City is another cemetery from which the Irish tombstones have been extracted by Joseph Michael Silinonte. His work is *Tombstones of the Irish Born: Cemetery of the Holy Cross, Flatbush, Brooklyn* (Bowie, Maryland: Heritage Books, Inc., 1994) and demonstrates, along with Ardolina's, the principle of individuals recognizing the importance of the Irish Catholic tombstones with birthplaces.

The second example, although bizarre, affects many of the Scots-Irish in the Tennessee Valley area of the Mid-South. When the Tennessee Valley Authority (TVA) began building dams and flooding the valley in the 1930s, it had to move entire communities, cemeteries, and tombstones, resulting in a trove of records. The registers for the cemetery

TVA 714 **GRAVE REMOVAL MASTER FILE**

Name: McCullah, George
Last Name / First Name / Middle Name

Reinterment Cemetery: Bakers Forge Memorial, EH Sec K, Block X, Lot 3 — No. R 4

Original Burial in Gr. No. 97, Cedar Hill — Cem. No. 10

Nearest Relative: Mike McCullah, LaFollette, Tenn. (Address)

Removed By: TVA — Contract By: M. H. Bivins

Removal Date: November 27, 1934

Remarks:

Figure 3: Master File Relocation Card Index for Grave and Cemetery Removal and Relocation, 1934-1954. Records of the Tennessee Valley Authority. (Image courtesy of the National Archives Record Office, East Point, Georgia. This work is in the public domain in the United States because it is a work prepared by an officer or employee of the United States Government as part of that person's official duties under the terms of Title 17, Chapter 1, Section 105 of the U.S. Code.)

relocations have been digitized and are on Ancestry.com in the database "Tennessee Valley Cemetery Relocation Files, 1933-1990."

The digitized books can be searched by state (Alabama, Georgia, Kentucky, North Carolina, and Tennessee); by dam projects, such as Chickamauga Dam; and cemetery removals. The field books are the surveys of the graveyards, whether stones had inscriptions or not; inscriptions; and conditions of the graves. For more recent dam projects, records differ because various maps and surveys were included, but the information is basically the same. These records are priceless because among those removed were early pioneers into the Tennessee Valley as well as veterans of the Revolutionary War, the War of 1812, and the Civil War. Even if a tombstone no longer exists but did in the 1930s and 1940s, a record of it is preserved in the field books of the TVA surveys and relocation files.

The third example is from the city of San Francisco. It was not uncommon for graveyards to be removed as cities expanded. Geographically, San Francisco is a peninsula, and so space was limited. As the city grew and the graveyard filled, the majority of the graves were removed and relocated south to Colma, San Mateo County, which to this day is known as the "City of Souls." It has 1.5 million burials and only 1,509 residents.

As graves were relocated, they were brought to mass pits for reburial in

Counties in which Research of TVA Projects Should Be Considered along with the Dams by which they are Accessed

State	County	Dam/Other	Dates Built
Alabama			
	Franklin County	Cedar Creek Dam	finished 1979
	Jackson County	Bellefonte Nuclear Generating Station	1975-(halted)
	Lauderdale County	Wheeler Dam	1933-1936
	Lawrence County	Wheeler Dam	1933-1936
Georgia			
	Union County	Nottely Dam	1941-1942
Kentucky			
	Livingston County	Gilbertsville Dam	1938-1944
	Livingston County	Land Between the Lakes/Barkley Dam	finished 1966
	Lyons County	Land Between the Lakes/Barkley Dam	finished 1966
	Marshall County	Guntersville Dam	1935-1939
	Marshall County	Gilbertsville Dam	1938-1944
	Trigg County	Land Between the Lakes/Barkley Dam	finished 1966
North Carolina			
	Cherokee County	Hiwassee Dam	1936-1940
	Clay County	Chatuge Dam	1941-1942
	Graham County	Fontana Dam	1942-1943
	Swain County	Fontana Dam	1942-1943
Tennessee			
	Anderson County	Bull Run Fossil Plant	1962-1967
	Anderson County	Norris Dam	1933-1936
	Bedford County	Normandy Dam	finished 1976
	Blount County	Fort Loudon Dam	1940-1943
	Campbell County	Norris Dam	1933-1936
	Carter County	Watauga Dam	1942-1948
	Claiborne County	Norris Dam	1933-1936
	Cocke County	Douglas Dam	1942-1943
	Coffee County	Normandy Dam	finished 1976
	Franklin County	Tim's Ford Dam	1966-1970
	Grainger County	Cherokee Dam	1940-1941
	Hamblin County	Cherokee Dam	1940-1941
	Hamilton County	Chickamauga Dam	1936-1940
	Hardin County	Pickwick Dam	1935-1938
	Humphries County	Johnsonville Fossil Plant	1951-1959
	Jefferson County	Douglas Dam	1942-1943
	Johnson County	Watauga Dam	1942-1948

Counties in which Research of TVA Projects Should Be Considered along with the Dams by which they are Accessed

State	County	Dam/Other	Dates Built
Tennessee (cont)			
	Knox County	Norris Dam	1933-1936
	Knox County	Fort Loudon Dam	1940-1943
	Loudon County	Fort Loudon Dam	1940-1943
	Loudon County	Tellico Dam	1967-1979
	Marion County	Nickajack Dam	1964-1967
	Meigs County	Chickamauga Dam	1936-1940
	Meigs County	Watts Bar	1939-1942
	Monroe County	Tellico Dam	1967-1979
	Moore County	Tim's Ford Dam	1966-1970
	Rhea County	Watts Bar	1939-1942
	Rhea County	Chickamauga Dam	1936-1940
	Roane County	Norris Dam	1933-1936
	Roane County	Watts Bar	1939-1942
	Sevier County	Douglas Dam	1942-1943
	Sullivan County	South Holston Dam	1942-1950
	Sullivan County	Bear Creek Dam	finished 1965
	Sullivan County	Boone Dam	1950-1952
	Sumner County	Gallatin Fossil Plant	1956-2000
	Union County	Norris Dam	1933-1936
	Washington County	Boone Dam	1950-1952
Virginia			
	Washington County	South Holston Dam	1942-1950

Colma. The tombstones did not inevitably go with the remains, and the engravings on the removed stones were not copied. Many of the stones were dumped at Ocean Beach, and others created breakwaters in San Francisco Bay, where they still are exposed by the waves.

To fully appreciate the situation in Colma, its history should be understood. By 1900, San Francisco had banned further burials because of lack of space, but before then, Colma was the site for interring San Francisco residents. The Roman Catholic Archdiocese established Holy Cross Cemetery there in 1887.

In 1914, San Francisco issued eviction notices to cemeteries to remove the graves and monuments. Many people could not afford the $10 fee for each one. Regardless, Colma received hundreds of thousands of bodies. For those who could pay, the monuments were

Study of Old San Francisco Cemeteries Relocated to Colma

Old Cemetery	Established	Removed	Colma Cemetery
Calvary (Catholic)	1860	1937-1940	Holy Cross
IOOF	1864	1933	Green Lawn, Woodland Memorial Park
Lone Mountain/ Laurel Hill	1854	1940	Cypress Lawn
Masonic	1864	1934	Woodland Memorial Park (most), Holy Cross, Cyprus Lawn, National Cemetery
Old Mission	1776	---	Holy Cross
Yerba Buena	1850	1930s	Holy Cross
Golden Gate	1868	1909	various or only stones removed

removed with the bodies. Otherwise, remains went to the mass graves. The relocation projects lasted until after World War II. Since many people did pay the costs for removals, it cannot be assumed that a tombstone is now landfill. Regardless, in tracking down any records for the removal process, an understanding of the old cemeteries and what happened to them is necessary. At that point, the cemetery can be contacted. A study of cemeteries where the Irish, Catholics, and Protestants were buried would look something like the chart at the top of this page.

Some of the tombstones were transcribed before they were moved, but for the others, only the relocation records to Colma exist. A place to start with the search is the digitized collections on FamilySearch.org. For cemetery removals or tombstone transcripts not on the site, contact the new graveyard in Colma or consult various websites such as Findagrave.com and Billiongraves.com. Fascinating details of this convoluted and dark history can be found on Sanfranciscocemeteries.com.

The Cemetery Registers
The other part of cemetery research is determining what documents were constructed by the cemeteries themselves. These are typically burial records and should list every interment from the dates the records began. Rural graveyards most likely do not have files or books until at least the twentieth century, but some of the records for urban areas can date back to the years the cemeteries were established. For small church graveyards, the church burial registers may be the cemetery registers. Registers are not standardized and can consist of plot books, burial registers, and day books. Cemeteries are accustomed to genealogy requests; however, in some states, laws restrict access.

On websites such as Findagrave.com, computerized indexes to the cemetery burial records have regularly been downloaded and added. But, sometimes, it is a little difficult to be certain from where these were acquired. Some cemeteries index their burial registers and place them on the cemetery websites, where they can be searched by name, plot number, or date. Finding them is often as simple as an Internet search for the cemetery in question. Occasionally, a Catholic diocese has a master website with all the burials.

When researching in urban areas, it is essential to identify everyone in the family plot. An urban plot was initially bought by one person, and over the decades, family members were buried in them, many without tombstones. Yet the people should be listed in the registers with at least names, dates of burials, and even maps for where the coffins were placed because the cemetery thus can ensure where the next coffin can be situated. Be aware that in urban cemeteries, some non-family members may also be in the family section. Because of the limited space, family plots were sold for profit.

Birthplaces in Ireland may be in the burial registers themselves. Again, cemeteries do not have standardized records.

A striking example of where birthplaces are noted is St. Joseph's New Cemetery in Cincinnati, Ohio, an important record for Irish Catholics in the city. It was the Irish graveyard, as opposed to Old St. Joseph's Cemetery, which was German. Because the courthouse was burned in 1884 during a riot, many of the primary records for Hamilton County were lost, and so St. Joseph's New Cemetery records are a primary source of birthplace data. The St. Joseph's New Cemetery records are online at the cemetery website, but the extractions do not have entire listings, such as birthplaces. It does provide the addresses for how to obtain the records that do contain that information. These are on microfilm in several repositories, including the Family History Library.

Irish Protestants were buried in numerous Cincinnati cemeteries. One of the best known is the historic Spring Grove Cemetery, whose books usually include birthplaces and parents' names. Its registers were transcribed by the Cincinnati Chapter, D.A.R. in 1963 as "Earliest Records of Spring Grove Cemetery, Cincinnati, Ohio, Hamilton Co., 1826-51." Extractions from the lists of some of those buried there in 1849 with birthplaces specified indicate the large number of Irish Protestants. The records are digitized on FamilySearch.org:

> 545. Smith, Olivia Hannah (John B./Jane M. Smith)
> b. about 1835, Kells, Co. Meath, Ire.
> d. Mar. 30, 1849; rem. fr. Episcopal Cem. Ap. 5, 1849
>
> 679. Love, Robert (John/Mary Love)
> b. 1825, Co. Tyrone, Ire.
> d. June 30, 1849
>
> 698. Stephens, Hellen (Henry/Catherine Kelly)
> b. Feb. 14, 1782, Dublin, Ire.
> d. Jl 7, 1849
>
> 699. Davidson, John (James/Eliza Davidson)

b. about 1824, Co. Tyrone, Ire.
d. July 12, 1849

751. Burland, William H. (John/Elizabeth Burland)
b. Mar. 17, 1810, Tipperrary, Ire.
d. Jl 5, 1849, rem. from Mt. Harrison, Storrs Twp., Hamilton Co., O, Jl 6, 1849

772. Gamble, David (William/Jane Gibbs)
b. Oct. 13, 1826, Dublin, Ire.
d. Ag. 15, 1849

808. Roberts, Thomas
b. Dec. 1808, Ireland
d. Ag. 7, 1849

821. Hampton, John (William/Clementia Hampton)
b. 1829, Dublin, Ire.
d. Ag. 23, 1828 (*sic*)
rem. fr. G. Yeatman's vault ag. 24, 1849

822. Mills, James (Robert/Margaret Mills)
b. 1815, Tatnadarria?, Ire.
d. Sept. 21, 1849

825. Moon, Elizabeth
b. 1831, Co. Derry, Ireland
d. Sept. 22, 1849

858. Sands, Nancy Eliza (James/Barbara Murdock)
b. 1823, Belfast, Ire.
d. Oct. 24, 1849

The prudent approach is to make sure nothing from a cemetery has been missed and not to limit the search to the presence or absence of a tombstone.

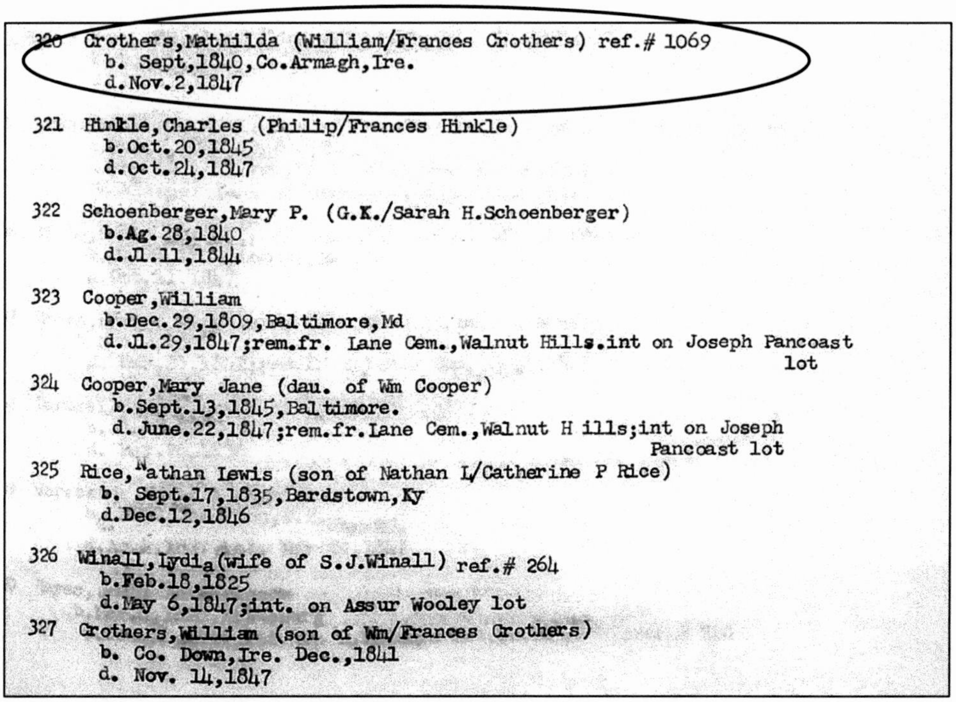

320 Crothers,Mathilda (William/Frances Crothers) ref.# 1069
b. Sept,1840,Co.Armagh,Ire.
d.Nov.2,1847

321 Hinkle,Charles (Philip/Frances Hinkle)
b.Oct.20,1845
d.Oct.24,1847

322 Schoenberger,Mary P. (G.K./Sarah H.Schoenberger)
b.Ag.28,1840
d.Jl.11,1844

323 Cooper,William
b.Dec.29,1809,Baltimore,Md
d.Jl.29,1847;rem.fr. Lane Cem.,Walnut Hills.int on Joseph Pancoast lot

324 Cooper,Mary Jane (dau. of Wm Cooper)
b.Sept.13,1845,Baltimore.
d.June.22,1847;rem.fr.Lane Cem.,Walnut H ills;int on Joseph Pancoast lot

325 Rice,Nathan Lewis (son of Nathan L/Catherine P Rice)
b. Sept.17,1835,Bardstown,Ky
d.Dec.12,1846

326 Winall,Lydia(wife of S.J.Winall) ref.# 264
b.Feb.18,1825
d.May 6,1847;int. on Assur Wooley lot

327 Crothers,William (son of Wm/Frances Crothers)
b. Co. Down,Ire. Dec.,1841
d. Nov. 14,1847

Figure 4: From "Earliest Records of Spring Grove Cemetery, Cincinnati, Ohio, Hamilton Co., 1826-1851," by Cincinnati Chapter, D.A.R. (Image courtesy of Genealogical Records Committee, Cincinnati Chapter, D.A.R.)

Selected Quick-Reference Observations for U.S. Censuses

1790: The 1790 federal population count was not completed until March of 1792 and thus encompassed individuals who may have been born after 1790. Vermont was admitted to the union in 1791 and was a special addition to the 1790 census, being taken as the family existed in April 1791 rather than in August 1790.

1810: The 1810 enumeration was the first census to separate the District of Columbia from those of Maryland and Virginia even though the district had been created in 1792.

1820: An individual could appear in both the 16-18 and the 16-26 age categories, giving the impression of a larger than actual household. This was the first census to ask for the number of persons in the home not naturalized.

1830: The 1830 census was the first to provide printed forms for enumerators. It also asked for numbers of "aliens" (persons not naturalized).

1840: This census asked for the specific ages of Revolutionary War pensioners in the home.

1850-1870: The 1850 census began the practice of listing each member in the household by name, age, sex, color, and birthplace. Although the information was slightly different for each decade, the next two censuses, in 1860 and 1870, were similar in content. They included questions about who was married within the year, whether a person was blind, insane, or "idiotic," and occupations of those over age 15.

Other important questions for each person were: for 1850, school attendance within the year; 1860 and 1870, value of real estate and personal estate; 1870, ability to read or write and whether father or mother was of foreign birth.

If your ancestor lived in the Indian Territory in 1860, now known as Oklahoma, and was not Native American, check the 1860 census index for the state of Arkansas.

1880: In addition to previous questions, this census asked for each household member's marital status, relationship to head of household, and birthplace of parents.

1900: This census added questions about how many children were born to the mother and how many were still living, each person's exact month and year of birth instead of just an age, how many years married, and year of immigration.

1910: Questions added about primary language spoken and service in the Civil War.

1920: Added questions about whether naturalized and year of naturalization.

1930: Asked for age at first marriage.

1940: Asked for place of foreign birth as it was known on 1 January 1937, thus avoiding place-name changes occurring during World War II. It also asked for a person's residence in 1935 for comparison to residence in 1940.

Chapter Two

Census Records

The federal and state censuses in the United States are vital to Irish immigrant research. For most of them, countries were recorded as the places of births, but the enumerators on occasion named counties or cities as well. Because the censuses often have Ireland in some schedules and a different place in another schedule, they can be exasperating. Remember that who provided the information and under what circumstances are not known. Therefore, neighbors, children, or grandchildren might have answered the enumerators' questions if the heads of households were not available. Ultimately, the census takers did not care.

Censuses are a fascinating topic and have been a part of American history since 1790. Entire books have been written about how to use these indispensable record collections for genealogy. Foremost among them are:

Dollarhide, William. *The Census Book: Facts, Schedules & Worksheets for the U.S. Federal Censuses*. Orting, Washington: Family Roots Publishing, 2019.

Hinckley, Kathleen W. *Your Guide to the Federal Census for Genealogists, Researchers, and Family Historians*. Cincinnati, Ohio: Betterway Books, 2002.

Lainhart, Ann S. *State Census Records*. Baltimore, Maryland: Genealogical Publishing Company, 1992.

Szucs, Loretto Dennis and Matthew Wright. *Finding Answers in U.S. Census Records*. Orem, Utah: Ancestry Publishing, 2001.

The United States censuses from 1790 to 1940 are widely accessible online. The most frequently used websites are Ancestry.com, FamilySearch.org, Findmypast.com, and MyHeritage.com.

General Research Strategy
Spellings, names, and the indexes themselves can potentially be issues in any of the United States censuses. Never take for granted that a search is over if no applicable results are found. If a county or town where the ancestors lived is known, a page-by-page search of that particular schedule may need to be undertaken. An indexer might not have recognized the name and thus inaccurately interpreted it into the database index. Sometimes, because the writing is so poor, it is not the

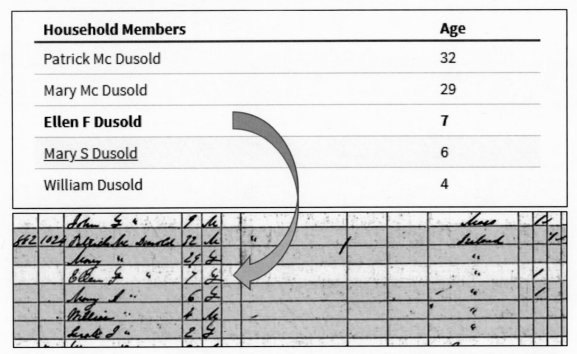

Household Members	Age
Patrick Mc Dusold	32
Mary Mc Dusold	29
Ellen F Dusold	7
<u>Mary S Dusold</u>	6
William Dusold	4

Figure 5: 1860 Federal census of Spencer, Worcester County, Massachusetts, showing Ellen F. Dusold in an online index although the census reads Ellen F. McDonald. This is a frequent challenge for researchers when indexers are not experienced enough to decipher older handwriting styles. (Image courtesy of the National Archives and Records Administration.)

fault of the indexer, as the name would have to be known ahead of time. Assume that, as the researcher, the surname being sought will be recognized no matter how mistakenly or sloppily it might have been written. If that fails, again read one page at a time for first names, not surnames.

One important consideration when using indexes is that the censuses might not have been created by American indexers. The number of times Ireland, especially when abbreviated as "Ir" or "Ire" becomes "Indiana" or "India" is stunning. If problems are encountered when using indexes, it may be sensible to omit Ireland as the birthplace. Also are cases in the post-1850 census schedules where counties are listed, such as "Co. Cork,

Ireland," and it is indexed strangely as "Central African Republic." Such indexing issues have provided researchers with hours of frustration and amusement.

Often, it is wise and helpful to double-check findings with indexes produced by counties' genealogy societies or genealogists. They are familiar with the names, and, habitually, their publications or websites note how they were recorded versus what they should be.

When searching a census, confirm first that a family was or was not enumerated. Reading through the neighborhood in which the ancestor was thought to be residing and then reconstructing it in the census to where the ancestor seems to be missing is a strategy that is successful, particularly in farming areas where people owned property and were physically and geographically stable. It does not work quite as well in urban areas because people moved every couple of years and rented their apartments. This tactic can avoid problems such as common-law arrangements, children with step-fathers' surnames, or even blended families. Yet, it might be the final confirmation that the census enumerator did overlook the family in the census.

The blended family in the census reports can be easily missed, especially when it is not expected. A merged family is his children, her children, and, possibly, their children, and they can be obfuscated if civil or church marriages are incomplete, destroyed, or nonexistent in an area. They also may be indistinguishable without death records and tombstones. This discussion applies to post-1850 censuses.

What makes this topic important in reconstructing an Irish immigrant family is that a man might have had three wives over the decades, all named Mary. In Irish culture, especially among Catholics, this was not unusual. Unless the researcher is paying close attention to ages, it may seem like they are all the same Mary. If all the Marys were born in Ireland, inconsistencies in the children's ages are a needed clue. However, historically, the high rate of infant mortality can also explain years between births without the families having been blended. If intervals of time between children's ages are noted, sorting through the multiple marriages in databases under the name of

the husband is advantageous, especially if the marriages occurred between the gaps in the children's births as listed in the censuses.

Common-law marriages can conceal the presence of blended families and explain the absence of registered marriages. They occurred with some regularity in bygone eras, and a hundred years from now, researchers will be saying the same about the present time. In common-law marriages, where there were the husband's children, the wife's children, and the children of the couple, the surnames as recorded in the censuses are another clue. Be aware, though, that the names could be in the following enumerations with the fathers' or the step-fathers' surnames. This is predictable and does not consequently signify "adoptions" between the two census reports, as many researchers surmise. Additional evidence of a blended family from the census reports is two children with the same name but with different ages, for example, two Catherines, aged 7 and 9, with the same last name.

Another pivotal strategy is required for using indexes, if not the censuses themselves, when O and Mc (Mac) are before surnames. Researchers should not be looking for exact surnames. Illiterate or semi-literate cultures were not thinking in precise terms, and so O'Donnell became Donnell. When the census enumerator questioned the family, it could have evolved to Donald, McDonald, or O. Donald. Therefore, Patrick O'Donnell is Patrick O. Donnell. If the search ability of a website is sophisticated enough, it will pick up these familiar issues. The *Mc* is the same, in that Andrew McDonald becomes Andrew M. Donald or Andrew Donnell. The use of wild cards, usually a * or %, can be an enormous aid in circumventing these database problems.

Lastly, never expect certain names to be spelled in a recognizable manner; doing so throws off database searches. Once the family historian is aware that Gearity or Dougherty can be spelled numerous ways, research progresses more quickly. The census taker was not asking how to spell the name, and the family might not have known how. That is when the use of wildcards or a page-by-page search of a targeted area is essential.

United States Federal Censuses

Most researchers approach the federal enumerations as categories, being pre-1850 and post-1850. The reason for this is that the 1850 schedule was the first to ask for the names, ages, occupations, and birthplaces for everyone in each household. The 1840 census and those before it list only the heads of the households and statistics for the ages of white males and females. If the families were free color, the heads of households were named and statistics provided. Slaves also had statistics but no names.

In certain censuses, notably 1850, 1860, and 1870, for unknown reasons, the enumerators recorded more information than just Ireland for birthplaces. They are incredible research tools. For example, if an ancestor was listed as born in County Wicklow, and in his or her neighborhood

were others from County Wicklow, regardless of surnames, several questions need to be asked. Did they all know one another in County Wicklow? Are they somehow related? In essence, these questions are the beginnings of developing a viable immigrant research strategy, especially if the ancestor's christening or marriage is not in the church register databases for County Wicklow. At that point, conduct research for the others from County Wicklow in the church records' databases. If everyone in the neighborhood was from the same area of Ireland, the problem is solved.

A case in point is the census of 1860, 4th Ward of Milwaukee, Milwaukee County, Wisconsin. The 4th Ward of the city was the location of the Irish community, historically. The census enumerators listed counties of birth in the schedule. They have provided decades of study for historians and genealogists alike. When conducting research on the Milwaukee Irish, this census is one of the first records to read. Another example, just as extraordinary, is the 1860 Census of the First District of Savannah, Chatham County, Georgia. When looking for these kinds of anomalies, be aware that the names of the Irish counties may not be in the general database indexes, that is, only Ireland may be displayed. However, when an index does pick up the county names, worthy research possibilities are created.

Another excellent lead to origins is in the 1930 census because birthplaces are "Irish Free State" or "Northern Ireland."

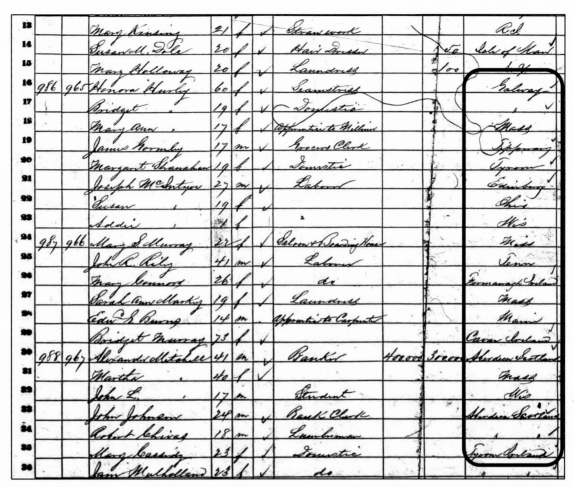

Figure 6: Note the use of counties in Ireland for birthplaces in the 4th Ward of Milwaukee, Wisconsin, in this 1860 census. Such enigmas can be found on occasion in various United States communities from 1850 onward. Counties Galway, Tipperary, Tyrone, Fermanagh, and Cavan are represented in just three households on this page. (Image courtesy of the National Archives and Records Administration.)

The island was partitioned into the two areas in 1921. The Irish Free State is today the Republic of Ireland, and Northern Ireland remains part of the United Kingdom. In the case of common names, even a small hint such as this can be an enormous one for narrowing a search.

One thought people have is whether an Irish-born wife is from the same place as her Irish-born husband. Where the children were born, as listed in the census schedules, is the surest way to know. If some were born in Ireland, the husband

and wife were from the same area. If they were all born in the United States, the answer is not as certain. Even if a marriage record is found for them in an American county or church record, the answer still may not be clear.

The pre-1850 census schedules are considered the most challenging for research by genealogists, especially for immigrants who died before 1850. These early enumerations do have a category for foreign born, but they do not identify which person in the household was foreign born. This is where other county and state records, such as naturalizations, supplement the census information. Another method is to identify the children of the person who died before 1850 and find them in the 1880 census, the first enumeration to ask where a person's father and mother were born. While not always correct, they do at least provide an indication about whether one or both parents were born in Ireland.

Often, pre-1850 schedules do not name the immigrant but do push the lineage as a whole back to the immigrant. Sometimes, the family has been in the United States since the colonial days, and what is needed is a method to continue tracing the lineage until the immigrant is recognized. Therefore, links are needed to prove, for instance, that individual in 1840 Indiana was the one in 1820 Pennsylvania.

One of the best ways to do that is to find the people in Indiana in 1840 who associated with the person being investigated to determine whether a group of people might have migrated together to Indiana from Pennsylvania. The pre-1850 censuses are in two formats. Occasionally, names are on the pages by the first letters of the surnames. That is frustrating and can destroy a research strategy because the neighborhood is not intact, as the census taker found it. When the neighborhood is intact, the neighbors of the ancestor are identified, and then the task can begin to see if they were all from the same area. The American frontier was not a safe place, and so people traveled in groups. Thus, neighbors in Pennsylvania in 1820 became neighbors in Indiana by 1840.

State Census and Census Substitutes

Besides the federal enumerations from 1790 to 1940, researchers use two sources to locate people, state censuses and what are termed "census substitutes." The current guide to these types of records, including census substitutes, is a series of 52 state manuals by William Dollarhide, *Census & Substitute Name Lists* (Orting, Washington: Family Roots Publishing Company, 2017-2018). New for 2020 is Dollarhide's *Census Substitutes & State Census Records,* 3rd edition (Orting, Washington: Family Roots Publishing Company, 2020), covering 50 states in five volumes.

State censuses were conducted by each state and may or may not include agricultural enumerations. Not all states kept these. Censuses of each state were unique, and so the information is not uniform. Some named heads of households only, with other family members as statistics. Others were full censuses with personal information similar to that in the federal enumerations. Some are vague, and some are detailed. Until each is studied, what can be helpful cannot be determined. These records are so important that several genealogical guides are devoted to the topic. State censuses are either online or being placed online with indexes and digitized images. The collections most accessed are those on Ancestry.com and FamilySearch.org.

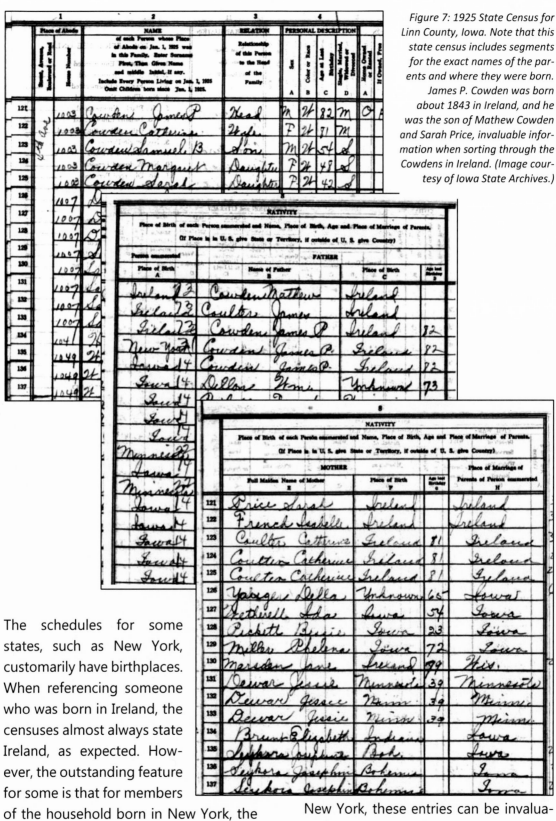

Figure 7: 1925 State Census for Linn County, Iowa. Note that this state census includes segments for the exact names of the parents and where they were born. James P. Cowden was born about 1843 in Ireland, and he was the son of Mathew Cowden and Sarah Price, invaluable information when sorting through the Cowdens in Ireland. (Image courtesy of Iowa State Archives.)

The schedules for some states, such as New York, customarily have birthplaces. When referencing someone who was born in Ireland, the censuses almost always state Ireland, as expected. However, the outstanding feature for some is that for members of the household born in New York, the county is often listed. As people moved westward onto the frontiers of Upstate New York, these entries can be invaluable because people's names may not appear in county records. Even if they did, there is no way to find them without a state-wide index. The state censuses were taken between the federal schedules, and so they show migrations.

Although a source such as this may not solve the immigrant origins' question, it is the first measure. With common names, finding where someone was naturalized can be an impossible quest, but if a state census reveals in what counties the children were born, the records documenting citizenship can be searched for those localities. Continuing with this example, a person could take out a declaration of intention in one county in eastern New York, finish the process of naturalization in the middle of the state, and then move to western New York State. The birthplaces of the children as recorded in the state census for that western New York county leave a trail for searching relevant records.

The idea of census substitutes is different than it is for state censuses, but the principle of using them is basically the same. A "census substitute" or "census alternative" is a record to fill in information for missing federal censuses. These can be any records that cover times for which state or federal censuses are absent. While some states have complete enumerations from 1790, others have significant time lapses between them.

Generally, tax lists close these gaps and locate people. One of the popular substitutes is the 1787 "census" of Virginia, which, because of the year, also includes what is now Kentucky and West Virginia, areas that were part of Virginia. The three-volume work *The 1787 Census of Virginia* (Springfield, Virginia: Genealogical Books in Print, 1987), by Netti Schreiner-Yatis and Florene Speakman Love, names all of the white male tithables over 21 years of age and all persons to whom ordinary licenses and physicians' licenses were issued. It is unsurpassed for tracing people during the time and is a standard in the industry in Virginia research because the 1790 census did not survive.

Another example of how tax lists can assist in locating people is New Jersey's. The first complete census for New Jersey was in 1830. An index to the tax lists for the entire state is in Ron Vern Jackson's *New Jersey Tax Lists, 1772-1822* (Salt Lake City, Utah: Accelerated Indexing Systems, 1981). This source not only substitutes for the 1790, 1800, 1810, and 1820 federal enumerations but also does so for the censuses before the 1772 to 1799 period. Once a person is found in this index, which has his or her name, town, and county, other records can be searched for Irish origins. Jackson's index to the tax lists has been added to the Ancestry.com database "New Jersey, Compiled Census and Census Substitutes Index, 1643-1890." It is not labeled except in the explanation about the database, that is, that Jackson's tax compilation is a part of it, thereby obscuring its tremendous merit.

Chapter Three

Church Records, Part I

> ➤ **Introduction**
> ➤ **Congregational**
> ➤ **Presbyterian**
> ➤ **Baptist**
> ➤ **Episcopal**
> ➤ **Methodist**
> ➤ **Stone-Campbell Restoration Movement**
> ➤ **Moravians**

Because of the separation of church and state in America, thus preventing mandates for religion, many people lost European church traditions, experimented with denominations, or had none. Congregations moved, changed names, disbanded, split, united, and switched denominational loyalties. The disarray tends to discourage researchers, rendering church records an underdeveloped topic. Nevertheless, although church registers in the United States are not the main source for documenting people as they are in some countries, family

historians should not neglect to include them. They can be overlooked for research because they can be in the custody of regional congregations or deposited in archives and so are difficult to find. When identified and studied, they can be rewarding. The process of locating them has to be thought of as part of an integrated research approach.

Since each denomination and congregation kept records differently, whether they hold the key to immigrant origins cannot be predicted. Sometimes, birthplaces can be in marriage and burial records, and oddly enough, those of parents were sometimes recorded at their children's christenings. In entire sections of the United States, most of the churches practiced only "believers' baptisms," and so there are no christening records from which to reconstruct a family. In these cases, research must be tailored. To explain these variances, additional space is dedicated herein for this complex subject.

Although few reference books are on the market about the genealogical use of church registers, several noteworthy ones as well as ones with chapters about the subject are:

Greenwood, Val D. "Church Records and Family History." *The Researcher's Guide to American Genealogy*. 4th ed., Baltimore, Maryland: Genealogical Publishing Company, 2017, pp. 585-623.

Hansen, Holly T., Arlene H. Eakle, Ruth E. Maness, and James L. Tanner. *Discovering the Evidence in Church Records*. Morgan, Utah: Family History Expos, Inc., 2017.

Henderson, Harold A. and Sunny Jane Morton. *How to Find Your Family History in U.S. Church Records*. Baltimore, Maryland: Genealogical Publishing Co., 2019.

Szucs, Loretto Dennis and Sandra Hargreaves Luebking. "Church Records." *The Source: A Guidebook to American Genealogy*, 3rd ed., Provo, Utah: Ancestry, 2006, pp. 221-254.

All provide an overview of major denominations, but not one deals with immigration studies since that is not their purpose. These works are excellent as an introduction to the kinds of records produced. As is any book published in the technological age, information about where records are located, indexes, and databases available are dated. However, the discussions of the records and strategies remain reliable.

This chapter focuses on faith groups that are known to have appealed to the Irish immigrants in the United States or that might have arrived as members of specific faiths. All are current faiths except one, the United Society of Believers in Christ's Second Appearing (Shakers), whose historic communes are still notable sites. All left behind records that might have listed where a member was born or from which Irish congregation he or she transferred. Even if they do not supply that information, they can be used as a part of the process of leading to another document that does.

Take into account that just because a person immigrated as a Catholic does not mean he or she remained one. The same applies to the incoming Scots-Irish (Ulster-Scots) Presbyterians, and because of the strict nature of early Quakerism, it definitely applies to them! Never expect an ancestor to do what the family today might do. People are people, and in this type of research, an open mind is required.

Many denominations are worthy of inclusion in this chapter, but the ones chosen are examples of what can be accomplished when properly understood. They are:

- Congregational Church
- Presbyterian Church
- Baptist Church
- Episcopal Church
- Methodist Church
- Stone-Campbell Restoration Movement
- United Brethren (Moravians)
- Roman Catholic
- Religious Society of Friends (Quakers)
- United Society of Believers in Christ's Second Appearing (Shakers)
- Church of the New Jerusalem (Swedenborgism)
- Church of Jesus Christ of Latter-day Saints (Mormons)

As the generations pass, researchers are frequently uncertain about to which denominations their ancestors belonged, if they did at all, and whether the families were Irish Catholic or Irish Protestant. There are many explanations for this, the foremost being that in Protestantism, loyalty is not primarily to the church as an institution but to Christ as the head of the "universal church," which includes all believers in Christ. Denominations are not viewed as divine institutions, and so switching institutional affiliations is as simple as transferring a membership. Even though variations and exceptions to this are undeniable, it is the basis.

When any knowledge is passed down, it is because some faith groups do deem their churches as divine institutions. Each speaks of its own church as the "Bride of Christ," with some reference to mean exclusively its denomination, which carries expectations of a different level of loyalty. In these cases, the church culture and family culture are the same. Examples are Roman Catholics and Mormons. If families fell away from these churches or converted to another, the chance is good that a memory of church fellowship might have remained in family lore, for instance, "Great grandpa left because the priest [fill in the blank]" or "Great grandma just could not get on board with polygamy." Great clues indeed!

If researchers do not know to which denomination the ancestors belonged, the indication is that they usually, although not always, were Irish Protestant. Irish Catholicism was a distinct culture, and thus the chances are good of a memory being passed down. Indications of denominational affiliation can also be in a civil marriage record. Who married the couple? If a minister did, discover where he pastored and then look for the church version of the marriage to see if it may state where the couple was born.

Religion in America

When studying church registers, a cursory history of how it affects average people is helpful. It is easy to break it into pre-1776 and post-1776 periods. Before 1776, what is now the United States was under various colonial powers. Great Britain, France, the Netherlands, and Spain all held tracts of land. Each had its own state or, at least, its prominent religion, and incoming settlers to its territories had to adjust. For the French and Spanish governments, it was the Roman Catholic Church; for the British, Anglicanism, better known as the Church of England; and for the Dutch, the Reformed Church. Territories' boundaries shifted because of wars and political compromises. Average persons did what they had to do to retain their lands and prosper economically, regardless of which European power was in charge.

A state religion meant everyone in its boundaries had to conform to that church. If they did not, they were considered nonconformists, or dissidents. A large portion of New England is a good example of nonconformists becoming the majority. New England was settled by English Calvinists, who emerged as the Congregational Church, and they held power in the colonial towns. Although they arrived as religious refugees, beginning with the Mayflower, it did not take long for them to banish those they considered to be nonconformists, which is why Quakers and Baptists founded Rhode Island. Like Rhode Island, Pennsylvania became a haven for almost anyone seeking refuge. It was founded by William Penn, a Quaker, and became home to a startling diversity of religions.

In the 1600s, the Church of England, renamed the Episcopal Church after 1776,

Figure 8: A Puritan husband and wife walking through snow on their way to church, he carrying a rifle, and she, a prayer book or bible. (Image of print courtesy of Library of Congress. Engraving by Thomas Gold Appleton [1812-1884]. Copyright expired.)

do not expect a Catholic on the plantations in Virginia in the pre-1776 period to have continued as such.

Maryland was founded as a refuge for Catholics and has always been the center of historic Catholicism in the English colonies. Remaining with the Church was possible for these families. The opposite was true for South Carolina, founded as a Protestant colony buffer against Spanish Florida, which was Catholic. South Carolina was a hotspot for Protestant nonconformity, and although it was an English colony, it nonetheless was populated by loyal Protestants.

held strength in the Southern colonies. The incoming Roman Catholic Irish indentured servants and convicts working on the tobacco plantations had no priests, nor were priests allowed. If these people upon release after bondage did not move on, they were documented in the Church of England registers or in nonconformist churches as they were established in their areas. In other words,

With the separation of church and state after the Revolutionary War, a state religion was relegated to the dust heaps of history. Some academics contend that what arose was a type of "public religion" or "civil religion," in which values were not built upon a denomination but upon a universal belief in what was morally and ethically acceptable and what was not.

The Spanish territories offer a unique example of why people changed religions, often in name only, and why research has to be open minded about records. After 1776, both Irish Catholic and Protestant settlers flooded into Spanish and, later, Mexican territories from the expanding United States. To receive a land grant, the settler had to conform to the Catholic Church. For Irish Catholics, this was not an issue. Irish Protestants also conformed to receive land grants, explaining why known Protestants are found in the Catholic registers. However, many of these regions were so rural that they had no priests, and conversions were paper events only. When the ever-spreading United States took over these areas, the issue became the rights by which the land had been obtained, not the conformity to religion.

Two Great Awakenings were in American religious history. The original, known in the history books as the Great Awakening or the First Great Awakening, was during the colonial period. It started in the late 1720s, peaked in 1740, and continued to some degree into the 1770s, setting the foundation for Protestant evangelicalism to develop into a dominant force in America. It emphasized the need for conversion and acceptance of Christ as one's personal savior, becoming embedded within the various Protestant churches and sweeping the Northern and Middle colonies. One of the goals was to eliminate a formalistic worship style.

The core leaders during the Great Awakening were from Calvinistic churches (Congregational, Presbyterian, and Reformed), although the revivalism grew more slowly in the Southern colonies.

The Baptist surfaced as the predominant evangelical Church in Virginia. The colonial Anglicans, mainly those aligning themselves with the growing Methodist element within their ranks, also prospered. Methodism was originally study classes within the Church of England. After the Revolutionary War, though, these Methodist societies separated from the newly formed Episcopal Church, creating the Methodist Episcopal Church. The beginning of the Revolutionary War brought an end to the Great Awakening.

The Second Great Awakening is better known in history than the original revival movement. It occurred in various locations throughout the United States between 1790 and 1830. Like the Great Awakening, it had corporate and individual elements. Not only did it emphasize the personal nature of salvation but also it underscored that a special divine blessing had been bestowed upon America by God, an attitude that is still felt. In addition, the preachers stressed that individuals could reform their own lives and society.

The Second Great Awakening was meant to bring civilization to the frontiers, which had few churches and schools. It was then that so many Irish immigrants or their descendants, along with the rest of the populations on the frontiers, became religious and began the process of becoming literate. Its cultural impact on the South and the Midwest frontier areas should not be underestimated because by then, residents had been removed from church and education for a generation or two. In other words, a Scot-Irish family originally of Presbyterian heritage converted or reunited with Presbyterianism as a denomination of choice, not necessarily of birth. The Presbyterian Church and the Baptist or the Methodist attracted all kinds of people en masse.

One of the most famous of the frontier revivals was at Cane Ridge, Bourbon County, Kentucky, during 1801. Over 10,000 people took part in the immense event, and it was symbolic of the changes occurring throughout the United States. As revivals sprang up in Tennessee, Kentucky, and southern Ohio, tens of thousands of previously unchurched settlers became part of Protestant denominations.

The Second Great Awakening also gave rise to new expressions of American Protestantism, such as the Stone-Campbell Restoration Movement and the Cumberland Presbyterian Church. The Methodist Church expanded widely on the frontiers because it was at the forefront of the revivalism. Although the fires of the Second Great Awakening had dimmed by the 1830s, they ignited for a second time, with fervor, in Upstate New York. This area is known in American religious history as the "Burnt-Over District" because of the revival fires. From the Burnt Over District revivals, new and distinct religious movements, such as Mormonism (1830), Adventism (1844), and Spiritualism (1848), transformed the American landscape, all of them birthed in Upstate New York.

An excellent treatment of "made in America" versions of faith can be found in Paul K. Conkin's *American Originals: Homemade Varieties of Christianity*

(Chapel Hill, North Carolina: The University of North Carolina Press, 1997). The classic of the Burned Over District period is Whitney R. Cross's *The Burned-Over District: The Social and Intellectual History of Enthusiastic Religion in Western New York, 1800-1850* (Ithaca, New York: Cornell University Press, 1950).

Congregational Church

The Congregational Church has a long history in the United States. Some people use the term "New England Congregational Church." The location has always been the strength of this denomination in the United States, but it is by no means limited to New England. Today, American Congregationalism is split into three branches:

- United Church of Christ (Cleveland, Ohio)
- National Association of Congregational Christian Churches (Oak Creek, Wisconsin)
- Conservative Congregational Christian Conference (Lake Elmo, Minnesota)

The largest expression, multi-ethnic and liberal Protestant, is the United Church of Christ. Its stately and beautiful historic buildings still dot towns and villages throughout New England. When the United Church of Christ was created, many evangelical and conservative congregations formed the remaining two denominations. Only the United Church of Christ is considered a mainstream Protestant denomination.

The Congregational Church is the English version of Calvinism. The early

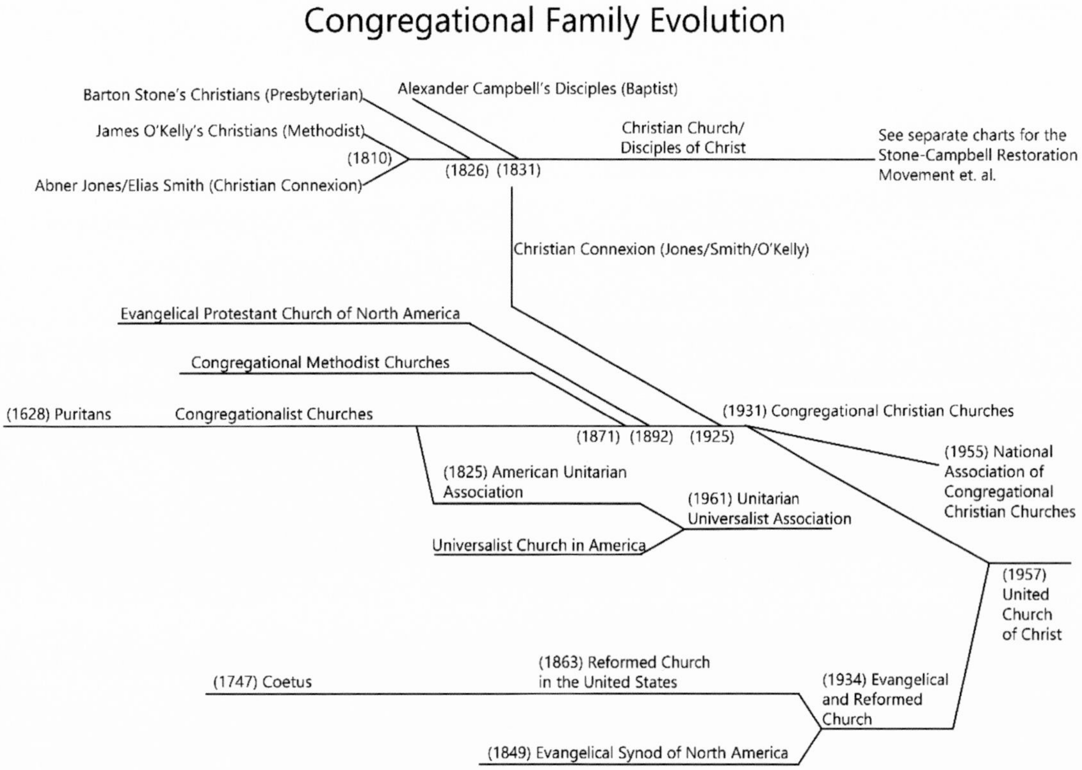

Congregational Family Evolution

Barton Stone's Christians (Presbyterian)   Alexander Campbell's Disciples (Baptist)

James O'Kelly's Christians (Methodist)

Christian Church/
Disciples of Christ

See separate charts for the
Stone-Campbell Restoration
Movement et. al.

(1810)   (1826) (1831)

Abner Jones/Elias Smith (Christian Connexion)

Christian Connexion (Jones/Smith/O'Kelly)

Evangelical Protestant Church of North America

Congregational Methodist Churches

(1628) Puritans   Congregationalist Churches

(1931) Congregational Christian Churches

(1871) (1892) (1925)

(1955) National
Association of
Congregational
Christian Churches

(1825) American Unitarian
Association

(1961) Unitarian
Universalist Association

Universalist Church in America

(1957)
United
Church
of Christ

(1863) Reformed Church
in the United States

(1747) Coetus

(1934) Evangelical
and Reformed
Church

(1849) Evangelical Synod of North America

Figure 9: Congregational development in the United States.

Congregationalists in New England were of English origin, and although they are not the subject of this discussion, neither can they be separated from it. This is because the main church, such as the one in Massachusetts, was state supported, and incoming immigrants from Ireland had to conform to it. Frankly, it was often the only church in town. Therefore, it is possible to find Anglicans, Catholics, Scots-Irish Presbyterians, French Huguenots, and just about anyone else either conforming to or exiting from Congregational strongholds.

It was not until clergy from other denominations, such as Catholic priests and Presbyterian ministers, arrived that immigrants could then form their own churches. Before the dates of the establishments of new denominational churches, the Congregational Church records are the primary source for documenting early New Englanders with Irish origins.

The incoming Irish, especially Presbyterians who were also Calvinists, did not always find a welcoming church home among descendants of the English Congregationalists. The Ulster-Scots began immigrating in droves in 1718, and, by then, the descendants of the original English Congregationalists had already been in America for a hundred years. This made it important for the Scots-Irish and the arriving Scots to secure Presbyterian ministers from either Ulster or Scotland and to separate from regional Congregational churches.

Understanding the Differences Between Pilgrims and Puritans

Colonial America was paved with the history of Pilgrims and Puritans. Although these original groups were English and not Irish, the Irish can be documented in the records of these colonial New England believers. Indentured servants of the 1600s and Scots-Irish of the 1700s became part of a distinct New England Congregationalism as it organized. A quick reference is warranted.

Similar Roots Shared by Both Pilgrims and Puritans
Originated in England.
Roots in Calvinism.
Disagreed with the Church of England.
Fled religious persecution and hoped to find religious freedom.
Settled in present-day Massachusetts.

Recognizing the Distinction

Pilgrims	Puritans
Arrived on the Mayflower in 1620	Arrived in America in 1629/30 aboard various ships
Settled in Plymouth, Massachusetts	Settled in Massachusetts Bay Colony (Primarily Boston and Salem)
Wanted to separate from the Church of England	Wanted to purify the Church of England
Led by William Bradford	Led by John Winthrop
Sponsored by the Virginia Land Company	Sponsored by Massachusetts Bay Company
Were mostly poor and uneducated	Mostly middle and upper class and were well educated
Mayflower Compact: All men participated with majority rule	Led by Puritan Ministers who dictated law according to the Bible
Had good relationship with Native Americans, trading food and furs	Had poor relationship with Native Americans, preferring they be exterminated
Held town meetings to discuss important issues	Only ministers could govern and make decisions
Faced starvation and disease	Built public schools and libraries. Founded Harvard College
	Puritan minister, Roger Williams, separated and formed the first colonial Baptist Church in present-day Rhode Island

During the Great Awakening, many joined the Congregational Church; however, it also split congregations into various factions. In New England, the New Lights supported revivals, and the Old Lights did not approve of the emotional nature of these revivals. Many New Lights returned to traditional Congregationalism while others became Baptists. For the traditional Old Lights, a rational religion was sought, spawning Unitarianism from within Congregationalism. The American Unitarian Association was formed in 1825. Today, this is the Unitarian-Universalist Church.

Because of the rise of Unitarianism, the Congregational Church was not the officially favored and tax-supported Church in Massachusetts in 1833. Until that year, it was state supported, regardless of what the United States Constitution declared about separation of church and state. At that point, the Congregational Church became one of many churches.

Historically, Congregationalism and Presbyterianism are similar enough that the differences were in non-theological matters. To serve the needs of the frontier, the Presbyterian Church and the Congregational Associations of New England consented to a plan in 1801 that allowed one denomination to call a pastor from another denomination. The "Presbygational" agreement ensured that new churches could be staffed in the expanding areas of western New York State and farther westward. Under the arrangement, Presbyterians and Congregationalists were a single denomination in Illinois, Indiana, Michigan, New York, Ohio, and Wisconsin. Many Presbyterian congregations rejected the union in 1838, and in 1852, it was discarded by the Congregational Church, which is another reason to always check the Presbyterian registers for someone who might have been Congregational or vice versa.

In 1957, after several mergers with other like-minded denominations, the United Church of Christ was created, with a Liberal Protestant outlook. Today, it is the largest within American Congregationalism, but not all churches joined. The Conservative Congregational Christian Conference was formed in 1948, which is conservative and evangelical in thought.

Congregational Records

The records of New England Congregationalism are so renowned that they have been published typically up to 1850 in compilations and are based upon the town. To clarify this, in New England, the town is the main governmental unit, especially outside of urban areas. The county also kept records, but it is the town records that documented the locals and their immediate concerns. The original concept of a town was a surveyed piece of ground with a "town center" and various villages and communities within the surveyed boundaries. Over the years, towns were partitioned, and the process started all over again until New England was filled with towns. Therefore, for the 1700s period especially, when the Ulster-Scots were arriving, and for the earlier 1600s, when there were Catholic indentured servants, the town should have documented them. The records include births, marriages, and deaths, along with other records of day-to-day affairs.

The vital records in the town registers, as extracted and indexed by historians and genealogists, could be the same as the Congregational Church records. The vitals are often extracted and combined with tombstone transcriptions, records of other denominations, family papers, and similar documents that have births/christenings, marriages, or deaths/burials. These books are usually in the public domain and can be found on major websites such as AmericanAncestors.org, Ancestry.com, FamilySearch.org, and others.

The compilations, first and foremost, had no purpose for assigning birthplaces in Ireland for immigrants. Nevertheless, because they are indexed and readily available in databases, the information can be used in several strategies, which can at some stage answer the question of origins. Among the strategies is one to determine who else in the town might have been related to the ancestors and was from Ireland.

Towns are not huge tracts of real estate, and so it could be assumed as a starting point that all persons by the surname of the ancestor being investigated were relatives. They might not have been, but research has to begin somewhere. Take the year of the ancestor's marriage and search all marriages for ten years before and after, at first limiting them only to that town. To begin, presuppose these are the ancestor's siblings or perhaps cousins. In other words, they were all descended from the same immigrant ancestor, or if they were the immigrants, they all came together. Research the other people through published town and family histories. Does a pattern materialize? The aim is to establish a commonality back to the immigrant and trace forward for who might or might not have been related. For anyone related, is the place of birth in Ireland preserved among any of the branches?

Manuscripts of the Congregational Church can be at several repositories. As primary records for New England, they have been gathered and preserved. The Congregational Church Library & Archives in Boston is a major repository for all materials related to New England Congregationalists. Its website, Congregationallibrary.org, offers a great amount of help and databases, one of which is a list of ministers and missionaries from the 1600s to the present.

In its collections are family papers and denominational records. A main initiative of the library is its program "New England's Hidden Histories: Colonial-Era Church Records." Started in 2005 in partnership with the Jonathan Edwards Center at Yale University, old church records from across New England have been rescued, preserved, and made available for study. New material is constantly being obtained. The collection is arranged in three ways: registers made by local churches, items created by individuals, and records produced by conferences, associations, and other church bodies. Another place to document Congregationalists is the New England Historic Genealogical Society in Boston, which hosts outstanding databases at its AmericanAncestors.org website. This is the oldest and one of the most respected genealogy societies in the country. It operates a large research library in Boston. Its online databases and library holdings have successfully identified Irish origins of immigrants.

An additional major library for Congregational research is the Family History Library in Salt Lake City, which hosts the massive FamilySearch.org website. It has digitized images of the original Congregational registers as well as one of the largest genealogy-related book collections in the country.

The Congregational Church Library, New England Historic Genealogical Society, and the Family History Library are all registered non-profit organizations. Congregational Church records, indexes, and databases are readily available from the three of them.

Presbyterian Church

The Presbyterian Church is the Scottish version of Calvinism, founded by John Calvin (1509-1564). He was born in France and was a leader in the Protestant Reformation of the sixteenth century. He laid a theological foundation upon which the Reformed tradition was built. The Calvinist churches took different names in various countries. It was Presbyterian in Scotland and Ireland; Congregational (Puritans) in England; the Reformed Church in Germany, Hungary, the Netherlands, Poland, Romania, and Switzerland; and Huguenot in France. John Calvin's monumental, systematic theology of the Christian faith, *Institutes of the Christian Religion* (1559), may be remembered as one of the most influential Christian books of the last 1,000 years.

Irish Presbyterianism originated within Scottish Presbyterianism. The father of Scots Presbyterianism was John Knox (1514-1572). He fled Scotland and then England, arriving in Geneva in 1555. He served as pastor of the English-speaking exiles while studying under Calvin. In 1559, he returned to Scotland to head the Scottish Reformation. In Scotland, Presbyterianism eventually became the established church instead of Anglicanism. In Ireland, it was the opposite, Anglicanism became the state religion. This branch of Calvinism in Scotland was known as the Church of Scotland, and in Ireland, as the Presbyterian Church. Although the Irish people of French Huguenot descent also immigrated to America, this section focuses on the Scottish version of Calvinism because of its large numbers. However, while distinct French Huguenot settlements were in Ireland, most of them merged into Anglicanism.

The Ulster-Scots were almost entirely Presbyterian, but this does not mean they remained so either in Ulster or America. Many married outside the Scots-Irish community, and so for this reason alone, to assume an Ulster immigrant was Presbyterian, especially with a Scottish surname, is not safe.

The Ulster-Scots began arriving in American colonies during the 1600s but not en masse and in identifiable waves until 1718. They intermarried with other ethnic and religious groups they encountered. They also are well documented as intermarrying with the Native American tribes. For example, the Cherokee probably have the most Scots-Irish, mixed-race, documented genealogies, but they can also be found in the Catawba, Chickasaw, Choctaw, Muscogee (Creek), and others. A more detailed study of how to use Native American records in the search for Irish origins can be found in Dwight A. Radford's Special Strategy chapter "Southeastern Native American Connection" in *American Scots-Irish Research: Strategies and Sources in the Quest for Ulster-Scots Origins* (Orting, Washington: Family Roots Publishing, 2020).

Again, while it is all right to begin by at least presuming the Scots-Irish were originally Presbyterian, once they headed into the inland frontiers, few ministers and congregations were there. It was not until the Second Great Revival that Presbyterian churches were planted

and schools established to serve the population. Families who might have had no connection with Presbyterianism for a generation or two converted or reunited with the Presbyterian Church. Similar numbers of others joined the Baptists, Methodists, or Disciples/Christians. All four churches attracted the largest number of adherents as the frontiers became less harsh and institutions were a part of daily life.

Note that Presbyterianism previously, and to this day, is not one monolithic church. It has had several divisions as well as unions that occurred in Ulster and America.

In the colonial times, because Presbyterian congregations were often in short supply, it was common for believers to

Select Presbyterian Church Evolutions

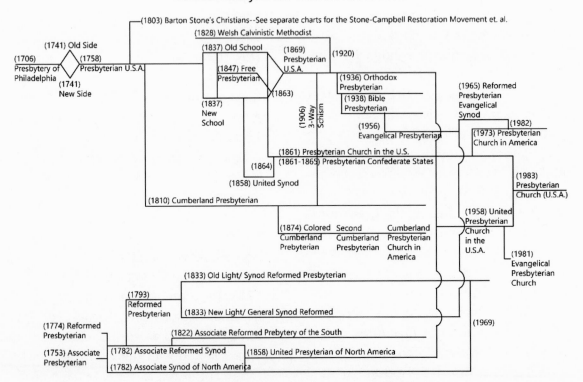

Figure 10: Presbyterian development in the United States

be found in the records of their dominant area churches, including the Congregational and the Reformed. Both denominations are also branches of Calvinism, and so the theological distinction is not great even if they were quite different culturally. Irish Presbyterians routinely attended Dutch Reformed or German Reformed congregations or at least had their marriages and children's christenings performed in them. New England Congregationalists were not in the same situations because they also spoke English. Culturally, the old New England families were vastly unlike the incoming Scots-Irish Presbyterians, and this brought conflict. Yet, seen all over New England were Presbyterian churches established separate from the Congregational churches once Presbyterian ministers from Scotland or Ireland could be obtained.

Before 1776, the same principle applies to the colonial Church of England, which became the Episcopal Church. In the early days, it was customary, especially in the Southern colonies, for Presbyterians to be married and baptized by Anglican clergy. After more Presbyterians arrived and ministers were employed, they formed congregations of their own.

Because of the associations of Presbyterians with the dominant or only faiths in their communities, Irish origins might have been preserved in their records as well. The fact pertains to most denominations, whether Anglican, Congregational, Lutheran, or Reformed.

One research strategy that needs to be addressed is the congregational migration of Presbyterians. One group after another came with its minister and established a colonial congregation. If this occurrence is suspected of an ancestor's church community, switch research to the minister. Collections, called fasti books, have been published from the Irish Presbyterian perspective with biographical sketches of ministers. The Presbyterian Historical Society of Ireland in Belfast has these on its website, Presbyterianhistoryireland.com. The books can solve any immigrant origins' questions because each congregation lived only a short distance from its pastor and church building in Ulster.

Branches of Presbyterianism and Records

The first and perhaps most prominent feature of Presbyterianism is that it extends from ultra-conservative, sometimes called "Hyper-Calvinism," to ultra-liberal, which embraces modern Liberal Protestantism, to just about everything in between. The story of Presbyterianism, whether in Scotland, Ulster, or in the United States, is the adherence to reevaluation of polity and theology that has led to many divisions as well as unions. This affected what happened to records because many of the old denominations no longer exist but were grafted into new denominations. The largest Presbyterian denominations in the United States are shown on page 32, but the years they were established are not relevant because of mergers and divisions (see page 30, figure 10). Just be aware that an older congregation can significantly predate the founding of the current denomination.

Largest Presbyterian Denominations in the United States

Denomination	Founded	Headquarters
Associate Reformed Presbyterian Church	1803	Greenville, South Carolina
Cumberland Presbyterian Church	1810	Memphis, Tennessee
Cumberland Presbyterian Church in America	1874	Huntsville, Alabama
A Covenant Order of Evangelical Presbyterians	2012	Goleta, California
Evangelical Presbyterian Church	1981	Orlando, Florida
Orthodox Presbyterian Church	1936	Willow Grove, Pennsylvania
Presbyterian Church in America	1973	Lawrenceville, Georgia
Presbyterian Church (USA)	1983	Louisville, Kentucky

The Presbyterian Historical Society in Philadelphia is a major repository of all American Presbyterian documents from all branches and denominations that choose to deposit archival material. It is also the national archive of the Presbyterian Church (USA), the largest Presbyterian denomination in the country. A catalog on its website can be searched by location for congregational registers that have been deposited. The website also has a short history of the congregations, which identifies branches to which they currently belong or did at one time. This is a main repository with biographical information on ministers, missionaries, and prominent historical persons. The Presbyterian Historical Society with its resources is one of the first stops in this research.

Aside from the growing collection at its archive, registers from its collection are available at the Family History Library in Salt Lake City. The archive also has been digitized by Ancestry.com and indexed in the database "U.S., Presbyterian Church Records, 1701-1970," which is a foremost, nationwide collection of records. It must be understood that as remarkable as the deposits of Presbyterian collections are, not one of them is complete.

Therefore, if a congregation is not found on deposit or on a database, consider one of the smaller denominations. Do not expect all documents at the Presbyterian Historical Society to be digitized at either the Family History Library or online at Ancestry.com.

Two denominations are especially essential in the search for Scots-Irish ancestors, the Cumberland Presbyterian Church and the Associate Reformed Presbyterian Church, each with its own archive and record collections. The Cumberland Presbyterian Church arose from the Second Great Awakening on the American frontier. It began in 1800 and was formally organized in 1810 in Dickson County, Tennessee. The members were revivalists who disagreed with the mother Presbyterian Church. They saw that revivals were extraordinary events and allowed exceptions to both educational requirements for ordaining ministers and the required subscriptions to the Westminster Confession of Faith. Originally a frontier, Southern Scots-Irish movement, the Church quickly swept beyond those roots. It is primarily concentrated in the American South or where Southerners migrated, mainly Tennessee, Kentucky, Alabama, Missouri, southern Illinois, Arkansas, and Texas. Some of its innovations have been along social lines, the first Presbyterians to ordain women to the ministry (1889) and among the first denominations to admit women to its higher educational institutions. It also began to ordain African Americans to the ministry around 1830. The African American denomination is Cumberland Presbyterian Church in America.

For the family historian, the archive for both denominations is at the Historical Library of the General Assemblies in Cordova, Tennessee. The website, which is in various stages of being reconstructed, has an inventory of ministers.

Some of the sketches of the ministers have only basic information involving church service. Others have details about their lives. Considering the Church was not officially organized until 1810, most of the ministers were not born in Ireland, but they were the children and grandchildren of the immigrant generation. Hence, a sketch about the minister's family history may be more relevant than what was written about him. Also remember that the purpose of these biographies is not the genealogy in Ireland but is the reconstructions of the lives and church service of the ministers in America. Two examples of information extending back are for Finis Ewing (1773-1841) and Ezekiel Cloyd (1760-1851):

> *"FINIS EWING was born on the 10th of July, 1773, in Bedford county, Virginia. His father and an uncle had settled there on their emigration from Ireland to this country, a number of years previous to the American Revolution. The two brothers seem to have ranked among the most respectable and prosperous farmers of the county. The older of the two, Robert Ewing, was for many years Clerk of Bedford County Court, and an elder in the Presbyterian Church. He married Miss Mary Baker. They had twelve children--nine sons and three daughters. The subject of this sketch was their twelfth and last child, and from his being the last, his parents gave him the fanciful name of Finis--the end..."*

> *"EZEKIEL CLOYD was born on the 12 of February, 1760. His parents are supposed to have lived at the time in Montgomery county, Virginia. He was the son of John and Margaret Cloyd. His mother's name before her marriage was Scott. His parents emigrated from Ireland and settled in Virginia in 1758. They were, however, of Scotch origin. The name seems to have been originally Clyde. Of course the family were thoroughly Scotch. The parents were both members of the Presbyterian Church. I have in my possession the mother's certificate of Church-membership in Ireland. It is dated August 14, 1758, and given to Margaret Clyde, alias Scott..."*

In these two examples, a place in Ulster is not given but was made in passing, and these were extensive biographies of the lives of these two ministers. Yet, enough clues about both families were presented that an issue would not be the reconstruction of the parents' lives in America with the goal of finding where they lived in Ireland.

Another branch of the American Presbyterian family tree is the Associate Reformed Presbyterian Church (ARP), which is also strongly centered in the South and is Scots-Irish. Its history reaches from Scotland to Ulster and then into the American colonies. As with Presbyterianism in general, it had its beginnings in the preaching of John Knox in Scotland. When it became the state religion in 1560, controversy and bitter strife over control became a way of life for church and state alike.

Despite improvements in 1688 under William III, a great number of problems remained. In 1733, Ebenezer Erskine led a group of Presbyterians in forming a separate Associate Presbytery, and thus the term "Associate" came into being within the developing denomination's name. Ten years later, another group, which for years had suffered problems with the Church of Scotland, organized into the Reformed Presbytery, bestowing the second part "Reformed" to the ARP Church denominational name.

Both branches of Calvinism were carried to Ulster as the Scots settled there en masse. These distinct branches followed the Ulster-Scots as they immigrated to the colonies, settling first in Pennsylvania, where an Associate Presbytery and a Reformed Presbytery were organized in the 1750 to 1770 period.

Formal union talks between the Associate Presbytery and the Reformed Presbytery began in 1777, and by 1782, the Associate Reformed Synod was created in Philadelphia. Even at this creation of the new Associate Reformed Synod, not all congregations from either branch joined. Congregations that did not were concentrated in Pennsylvania, New York, Ohio, North Carolina, South Carolina, and Georgia.

In 1790, another Associate Reformed Presbytery was created, formed in Abbeville County, South Carolina, to minister to the members in North Carolina, South Carolina, and Georgia, known as the Carolinas Presbytery. By 1803, the entire Church was served by four Synods and one General Synod. The Synods were those of the Carolinas, Pennsylvania, New York, and Scioto (in Ohio), with the headquarters of the Church in Philadelphia.

In 1822, the Synod of the Carolinas was granted separate status, and by the end of the nineteenth century, it was the sole remaining body of the ARP Church as several mergers over the years had absorbed the other presbyteries forming the old United Presbyterian Church. It is through these remaining Associate Reformed Presbyterians in the Southeast that the denomination continues today.

In the past, the ARP Church has had its highest concentrations in western North

Carolina (especially Rowan, Mecklenburg, Cabarrus, and adjacent counties), upper South Carolina (especially Lancaster, Chester, York, Fairfield, Newberry, and Abbeville Counties), and in Tennessee (particularly Tipton County).

The McCain Library genealogical collection is in the Erskine College of the ARP Church, and it is noteworthy because many families in this part of South Carolina were interconnected. Accordingly, the ARP Church records are a leading source for Abbeville County and the surrounding counties as well.

The official repository for the ARP Church is the Presbyterian Historical Society, which holds congregational registers as well as presbytery and synod books. It has the most complete collection of ARP Church periodicals. The index "Associate Reformed Presbyterian Church (1782-1858)" also is at the Presbyterian Historical Society. Two indexes to the vital records were published in these periodicals by Lowry Ware as *Associate Reformed Presbyterian Deaths & Marriage Notices From The Christian Magazine of the South, The Erskine Miscellany, and The Due West Telescope, 1843-1863* (Columbia, South Carolina: SCMAR, 1993) and *Associate Reformed Presbyterian Death & Marriage Notices, Volume II: 1866-1888* (Columbia, South Carolina: SCMAR, 1998).

Before the establishment of Clark and Erskine Seminary (now Erskine Seminary) in 1837, ministerial students were apprenticed to other ministers. Biographical material on many of the early ministers can be found in Robert Lathan's 1882 *History of the Associate Reformed Synod of the South, 1782-1882* (Greenville, South Carolina: Associate Reformed Presbyterian Center, 1982) and in *Centennial History of the ARP Church, 1803-1903* (Charleston, South Carolina: Walker, Evans & Cogswell, 1905). Both are digitized through FamilySearch.org.

Baptist Church

The Baptist tradition is so interwoven into American history that it cannot be separated. Nevertheless, it must be placed into a context. In Ireland, the Baptist Church was a minority denomination. Irish Baptists did indeed immigrate to America, but most Irish, typically Protestants, became Baptists in the United States, not in Ireland. This was a result of the large-scale revivals, especially during the Second Great Awakening.

In documenting a Baptist family, the first question to ask is, What kind of Baptist? Today, the second largest religious grouping in the country comprises all Baptists combined, and the Southern Baptist Convention is the largest Protestant denomination.

Baptist congregations range from militantly independent conservatives on the right to socially oriented and ecumenically minded on the left and everything in between. There are those who worship on Saturday or Sunday. Rigid, small groups are in almost compound-like settings, and mega churches host thousands of worshipers at a time.

Congregations can become part of like-minded conventions and associations, or they can stay independent.

The earliest Baptists came from England, with the first congregation founded in Providence, Rhode Island, in 1639 by William Rogers. Because there were Baptists in New England, if an ancestor disappears from the predominant Congregational Church registers, the reason could very well be that he or she joined the Baptists.

During the Second Great Awakening, Baptists expanded into new areas and converted more people. It was also the Baptists, along with the Methodists, who won the hearts of African Americans. Therefore, whether tracing a white, black, or a mixed-race family, chances are a Baptist family will be discovered along the way.

Baptists often divided over cultural, racial, political, polity, and doctrinal issues. Knowing a little history about how a congregation came to be united with a denomination or convention is important in the search. In the United States, Irish ancestries are interwoven in the white, black, and native communities, and so knowledge of denominations and types of Baptists is helpful:

American Baptist Churches USA. Considered mainline Protestant, it has historically been known as "Northern Baptist." The American Baptist Church is traced to the first Baptists, with the convention itself back to 1814. This nationwide, multi-ethnic denomination is concentrated in the Midwest and Northeast.

Free Will Baptists. Concentrated mainly in the South and Midwest, although at one time strong in New England, it is the largest organization, the National Association of Free Will Baptists. Its lineage is from two different lines, dating back to 1727 and 1780.

General Baptists. Located primarily in the Midwest, the General Association of General Baptists is rooted in 1823 Indiana.

Independent Baptists. Congregations that have maintained their independence are commonly called "Independent Baptists," which is a general description. Independent Baptists as a movement began in the late nineteenth and early twentieth centuries in reaction to liberalism and modernism. Congregations are nationwide.

National Baptists. An African American denomination founded in 1880, the National Baptist Convention, USA, is the world's second largest Baptist denomination. It is found nationwide.

Primitive Baptists. Historically known as Hard Shell, Anti-Mission, or Old School Baptists, the Primitive Baptists formed in the early 1800s chiefly in the mountainous regions of the Southeast. There are the white Primitive Baptist Church and the African American denomination known as the National Primitive Baptist Convention, USA.

Seventh Day Baptists. Emerging from English Baptists, the first congregation was formed in Newport, Rhode Island, in 1671. The Seventh Day Baptist General Conference worships on Saturday.

Baptist Church Evolution in the United States

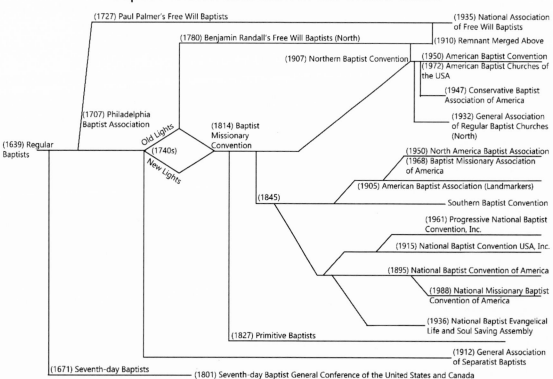

Figure 11: Baptist development in the United States.

Southern Baptist Convention. The Southern Baptist Convention is the largest Baptist denomination in the world. Founded in 1845 over slavery issues, it is nationwide, although it is heavily concentrated in the American South. Historically, it was predominately white.

The foregoing is a synopsis of the main Baptists in the United States but these are still not the only ones. The Baptist tradition has more regionalized versions, such as the United Baptist Church, strong in Tennessee and Kentucky, and the Baptist Church of Christ, chiefly in Middle Tennessee. Central to this discussion is that each tradition generated a paper trail and wove itself into the national experience, helping define what it meant to be an American.

Baptist Record Keeping

Baptist records are a direct reflection of Baptist attitudes and theology. On the American frontiers, Baptists burgeoned during the Second Great Awakening. However, records were not always kept for those converting in revival meetings. Some Baptists maintain they are not even Protestants but are part of an underground group of believers who can be traced back to the New Testament Christians, bypassing Catholicism and Protestantism.

The use of Baptist congregational records is not necessarily to find where someone was born in Ireland. That these records contain birth information is unlikely, but they are valuable portals to other documents that may have it.

History books, obituaries, convention reports, and transfers in and out of the congregations all hold potential to locate a member of the congregation, especially the transfers of early members into congregations. Where did the members transfer from? If they were on the frontiers of the Midwest or South, it can be so easy to lose them, not knowing where they originated.

Historically, many frontier ministers were not professionally trained. They "received a call from God" to preach, their only credential. A literate or semi-literate frontier minister was secondary to the "call to preach" because a person's salvation was based upon a personal experience with God. Literacy was not a prerequisite for salvation, and God's word was open to *all* people. This does not mean there are no records for ministers. Convention reports are an excellent source from which to find directories of ministers. These can be found at websites such as HathiTrust.org or Archive.org. Often, these reports have published obituaries of ministers who died during that year and can offer excellent clues.

As the frontiers were settled, congregations were established, education was more available, and records were generated, assisting in documenting members. All record keeping was at the judgment of each congregation. The believers, as the congregation, together make up the body of Christ. The individual congregation of believers is a sacred Baptist concept.

In Baptist theology, salvation is an experience based upon the faith and confession of the believer. It is not based upon baptism. Baptism is by total immersion as a sign of commitment, faith, and admission into the Church. "Believers' baptisms" might or might not have been recorded. An exceptional work detailing the scope of Baptist thought is James Leo Garrett's *Baptist Theology: A Four-Century Study* (Macon, Georgia: Mercer University Press, 2009). This work covers all expressions of Baptists and thus is useful for the family historian, although that was not its intended audience.

One of the difficulties in Baptist research is that a congregation might not have kept records. Another is determining what happened to a congregation, let alone its records. Types of records that can be helpful include memberships, transfers in and out, disciplinary, believers' baptisms, and general minutes.

In rural areas, congregations arrived and left. On the frontier, especially in places such as the Mid-South in the 1830s, entire congregations were swept up in the rising tide of the Stone-Campbell Restoration Movement. A Baptist Church could have become a Christian Church. On the other hand, in New England, a Baptist congregation might have been in the same town for several hundred years. In other parts of the country, congregations united with others or changed their names when they moved to new buildings in new localities.

Baptist records may still be with the congregations. In the quest, look first at the collections through the FamilySearch Catalog on FamilySearch.org for a microfilm or digitized copy of the needed record. Some records may be at a state archive. Also, major Baptist repositories have websites and contact information. Among them are American Baptist Historical Society, Free Will Baptist Historical Commission, The Primitive Baptist Library of Carthage, Illinois, Southern Baptist Historical Library & Archives, and the Seventh Day Baptist Historical Society.

Episcopal Church

The Episcopal Church of the United States is a member of the Worldwide Anglican Communion. In different countries and regions, the Church takes on differing names, such as the Anglican Church of Canada, Church in Wales, Church of England, Church of Ireland, and the Scottish Episcopal Church. Worldwide, these national churches are diverse culturally, theologically, and socially. National churches and the parishes within them range from extreme conservatism to extreme liberalism, with everything in between.

The Anglican tradition has had to define what happened after the break with Rome by King Henry VIII (1491-1547). Part of Anglican history is that its *development* has had little to do with King Henry VIII and the issue of his various wives. People habitually state that the Church of England was founded because the King wanted a divorce. To define Anglicanism in those terms is to simplify complex issues while ignoring the deeper ones. The 400 years since were shaped by Elizabeth I and her efforts to give meaning to a "reformed Catholicism," which was neither Roman Catholic nor Protestant. The process of defining

the tenets was profound and was not about King Henry VIII wanting a divorce. Anglicanism never had a need to make claims of originality since it has always seen itself as the continuing Catholic Church in its reformed condition. This is why in Ireland, the Church of Ireland could define itself in terms of being both ancient and Celtic.

In Ireland, the Church of Ireland was the state religion from 1536 through 1870, with all others being dissenting Protestants. After it was disestablished on 1 January 1871, it became one of many churches in Ireland and accounted for more than 12% of the population. It shares a separate history from Anglicanism in other parts of the world. In Ireland, although it was the state religion, it was a minority. In Ulster, it was often outnumbered by Presbyterians and in other provinces, by Roman Catholics. The Church of Ireland was on the edge of Europe; therefore, it was often ignored and underfunded from its home base in Canterbury, England.

From the 1600s, members of the Church of Ireland have been immigrating to the American colonies, where Anglicanism was known as the Church of England. It was the established Church in many of the colonies and was markedly strong in the Southern colonies. During and after the Revolutionary War, many Irish Anglicans were exiled as Loyalists and helped to create what became Canada. Those who sided with the Americans in the war were tainted, and thus the Church of England became its own national Church, the Episcopal Church, in 1785.

ST. PAUL'S CATHEDRAL (EPISCOPAL), WOODWARD AVE., CORNER HANCOCK AVE., DETROIT, MICH.   245

Figure 12: St. Paul's Episcopal Cathedral in Detroit. (Postcard dated 1933, from collection of E. Wade Hone, West Jordan, Utah. Copyright expired.)

From an immigration perspective, the records of the Episcopal Church in America are significant because of the condition of Church of Ireland registers. The average Church of Ireland register began in only the late 1700s or early 1800s, unlike those in England or Wales, where the Anglican registers can date back hundreds of years, into the 1500s and 1600s, with vast collections of them indexed. In fact, most Episcopal registers in the United States predate by many years the ones for Ireland. Moreover, half the Church of Ireland parish registers were in the 1922 Four Courts Fire, in which the archive in Dublin was destroyed.

Episcopal Records

The Episcopal Church has national headquarters in New York City. It is also referred to as the Protestant Episcopal Church or simply P.E. Church, and the two terms are standard in old records. The General Convention governs the Church. Within the United States are many dioceses, each headed by a bishop who serves the needs of the diocese. Within each diocese are many parishes, every one with a priest who serves the membership within the parish boundaries. For almost every family historian, the records generated by the local parish of an ancestor are the most helpful.

The Archives of the Episcopal Church, in Austin, Texas, has documents on the General Convention, missionaries, organizations, and a collection of personal papers of select individuals who have had an impact on the Church. It accepts genealogical inquiries, but its holdings are limited to the national church. It has few parish registers or membership lists. One area of its holdings that may be helpful is the collection of diocesan newspapers along with diocesan and parish histories. The archive has made a concerted effort to identify and collect these. The archive website has directories from which parishes and dioceses can be identified and contacted.

Ancestry.com has a growing collection of digitized and indexed registers from various Episcopal dioceses. FamilySearch.org also has its own digitized collection. It is not uncommon for some of the older and historic parish registers from a given locality, such as Virginia or Maryland, to have been published. These can extend into the 1600s. In some urban areas, the Episcopal Church buildings occupy prominent places in the downtown areas and attracted the business class, freemasons, and literate and wealthy families. In the rural areas, the parishes often were simple buildings with no standings. The distinctive ones in the communities were those that might have belonged to Baptist or Methodist churches.

Records generated by a typical Episcopal parish include registers and vestry books. A parish register has the births/baptisms, marriages, and

deaths/burials. The vestry minutes are the business minutes of the parish. Each has the potential to provide birthplaces in Ireland. If a birthplace can be found, it most likely will be in a marriage or burial register, but it can be mentioned in passing as the result of some vestry inquiry. Membership books, often in the form of family books, can also be located within the Church documentations. Transfers in and out of the parish can be helpful in tracking the movements of people.

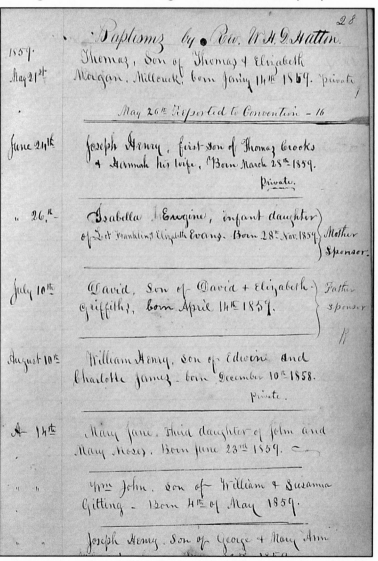

Figure 13: Baptism registry page from Holy Apostles Episcopal Church in St. Clair, Schuylkill County, Pennsylvania. (Image courtesy of Holy Apostles Episcopal Church)

Episcopal Provinces and Dioceses Across the United States

Province 1-New England

Province 2-Atlantic

Province 3-Washington

Province 4-Sewanee

Province 5-Midwest

Province 6-Northwest

Province 7-Southwest

Province 8-Pacific

Figure 14a and 14b: Episcopal provinces and their dioceses for the United States.

Tracing an Episcopal Priest

In the Anglican tradition, priests may marry. The priest is set aside as a servant of Christ. The bishops are priests who serve as pastors to the pastors. The Anglican tradition is not democratic, and priests are under obligation to be obedient to the episcopate. On the other hand, in some areas of the Church, ecclesiastical policy can vary, with the bishops, priests, and the laity sharing responsibilities in a somewhat democratic manner. Most geographical areas of the Anglican Communion currently ordain women as priests, although this has not been without contention. The Church of Ireland was the first in the Anglican Communion to do so, in 1990.

If a priest was born in Ireland, consider that he might have been trained at Trinity College in Dublin, or that he was from a moneyed family in Ireland. If so, university records and pedigrees with birthplaces may be on file for the family at the Genealogical Office in Dublin. Also, clergy were typically respected in their American communities, and so informative obituaries usually have been published. They may state birthplaces.

The Archives of the Episcopal Church, in Austin, Texas, holds an "Archives Biographical Files" with information on many ordained ministers that can consist of obituaries, photographs, newspaper clippings, personal papers, and even some genealogies. Keep in mind that Episcopal ministers were well educated and trained, and so a variety of records were potentially created throughout their lives.

Methodist Church

Methodists were the radicals of the 1700s. They arrived in Ireland from England and then emigrated from both countries to colonial America. The chief founder and theologian of Methodism was John Wesley (1703-1791). A son of the Church of England parish rector, he was born at Epworth, Lincolnshire, England. John Wesley studied at Christ Church College in Oxford and was ordained into the ministry in 1725. In 1727, his brother Charles Wesley (1707-1788), an undergraduate in Christ Church College, gathered some like-minded students to study the Bible. John became a leader of this group. The name Methodists was given to these students because of their regular (methodical) observance of the rules found in the Anglican Book of Common Prayer regarding works of piety and charity.

On 24 Mary 1738, while attending a Moravian meeting, John Wesley experienced what he called his evangelical conversion. This gave him a sense of mission, and he spent the next fifty years preaching his evangelical insights. He first visited Ireland in 1747. His was originally a reform movement within Anglicanism, not its own denomination, affecting how records are pursued, whether in Ireland or in America.

John Wesley began sending his missionaries, mainly from England, specifically to the American colonies in 1769. The Irish Methodists had already been in the colonies since about 1760. For example, Robert Strawbridge (c. 1732-1781), born in County Leitrim, worked from his farm in Frederick County, Maryland, and established Methodist societies in Maryland and northeast Virginia. Philip Embury (1723-1773) from County Limerick emigrated about 1760 and settled near Albany, New York, where he established Methodist societies. Barbara (Ruckle) Heck (1734-1804), also from County Limerick, emigrated in 1760 and settled in the Camden Valley in Upstate New York. She helped establish the first Methodist society in New York in 1766. She and her family left America as Loyalists in 1785 for Upper Canada (now Ontario), where they continued to establish Methodism.

Many of the earliest Methodist ministers were not ordained. They were a lay ministry who preached to anyone who would listen. They took religion to the people rather than requiring the people to come to them, which is principal in understanding the explosion of Methodism on the American frontiers as well as in the urban cities.

Methodism took root differently in various parts of the American colonies, and the Irish were instrumental in its progress. In America, as it did in the British Isles, it functioned first within the Church of England. As a result of friction between Anglicans and Methodists in Virginia and New York, some American Methodist congregations began meeting by the 1760s. The denomination took root among English settlers on the Delmarva Peninsula (Maryland and Delaware) in the 1770s. There, in an environment somewhat unsuitable for formal Church of England practices, it was received with enthusiasm by Anglicans. On the tough frontiers of the Delmarva Peninsula and elsewhere, Methodist

missionaries found a suitable audience and began the process of creating their own frontier Methodism.

As a result of the Revolutionary War, many Loyalist Anglican priests fled the colonies, leaving Methodists without access to clergy who could perform Holy Communion, baptisms, and other acts reserved for the clergy. Consequently, John Wesley and two other Anglican priests began ordaining an American Methodist clergy in 1784, creating the Methodist Episcopal Church (M.E. Church) in Baltimore. At that time, Wesley appointed Thomas Coke (1747-1814) and Francis Asbury (1745-1816) as superintendents over the M.E. Church.

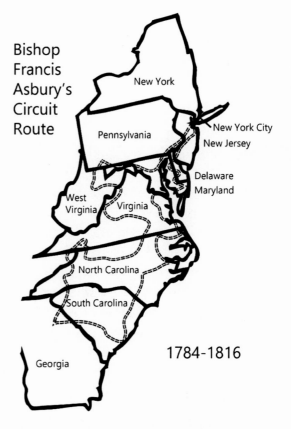

Figure 15: Francis Asbury was a Bishop of the Methodist Church from 1784 to 1816 and was famous for his circuit riding to preach to more congregants than was possible with a stationary pulpit.

Select Methodist Church Evolutions

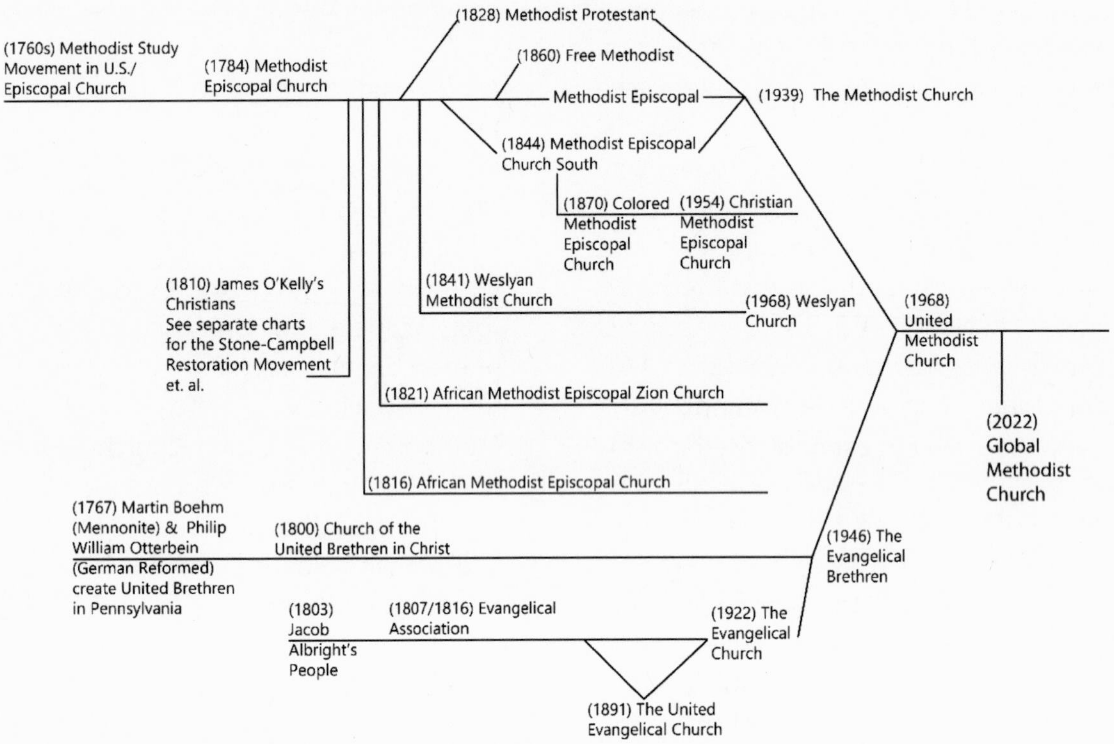

(1760s) Methodist Study Movement in U.S./ Episcopal Church

(1784) Methodist Episcopal Church

(1828) Methodist Protestant

(1860) Free Methodist

Methodist Episcopal — (1939) The Methodist Church

(1844) Methodist Episcopal Church South

(1870) Colored Methodist Episcopal Church

(1954) Christian Methodist Episcopal Church

(1810) James O'Kelly's Christians
See separate charts for the Stone-Campbell Restoration Movement et. al.

(1841) Weslyan Methodist Church

(1968) Weslyan Church

(1968) United Methodist Church

(1821) African Methodist Episcopal Zion Church

(2022) Global Methodist Church

(1816) African Methodist Episcopal Church

(1767) Martin Boehm (Mennonite) & Philip William Otterbein (German Reformed) create United Brethren in Pennsylvania

(1800) Church of the United Brethren in Christ

(1946) The Evangelical Brethren

(1803) Jacob Albright's People

(1807/1816) Evangelical Association

(1922) The Evangelical Church

(1891) The United Evangelical Church

Figure 16: Select Methodist Church development.

Francis Asbury had an enormous impact on the growth of American Methodism. Asbury became known as America's Bishop. He almost single-handedly led the newly formed M.E. Church through its formative years. He traveled 6,000 miles each year on horseback, through all kinds of terrains and weather, to preach anywhere and everywhere. After the beginning of the M.E. Church in 1784, Asbury led it for the next 32 years, seeing the Church rise to some 214,000 members at the time of his death.

Circuit riders took Methodism to diverse areas. Aside from preaching the message of justification by faith, they taught John Wesley's General Rules, which touched upon social problems such as smuggling, gambling, drinking or selling spirituous liquors, slaveholding, and other practices of the late eighteenth century, into the early part of the nineteenth century.

Methodists soon were a major participant in the Second Great Awakening (1790-1830), with Asbury as their most active leader. He became an example to other circuit-riding preachers for how to effectively spread Methodism on the frontier. Through the circuit-riding method and planned revivals, Methodism reached across the Appalachian Mountains and deep into the frontiers. As advocates of the outdoor camp meeting form of revivalism, Asbury and others established the Methodists as the most vigorous denomination of the period.

John Wesley's theology on personal and human freedom resonated in the frontier mind.

In the North, race became a major issue, and the M.E. Church was challenged with whether to ordain black ministers. African Americans were among some of the earliest Methodists. Although the first conference in 1784 declared that all slaves owned by Methodists would be free, the reality was much different. The church drifted from this position and allowed individual churches to decide the status of slavery. Free blacks and slaves had been a part of its home societies since early days, yet they were not treated as equals to whites. By 1790, 20% of Methodists in the United States were black. African Americans began separating from the main Church as early as 1793 in Philadelphia, giving birth to the African Methodist Episcopal Church (AME Church). By 1796, in New York City, blacks began leaving, and another denomination, the African Methodist Episcopal Church Zion (AMEZ Church), was founded. It ordained its own bishops and went on to have an enormous impact on African American culture and history.

By 1840, one million Church members were in the North and the South. John Wesley left a legacy that was strongly anti-slavery in his 1774 publication *Thoughts Upon Slavery*. The American Methodists continued to live in the shadow of this surprisingly blunt condemnation of slavery.

The greatest schism occurred in 1845 when Methodists in the Southern and Border states withdrew and formed the Methodist Episcopal Church, South. In this new denomination, the ownership of slaves was acceptable. While the Southern Methodists made room for slavery, the Northern Methodists continued to aggressively work against slavery as an institution. The division of the Church and the upcoming Civil War were major issues within the Church in the North and the South because even with two white denominations, each was the largest and wealthiest Protestant body in its region heading into the Civil War.

After the defeat of the Confederate States of America, the Southern Methodists were in shambles. In the fifty years after the War, the Northern and Southern Methodist churches grew fourfold. The members in the North increased from one million to four million, and in the South, from 500,000 to two million. African Americans in the Methodist Episcopal Church, South, in 1870, with the blessings of the white denomination, formed the Colored Methodist Episcopal Church. Today, it is known as the Christian Methodist Episcopal Church, and like the AME Church and the AMEZ Church, all three remain an influential presence in the African American community.

At a conference in 1939, three Methodist denominations united, including the Northern and Southern branches, renamed the Methodist Church. In 1968, the Methodist Church united with the Evangelical United Brethren Church (a Germanic Wesleyan body), and the United Methodist Church was born. It became the second largest Protestant denomination in the country.

Like the Baptists and Presbyterians, the Methodists continue to suffer from divisions in the American culture wars. In 2020, the largest Methodist denomination, the multi-ethnic United Methodist Church, voted to divide because of disagreements about ordaining LGBTQ clergy and same-sex marriage. This move created a new "traditionalist Methodist" denomination.

From a genealogical perspective, although three of the four largest Methodist bodies are African American, descendants of Irish immigrants are in all of them. Therefore, any discussion of finding the Irish origins of an Irish immigrant using Methodist documents crosses racial and cultural lines to no small degree.

Methodist Records

The place of the Methodist Church in the United States is unique. It was somewhat of a "community church" historically and drew many people for various reasons. If a family cannot be found in the records of the denomination to which it should have belonged, searching the registers of the Methodist Church closest to the family home is always wise. This not only includes all Protestants but also Roman Catholics. Just one example of the unexpected Catholic connection is William Scott Fisher's work *New York City Methodist Marriages, 1785-1893* (Camden, Maine: Picton Press, 1994). By surveying its index, Catholics with traditional Irish surnames are apparent, certainly more than would typically be expected, although they are not specifically named as Catholics.

The Methodist form of government, which affects records, is present in the United Methodist Church. It is based upon the General Conference, then local conferences, and finally, congregations within the conference. Each conference does keep its own records and serves its communicants on a regional level. The General Conference cannot be thought of as a headquarters, as it is not. Overall, it is where district conference leaders conduct business.

Ancestry.com has a growing collection of digitized and indexed United Methodist records from various archives and especially local Methodist conference repositories. FamilySearch.org also has its own digitized collections.

If the records for a congregation are not yet online, contact its local conference archive. A directory can be found on the General Commission of Archives & History website, Gcah.org. The General Commission does not collect records belonging to individual churches but has all the resources needed to identify them and have them searched. They do offer some genealogical references online. A foremost online index is the "Annual Conference Journal Memoirs Index," which has conference memorials (obituaries) and Honor Rolls taken from the annual conference journals held by the General Commission of Archives & History.

Many of the historic area conference reports are digitized and online at Archive.org, which links the General Commission with the collection "American Methodism Internet Archives." Drew University in Madison, New Jersey, has a large collection of district conference journals from many branches of Methodism as well as the African American denominations and the Wesleyan-Holiness denominations, located in the Methodist Library of the United Methodist Archives and History Center. An inventory of holdings is on the university's website.

The separate congregations kept records aside from the regional Conferences to which they belonged. While many have been gathered for the conference archives, many remain with the congregations. These include some of the following:

Class Lists. These are lists of names of people attending.

Subscribers Lists. These are very similar to Class Lists because they are lists of names of members.

Baptisms. The baptismal registers are a combination of infant baptisms, teenage baptisms, and adult baptisms. Rituals are performed by sprinkling, pouring, or immersion, and the method will not be noted in the register itself. Ages of believers are often attached to the baptism entries. For infant baptisms, birth and baptism dates might have been noted.

Marriages. These registers have the names of the couples, the dates, and any notes the minister might have appended. As with any record, what the ministers documented differs between congregations and ministers.

Probationers' Lists. These records are about persons not in full membership. They can show the person's residence, when received into the congregation, when removed from the congregation, or reasons for not being accepted into the fellowship of the congregation.

Membership Lists. Records of when members in full connection were received into congregations and how they were received, such as by transfers or baptisms.

Contributors. Members' names and their amounts of contributions.

Some of the records, especially for marriages, have birthplaces in Ireland, which is why they need to be searched.

Tracing a Methodist Minister

The Methodist Church has stressed educational requirements for its clergy, but this has different meanings at different times. For example, for the early Methodist clergy, the ministry was a demanding and disciplined vocation. Standards were set during the first conference in 1784, and ministers were expected to study and interact with the members. Many had to supplement their incomes by selling Methodist publications. Because of low wages, the earliest ministers often did not marry or married later in life.

If a legend of a "Methodist preacher" is in family lore, be aware that this could be interpreted a couple of ways. The term preacher could refer to an ordained minister or to a lay person who had many of the same duties as an ordained minister. If he was a lay person, the position was regional, and records are with the congregation or conference. If he was ordained, the records of the General Commission on Archives & History or the

Methodist Library at Drew University should be able to help.

The 1816 General Conference recommended that the annual conferences organize courses in reading and study for any candidate for the ministry. It was not uniformly implemented in all the conferences. Some conferences developed workable programs, thus leaving records, while others were lackadaisical in complying. The early M.E. Church, like other American denominations, had a disdain for formal theological seminary training, but by 1841, the Methodists in New England had succeeded in establishing a seminary for theological instruction, Newbury Biblical Institute in Newbury, Vermont.

Most of the early Methodist ministers had no formal theological training. Their qualifications were literacy and being well read. The Conference records and journals have the records of ministers in training.

Understanding Wesleyan Arminianism

Founders John and Charles Wesley's approach to theology was Arminian even though other Wesleyans' beliefs were more Calvinistic-Methodist. The Arminian doctrine developed by John Wesley came to be known as Wesleyan Arminianism, a theological system originally proposed by James Arminius (1560-1609) that deals with the relationship and bond between God and humanity. Arminianism decrees that God, with the goal of every person's salvation, loves all who have fallen, and, at the same time, his sovereignty over the will of humans is freely limited. The belief is the opposite of traditional Calvinism, which teaches the complete sovereignty of God over humanity through predestination. John Wesley, however, refined Arminianism with a strong evangelical emphasis on the Reformed doctrine of justification by faith. He departed from Classical Arminianism in the following areas:

Atonement. Wesley sought a coexistence of God's love for people and God's hatred of sin. To him, it was not a legal demand for justice so much as an act of mediated reconciliation.

Possibility of apostasy. The Classical Arminian theology that Christians could apostatize and forfeit their salvation was accepted by Wesley. In Wesleyan Arminianism, losing salvation is not based on the sin committed but is more closely related to experiences that are profound and prolonged. Wesley saw two areas in which a person could be deprived of salvation: unconfessed sin and the actual expression of apostasy. Wesley disagreed with the Classical Arminian theology, stressing that these were not permanent states, and the sinner could return.

Christian perfection. Wesley taught that Christians could attain a state of practical perfection wherein they lack all voluntary sin through the Holy Spirit. This was a condition of perfect love and could happen during their lifetimes. Also termed "entire sanctification," it had an enormous impact on the Wesleyan-Methodist and Wesleyan-Holiness movements in America.

(continued....)

Understanding Wesleyan Arminianism (cont.)

To Wesley, entire sanctification was not only to the favor of God but also to the very image of God. Perfect Christians did not refer to those who no longer violated the will of God because involuntary transgressions remained. In this view, Christians are still subject to temptation and need to pray for forgiveness and holiness. It is not an absolute perfection but a perfection of love. Wesley regarded the practice of prayer, scripture, meditation, and Holy Communion as the means of grace whereby God sanctifies and transforms the believer, considered by some to be Wesley's greatest theological contribution to evangelicalism.

The Arminian theology was truly as radical as it was practical, providing an alternative to traditional Calvinism. To assist in fully understanding Wesleyan-Arminianism as well as Classical Arminian thought, several noteworthy books explore the depths of this theological system:

Collins, Kenneth J. and John H. Tyson. *Conversion in the Wesleyan Tradition*. Nashville, Tennessee: Abingdon Press, 2001.

Collins, Kenneth J. *John Wesley: A Theological Journey*. Nashville, Tennessee: Abingdon Press, 2003.

Collins, Kenneth J. *The Theology of John Wesley: Holy Love and the Shape of Grace*. Nashville, Tennessee: Abingdon Press, 2007.

Maddox, Randy L. *Responsible Grace: John Wesley's Practical Theology*. Nashville, Tennessee: Kingwood Books, 1994.

Olson, Roger E. *Arminian Theology: Myths and Realities*. Downers Grove, Illinois: IVP Academic, 2006.

Wynkoop, Mildred Bands. *Foundations of Wesleyan-Arminian Theology*. Kansas City, Missouri: Beacon Hill Press of Kansas City, 1972.

Stone-Campbell Restoration Movement

The concept of restoring primitive Christianity as read exactly from the pages of the New Testament is not new. In nineteenth-century America, the idea erupted and proliferated through the Stone-Campbell Restoration Movement, sometimes referred to as "Stone-Campbell Movement." It was rooted in the Scots-Irish experience. By 1860, it was the fourth largest church in America with 200,000 members.

The Restoration Movement began as the merging of two distinct philosophies. The first came out of Kentucky Scots-Irish Presbyterianism during the Second Great Awakening. Barton W. Stone preached at the famous Cain Ridge Revival of 1801. Soon afterward, he and others withdrew and became known as "Christians." The second was founded by

Alexander Campbell and his father, Thomas Campbell, Presbyterian immigrants from Ballymena, County Antrim. The Campbell family tentatively aligned itself with the Baptists. By the 1820s, the Campbells left and became known as "Disciples."

Christians and the Disciples shared convictions: believers' baptisms by immersion, Christian unity free from denominationalism, and a restoration of the New Testament Church. These parallel movements united in 1832 with origins in frontier reformers who were dissatisfied with Baptists, Methodists, and Presbyterian teachings. In many ways, the story represents the dissent within Ulster and Scottish Presbyterianism as it played out on the frontier.

The core message was to restore non-denominational Christianity, bypassing all forms of what they saw as man-made Christianity. In their eyes, they were going back to the beginning, planting the same church described in the New Testament. Thus, like-minded congregations were established and considered to be the church that Christ founded 2,000 years ago and not as a creation of the 1830s. Their ability to successfully communicate that message to the general frontier mindset is unsurpassed. Mottos, such as "Where the Bible speaks, we speak and where it is silent, we are silent," and "Christians only, but not the only Christians," became catch phrases associated with the Disciples/Christians. Because of their message of non-denominationalism, each congregation was autonomous, and what it called itself was more of a description than a Church name. Some went by Christian Church; others, Disciples of Christ; others, Churches of Christ; and some wore all three descriptions at the same time. Although the Restoration Movement was considered heretical by many evangelical preachers, the message of a restored 2,000-year-old church and Christian unity proliferated. Although found in all states, it is to this day particularly concentrated in Ohio, Indiana, Illinois, and Missouri in the Midwest, and Arkansas, Kentucky, Oklahoma, Tennessee, and Texas in the South.

The emphasis on restoring the primitive church of the New Testament and becoming "Christians Only" opened the doors to controversy and dissent over what that meant and how far was too far. In 1849, efforts to organize a missionary society outside the local congregation to pool resources became an issue. Another controversy was whether instrumental music in worship was scriptural or not. During the 1840s and 1850s, most American denominations were faced with the introduction of instruments of music to worship services. It was especially divisive among the Reformed and Anabaptist churches. While most eventually accepted the matters without division, the Stone-Campbell Restoration Movement did not.

Heated debates ensued in the religious press over instrumental music in worship, centered on the biblical nature of music. Instruments began to become more prevalent in the urban areas of the North, and the Southern congregations overwhelmingly refused them. Some scholars have argued that the division in the movement was cultural and not about instrumental music. After the Civil War, the congregations in the North were constructing large buildings, purchasing costly stained-glass windows, hiring educated ministers, and installing expensive organs. In the South, the churches were poor, rural, and in ruins.

The Restoration Movement still fared better than most of the period's denominations that were splitting along various lines, typically progressive and conservative ones. The Restoration Movement had more success because each congregation was independent. It is difficult to divide a church over theological or cultural lines without a headquarters or a governing body beyond those of individual congregations.

The United States Religious Census of 1906 listed non-instrumental Churches of Christ separately from the Christian Church for the first time. The census showed 982,701 Disciples of Christ and 159,658 non-instrumental Church of Christ members. The Restoration Movement now officially accepted what had been known for years, that there were two separate church bodies of divergent believers.

The liberal-conservative divide only widened as three main branches of this movement appeared. The Christian Church (Disciples of Christ) took the path of Liberal Protestantism. As a result, more middle conservative congregations in 1968 became the Christian Church/Churches of Christ. The non-instrumental Church of Christ took a more varied path, from ultra-conservative to liberal. The ecumenical approach adopted by the Christian Church (Disciples of Christ) advanced it beyond its Restoration Movement roots by cooperating with other churches, being one of many Christians. This is the opposite stance of many conservative non-instrumental Church of Christ congregations, who differ and can swing from being "Christians only" to being the "only Christians."

A standard reference work covering all three branches is Douglas A. Foster, Paul M. Blowers, Anthony L. Dunnavant, and D. Newell William's *The Encyclopedia of the Stone-Campbell Movement* (Grand Rapids, Michigan: Wm. B. Eerdmans Publishing Col, 2005). Other theological works for the three movements include:

Cottrell, Jack. *The Faith Once for All: Bible Doctrine for Today*. Joplin, Missouri: College Press Publishing, 2002. (Conservative work from the Christian Church/Churches of Christ perspective.)

Turner, Rex A., Sr., Don Shackelford, ed. *Biblical Theology: Fundamentals of the Faith*. Rev. ed. 1989. Montgomery, Alabama: Amridge University Press, 2010. (Written from a non-instrumental Church of Christ perspective.)

Williamson, Clark M. *Way of Blessing, Way of Life: A Christian Theology*. St. Louis, Missouri: Chalace Press, 1999. (Written from a Christian Church [Disciples of Christ] perspective.)

Stone-Campbell Movement Records

The records of the Stone-Campbell Restoration Movement are much like those kept by Baptist congregations. The records of the congregations themselves

Stone-Campbell Restoration Movement

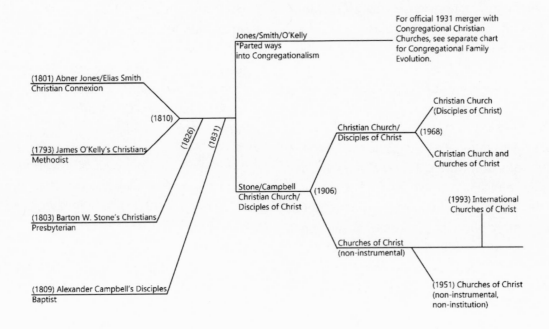

Figure 17: Stone-Campbell Restoration Movement.

are not necessarily used to identify immigrant origins. Their worth is in documenting persons and tracking their movements before they entered congregations and after leaving them. They are part of the holistic approach in working back to the immigrant. Because of its large membership of Scot-Irish heritage, anything they document about a person is significant.

There are records that may help with this goal. The abundant religious periodicals have obituaries and information on ministers. The emphasis on being able to read the Bible was a prized educational achievement within the movement from its first days, and the early ministers were educated men. The educational pursuits increase the chances of additional records being left.

The records for the three branches of the Restoration Movement can be found in several places. Many are still with the congregations. Others have been microfilmed or digitized through FamilySearch.org. The Disciples of Christ Historical Society in Bethany, West Virginia, collects for all branches of the Restoration Movement at Discipleshistory.org.

Considerable materials about the Restoration Movement are at the "Discipliana Collection" at Barton College in Wilson, North Carolina, a Christian Church (Disciples of Christ) institution. It is part of the Disciples Seminary Foundation at the Willis N. Hackney Library. It has the works of early leaders of the movement as well as many individual church registers. The congregational registers it holds are digitized through FamilySearch.org. Aside from the congregational registers, the "Discipliana Collection" has material on historical persons and institutions. The Collection consists of some 3,000 volumes and two dozen periodicals including Disciples' periodicals, pamphlets, rare books, microfilm, memorabilia, and other research materials for Disciples' history.

A sizeable archive, mainly concentrated on material from the non-instrumental Church of Christ, is the Center for Restoration Studies at Abilene Christian University, Abilene, Texas. For the genealogist, the "Personal Papers" and "Vertical Files" are the most valuable. The Vertical Files is subdivided further, with pertinent collections for churches, leaders, and miscellaneous papers. All of these are inventoried on the "Center for Restoration Studies" website. The extensive "Miscellaneous Collections" has information on most topics of concern to the Church of Christ. For information on individual congregations, the "Churches Collection" is the most beneficial. The breadth of data is from membership registers to histories. While the "Churches Collection" embraces the entire United States, most of it centers on Oklahoma, Tennessee, and Texas.

Whether a congregation from any of the three branches has surviving records or even produced records is the first step in research. Once this has been determined, locate where they are deposited. The FamilySearch Catalog online is one of the first places to consult, as is the Disciples of Christ Historical Society. If they are not at either, contact the ancestor's

local congregation. Each congregation kept its own records, and so they vary in content even in the same town.

The earlier congregation records are usually in the form of minutes and are similar to minutes in most churches. They are seldom indexed and can have hundreds of manuscript pages that could cover transfers in and out of the congregation, membership lists, disciplinary actions, subscriptions of contributors and the amounts given, and adult baptisms. Some congregations kept separate books for memberships or vital information such as baptisms, marriages, and deaths, but most are intermixed with the narrative of the minutes.

Another statement needed about the middle-of-the-road conservative Christian Church/Churches of Christ (also seen as Christian Church and Churches of Christ) is that these congregations can go by Christian Church *or* Church of Christ. In places, such as Ohio, they outnumber the non-instrumental Church of Christ congregations, and often have that name, even if the two are in the same town. In the South, where the non-instrumental Church of Christ is the most prominent, it is always known as the Christian Church (or the colloquial Independent Christian Church). Efforts to seek records still with local congregations in places like Ohio can be hampered because the name Church of Christ may be used by non-instrumental congregations and the ones that have organs and choirs. Yet, the two are not associated. If seeking old records in a particular town, it may be easier to simply contact both as well as the Christian Church (Disciples of Christ) because before 1906, all congregations were technically of the same Church even though all congregations were autonomous.

Moravian Church (United Brethren)

The Moravian Church, formally known as *Unitas Fratrum* (Latin for Unity of the Brethren or United Brethren), is a pre-Reformation body. Organized in 1457 in Bohemia, it, along with the Waldenses, was founded in 1170 in what is now Italy, and both were the predecessors of the Protestant Reformation. At the birth of the Reformation, the Moravians stood alongside Martin Luther and other Reformation leaders who were merging into the rising tide of Protestantism.

The Moravian Church can be traced back to the preaching of Jan Hus (English John Huss) (c. 1372-1415) in what became the Czech Republic. He wanted to return the church in Bohemia and Moravia to the earlier practices, when those areas were Eastern Orthodox. He objected to some practices of the Roman Catholic Church. He demanded that the liturgy should be in the language of the people, lay people should receive both the bread and wine, priests could marry, and indulgences and the doctrine of Purgatory should be eliminated. He believed that the authority of scripture was higher than the authority of the church. By rejecting indulgences, Jan Hus, by default, adopted the doctrine of justification by grace through faith alone. This, in effect, made the Moravians a Protestant church even though it predated Protestantism. He was tried by the Council of Constance, declared a heretic, and burned at the stake on 6 July 1415, 102 years before Martin Luther ignited the Protestant Reformation.

Culturally, many Moravian customs have unfolded across the world, with their origins lost to the public. For example, Easter Sunrise Service was popularized internationally by Moravian missionaries. The first recorded Sunrise Service was in 1732 in the Moravian congregation at Herrnhut, Saxony. Another commemoration that can be traced back to the Moravians is New Year's Eve worship service, derived from the tradition of the "Night Watch." It was popularized by Methodist John Wesley, who learned it from the Moravians.

Moravian Distinctives

Moravian distinctives cannot be thought of in terms of special doctrines since the theology parallels that of historic Protestantism, but how traditional Protestant doctrines are approached and applied are distinct. Moravian theology tends to be relational rather than academic and systematic. It consists of God's relationship to humanity, humanity's relationship to God, and humanity's relationship to one another. The approach is applied to doctrines such as the Holy Communion. For example, how Christ is present in the Holy Community is not as necessary as appreciating the presence. Another example is baptism. Knowing that baptism initiates one into the church is more essential than how that is accomplished (sprinkling, pouring, or immersion).

The Moravian Church has always allowed a great deal of freedom in doctrinal thinking. Its motto is "In essentials unity, in non-essentials liberty and in all things charity." This underscores its commitment to Christ and has allowed the members to participate in numerous influential charities and educational ventures. Works detailing Moravian thought include:

Crews, C. Daniel. *Confessing Our Unity in Christ: Historical and Theological Background to "The Ground of the Unity"* 2nd ed. Winston-Salem, North Carolina: Moravian Archives, 2000. Crews, C. Daniel. *This We Most Certainly Believe: Thoughts on Moravian Theology.* Winston-Salem, North Carolina: Moravian Archives, 2005.

Freeman, Arthur. *An Ecumenical Theology of the Heart: The Theology of Count Nicholas Ludwig von Zinzendorf.* Bethlehem, Pennsylvania, and Winston-Salem, North Carolina: Moravian Church in America, 1999.

As a historic ecumenical denomination, the Moravians do not engage in debates about denominational differences but concentrate on what unites them. They see that the issues that divide Christians can also enrich them, and so the church has a tradition of working alongside other denominations to accomplish particular goals. At times, the Church has even turned its missions over to other denominations who have been better equipped to operate them.

Moravian Immigration Strategy

The number of Moravians in Ireland during the eighteenth and nineteenth centuries is uncertain, but John Taylor Hamilton's *A History of the Church Known as the Moravian Church* (1900. Reprint, New York: A.M.S. Press, 1971) places it at 4,673 in 1824 and 5,000 in 1834. Historically, the strength of the Moravian Church was in Ulster. Still, its numbers cannot be accurately calculated because of the constant flow of emigration.

At first glance, it may seem that immigrant origins are solved because the places these congregations existed are known in Counties Antrim, Cavan, Clare, Down, Dublin, and Londonderry (Derry). In fact, many remain in Northern Ireland and in Dublin. If an ancestor is found in any extant registers for one of these congregations, the question of immigrant origins is answered. Many of the registers are at the PRONI in Belfast or indexed on RootsIreland.ie. In numerous cases, however, locating them is not that simple.

In America, it was common for people to convert to the Moravians. They were missionary minded with high standards and a stable, substantial lifestyle that was attractive to many people who had no connections with the Moravians in Ireland. Therefore, always consider this when researching an American Moravian ancestor who just happened to have been born in Ireland.

Moravian immigration to America was primarily to Pennsylvania and North Carolina, where Moravians organized towns and supported institutions. Moravian immigrants of all nationalities first located in the settlements at Forsythe County, North Carolina, and the communities of

Bethlehem, Nazareth, and Lititz, Pennsylvania. Records from these communities can indicate a member's congregation of origin. Those who joined in America might have had no connection to the North Carolina or Pennsylvania Moravian communities.

Moravian Records

Large Moravian collections can be found at two archives. The Moravian Archives, Northern Province of the Moravian Church of North American in Bethlehem, Pennsylvania, and the Moravian Archives, Southern Province of the Moravian Church of North America, in Winston-Salem, North Carolina, are where most registers are housed. The Moravian Archives in Bethlehem has a "Moravian Roots Genealogy Database" on its website that can be searched by name. The database contains information on baptisms, marriages, and funerals. The source is the records held at its archive. The heart of the collection in Winston-Salem is the "Memoir Collection," with over 14,000 records of individual members.

Most Moravian Church records of births/baptisms, marriages, and deaths do not have the birthplaces of the members. The record that may have this information is called a memoir. Memoirs are similar to eulogies. Before death, a person might have had a memoir written about his or her life and service to the church. If one was not written before the member's death, the minister could have done so afterward. Memoirs can be basic or remarkable in their details.

The memoirs for the Forsythe County congregations are at the Moravian Archives in Winston-Salem. Those for non-Germanic people have been translated from the original German. All the North Carolina memoirs are indexed at the Archives. The index is completely cross-referenced for the married women. The following are examples of Irish-born Moravians from the memoir index cards:

Brietz, Margaret (nee Marrow). b. 02 Jan. 1829, Magherafelt, Derry Co., Ireland; d. 14 Jan 1886, Salem; m. Charles G. Briety, 1857

Craig, William. b. 23 Jan 1801, Gracehill, Ireland; d. 25 Sep. 1823, Salem.

Douthit, John (Sr.). b. 09 May 1709, Coolrain, Ireland; d. 22 Feb 1784, Hope, NC; m. Mary Scott, 1738; 11 children.

Mack, Mary (nee Grant). b. 01 Aug 1755, Ballinderry Co., Antrim, Ireland. Called to service in W.I. [West Indies], 1799 & to marry Hanan. Trying trip, including capture by Irish rebels. M1. I. J. Hanan; m2. Jacob Mack.

Quinn, William. b. 17 Mar 1846, Galway Co., Ireland; parents: John & Catharine Quinn.

Rights, Margaret (Waterson). b. 16 Jun 1793 Gracehill, Ireland. d. 12 Jul 1863.

Waterson, George. b. 21 Jan 1751 at Lisnamara, Ireland; d. 13 Apr

Figure 18: Otterbein United Brethren (Moravian) Church, Baltimore, Maryland. (Image courtesy of the Library of Congress. Photographer E.H. Pickering, Historical American Buildings Survey. This work is in the public domain in the United States because it is a work prepared by an officer or employee of the United States Government as part of that person's official duties under the terms of Title 17, Chapter 1, Section 105 of the U.S. Code.)

1821, Salem; m. Martha
Hammond, 1782, in Ireland.

Waterson, Martha (nee
Hammond). b. Feb 1757,
Ballyronan, Londonderry Co.,
Ireland. m. George Waterson. 7
children.

Worthington, John. b. 03 Nov
1725, Dublin, Ireland. d. 1789.

It is obvious from the places that some of these were Moravian in Ireland, such as Gracehill, but this is not always the case. William Quinn, born 17 March 1846, was from County Galway, and no Moravian congregation was in that part of Ireland. Consequently, American Moravian records need to be searched to learn more about him.

Another source for immigrant origins is the eleven-volume set of minutes of the North Carolina congregations. The minutes from 1752 to 1879 have been published in the series *Records of the Moravians in North Carolina* (Raleigh: Edwards and Broughton Printers, 1922-1969), with volumes 6 and 7 reprinted by the North Carolina Department of Archives and History. These books mention Irish families and sometimes the congregations in Ireland from where they came. Examples of the Irish identified in the published church minutes are:

April 5, 1810. Mr. George
Waterson, of Lincoln County, this
state, who has spent some time
here, left today for Norfolk. From
there he will return to Ireland,

and, God willing, will bring his
family to America. Our best
wishes go with him. ("Extracts
from Salem Diary," Volume VII
[1809-1822], p. 3109).
November 8, 1826. John Spence,
the journeyman tailor who is
working for Br. Charles Levering,
was formerly a Society Brother at
Gracehill, Ireland. ("Salem Board
Minutes," Volume VIII [1823-
1837], p. 3777).

December 27, 1840. ...In the
evening there was a final meeting
of these festival days in which the
married Agnes Jane Whicker, m.n.
Morrow, was numbered among
the nonresident section of the
congregation. She was baptized
and confirmed in Ireland in the
Episcopal Church and became
acquainted with the Brethren's
congregation before she
migrated to America. Here in
Salem where she has relatives (Br.
and Sr. Waterson) she lived a long
time as a single person... ("Diary
of the Congregation in Salem,"
Volume IX [1838-1847], p. 4526).

Chapter Four

Church Records, Part 2

> ➤ **Roman Catholic**
> ➤ **Religious Society of Friends (Quakers)**
> ➤ **Society of Believers (Shakers)**
> ➤ **Church of the New Jerusalem (Swedenborgians)**
> ➤ **Church of Jesus Christ of Latter-day Saints (Mormons)**

Roman Catholic

The Spanish Roman Catholic Church was in what is today the United States 42 years before the arrival of the Protestant English in Virginia. St. Augustine, Florida, was founded in 1565, and Santa Fe, New Mexico, in 1610, just three years after the English Jamestown, Virginia, settlement in 1607. The Puritans and the Mayflower were latecomers in 1620. These former Spanish and French colonies, dominantly Catholic, were annexed or purchased by the ever-expanding United States. French and Spanish Catholicism accompanied the new territories.

The Irish entered these areas either from the United States as settlers seeking land grants or straight from Ireland. They found themselves in ethnically Spanish or French parishes until they could create their own English-speaking parishes.

These areas, unlike others in the evolving United States, had established parish systems. Large Irish populations also were in places such as St. Louis, Missouri, a former French stronghold, and New Orleans, which had been under several flags over its history. Other localities under English control, such as Maryland, also had parish systems. Maryland had been set up as a refuge for Catholics.

A long-standing notion is that the Irish all came during the Potato Famine beginning in 1845, but they had been on the frontiers as workers before then. They were often served by visiting priests instead of traditional parish priests. These early Catholics met in homes with the priests when they went through their localities. At some time, sufficient Catholics warranted buildings and resident priests. This was customary in Upstate New York, where the workers and farmers saw their home churches grow into large and often Irish-dominated parishes.

Catholics settled across the states in wilderness regions like Kentucky. Coming from Maryland, they traveled together, founding what became parishes. In places, such as on the frontiers of neighboring Tennessee, the number of Catholics did not compare to that of Kentucky. Those early Tennessee Catholics tended to become blended into the local Protestant population because of few priests or other Catholics.

Each area has to be judged by its own history. If the Catholics were on the frontiers, were they being served from a mission? It might have been from a larger urban area, such as Albany, New York, or farther afield, such as Baltimore or Quebec. An old county history book will usually have some of this history and the regions the early missions attended. If not, learning where the itinerate priests were based answers the question. Records can then be located and searched.

The urban areas were different because they had resident priests, although only one or two parishes might have been in each larger city before the influx of immigrants, such as the Irish. The search for records is easier. New strategies need to be employed for after the time the parish system rapidly began expanding and immigrants from multiple countries arrived.

When considering Catholic ancestors, some issues need to be carefully thought through. First is whether they were even served by a priest. If there were no priests or parish system, chances are they were unchurched or they went to other denominations. Do not be surprised if this is found to be the case. It is no different than the relationship of Protestants with religion, where they either became unchurched or attended a denomination unfamiliar to them, such as an ethnic German Lutheran or Dutch Reformed congregation.

In addition, a mixed marriage might have accounted for the Irish branch of the family being in the Catholic Church. For example, in places such as Ohio, it was common over the years for German Catholics to intermarry with the large population of Scot-Irish Protestants, and if so, the Catholic faith does not come from the Irish side but from the German side.

The opposite occurred also. Ancestors may not be found at all in the Catholic registers because they converted to another church. This happened often through intermarriage. If the children were not baptized Catholic, probably this was exactly the case.

Because of the Catholic attitude about divorce, couples not living together in the censuses can be found. Typically, but not always, the husband is missing. Determine whether the couple is buried together, and if not, a safe assumption is that something out of the ordinary occurred. A husband or wife abandoning the family and going his or her own way was not remarkable. Both circumstances can be documented. Some men went to California or to the gold fields of Alaska and the Yukon and were never heard from again.

Some spouses were committed to institutions such as prisons or mental health facilities, where they died, and nobody talked about them ever again. Some men died in war and were buried far from the family homes. Still others simply slipped off and had other families, never to return to the first family. When trying to sort through this, recall that because of

Catholic culture and doctrine, certain customs were in place, and if violated, for instance, by a missing spouse, something unusual took place.

Reading between the lines, what a Catholic family was supposed to do and what is seen in the records present some of the most interesting clues. For example, divorce not being an option explains why a divorce was never filed. Since Catholic graveyards were consecrated ground where only Catholics could be buried, the question arises about why the spouse was not buried there. A suicide could not be buried in the consecrated ground. Sometimes, newspaper articles can help solve some of these riddles. And there were times when people did not want to be found, and they succeeded!

Finding the "Irish Parish"

Often among genealogists there is a tendency to speak off-the-cuff about the "Irish Parish" in a city or community. Typically, this means that it was where the Irish were concentrated. Even though it might have been more of an English-speaking parish than an Irish one, the difference may only be slight. What is inferred is that they were not the parishes in the French, German, Hungarian, Italian, Lithuanian, Polish, Spanish, or other neighborhoods in any sizeable urban area. While unindexed records in large metropolitan areas can be daunting, it is certain that in the search for an ancestral parish, St. Patrick's Parish is a safer bet than Our Lady of Pompeii. With a little logic, even in the largest of urban areas, parishes can be narrowed to some extent just by using the name of the church as a guide.

The name of the parish in urban areas is not the only key to finding the Irish-dominated parish or, at least, the English-speaking parish. In large urban areas, people tended to live in apartment tenements. They moved every year or so in the search for jobs or cheaper rents, and so an ancestor's family might have been in several parishes. Now that many records for major dioceses are coming online at Findmypast.com or for Boston at Ancestry.com, documenting is easier. However, not all dioceses with major urban areas are online currently.

In these cases, identifying the correct parish is a matter of aligning the English-speaking one to the neighborhood where the ancestors lived, which can be done through the city directories for the ancestor's address and the address of his or her local parish. With current technology, it is simpler than ever. If the old parish churches are still in existence, a "street view" map can easily highlight the buildings. The signs on the fronts of the buildings should also be in the pictures. If the buildings have been sold by the dioceses but are still standing, the architecture might identify them along with the initial search of the city directory. With a map website, it is possible to plot the distance from the church address to the ancestor's home. There may be several parishes to choose from. Be aware that even if one was not English speaking, the Irish might still have been associated with it because it was the closest to their homes.

When potential parishes are identified in conjunction with the ancestor's address, the next step is finding records indexed

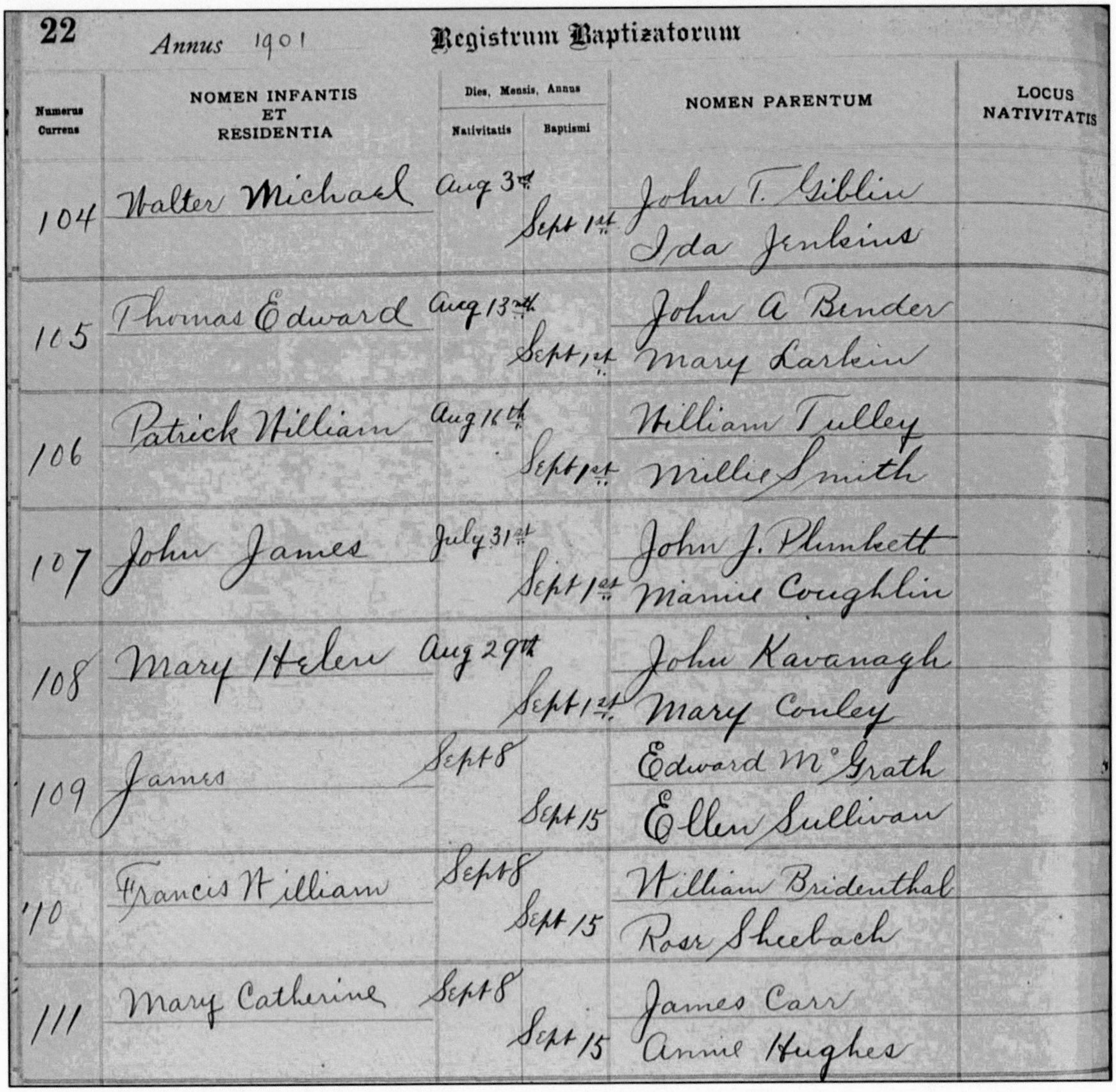

22	*Annus* 1901		**Registrum Baptizatorum**		
Numerus Currens	**NOMEN INFANTIS ET RESIDENTIA**	**Dies, Mensis, Annus**		**NOMEN PARENTUM**	**LOCUS NATIVITATIS**
		Nativitatis	**Baptismi**		
104	Walter Michael	Aug 3rd	Sept 1st	John T. Giblin / Ida Jenkins	
105	Thomas Edward	Aug 13th	Sept 1st	John A Bender / Mary Larkin	
106	Patrick William	Aug 16th	Sept 1st	William Tulley / Millie Smith	
107	John James	July 31st	Sept 1st	John J. Plunkett / Mamie Coughlin	
108	Mary Helen	Aug 29th	Sept 1st	John Kavanagh / Mary Conley	
109	James	Sept 8	Sept 15	Edward McGrath / Ellen Sullivan	
110	Francis William	Sept 8	Sept 15	William Bridenthal / Rose Sheebach	
111	Mary Catherine	Sept 8	Sept 15	James Carr / Annie Hughes	

Figure 19a: A 1901 baptism register from former St. Patrick's Catholic Church in Chicago. Note the marriages recorded for these individuals. (Image courtesy of Catholic Archives and Records Center, Chicago, Illinois.)

online. If they are not, they may still be with the parishes, or they were turned over to the dioceses or other repositories.

While early Catholic parishes tended to be divided along ethnic lines, as were the cemeteries, they all were not. Throughout rural America, only one parish might have served each area, and the parishioners might have been both Germans and Irish with either a German or Irish priest. Consider the nationality carefully when reviewing an index. If the priest writing the records was German, how did he hear and interpret Irish surnames? This can throw off an index search to no small extent. In these areas, even if registers are indexed, it might be prudent to just look at the registers page by page so that nothing is missed. As many are digitized at the FamilySearch.org and Findmypast.com websites, the task is achievable.

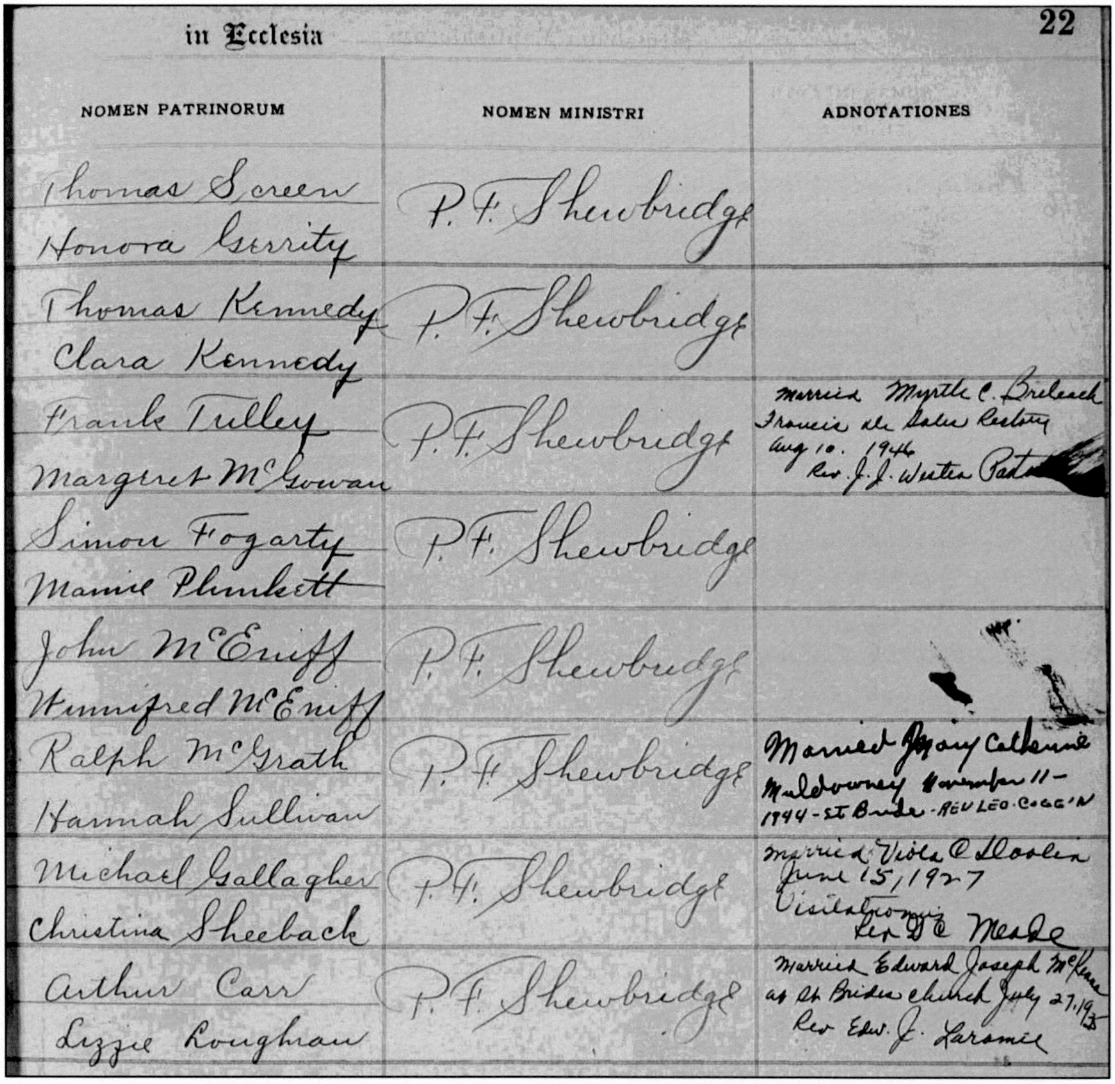

in Ecclesia 22

NOMEN PATRINORUM	NOMEN MINISTRI	ADNOTATIONES
Thomas Screen Honora Gerrity	P. F. Shewbridge	
Thomas Kennedy Clara Kennedy	P. F. Shewbridge	
Frank Tulley Margaret McGowan	P. F. Shewbridge	married Myrtle C. Brilesch Francis de Sales Rectory Aug 10. 1946 Rev. J. J. Wester Pastor
Simon Fogarty Mamie Plunkett	P. F. Shewbridge	
John McEniff Winnifred McEniff	P. F. Shewbridge	
Ralph McGrath Hannah Sullivan	P. F. Shewbridge	Married Mary Catherine Muldowney November 11- 1944-St Bride-REV LEO COGG'N
Michael Gallagher Christina Sheeback	P. F. Shewbridge	married Viola C Doolin June 15, 1927 Visitation Rev D C Meade
Arthur Carr Lizzie Roughan	P. F. Shewbridge	married Edward Joseph McKenna at St Brides church July 27, 1935 Rev Edw. J. Laramee

Figure 19b: A 1901 baptism register from former St. Patrick's Catholic Church in Chicago. Note the marriages recorded for these individuals. (Image courtesy of Catholic Archives and Records Center, Chicago, Illinois.)

What to Look for in a Parish Register

Catholic parish registers can be with parishes, the dioceses, or online. Therefore, some effort is required to determine just where relevant records are on deposit. The website Findmypast.com has been obtaining contracts with dioceses to digitize and index their records, and so it needs to be periodically consulted for additions. Over the decades, the Family History Library has microfilmed and digitized various parish registers and entire diocesan records, and thus it is another major repository.

Many historic parishes no longer exist. They were either disbanded as the neighborhoods changed, for example, from predominantly Irish to African American. Do not be surprised if the old St. Patrick's parish is now an exclusively Spanish-speaking or Filipino parish. In other cases, parishes merged, and the records went into the merger or were deposited at the diocesan offices or archives. Because of the interest in family history, it is not uncommon for a simple search engine task to reveal that someone has written the history about a now defunct or merged parish. The diocesan offices also have knowledge of what happened to old records.

From an immigration strategy perspective, the local parish registers need to be consulted because they might contain a birthplace in Ireland. If a birthplace is listed, it will be in a marriage record, and depending on the record-keeping practices of the parish, it can be an unparalleled discovery. If a parish kept burial registers, birthplaces can also be recorded in them, usually as county names. Burial is not a sacrament of the Catholic Church, and so most parishes did not document them. In rural areas, the Catholic cemeteries and the parishes may have the same burial records. Urban areas typically do not. Oddly enough, some parish priests, but certainly not all, noted where parents were born in the children's christening records. When found, they are marvelous exceptions, which is another reason to search all the christenings of the immigrant's children.

Many beginning researchers overlook the christening records of the children simply because the children were not the immigrants. The christenings are among the most important Catholic parish records because of the names of the godparents (sponsors). They were valued people to the parents, and their presence in the search for Irish origins is straightforward. A sponsor at a baptism is different than a witness at a marriage.

Foremost is that in marriages, the witnesses do not even have to be related or even know the couple. In the case of godparents, they are trusted friends or family who were responsible for the child's physical and spiritual well-being if something happened to the parents. Who were these people?

If their surnames are the same as the father's or the mother's maiden name, the natural assumption is that they were siblings or, at least, cousins from Ireland—and not only from Ireland but also in the same parish in Ireland. That is a major clue, warranting tracing the lives of these sponsors for where they were from in Ireland. Their attendance may also be the first indication that other family members immigrated. Even if they do not have the same surnames, they might have been cousins or friends from Ireland. Be conscious that not everyone immigrated with family. Sometimes, they came with friends, especially among young people seeking better lives and footholds. In theory, like the family, the friends were from the same parish in Ireland. Therefore, if research on the immigrant ancestor does not reveal a birthplace in Ireland in any of the records, look to the sponsors at the christenings.

When deciphering parish registers, men's surnames are certain. First names may vary, such as Eugene and Owen being interchangeable or Con or Corny for Cornelius. Irish women's names are more complicated. First, question whether the priest was recording the maiden or married names for women, as it affects witnesses to marriages and what is in the christening records. Occasionally, it is not clear, and in other cases, it is obvious. Make this an area of concern. For female given names, do not be alarmed to see Bridget for Delia or Hannah for Anna and Johanna. They are prevalent enough to be almost forgettable. Female first names do present a problem. The same woman might have been listed three times as a godparent, but her first name is different each time.

Dispensation Records

A marriage dispensation was issued if a question arose about a couple seeking to marry in a Catholic church by a priest. The matter went before the bishop of the diocese for a dispensation (permission) to be granted for the marriage to be performed. A dispensation was an exception to what was normally forbidden. The papers are usually kept at the diocesan offices, not being part of the parish registers, although the parish marriage registers might have a "disp," indicating the dispensation was granted. The records can be considered somewhat sensitive, with many dioceses restricting access to them. Contacting the diocesan archives should clarify its policy.

From a genealogist's perspective, dispensations are ordinarily tame, for instance, the couple being distantly related (*consanguinity*), an issue with the reading of the marriage banns in church, or bringing a common-law marriage into a Church marriage. From the perspective of an immigration strategy, the most important one is a priest's performing the marriage of a Catholic to a non-Catholic, which generated a record with additional information. Catholics married Protestants all the time. A dispensation might not have personal details about the non-Catholic party, but it should about the Catholic party. It can include birthplaces in Ireland and parents' names. Each diocese kept the records differently. For some immigrants, the dispensations might have been the only records in which birthplaces and parents' names were recorded.

The wording of the dispensation record holds weighty clues. The Catholic Church accepted that Protestants were baptized Christians, and, therefore, in the registers, when *mixtae religionis* is found, it means a "mixed religion" marriage between a Catholic and non-Catholic Christian. When *disparitatis cultis* is recorded, it is "disparity of cult," referring to a marriage between a Catholic and non-Christian. In Utah or areas of the Intermountain West where Mormons overwhelmingly outnumber Catholics, terms became more blurred.

In the areas of the United States, especially Utah, where Catholics were associating and marrying Mormons, a dispensation was defined with the new phrase *mixtae religionis et disparitatis cultus ad cautelam* or "mixed religion with disparity of cult as a safety." It covered the grounds for a marriage when a Mormon might or might not have been Christian. In the early years of Utah, it appears as though Catholics did not consider Mormons to be valid Christians. Under this interpretation, the dispensation could also be listed as a *disparitatis cultis* or "disparity of cult." It is both ways in the registers, depending on the bishop at the time.

Figure 20: St. Mary's Cathedral, Cheyenne, Wyoming. (Credit: Dwight A. Radford, 2019)

Understanding Canon Law

In America, the intermixing of cultures and religions created situations that puzzle researchers. One of them is about conversion to the Catholic Church. What does that really mean? In a mixed marriage ceremony performed by a Protestant minister, what are the ramifications? Having a basic understanding of Canon Law is helpful.

When reading the old records, remember that before the Second Ecumenical Council of the Vatican (1962-1965), also known as the "Second Vatican Council" or simply "Vatican II," the Roman Catholic Church was different than it is today. Vatican II modernized the Church for a contemporary membership by redefining and clarifying centuries' old ideas and dogma. The most obvious was the reciting of the Masses in the language of the people instead of Latin. The altars of the Church were turned around to face the congregations so that the priests are participants in the Masses along with the people. Studying the Bible is encouraged rather than relying on the priests or Church devotional booklets. The Church moved away from biblical literalism in favor of critical modern scholarship. Its position toward other Christians and non-Christians was redefined to be more open. An overall emphasis on renewal and care for the poor was also a part of Vatican II. Therefore, what is in the records before Vatican II can be unlike what is in them afterward.

The Church still sees itself as being exceptional but not in exclusive terms, as it is thought to be in some conservative Protestant denominations in which the belief in a particular theology dictates whether someone is a valid Christian or not. The view of the Catholic Church as being holy and more than simply a human-created institution is the key to understanding some of the questions that genealogists have in grasping exactly what the records and period attitudes mean. Canon Law sets a standard for some conclusions.

As with any denomination, what is preached from the pulpit and what is practiced in the pews are often not the same; hence, despite Canon Law, priests or parishioners may be doing something else. People are people, and the family historian has to keep that in mind. How Catholicism was practiced on the frontiers and mining camps of the American West was dissimilar to how it was practiced in Boston or St. Louis. On the frontiers, where priests were scarce, a Catholic's relationship and understanding of the Church might have been nominal at best, explaining, in part, why so many Catholics fell away or joined other denominations. Until the infrastructure of the Church was solid across the country, options were limited.

Canon law as understood and pronounced by the Church authorities has a long history. Its reference book dates to 1917 with the publication of the first codification of Latin canon law. It was enforced through 1983, when it was replaced. With the publication of *Code of Canon Law* (in Latin: *Codex Iuris Canonici*), Church leaders had a reference from which to study. During its first 65 years, the *complete* translation was not public nor was it translated into other languages. In 1918, the English version summary, *The New Canon Law: A Commentary and Summary of the New Code of Canon Law* (New York: New York: Joseph F. Wagner, Inc., 1918), was published.

The English edition assists family historians in finding and understanding a wealth of information about the pre-Vatican II policies and doctrines of the Church, which, in turn, created the records. The English edition can be found at websites such as Archive.org. It is a fascinating work and crucial to Catholic research. For example, the 1917 publication cited in part the Canon Law 946:

> *The pastor shall also, according to Canon 470 §2, note in the baptismal record that the parties contracted marriage in his parish*

that day. If one or both parties were baptized in another parish, the pastor in whose parish the marriage was contracted shall send notice of the fact to the pastor where the parties were baptized, which he may do either directly or through the Curia of his diocese

This instruction alone has solved many immigration problems for family historians. Also, it has aided in tracking "who went where" among siblings, which, in turn, has accomplished the same purpose. By recording the marriage information into early baptismal records, Canon Law altered what is in the parish registers.

Some of the main laws surrounding baptisms, marriages, burials, and even related excommunications are:

Baptism

591. Infants that have been abandoned and found shall be conditionally baptized, if after careful investigation there is no certainty about their Baptism.

593. An infant of infidel parents can lawfully be baptized even though the parents object, in case the danger of death is such that it may be prudently judged the child will not live until he comes to the use of reason.

Outside danger of death the infant may be licitly baptized, provided there is guarantee for the Catholic bringing up of the child, (1) if the parents or guardians, or at least one of them, consent, (2) if there

are no parents, i.e. father or mother, nor grandfather or grandmother, nor guardians, or if they have lost the right to the child, or cannot in any way exercise that right.

594. Regarding the child of two Protestants or schismatics, or two fallen-away Catholics, the rules of the above Canon shall generally be followed.

595. An adult should not be baptized except with his own knowledge and will, and after due instruction. He is, moreover, to be admonished to repent of his sins.

In danger of death, if he cannot be thoroughly instructed in the principal mysteries of faith, it is sufficient for the conferring of Baptism that he show in some way his assent to these points of faith, and earnestly promises that he will keep the Commandments of the Christian religion.

If he cannot even ask for Baptism, but has either before, or in his present condition manifested in some probable manner an intention of receiving Baptism, he may be baptized conditionally. If afterward he gets well, and there remains doubt as to the validity of the Baptism, he may be baptized again conditionally.

597. Insane and delirious persons should not be baptized unless they have been such from birth, or became such before they had obtained the use of reason, in which case they should be baptized like infants.

If they have lucid intervals, they may in those moments be baptized if they desire it. They may also be baptized in imminent danger of death, if before became insane they have shown a desire for Baptism.

Those suffering from lethargy or delirium should be baptized only while conscious and desirous of Baptism; if the danger of death is imminent, the rule of the foregoing paragraph of this Canon is to be followed.

602. In danger of death private Baptism may be given. If it is administered by one who is neither a priest nor a deacon, only that should be done which is necessary for the validity of the Baptism. If a priest or a deacon baptizes, and there is time, he should perform the ceremonies that follow Baptism.

Outside the case of danger of death, the Ordinary cannot allow private Baptism, except in cases of adult converts from heresy who are baptized conditionally.

The ceremonies of Baptism, which for any reason had been omitted in the conferring of Baptism, would as soon as possible be supplied, except in the case mentioned in the preceding paragraph.

603. If Baptism is given again conditionally, the ceremonies should be supplied if they were omitted in the first Baptism, saving the exception of the foregoing Canon. If the ceremonies were observed in the first Baptism, one is at liberty to go through them again or not.

613. Infants should be baptized as soon as possible. Pastors and preachers should often remind the faithful of this grave obligation.

620. The pastor should, carefully and without delay, enter into the records the name of the one baptized, the minister, parents and sponsors, date and place.

In the Baptism of illegitimate children the name of the mother is to be entered, if her motherhood is publicly known, or if she of her own accord demands this either in writing or before two witnesses. Also the name of the father, provided he himself demands it either in writing or before two witnesses, or if he be known from some public document. In all other cases the child should be entered as one whose father or parents are unknown.

Marriage

903. The Church forbids most severely and in all countries marriage between a Catholic and an heretic, or schismatic. If there is danger of perversion for the Catholic party and the offspring,

such marriage is also forbidden by the Divine law.

904. The Church does not dispense from the impediment of mixed religion unless: (1) there are good and serious reasons; (2) the non-Catholic party promises to remove all danger of perversion of the Catholic party, and both parties promise that all their children shall be baptized and brought up as Catholics; (3) there is moral certainty that the promises will be kept. The promises are, as a rule, to be made in writing.

905. When the Church has given the dispensation from the impediment of mixed religion, the parties are not allowed, either before or after the Catholic wedding, to approach either in person or through proxies a non-Catholic minister as such, to give or renew the consent in the Protestant Rite.

If the pastor knows that the parties will certainly violate or have already violated this law, he shall not assist at the marriage, except for very serious reasons, and only after scandal has been removed, and the Ordinary has been consulted.

The Church does not censure parties who are forced by civil law to appear before a non-Catholic minister, who acts as an official of the government, but their intention must be to merely comply with the requirements of law and to gain the civil recognition of their marriage.

910. A boy under sixteen years of age and a girl under fourteen cannot validly contract marriage.

Though marriage is valid when these years are completed, the pastors of souls should dissuade young people from marriage at an earlier age than is commonly the custom in the respective countries.

913. The marriage between a person baptized in the Catholic Church, or received into the Church from heresy or schism, and a non-baptized individual is null and void.

If a certain party at the time of the marriage was commonly held to have been baptized, or if his baptism was doubtful, the validity of such marriage must, according to the rule of Canon 1014, be upheld until it is proven with certainty that one party was, and the other was not, baptized.

961. The valid marriage of Christians, consummated by the conjugal act, cannot be dissolved by any human authority for any reason; death alone can dissolve the bond.

Burial

1046. The bodies of the faithful must be buried; cremation is forbidden.

If anyone has in any manner ordered his body to be cremated, it shall be unlawful to execute the desire; if this order has been attached to a contract, last will, or any other act, it is to be considered as not added.

1048. The bodies of the faithful are to be buried in a cemetery which has been blessed according to the rites given in the approved liturgical books, either with the solemn or simple blessing by the persons mentioned in Canons 1155 and 1156.

In churches bodies shall not be buried except those of residential bishops, abbots or prelates nullius in their own churches or the Roman Pontiff, royal personages and Cardinals.

1049. The Catholic Church has the right to possess her own cemeteries.

Where this right of the Church is violated without hope of regaining the same, the Ordinaries should take care that the cemeteries belonging to the State are blessed, if those to be buried there are for the greater part Catholics, or at least that the Catholics may have a part of the cemetery reserved for themselves, which part is to be blessed.
If even that much cannot be obtained, the individual graves ought to be blessed according to the ritual, each time the body of a Catholic is buried.

1082. Unbaptized persons must not be buried from a church, with the exception of catechumens who die without having, through no fault of theirs, received Baptism, and are therefore to be counted among those baptized.

All baptized persons are to receive ecclesiastical burial, unless they are explicitly deprived of it by law.

Excommunication
1602. 1. Catholics who marry before a non-Catholic minister;

1602. 2. Catholics who contract marriage with the explicit or implicit understanding that either all or some of their children are to be brought up as non-Catholics;

1602. 3. Catholics who knowingly present their children to a non-Catholic minister for Baptism;

1602. 4. Catholic parents, or those who take the place of the parents, who knowingly have their children brought up or instructed in a non-Catholic persuasion;

1602. 7. Those who procure abortion, not excepting the mother, if abortion has actually taken place.

Catholic Archdiocese and Diocese Jurisdictions

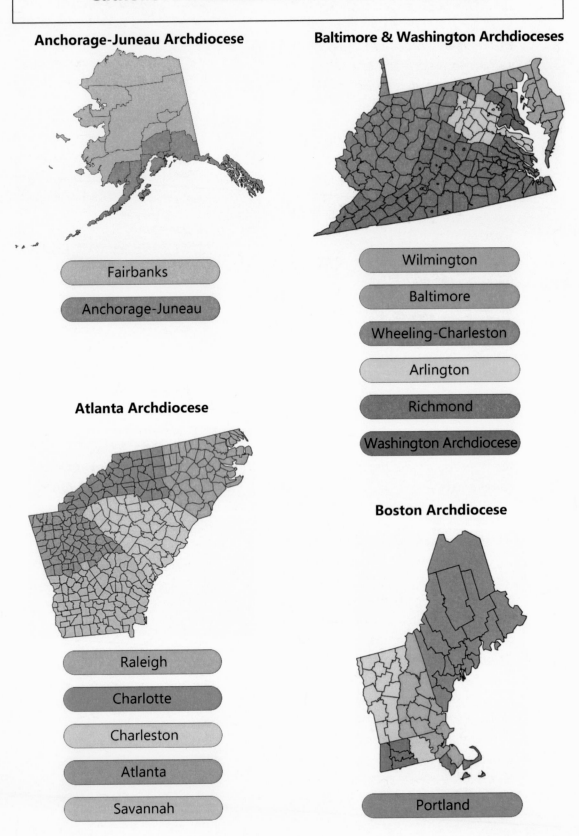

Anchorage-Juneau Archdiocese

Fairbanks

Anchorage-Juneau

Baltimore & Washington Archdioceses

Wilmington

Baltimore

Wheeling-Charleston

Arlington

Richmond

Washington Archdiocese

Atlanta Archdiocese

Raleigh

Charlotte

Charleston

Atlanta

Savannah

Boston Archdiocese

Portland

Manchester

Burlington

Fall River

Boston

Worcester

Springfield

Cincinnati Archdiocese

Youngstown

Cleveland

Toledo

Steubenville

Columbus

Cincinnati

Chicago Archdiocese

Chicago

Rockford

Joliet

Peoria

Springfield

Belleville

Denver Archdiocese

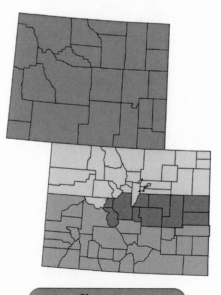

Cheyenne

Denver

Colorado Springs

Pueblo

Davenport

Des Moines

Detroit Archdiocese

Galveston-Houston Archdiocese

San Antonio Archdiocese

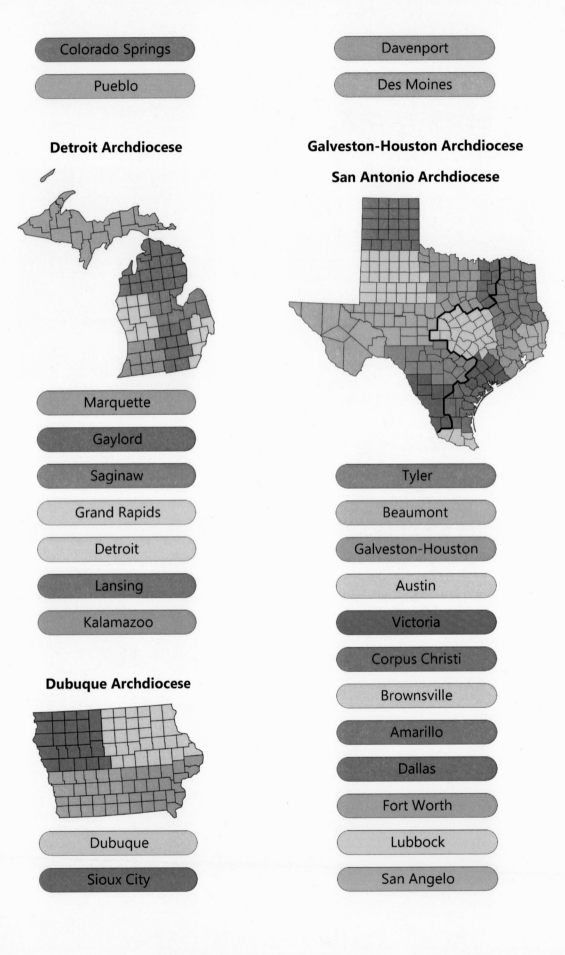

Marquette

Gaylord

Saginaw

Grand Rapids

Detroit

Lansing

Kalamazoo

Tyler

Beaumont

Galveston-Houston

Austin

Victoria

Corpus Christi

Brownsville

Amarillo

Dallas

Fort Worth

Lubbock

San Angelo

Dubuque Archdiocese

Dubuque

Sioux City

El Paso

San Antonio

Laredo

Hartford Archdiocese

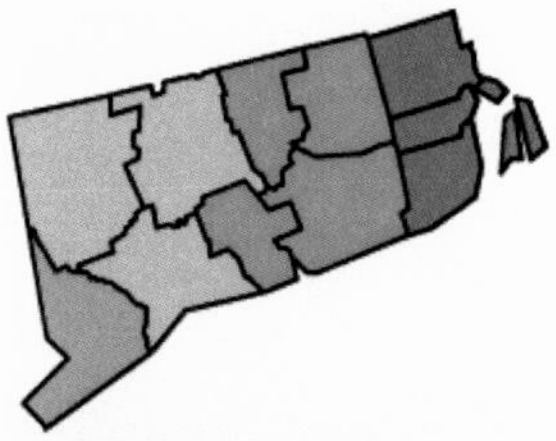

Providence

Norwich

Hartford

Bridgeport

Indianapolis Archdiocese

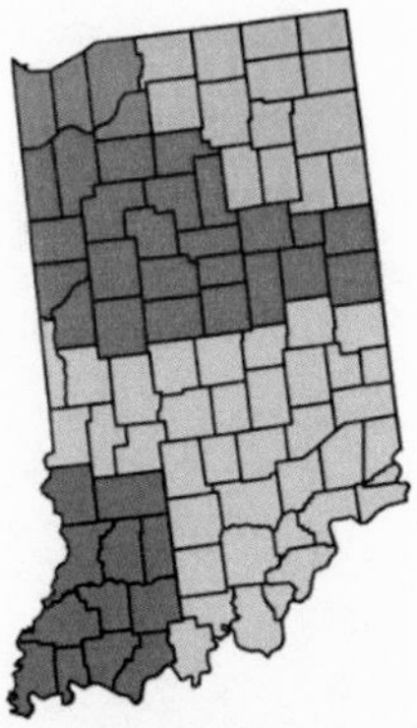

Fort Wayne-South Bend

Gary

Lafayette

Indianapolis

Evansville

Kansas City Archdiocese

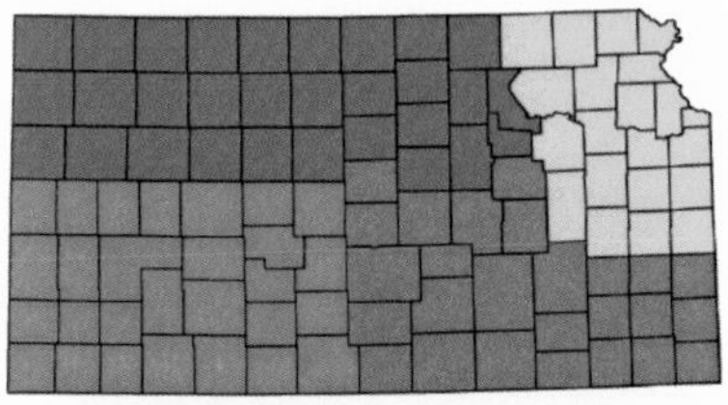

Kansas City

Salina

Wichita

Dodge City

Los Angeles Archdiocese

San Francisco Archdiocese

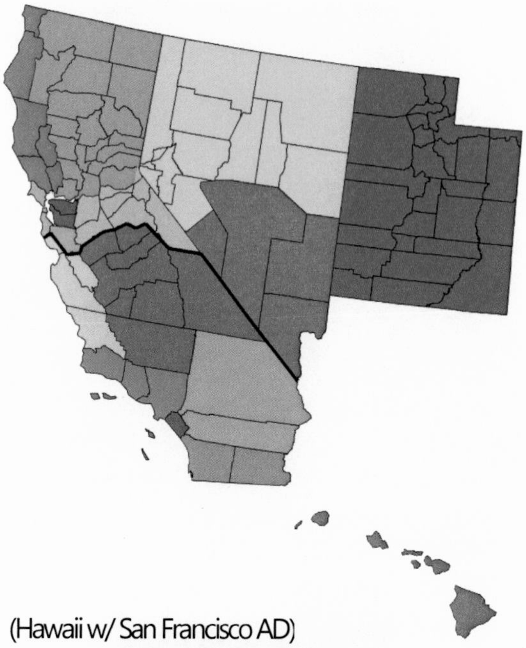

(Hawaii w/ San Francisco AD)

Salt Lake City

Reno

Las Vegas

Sacramento

Santa Rosa

Stockton

Oakland

San Francisco

San Jose

Honolulu

Fresno

Monterey

San Bernardino

Los Angeles

Orange

San Diego

Memphis

Miami Archdiocese

St. Augustine

Pensacola-Tallahassee

Orlando

St. Petersburg

Palm Beach

Venice

Miami

Louisville Archdiocese

Covington

Lexington

Louisville

Owensboro

Knoxville

Nashville

Milwaukee Archdiocese

Superior

Green Bay

La Crosse

Milwaukee

Madison

Lake Charles

Houma-Thibodaux

Mobile Archdiocese

Birmingham

Jackson

Mobile

Biloxi

New York Archdiocese

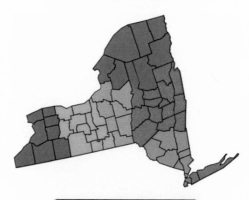

Ogdensburg

Albany

Syracuse

Rochester

Buffalo

New York

Brooklyn

Rockville Centre

New Orleans Archdiocese

Shreveport

Alexandria

New Orleans

Baton Rouge

Lafayette

Newark Archdiocese

Newark

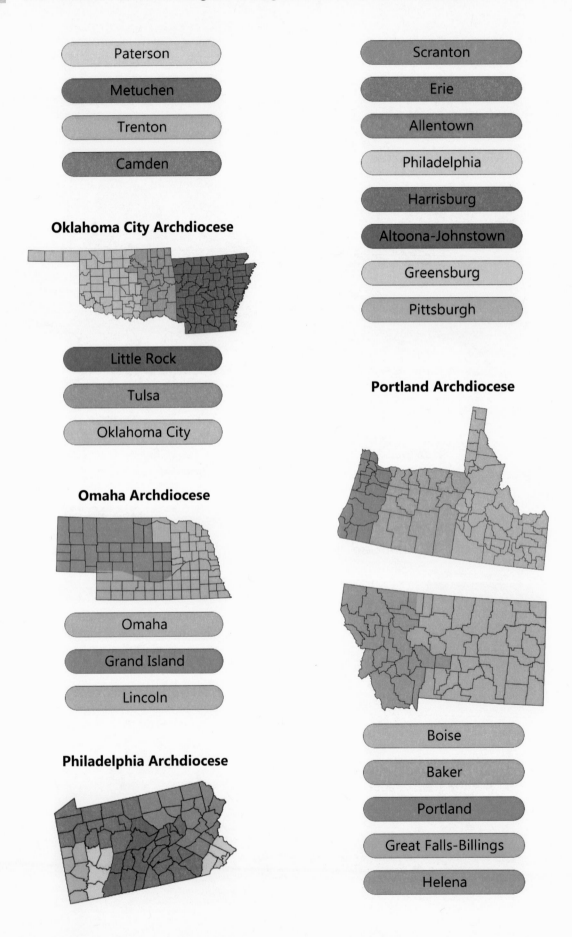

Paterson

Metuchen

Trenton

Camden

Scranton

Erie

Allentown

Philadelphia

Harrisburg

Altoona-Johnstown

Greensburg

Pittsburgh

Oklahoma City Archdiocese

Little Rock

Tulsa

Oklahoma City

Portland Archdiocese

Omaha Archdiocese

Omaha

Grand Island

Lincoln

Boise

Baker

Portland

Great Falls-Billings

Helena

Philadelphia Archdiocese

St. Louis Archdiocese

St. Louis

Jefferson City

Kansas City-St. Joseph

Springfield-Cape Girardeau

St. Paul and Minneapolis Archdiocese

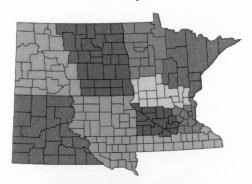

Duluth

Crookston

St. Cloud

St. Paul & Minneapolis

New Ulm

Winona-Rochester

Fargo

Bismark

Sioux Falls

Rapid City

Santa Fe Archdiocese

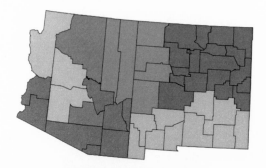

Santa Fe

Gallup

Las Cruces

Phoenix

Tucson

Seattle Archdiocese

Spokane

Yakima

Seattle

Religious Society of Friends (Quakers)

Members of the Religious Society of Friends, commonly called Quakers, have a long and sometimes tortured history in the United States. The first Quakers arrived in the Massachusetts Bay Colony from Barbados as early as 1656, and they migrated into Rhode Island, which was a haven for religious tolerance. The advent of Quaker culture was through Quaker William Penn's establishing the Pennsylvania Colony as a religious refuge in 1681.

It is not uncommon for people with roots in Colonial America to have a branch of the family that belonged to the Society of Friends. Canadians also may have Quaker ancestors because many American Quakers were exiled along with Loyalists during and after the American Revolution. Even so, few researchers have a clear understanding of just who these people were and what their impact was on society. They were considered dangerous radicals in not only England and Ireland in the 1600s and 1700s but also in the colonies.

The Quaker religion was formed in England in 1652 under the leadership of George Fox (1624-1691). Fox was born in the Church of England. As a young man, he became dissatisfied with the ceremonies of Anglicanism. He did not see that the priests could speak to his condition. In his pondering, he heard a voice that said, "There is one, even Jesus Christ, that can speak to thy condition." At this moment, he became conscious that God was working within him and that this faith was open to all men and women. It was the key to salvation.

From this simple beginning, the core tenets of the Friends were established: no clergy, no liturgy, no tithes to the established Church, no swearing of oaths, no taking up arms, religious and civil liberty for all, and living a simple lifestyle. Every day was to be a communion with God, an experience, not just on Sunday. All the positions were radical for the time. From their non-combatant beliefs to their equal treatment of women, the Quakers were not only considered a danger to the society but also a threat to the authority of the state religion. The Quakers suffered great persecution and imprisonment for their convictions.

Quakers emigrated from Ireland and settled in several American colonies, especially Maryland, New Jersey, Pennsylvania, Rhode Island, and Virginia. The largest migration was to Pennsylvania from 1682 to 1750. The influence of the Quakers on American history should not be underestimated because they addressed complex social issues that were centuries ahead of their time, especially regarding women's equality and the abolition of slavery.

Each congregation is called a Monthly Meeting, and Monthly Meetings are scattered throughout Ireland. Quakers began emigrating in the 1600s and continued throughout the early 1700s. Quaker research is difficult because many people in America as well as in Ireland did not remain Quaker. Someone could have been born a Quaker but did not immigrate as one. Also, he or she could have been Quaker in America for several generations, only to drift away or be "disowned" for some infraction.

Once the Quaker connection is identified, where the family was born in Ireland can be found in the Quaker records. The immigrant origins' question is then solved, and, moreover, the Irish Quaker records have some intriguing indexes and digitized images.

Two areas need to be clarified about Quakerism: the theology of the Inward Light and the disownment process that separates an individual from the Monthly Meeting. They seem like opposites at first glance. However, they both reflect how Quaker thought progresses through time, maneuvering through the hazards of popular culture and preserving a distinct identity.

The Inward Light
Lost upon the modern mind is how profound ideas from Quaker Monthly Meetings could affect the entire American society. Part of this has to do with the theology of the "Inward Light," also called the "Inner Light." Rooted within the Inward Light are many aspects of modern thought. In so many ways, society eventually caught up with Quaker discussions in the seventeenth and eighteen centuries.

Little has been written from a systematic perspective about Quaker theology (if there is such an organized belief system) and the Inward Light, but some quality works can explain the context:

Cooper, Willmer A. *A Living Faith: An Historical and Comparative Study of Quaker Beliefs*. 2nd ed., Richmond, Indiana: Friends United Press, 2001.

Dandelion, Pink. *The Quakers: A Very Short Introduction*. Oxford, England: Oxford University Press, 2008.

Dandelion, Pink. *An Introduction to Quakerism*. Cambridge, England: Cambridge University Press, 2007.

Scott, Janet. *What Canst Thou Say?: Towards a Quaker Theology*. London: Quaker Books, 1980.

Trueblood, D. Elton. *The People Called Quakers*. Richmond, Indiana: Friends United Press, 1966, 1971.

Today, the freedom to question, express thoughts, and enjoy religious liberty are taken as natural rights, but it is easy to forget they had consequences if practiced in the colonial period. Societal controversies were not created in a vacuum but were rooted in one or more historical currents of thought. The Quakers with their Inward Light is just one of those threads weaving in and out of society and leaving its mark on non-Quakers who adopted Quaker thinking stripped of the religious terminology.

The Inward Light is a metaphor to express that all people have access to the inspiration of the Holy Spirit, empowering individuals and groups with no need for a clergy. Quakers separate the Inward Light from conscience, which is a developed awareness of the merits or the faults of one's conduct, intention, character, and a sense of doing right. In Quaker thought, the Inward Light is an unmediated experience with the Divine. It is a direct revelation.

Historically, the typical Quaker Monthly Meeting was based upon silence. No one spoke unless guided by the Inward Light. At that time, all men and *women* can share their promptings in an *unedited* format. If the message was important and judged to be true, it was sent afar. It became a call to action.

By the religious standards of the seventeenth and early eighteenth centuries, these ideas were heresy and dangerous. Incomprehensible were people not relying on a well-informed clergy, expecting their own inspirations, and delivering those inspirations in *unedited* formats. Furthermore, a woman being equal to a man in this area was mind-boggling, indeed counter-cultural by the standards of the day. Consequently, Quakers were a despised religious group to be feared. Many parents gasped in horror when their children converted since there was no frame of reference from which these new ideas could be judged.

Without doubt, the concept of messages received by an individual through the Inward Light was divorced from the Anglican idea of a professional priesthood that delivered sermons in an *edited* form. For strict Calvinists, the very notion of the Inward Light was outside the Bible, which to them was the literal and final word of God. For strict Calvinists, all questions could be answered not through a person's inner promptings and revelations but through the Bible because it

constitutes the mind and will of God. The Quakers were beyond the mindset of most Anglicans and Calvinists.

Messages received through the Inward Light were as individual as were the members sitting in silence waiting for the promptings. They were often counsel or insight into local matters, but the major ones became defining markers in history. These could include opposition to war, governmental policies, the state religion, taxation, slavery in all its forms, and the equality of women to men. Even today, the best-known principle is the "Peace Testimony." This is a corporate commitment of Quakers to pacifism and nonviolence. The Peace Testimony is based upon the view "That of God" in everyone sets Quakers against war and killing and to work positively to remove the causes of conflict and injustice.

The Inward Light has allowed Quaker thought to advance over time, even giving them a profound and progressive voice ahead of the general culture. Certain positions accepted through messages of the Inward Light affected the larger society where they were living. Ideas originating from the Inward Light may be tame by today's standards, but historically, they threw governments and churches into chaos.

Quakers do not have a theology in the traditional sense. The doctrine of the Friends must be thought of in terms of a movement of believers toward a particular position. This progression of thought, however, did have a process and was not automatic. A message from the Inward Light was delivered by the individual to a

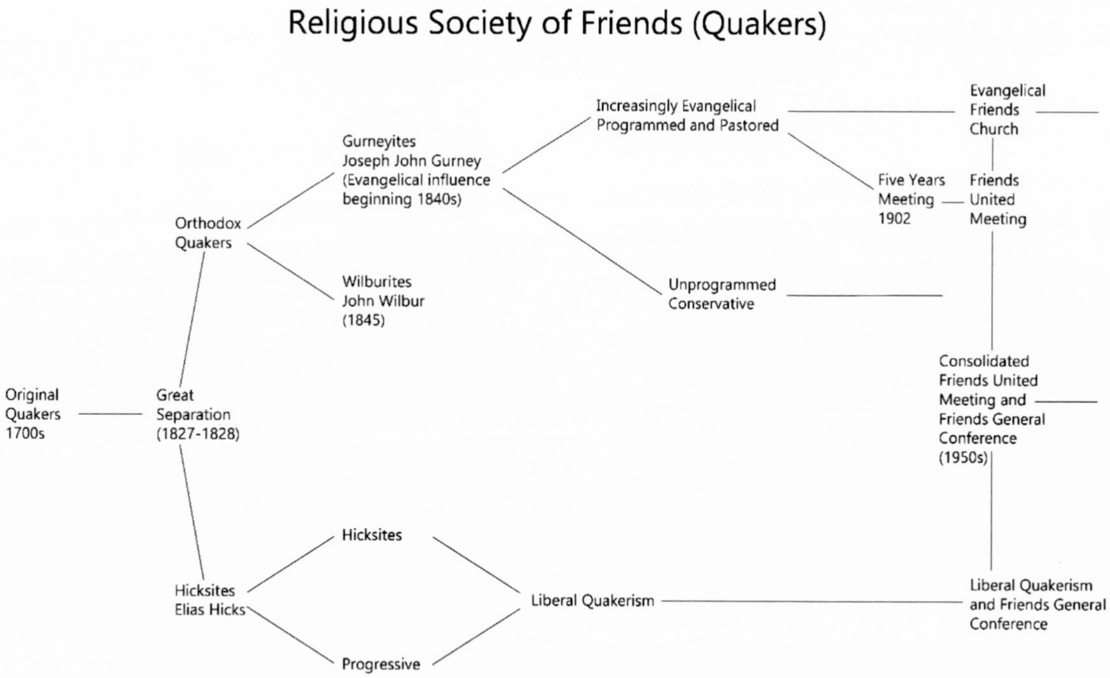

Religious Society of Friends (Quakers)

Figure 21: Evolution of the Religious Society of Friends.

Monthly Meeting, where it was judged. If approved, only then was it disseminated beyond the local level through "Traveling Friends," who could be men or women. To no small degree, the theology of the Inward Light and the dissemination of the messages have shaped and continue to shape the Quaker vision of what the world and its religious community could become.

As messages from the Inward Light were received beyond the level of a single congregation, they either filtered into the larger culture or, if they were crucial issues, were brought to the public arena directly by Quakers. When adopted by others, ideas were transformed and reworked. All ideas, when they leave their roots, transform into and combine with something else. When they do, the original roots are often forgotten, but they are not less powerful.

Two historic periods can be traced to some degree to the Quaker Inward Light. Both were in Upstate New York in 1848 and represent the Inward Light as radicalized time and again by non-Quakers or dissident Quakers. They are the rise of Spiritualism and women's suffrage.

In its radicalized form, the Inward Light by its very nature was only a step away from Spiritualism. With the birth of Spiritualism, dissident Quakers helped propel the new religion forward. Spiritualism drew from the Quaker idea of the Inward Light and the freedom of spiritual exploration it offered for the average person.

For background on the Quaker connection with the rise of Spiritualism, Bret E. Carroll's *Spiritualism in Antebellum America* (Bloomington, Indiana: Indiana University Press, 1997) is a standard text. Spiritualism was especially decisive in granting nineteenth century antebellum women a voice, even if the only one they had was from the spirits.

Women's suffrage was by no means a new idea to the Inward Light of Quakers. The first Women's Suffrage Convention in 1848 was attended by dissident and mainstream Quakers, who propelled the ideas of suffrage into the national spotlight through their own experiences.

While all Quakers were pro-suffrage, they were not all pro-Spiritualists. Yet, part of the roots of both movements can be traced to the freedom granted for personal expression, revelation, and validation through the Inward Light. Both served to empower women in a culture dominated by males.

The Disownment Process

The sister idea of the Inward Light, where the divine will is made known, is the disownment process, wherein that knowledge is preserved. Members not in unity with the divine will are disowned (disunity) from their Monthly Meetings. This is a form of discipline and created records within the Meetings. It explains how so many Quakers found themselves estranged from Quaker principles. To understand Quaker records and culture, an explanation of the concepts and use of the Inward Light and disownment is necessary.

It is recurrently through a record of disunity that many researchers first discover their Quaker ancestors. An indication of an ancestor having been Quaker is finding him or her living among or having dealings with Quakers.

Disownment from a Monthly Meeting was never popular historically and is almost never practiced today. In the past, it was a fact of life through the early twentieth century. To disown is to declare disunity with a person and to deny responsibility for that person's behavior. The practice is in complete opposition to Quaker critics, who believed reliance on the Inward Light would lead to chaos and anarchy. The practice of disowning a person was a clear, understandable parameter from which the community functioned. This disciplinary action reinforced Quaker ethics as followers of Christ.

Disownment cannot be thought of as excommunication as it is in other denominations. The difference may be subtle, but excommunication is toward the individual whereas disownment is a statement to the world about who Quakers and their standards are. Nothing is done to the person disowned. There is no shunning, denying privileges, or even banning that person from worship. The only denial may be the participation in the Friends' business meetings, but otherwise, the statement is: The behavior of the person disowned is not consistent with Quakerism, but he or she is no better and no worse than any other non-member.

Disownment or not disowning a person is a process. One or more Quakers were supposed to have already admonished the offender. If that was without success, the Monthly Meeting appointed a committee to investigate the facts reported and determine if the person was repentant. If so, a letter of apology was written (an acknowledgment). If not repentant, Overseers labored with the person, sometimes for years, because disownment was a serious matter. If not successful, a paper of disunity was written to clarify the matter for the records. A copy was given to the person disowned. The decision could be appealed to the Quarterly Meeting, and its decision was final. When final, a testimony against the person was published, and the case was closed.

People were disowned for specific reasons. The measure was not based on whether a person was liked or disliked. Only the transgression mattered, but it did not affect how Quakers associated in business or socially with a disowned person. In that regard, nothing changed.

A person could be reinstated as a Quaker. The process was basically the same as with the initial disownment, with a letter of acknowledgment, repentance, confession, and investigation of the matter. The typical time of reinstatement was a year or longer. Sometimes, decades elapsed. Disownment was never meant to be a final decision.

An excellent historical discussion, "Our Understanding of Disownment: As Historically Practiced in the Society of Friends," on the Quaker.org website compares several Monthly Meetings in Maryland, Ohio, Pennsylvania, and Virginia and has examples of disownments from older Monthly Meeting records. The study found that most disownments were the results of marrying outside the faith, not because it was the worst offense but because it was just the most common. The study also uncovered that some Monthly Meetings were stricter than others in disownment. Much depended upon how readily the offender acknowledged the error and how public the scandal was. Examples of the disownments are from the Hopewell Monthly Meeting (1760 to 1809) in Frederick County, Virginia:

#	Offense
280	going out in marriage
132	fornication
5	adultery
5	other sexual immorality
41	drinking to excess
28	a combination of offenses
22	military service
19	attending or conniving at an irregular marriage
13	quarreling or fighting
13	dancing
13	joining another denomination
9	nonattendance of meetings
4	taking the test of allegiance
3	false accusation
2	dishonesty
2	killing a mare
2	attending places of diversion
2	horse-racing
1	failing in business
1	nonpayment of debts
1	refusal to arbitrate
1	going to law
1	profanity

1	wife-beating
1	striking a man in anger
1	wounding a man
1	gaming
1	lending money for gambling
1	administering oaths
1	buying slaves
1	permitting fiddling and dancing at one's home
1	appointing meetings and preaching

Other Monthly Meetings had similar offenses listed along with more. The Pennsylvania Monthly Meeting (1682 to 1776) added:

#	Offense
408	showing contempt for the Society's authority over one's conduct
391	assault
359	loose conduct
214	entertainments
174	marrying too close a relative
142	neglecting family responsibilities
118	fraud
81	disapproved company
64	business ethics
61	theft
54	schism
35	voluntary withdrawal
23	courting and fraternizing
22	holding public offices that entailed activity contrary to Quaker ethics
21	lying
21	disobeying parents
21	dispensing liquor
17	violating laws
15	theological
11	destroying property
11	dress and speech
9	fleeing master
7	counterfeiting
7	printing
6	smuggling
5	misuse of the First Day of the week

Typically, on the frontier, when one was separated from the Monthly Meeting or married outside the community, all knowledge was lost. It is interesting that in some families, a particular attitude about the equality of women and men was passed down for generations but with no knowledge about where it came from. It can be a good suggestion that something of the faith was retained long after the family left or was disowned.

Religious Society of Friends Records

Quaker genealogy and history have no shortage of books, websites, and articles. One that is dated but standard in the field is Ellen Thomas Berry and David Allen Berry's *Our Quaker Ancestors: Finding Them in Quaker Records*. (Baltimore: Genealogical Publishing Co., 1987). A simple Internet search using terms such as "Quaker Genealogy" yields many quality sources, from library websites to personal genealogy pages.

Although Quaker record keeping excels that of other denominations, it also creates blind spots. It is easy to think all one has to do is look at a database or book and everything somehow instantly appears. If it does, it is rare. The first question to ask is whether an ancestor was a Quaker or had Quaker ancestors. This can be confusing because even if they came from Ireland, many Quaker names are common, such as Wilson in North Carolina. An odd or biblical first name sometimes can be another hint. For the population as a whole, though, a biblical given name is not exceptional, and so care needs to be taken. It is an indication only. An excellent clue is a residence among Quakers but is still not proof, as there are plenty of Baptist Wilsons in North Carolina, for example, living among Quakers. Nevertheless, if ancestors are found living among or dealing with Quakers, possibilities need to be explored.

In the county deeds, the Quaker rendering of dates may or may not support an association. This requires some explaining. Before 1751, the Julian Calendar was used in most of the English-speaking world and is reflected in the old records with regularly double years. Under this calendar, the New Year began on 25 March. When England and the colonies switched to the Gregorian Calendar, 1 January 1752 became the New Year. Quakers abided by this except for not using the names of the months and days, which they deemed to be of pagan origin. Instead, at that time, they opted to call April the 4th month instead of using its name. Before 1 January 1752, April was the 2nd month. The months September through December were exceptions because they were not named after pagan gods. Afterward, the custom was to apply numbers for all the months of the year with January being the 1st month. An excellent treatment of this can be found in the article "The Quaker Calendar" on the Swarthmore.edu website.

The dates are in records of Quakers, such as deeds, but what needs to be questioned is who the Quaker party was. Was he or she the buyer or seller of the property, or was it the clerk recording the deed? Thus, seeing the Quaker Calendar reflected in a county record is not proof of a Quaker connection. It still needs to be questioned further.

As Quakers were not restricted from associating or dealing with former Quakers or non-Quakers, the association with one may be evidence, although not decisive. Unless a Quaker record can be found proving that the ancestor was at one time a Quaker, research needs to be directed at an intermarriage or other distant familial relationship. These connections are more common than researchers think.

Quaker records are excellent in their content but not perfect. At times, what was documented about a person or family at various Monthly Meetings can be contradictory, but they are a solid source from which to work. Migration patterns, transfers in and out, births, marriages, and deaths are in the records as well as business minutes and disciplinary actions. The records can be extraordinarily detailed with multiple witnesses signing at the end. When accessing historical Quaker birth records, these are exactly what they are, births. Quakers do not baptize.

The database "U.S., Encyclopedia of American Quaker Genealogy, Vol. I-VI, 1607-1943" on Ancestry.com is William Wade Hinshaw's six-volume work

Encyclopedia of American Quaker Genealogy (Ann Arbor, Michigan: Edward Brothers Inc., 1938-1950). Known as *Hinshaw's* in genealogy circles, it has extracts from the minutes of Meetings in Georgia, Michigan, New Jersey, New York, North Carolina, Ohio, Pennsylvania, South Carolina, Tennessee, and Virginia. The minutes include information from certificates of removal, some giving the Meetings in Ireland from which Irish immigrants came. These are abstracts, and the database is a composite index to all six volumes. An ancestor not being found in this database could be because records did not survive or were not listed in Hinshaw's work.

Another major Ancestry.com database is "U.S., Quaker Meeting Records, 1681-1935," which encompasses the country and has digitized images of the original records. The original sources are from several repositories.

Other Ancestry.com databases have directories, periodicals, and obituaries. If a link is found to Ireland through an American record, numerous Irish Quaker records have been indexed and digitized on Findmypast.com.

Specific to Quakers from Ireland is Albert Cook Myers's classic work *Immigration of the Irish Quakers* (1902. Reprint, Baltimore: Genealogical Publishing Co., 1969), which undertakes a detailed study of the approximately 1,500 to 2,000 Irish Quaker immigrants who settled in Pennsylvania between 1682 and 1750. The origins in Ireland of many of these immigrants are identified. Genealogical data from this book was published separately as Myers's *Irish Quaker Arrivals to Pennsylvania 1682-1750*. Another book by Myers, *Quaker Arrivals at Philadelphia 1682-1750*, includes certificates of removal received at the Philadelphia Monthly Meeting from other Meetings in America, England, and Ireland.

For Irish immigrant research, records of births, deaths, marriages, and minutes recording members received by certificates are especially useful. Berry and Berry's *Our Quaker Ancestors: Finding Them in Quaker Records* is a genealogical guide to tracing members of the Society of Friends. Thomas C. Hill's *Monthly Meetings in North America: An Index* contains historical descriptions of each yearly Meeting and Monthly Meeting and where records of them may be found. *Quaker Genealogies: A Selected List of Books* has 897 genealogies and 13 collective genealogies for Quaker families, some of which had origins in Ireland. The Family History Library has microfilm or digitized copies of records from numerous Monthly Meetings.

United Society of Believers in Christ's Second Appearing (Shakers)

The term "Shakers" is an old, prejudicial term for members of the United Society of Believers in Christ's Second Appearing. A vast amount of information published on the Internet can be accessed about this community of believers. The Shakers, under the charismatic leadership of Mother Ann Lee, arrived in America in 1774 from England. They founded the first Shaker community in Watervliet,

Figure 22: Shaker South Family Dwelling House, Watervliet, Albany, New York, 1962. (Image courtesy of the Library of Congress. Photographers Bruster and Allen, Historic American Buildings Survey. This work is in the public domain in the United States because it was prepared by an officer or employee of the United States Government as part of that person's official duties under the terms of Title 17, Chapter 1, Section 105 of the U.S. Code.)

Albany County, New York. Mother Ann Lee is believed to be the Second Coming of Christ. Christ's counterpart in the feminine form was unique for the period. Coming from a dissident Quaker background, she saw men and women as equals. She diverged from the Quakers in her belief that sexuality was sinful and the sexes had to be separated to avoid temptation.

The faith advocated a communal lifestyle, pacifism, and celibacy for all members. Celibacy is probably what Shakerism is most remembered for in American history, but it is only part of its historical legacy. It is also noted for its development and production of a simplistic and distinctive style of furniture, known on the collector's market as "Shaker Furniture." Celibacy was expected also of married couples who joined the faith. Men and women lived apart in separate houses in the communes.

By the mid-1800s, the communal colonies stretched from Maine to Kentucky and encompassed some 6,000 to 7,000 believers. The Church grew by accepting children as well as adult converts. There was a swell in conversions after 22 October 1844 as the post-Millerite Adventists had to come to terms with Christ not

Shaker Communities

State	County	Community	Existence
CT	Hartford	Enfield	1790 to 1917
FL	Osceola	Narcoossee	1896 to 1911
GA	Camden	White Oak	1898 to 1902
IN	Parke	West Union (Busro)	1810 to 1827
KY	Mercer	Pleasant Hill	1806 to 1910
KY	Union	South Union	1807 to 1922
MA	Berkshire	Hancock	1790 to 1960
MA	Worcester	Harvard	1791 to 1918
MA	Middlesex	Shirley	1793 to 1908
MA	Berkshire	Tyringham	1792 to 1875
MA	Berkshire	Savoy	1817 to 1825
ME	York	Alfred	1793 to 1932
ME	Cumberland	Sabbathday Lake	1794 to present
ME	Cumberland	Gorham	1808 to 1819
NH	Grafton	Enfield	1793 to 1923
NH	Merrimack	Canterbury	1792 to 1992
NY	Livingston	Groveland	1836 to 1895
NY	Columbia	Mt. Lebanon	1787 to 1947
NY	Albany	Watervliet	1787 to 1938
NY	Wayne	Sodus Bay	1826 to 1836
OH	Cuyahoga	North Union	1822 to 1889
OH	Warren	Union Village	1806 to 1912
OH	Montgomery	Watervliet	1806 to 1900
OH	Hamilton	Whitewater	1824 to 1916

returning as expected. Many of the former Millerites sought stability in the Shaker communes. Some of these left later to join Spiritualism, which was officially founded in 1848. By the 1850s, many associated themselves with other post-Millerite Adventists who were preaching a Sabbatarian theology. They emerged as the Seventh-day Adventist Church in 1860.

As a result of the lifestyle and stability of the Shaker communities, they attracted many members, but numerous people left as well. Thus, an ancestor may be found associating with a particular Shaker community for only a short while but long enough for a record to mention a birthplace in Ireland. The Irish immigrants as well as their descendants were among the converts. Non-members also lived among the Shakers. Irish-born Shakers joined in the United States after immigrating, as no Shakers were in Ireland.

The Shakers did not pressure people into joining the religion, but persons from all walks of life were attracted to their communes. One interesting case is Emily Brannan (1805-1881), who spent her life in the Enfield, New Hampshire, community. She was the daughter of Lord Dunraven of Ireland. On the other hand, impoverished or disabled Irish, among others, were regularly taken in and cared for by the Shakers. The communities were places of stability in an unstable world. It was not uncommon for the Shakers' local courts to assign indigent or orphaned children to live in and to be apprenticed in trades in Shaker communities.

Because of the unique arrangement in which Shakers employed and housed non-members, an Irish immigrant who never joined may have been noted in its records. Among adult converts were single women who had no means of support. Transient converts or residents were known as "Winter Shakers," families who had fallen on hard times. They went to the Shaker communities in the winter only to leave when their circumstances or the weather improved. Thus, an Irish immigrant might have been associated with the Shakers for a short while or for a lifetime. If an ancestor or an ancestor's family is known to have lived in a township or community where there was a commune, the Shaker records may be worth investigating.

The Shakers also often took in and brought up orphans or children of parents who could no longer support them. Although many of these children stayed and became a part of the community, others left and never returned. In addition, children were sent to the Shakers by their parents to learn a trade. Shaker communities were found in the localities in the table on page 92, but only the Sabbathday Lake community is left.

Numerous additional settlements that did not last long or that consisted of only a few families were as far west as San Diego and San Francisco, California. Other small communities were absorbed into the larger ones over the years.

Shaker Records

Countless records were produced by the Shaker communities for different intentions. Because of the interest in them by historians and genealogists, many have been extracted and alphabetized over the decades into their own collections.

One such compilation of documents is the "Shaker Membership Card Index," which lists members in New England as well as in other Shaker communities. It was assembled from various sources, including church and cemetery records. These cards can contain birth and death places and dates, admittances and transfers from the communities, and apostasies. The card index is at the Western Reserve Historical Society Library, Cleveland, with digitized images through FamilySearch.org. The membership cards vary in their content. Exact birthplaces are in some, but others hold only vital information or dates when members joined. Some Shaker records have the origins of members' parents even when the members were born in the United States. One example is Mary McBride. A brief biography of her from the Union Village, Ohio, community reads:

> *Mary McBride born in Baltimore, Maryland, 1832. Entered White-water Shaker So. 1852. Moved to Watervliet So. 1853, and to Union Village, 1900. Was second Eldress at Watervliet So. Father's name Denis, born in Londonderry, Ireland. Mother's name, Mary, American born, but do not know her birthplace.*

Another principal group is the "Shaker Collection at the Western Reserve Historical Society (1723-1952)." This enormous archive of records from the various communities is on 58 rolls of microfilm. They are deposited at the Western Reserve Historical Society in Cleveland, Ohio, and a set is at the Family History Library.

Church of the New Jerusalem (Swedenborgians)

Swedenborgianism as a philosophical system in America was always much larger than it was as the Church of the New Jerusalem denomination. The hidden aspect of this faith may explain why it is almost never mentioned in genealogy instruction books, but understanding it is relevant to genealogy.

The Church was built around the teachings of Emanuel Swedenborg, but although it was small, it disseminated and kept alive Swedenborg's ideas that profoundly affected American culture and religious history. If an Irish-born immigrant is found to be associated with the Swedenborgians, it is because he or she joined in the United States or perhaps after immigrating to England, before emigrating again.

Three denominations in the United States base their teachings on the writings of Emanuel Swedenborg. These include the Swedenborgian Church, founded in 1817; General Church of the New Jerusalem, founded in 1890; and the Lord's New Church, which is Nova Hierosolyma, founded in 1937. The history of Swedenborgianism in America through 1890 is of the original organization with its strength in Massachusetts, Michigan, Ohio, and Pennsylvania.

Aside from its influence on the various nineteenth-century reform movements, Spiritualism, Theosophical Society, and New Thought, many famous Americans were Swedenborgians, such as Helen Keller and John Chapman (Johnny Appleseed). Transcendentalists Ralph Waldo Emerson, Bronson Alcott, and Henry James, Sr., were profoundly influenced by Swedenborg's writings. Numerous poets and writers, for instance, Edgar Allen Poe, also acknowledged their debt to Swedenborg. Both Swedenborgians and the New England transcendentalists were involved in some of America's historic nineteenth-century communal experiments such as Brook Farm, the Hopedale Community, the Jasper Colony, and the Owenite Community in Yellow Springs, Ohio.

Emanuel Swedenborg and His Writings

The roots of Swedenborgianism go back to the revelations of Emanuel Swedenborg (1688-1772). In 1724, he was appointed to a position by the government on the Board of Mines. As a result of his publication of seven volumes of scientific works, he was recognized by the scientific community and became a corresponding member of the Royal Academy of Sciences in St. Petersburg, Russia. By 1736, Swedenborg's religious philosophy began to emerge when he started taking notes of his dreams and out-of-body experiences. By 1744, his thinking had evolved to a metaphysical dynamism. He believed that his intellectual pursuits were unsatisfying and that he must submit to divine guidance. Three years later, he made his views public and resigned his position with the Bureau of Mines. He spent the rest of his life developing his ideas.

His out-of-body experiences to other spirit realms included communications with angels and with the dead. When he returned to his body, his revelatory process happened only when he opened his Bible and studied, thus he was not a channeler by the standard definition. The word seer more accurately applies. The knowledge he received through this revelatory process concerned treatises on life, life and death, God, and biblical commentaries. His information from his visits with angels has been detailed in Robert H. Kirven's *Angels in Action: What Swedenborg Saw and Heard* (West Chester, Pennsylvania: Chrysalis Books Swedenborg Foundation, 1995), which brings the scattered angelology from all Swedenborg's books together into one readable work.

While his profound writings had little impact in Sweden, his philosophies found the greatest following in England. In 1787, the English readers of Swedenborg's works established the Church of the New Jerusalem, known more simply as the "New Church." By 1810, a publishing house was dedicated to the task of printing Swedenborg's writings. His 35 volumes are his beliefs in the Lord's plan for a rebirth of Christianity.

Swedenborgianism in America

Members brought Swedenborgianism to the United States in 1784 from the Church of the New Jerusalem in England. In America, Swedenborgianism found an audience eager for new ideas, but its reception was mixed. Compared to many radical sects surfacing during the time, the New Jerusalem Church seemed ultraconservative, yet to the older Christian denominations, it seemed extremely radical. By 1787, the first American editions of Swedenborg's works were published, and one of the early subscribers was Benjamin Franklin.

From Philadelphia, converts carried the Swedenborgian message into western Pennsylvania. By 1791, a society was being formed in Baltimore that became one of the notable centers for the Church on the East Coast.

CONTENTS.

HEAVEN.

Figure 23: Portion of the Table of Contents from Emanuel Swedenborg's "Heaven and Hell," originally published in 1758. (This work is in the public domain in its country of origin and other countries and areas where the copyright term is the author's life plus 80 years or fewer.)

HEAVEN AND HELL

ALSO,

The Intermediate State,

OR WORLD OF SPIRITS;

A RELATION OF THINGS HEARD AND SEEN.

BY

EMANUEL SWEDENBORG.

BEING A TRANSLATION OF HIS WORK ENTITLED
"DE CŒLO et ejus Mirabilibus, et de INFERNO, ex Auditis et Visis.
Londini, 1758."

THE SWEDENBORG SOCIETY,
1 BLOOMSBURY STREET, LONDON.
1896.

By 1817, in Philadelphia, a connection between the Quakers and the Swedenborgians appeared as many Quakers converted. It was among the Quaker converts that some of the more radical reform ideas entered the Church of the New Jerusalem. However, not all members were radical reformers.

For the family historian, the following classes of people were attracted to Swedenborgian ideas and the Church of the New Jerusalem in the nineteenth century:

- Quakers or of Huguenot descent in Pennsylvania.
- Members of a radical reform movement or commune.
- The well-educated, professional, and free-thinking families in the eastern United States.
- People involved in the rising Spiritualist movement after 1848.
- Common farmers who met Swedenborgian circuit-riding missionaries such as Johnny Appleseed (John Chapman), especially in Ohio and Michigan. This class was not necessarily well educated or professional, but it was literate.

As Swedenborgians moved west of the Alleghenies, the Church was confronted with frontier life and had to adjust. The first frontier societies to be organized were in Bedford, Pennsylvania (1794), Steubenville, Ohio (1795), Cincinnati, Ohio (1811), and Lebanon, Ohio (1812). By 1822, societies were formed in Jefferson, Indiana; St. Charles, Missouri; Knoxville, Tennessee; and Louisville, Kentucky. On the frontier, Swedenborgians used the Methodist circuit rider and camp meetings as a model for evangelism.

By the 1830s and 1840s, as Swedenborg's writings became widely distributed in the country, others who never joined the Church became extremely interested in them, and the Swedenborgian message had its greatest impact on American culture. Swedenborg's writings came to mean different things to a wide variety of people who proceeded to implement the message, often grafting it into their own new religious movements.

From 1890, the General Convention (Swedenborgian Church) membership slowly increased, but societies decreased. During the 1920s, Swedenborgian theology continued its American journey with the eloquent Helen Keller. She introduced her Swedenborgian beliefs in her classic book *My Religion*. Today, most Swedenborgian ideas continue to filter into American culture, transformed by the New Age movement.

Church of the New Jerusalem Records
The standard work on Swedenborgianism in America is Marguerite Beck Block's classic 1932 work *The New Church in the New World* (New York, New York: Swedenborg Publishing Association, 1984). It mentions many of the early members, controversies, congregations, migrations, and schools of thought within American Swedenborgianism. This is one

of the first places to start a search for background information on the Church, its history, and early personalities. A scholarly journal detailing Swedenborgian history and theology is *Studia Swedenborgiana,* available at the website "Center for Swedenborgian Studies."

As the Church of the New Jerusalem was historically a small faith, almost any record generated by and about Swedenborgians has a good chance of mentioning members. Records for the Church include the registers of area societies. Many society records can be found at the Family History Library, which has the ones for the historic societies in Boston and Cincinnati.

For most of the nineteenth-century congregations, records are in two repositories. The collections were split between the headquarters in Newtonville, Massachusetts, and the Center for Swedenborgian Studies in Berkeley, California. They were not separated along any type of geographical lines.

The records, which typically consist of membership lists, baptisms, confirmations, marriages, burials, and society minutes, varies between societies. Membership lists are in several formats, from simple names to a column format combining births/baptisms, marriages, deaths/burials, and transfers. Some societies have exact birthplaces. The Church of the New Jerusalem historically baptizes infants as well as adults.

Confirmation records are simple, listing the names and dates. Marriages also tend to be rather minimal with the names of the couples, the dates of the marriages, sometimes residences of couples, and the ministers' names. Burials can provide the ages of the deceased or even the exact dates of births, deaths, and burials.

Several periodicals have been published by regional societies, individuals, and the Swedenborgian denominations. The contents of these periodicals can encompass theological articles and local church news as well as genealogical information. For example, after 1865, births, deaths, and marriages were reported in *The New Church Messenger,* published weekly during the nineteenth and for half the twentieth century. Submissions to *The New Church Messenger* were voluntary. Yet, this is the best periodical for vital information. The *New Jerusalem Messenger* also is a source for some vital information.

The most noteworthy periodical collections are housed at the American Antiquarian Society, Bryn Athyn College, Library of Congress, Swedenborgian House of Studies, Urbana College, and the Van Pelt Library at the University of Pennsylvania. Many are also online. Publications to about 1850 to consider for understanding and documenting a Swedenborgian ancestor include the following found in the chart on the following page:

Early Swedenborgian Publications

Publication	Name	Place Published
1805	*The New Hampshire New Jerusalem Magazine*	Portsmouth, NH
1817 to 1818	*The New Jerusalem Church Repository*	Philadelphia, PA
1820	*The New Jerusalem Record*	Philadelphia, PA
1823 to 1824	*The New Jerusalem Missionary*	New York, NY
1825 to 1826	*Herald of Truth*	Cincinnati, OH
1827 to 1893	*New Jerusalem Magazine*	Boston, MA
1836 to 1842	*The Precursor*	Cincinnati, OH
1841 to 1844	*The New Churchman & Extra*	Philadelphia, PA
1843 to 1891	*New Church Magazine for Children*	Boston, MA
1847	*The Little Truth Teller*	Philadelphia, PA
1848 to 1856	*The New Church Repository and Monthly Review*	New York, NY
1848 to 1852	*The Medium*	Detroit, MI

The Swedenborg Library of Bryn Athyn College in Pennsylvania houses one of the most extensive Swedenborgian collections in the world. Known as "Swedenborgiana," it contains many dissertations that discuss early members.

For continued discussions about Spiritualism in America, see Chapter 18 of this publication: The Irish and American Spiritualism.

Church of Jesus Christ of Latter-day Saints (Mormons)

The Church of Jesus Christ of Latter-day Saints (by and large called the Mormons or LDS Church) furnishes a new twist in the search for Irish origins. The Church was founded in 1830 by Joseph Smith (1804-1844) in Palmyra, Wayne County, New York, as a result of the reignited fires of the Second Great Awakening. Smith remains a controversial figure in American religious history. Several excellent academic histories have been written about him, and one well-documented study is Richard Lyman Bushman's *Joseph Smith: Rough Stone Rolling* (New York, New York: Knopf, 2005).

Smith and his movement challenged American Christians in ways to which they were not accustomed. As Latter-day Saints reinterpreted the Bible and openly added their own scriptures to support and define their doctrinal positions, they forced evangelicals to solidify their theologies. These additional scriptures included the *Book of Mormon* and the open canon *Doctrine and Covenants,* wherein new scripture continues to be added periodically.

The theological tenets of the Church have been the reason why the largest genealogy program and library in the world was established. In the search for immigrant origins, records for Mormon converts should at some point reveal a county or townland of birth.

Even though it is not derived from Catholicism, Protestantism, or Orthodoxy, the Latter-day Saints digitize their records, making them available for free to the public. The present section, though, addresses those who converted to this new religion and then emigrated to join the Saints in their colonies.

An explanation about the word Mormon is in order. "Mormon Church" and "LDS Church" are colloquial labels for reference purposes only. In 2018, members of the Church of Jesus Christ of Latter-day Saints were instructed not to use either term because they are meaningless and do not convey the mission of the church. Until then, the names were tolerated and continue to be ingrained in the

languages of the world, especially the word Mormon.

The theory about why this religious movement can assist in tracing Irish origins is straightforward. One child in a family, either as an individual or with a young family, would join the new faith, and the others would not. This was not rare in the nineteenth century. As a result, genealogical information was preserved through the Mormon branch of the family and forgotten by the rest. Therefore, the Church records are essential for the descendants of the non-Mormon branches of the family.

Church of Jesus Christ of Latter Day Saints and Select Progeny

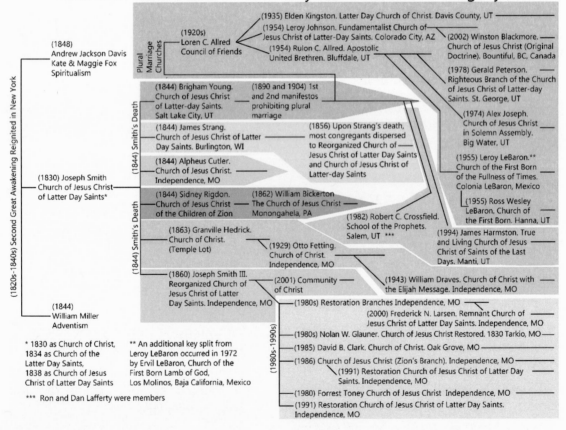

Figure 24: Development of the Church of Jesus Christ of Latter-day Saints and its subsequent branches.

Specifically, regarding those born in Ireland, the Church opened missions in Belfast and Dublin in 1840, just ten years after the Church was founded. American missionaries in Ireland had some success, but it was limited. The records of the Belfast and Dublin missions are available through the Family History Library, and they have residences of the converts. However, and this is a major point, most of the success was with the Protestant Irish who had already immigrated to Scotland and Lancashire, England. Therefore, most of the people born in Ireland were converted in England and Scotland, with only a minority in Ireland itself.

These converts were expected to gather with the Saints and promote building the Kingdom of God in the Mormon cities and colonies in the United States. Over time, because of persecution, the body of the Church had to move from gatherings in Kirtland, now Lake County, Ohio (1831-1837), to areas in and around Independence, Jackson County, Missouri (1831-1838), Nauvoo, Hancock County, Illinois (1839-1846), and for the westward bound Saints, to Salt Lake City, Utah, and the Rocky Mountain colonies from 1847.

After Joseph Smith's murder in 1844 in Illinois, a succession crisis appeared as many individuals claimed leadership. By 1847, Brigham Young led most of the Church membership out of the United States to what was then Mexico and established a kingdom built upon Church principles in the western deserts. They were leaving the United States as religious refugees. However, the United States annexed the entire region after the Mexican-American War in 1848, and the Mormons once again found themselves under the rule of a hostile United States government. The government was not sympathetic to a church-state theocracy operating within the new territories and utilized Mormon polygamy to dismantle the theocracy in 1890.

The Saints who did not follow Brigham Young remained in the Midwest and became one church of many in their communities. The largest organized in 1860 as the Reorganized Church of Jesus Christ of Latter Day Saints (RLDS). It is today called the Community of Christ.

Immigrants arriving overland on the Mormon Trail before the completion of the Transcontinental Railroad in 1869 resettled in a string of Mormon colonies. By 1900, those colonies ranged from southern Alberta, Canada, to northern Mexico in the states of Chihuahua and Sonora. Salt Lake City, the headquarters of the church, was at the center of this spider web of hundreds of organized colonies.

As the Church pertains to genealogy, Joseph Smith taught that all existing churches and religions were not complete, and God had revealed to him a divine order wherein the true religion was restored through him. He was God's modern-day prophet, seer, and revelator. Through visions and new scripture as well as the Bible, the restored true faith with all of God's authority was available to everyone, and thus the emphasis was missionary work. Missionary work also extends to the deceased who, in another dimension of this earth known as the

Spirit World, were being taught the correct gospel principles. Church ordinances, such as baptisms, marriages, and uniting of family units (sealings) were extended to the dead. Baptism is linked to salvation in the LDS Church.

The discussion therefore returns to the converts. To offer these ordinances to the dead, temples continue to be built worldwide, which are different than chapels. In the temples, baptisms for the dead and the sealings of couples and families are undertaken. For the deceased, this is through genealogy research. For the incoming converts, who want to submit their ancestors' names for "ordinance work" and to perform their own religious ordinances, questions are asked. These can include birthplaces and dates, marriage places and dates, and death information. These temple records, together with what was created in the congregational registers themselves, have documented people long lost in the Irish records. The average Catholic and Protestant record in Ireland began in the 1820s or 1830s, but the nineteenth-century, Irish-born converts contributing this information about their parents, grandparents, siblings, and cousins can easily trace entire lineages back into the 1700s.

As members continue to research and preserve their genealogies, online databases are created. Consequently, a non-Mormon branch tying into a Mormon line is not unexpected. For this reason, the databases are the first step in this type of research, and then it can extend into other records that might have documented families, such as congregational registers, diaries, published family histories, and general histories about Mormons. The first clue in a database is when an Irish-born person is identified as being married or dying in one of the following areas:

Western United States, especially in Arizona, Idaho, Nevada, Utah, and Wyoming, where the Church of Jesus Christ of Latter-day Saints remains either the largest or second largest church. Early Mormon colonies were also in California, Colorado, and New Mexico but not to the degree they were in the first states cited.

Southern Alberta, centered around Cardston, Lethbridge, Magrath, Raymond, and Stirling because Mormons colonized that area of Canada after arriving from the Latter-day Saint American communities. They remain a strong presence there.

Northern Mexico, in the states of Chihuahua and Sonora, where some of the Mormon colonies that survived the Mexican Revolution (1910-1920) can still be found. These areas are more mixed today, but the Anglo-American presence remains visible in their bi-lingual residents.

The website FamilySearch.org is owned and operated by the Church, but all persons are welcome to submit their genealogies to this program. Mormon pedigrees are also being added to commercial websites by users on Ancestry.com and MyHeritage.com.

The world's largest genealogy library, which also has records generated about early Mormons, is the FamilySearch Library in downtown Salt Lake City. Just a block away is the Church History Library, which is separate and concentrates on preserving original documents and Mormon History. The latter is also open to the public. A third, not associated with the Church, is the secular Daughters of the Utah Pioneer organization, also in downtown Salt Lake City. This is a lineage society, available to all people who can document ancestors who arrived in Utah Territory before the completion of the Transcontinental Railroad in 1869. It has a library and periodicals. All three organizations have websites, catalogs, and searchable indexes.

A more detailed study for the context of Latter-day Saints and their relationship to genealogy can be found in Dwight A. Radford's Special Strategy chapter "The Latter-day Saint Connection" in *American Scots-Irish Research: Strategies and Sources in the Quest for Ulster-Scots Origins* (Orting, Washington: Family Roots Publishing, 2020).

Figure 25: Idaho Falls Temple of the Church of Jesus Christ of Latter-day Saints, dedicated 1945. (Photo courtesy of Dwight A. Radford, 2020.)

BOSTON [M] DIRECTORY.   491

Murphy Mary, house 6 Fruit-st. ct.
Murphy Mary Mrs. h. Adams, c. Dorch. ave. wd. 16
Murphy Mary, widow, house 2 Dewerson ct.
Murphy Mary Miss, dressmaker, house 25 Rochester
Murphy Mary, widow, house 69 Pitts
Murphy Mary, widow, house 9 Rochester
Murphy Mary, widow, house r. 25 Eliot.
Murphy Mary Miss, house 1 Institute ave.
Murphy Mary, widow. house Culvert, n. Cabot
Murphy Mary A. widow, house 287 Federal
Murphy Matthew, clerk, 121 Brighton, b. 36 Auburn
Murphy Matthew, harnessmaker, house 208 Endicott
Murphy Matthew, laborer, house 29 Yeoman
Murphy Maurice, laborer, house 487 First
Murphy Maurice, blacksmith, h. 21 Hamilton alley
Murphy Maurice, laborer, boards 114 Broad
Murphy Michael, porter, 8 India, house 316 D
Murphy Michael, gasfitter, bds. 446 Commercial
Murphy Michael, laborer, house 414 Commercial
Murphy Michael, laborer, house 11 Columbia
Murphy Michael, stonecutter, house 122 Foundry
Murphy Michael, laborer, house 2 Stanhope place
Murphy Michael, typecaster, 52 Wash. h. 218 Fifth
Murphy Michael, teamster, house 42 Porter, E. B.
Murphy Michael, packer, 1 Dock sq. b. 1352 Tremont
Murphy Michael, laborer, house 74 Albany
Murphy Michael, laborer, house 71 Cove
Murphy Michael, laborer, boards 30 Oswego
Murphy Michael, laborer, house Lexington, n. Eagle
Murphy Michael, laborer, house 149 Kneeland
Murphy Michael, laborer, house 29 Yeoman
Murphy Michael, laborer, boards 33 Athens
Murphy Michael, boilermaker, bds. 202 Albany
Murphy Michael, laborer, house 5 Globe alley
Murphy Michael, house 1352 Tremont
Murphy Michael, carpenter, boards 68 Kingston
Murphy Michael, carpenter, boards 29 Pitts
Murphy Michael, moulder, house r. 111 Third
Murphy Michael, distiller, house I, near Fifth
Murphy Michael, papermaker, house 42 Mindoro
Murphy Michael, hostler, 154 Devonshire, house 322 Federal
Murphy Michael, teamster, house 327 Dorchester av.
Murphy Michael, laborer, house 150 Kneeland
Murphy Michael A. painter, house 47 Lenox
Murphy Michael J. porter, boards 142 Kneeland
Murphy Michael K. (Kinney, Gallagher, & Co.), 81 High, house at Woburn
Murphy Miles, gilder, house 195 Endicott
Murphy Montague C. carpenter, house 130 Brooks
Murphy Morris, laborer, boards Com'l, cor. Union, ward 16
Murphy Morris, laborer, house Com'l, near. Union, [ward 16
Murphy Nehemiah H. cardwriter, h. 85 Emerson
Murphy Owen, hostler, house 307 Federal
Murphy Owen, laborer, house 65 Hunneman
Murphy Owen, packer, house 26 Nashua
Murphy Patrick, wheelwright, house 395 Second
Murphy Patrick, shoemaker, house 82 Purchase
Murphy Patrick (McCann & Murphy), 327 North, boards do.
Murphy Patrick, laborer, house 120 Purchase
Murphy Patrick (Murphy & Gallagher), 21 Carney place, house 374 Shawmut ave.
Murphy Patrick, plasterer, house r. 28 Pleasant
Murphy Patrick, house 17 Hamilton
Murphy Patrick, coachman, house 145 Hudson
Murphy Patrick, horseshoer, 55 Emerald, house 45 Village
Murphy Patrick, laborer. house 250 North
Murphy Patrick, laborer. house 92 Cove
Murphy Patrick, laborer, house 30 Oswego
Murphy Patrick, teamster, boards 157 Havre
Murphy Patrick, laborer, house 1 Livingston place
Murphy Patrick, painter, boards 1320 Tremont
Murphy Patrick, currier, boards 12 Plymouth ct.
Murphy Patrick, laborer, house 2 Lane place
Murphy Patrick, blacksmith, 21 First, h. do.
Murphy Patrick, laborer, boards 97 South
Murphy Patrick, laborer, house 73 Middlesex
Murphy Patrick, laborer, boards 73 Endicott
Murphy Patrick, laborer, house 465 Commercial
Murphy Patrick, laborer, house 320 Federal
Murphy Patrick, tailor, house 201 Fourth
Murphy Patrick, painter, house 48 Orange
Murphy Patrick, laborer, house 32 Orleans, E. B.
Murphy Patrick, plasterer. house 97 Pynchon
Murphy Patrick, nailer, bds. Neponset ave. ward 16
Murphy Patrick, gardener, bds. Boston, cor. Pond, ward 16
Murphy Patrick, laborer, house 519 Harr. avenue

Murphy Patrick, bricklayer, house 13 Yeoman
Murphy Patrick, grocer, 41 First, house do.
Murphy Patrick, laborer, h. 417 Second
Murphy Patrick, laborer, h. 114 Broad
Murphy Patrick, laborer, house r. 134 Pynchon
Murphy Patrick D. laborer, house 88 Cove
Murphy Patrick E., Custom House, h. 552 Eighth
Murphy Patrick J. harnessmaker, h. 1 Medford
Murphy Peter, laborer, house 90 Warrenton
Murphy Peter, laborer. house 1327 Tremont
Murphy Peter, laborer, h. rear 82 Northampton
Murphy Peter, papermaker, h. 38 Dunlow
Murphy Peter, overseer, house Western ave.
Murphy Peter, laborer, house 1 Fillmore place
Murphy Philip, porter, 120 Pearl, house 92 Hudson
Murphy Pierce, laborer, house 24 Billerica
Murphy P. J. clerk, 100 Hanover, bds. 60 S. Margin
Murphy Richard, at Revere House, h. 13 S. Margin
Murphy Richard J. clerk, 80 Wash. h. 152 Third
Murphy Robert, liquors, &c. 111 Cambridge, house 20 Pitts
Murphy Robert, brassfinisher, b. 187 Harrison ave.
Murphy Sarah A. dressmaker, 237 Tremont, h. do.
Murphy Terrence, laborer, house 387 First
Murphy Theobald M. clerk, boards 26 E. Canton
Murphy Thomas, laborer, house 26 S. May
Murphy Thomas, laborer, house 218 Silver
Murphy Thomas, hostler, house 6 Hunneman place
Murphy Thomas, laborer, house 2 Wright's court
Murphy Thomas, puddler, house 34 K
Murphy Thomas, teamster, house 52 Middlesex
Murphy Thomas, gasworks, house 5 Medford
Murphy Thomas, painter, h. 4 Livingston place
Murphy Thomas, fisherman, house 47 First
Murphy Thomas, variety, 291 Bennington, h. 293 do.
Murphy Thomas, laborer, house r. 1291 Tremont
Murphy Thomas, laborer, boards 61 Northampton
Murphy Thomas, hostler, b. Northampton, corner Harrison avenue
Murphy Thomas, laborer, house 3 Sturgis place
Murphy Thomas, laborer, h. Green, n. Bowdoin, ward 16
Murphy Thomas, laborer, house r. 25 Silver
Murphy Thomas, porter, 115 Broad, h. 145 Second
Murphy Thomas, teamster, boards 86 Purchase
Murphy Thomas, laborer, house 88 South
Murphy Thomas, laborer, h. 1001 Harrison ave.
Murphy Thomas, plasterer, house 15 Mindoro
Murphy Thomas blacksmith, house 855 Albany
Murphy Thomas, collarmaker, 411 Federal, h. do.
Murphy Thomas, porter, house 82 Purchase
Murphy Thomas B. clerk, 74 Pleasant, boards 255 Dorchester
Murphy Thomas E. (Murphy, Leavens, & Co.), 28 Exchange, house at East Somerville
Murphy Thomas J. groceries, North Grove, corner Parkman, house do.
Murphy Thos. V. variety store, 71 Emerson and 145 Dorchester avenue, house do.
Murphy Timothy, laborer, house 112 Porter, E. B.
Murphy Timothy, laborer, house 8 Athens
Murphy Timothy, laborer, house 19 Everett, E. B.
Murphy Timothy, laborer, house 482 Commercial
Murphy Timothy, laborer, house E, n. Second
Murphy Timothy, laborer, boards 157 Havre
Murphy Timothy, paperhanger, house 47 High
Murphy Timothy, teamster, house 141 Beach
Murphy Timothy, laborer, h. rear Central avenue
Murphy Timothy, laborer, house 83 Fourth
Murphy Timothy, laborer, boards 557 Seventh
Murphy Timothy, blacksmith, boards 26 Third
Murphy Timothy, laborer, house 30 Oswego
Murphy Timothy, baker, house 11 Oneida
Murphy Timothy, laborer, boards 248 Federal
Murphy Timothy, mariner, house 134 Kneeland
Murphy Timothy, coachman, boards Mill, near Neponset avenue, ward 16
Murphy Timothy, laborer, house Commercial, near Linden, ward 16
Murphy Timothy, blacksmith, h. r. 1224 Tremont
Murphy Timothy, cabinetmaker, h. rear 14 Curve
Murphy Timothy, machinist, house 16 Tennyson
Murphy Timothy, file cutter, 92 Beverly, house 395 Second
Murphy Timothy, blacksmith, house 49 Pembroke
Murphy Timothy, teamster, house 17 Prentiss
Murphy Timothy, grocer, 37 Spring, house do.
Murphy T. J. porter, 86 Milk, h. at Charlestown
Murphy William, police station 5, h. 116 W. Canton
Murphy William, broommaker, at Blind Asylum, bds. 521 Harrison avenue

Figure 26: An 1870 Boston City Directory page for Murphys. Additional strategies must be utilized, including the 1870 census, to help determine which of the many identical fore-names was the correct ancestor. (This work is in the public domain in its country of origin and other countries and areas where the copyright term is the author's life plus 80 years or fewer.)

Chapter Five

Directories and Convention Reports

The idea of exploring Irish origins through published directories or almanacs does not occur to most researchers. Even though they are not the first sources to consult, they are valuable for a variety of strategies.

Currently, an explosion of directories is online. Ancestry.com is certainly a leader in city directories, and websites such as Archive.org and HathiTrust.org have an astounding array of county, farming, occupational, rural, and institutional directories. All also host an almost limitless supply of convention reports. FamilySearch.org has its own program wherein it is digitizing published books and booklets through a working partnership with archives and libraries.

At one time, not enough of these records were online, but there are now overwhelming quantities of them. Thus, the process of limiting a search to a source has become part of the research process itself. For example, using the word "almanac" on websites as well as "directory" can be helpful, but the number of hits is still too many. Additional key words, such as the name of a school, organization, and institution in a state or county, can narrow the search appreciably. Whether "convention" or "lists" needs to be inserted also is a consideration. Maybe what is being sought is not technically a directory but, rather, an annual convention report. Do not hesitate to try whatever works to determine whether needed material is online.

Of the many types of directories, reports, and almanacs online, principal ones to be discussed in this chapter include city, county, and agricultural directories and religious convention reports. There are certainly others, but these introduce the topic.

Developing an Immigration Strategy
Once a list of targeted material is located, the task is to develop a viable immigration strategy, which will vary by the source and the amount of information provided. Foremost, none of these records were generated for genealogists to identify where someone was born in Ireland. City directories had no reason to give birthplaces; however, they can act as annual "censuses" of localities. This can help in developing an account of when an ancestor was at specific addresses. On the other hand, rural farming directories may have biographical sketches with

birthplaces, as may convention reports. Some of the convention reports have yearly necrologies of members with biographical material. These are most often associated with religious conventions for memorializing clergy. Until they are examined, the contents are unpredictable.

The City Directory

Directories documenting residents of areas are in many forms. The most well known are the city directories that detail residents and businesses, a standard in genealogy research, especially in large urban areas. In metropolitan areas from Boston to Seattle, most immigrants rented their apartments, and families might have changed addresses every year or two. They did not have many possessions, and moving for cheaper rents or to be closer to jobs was to their advantage.

Irish names, such as Michael Walsh, can be so ordinary that knowing where the ancestral Michael was living from year to year in St. Louis is essential. The addresses could have affected what parishes the families attended. They can also assist in sorting through the various men by the same name in the censuses. Even if the entire family is known ahead of time, the chance of several Michael Walshes having a wife named Mary and some children named Bridget, Michael, Thomas, John, and Catherine is fairly high. Irish Catholic nicknames are not singular, and one census with Bridget as Delia or Catherine as Mary can make the census reports even more frustrating. Hence, knowing addresses is essential.

Often, with a prevalent name, the only way to differentiate one John Murphy from all the rest in a large city is by occupation, which can help follow the various movements of a family in an urban area. It can become a little confusing, and some side research may be necessary. First, not much can be accomplished with the occupation of a laborer. It is non-descriptive, and multiple John Murphys who were laborers can be found. However, for more specific or odd occupations, the search can be successful.

If John Murphy was in the 1860 Boston census as a mariner and not in the city directories as a mariner, possible alternatives for a mariner need to be taken into account. The odd occupation of a "stevedore" needs to be considered. A stevedore is a dockworker, longshoreman, or docker who does the manual loading and unloading of cargo from ships. At first glance, a mariner and a stevedore may not seem interchangeable, but they can be. Whether the perceived errors were those of the census enumerators in 1860 or the compilers of the city directories may never be known, and, ultimately, may not matter. The commonality is that John Murphy's occupation had something to do with the sea or docks, a difference that might not have been in the minds of the compilers of censuses or city directories.

In city directory databases, seeing who lived on a street or in an apartment building over the years is sometimes possible by simply searching a surname and the street address. A sibling from

Ireland might have resided with the ancestors for a short time, only to move on later. Therefore, if the birthplace in Ireland is not known, a door is opened to knowledge of a previously unknown sibling who can be traced, and the birthplace in Ireland might have been preserved in a record for him or her.

A major city directory database is on Ancestry.com as "U.S. City Directories, 1822-1995." It is a massive collection with large and small directories digitized and searchable. In the database, limiting a search by city and range of years is feasible. There is an inventory of what is on the database, and so it is possible to determine if accessing it is even necessary. Because of the good searchability of this database, it is worth investigating. However, be aware it does not have all city directories; no database does.

Ancestry.com does not have the only database online. Some can be found through USGenWeb.org, limiting the search to the state and county. Sometimes, genealogy societies have digitized images of directories. These can also be accessed through the USGenWeb.org site and are worth consulting. For directories not on Ancestry.com, be aware that Archive.org and HathiTrust.org also have digitized directories.

Although city directories had no reason to mention deaths, they can often be extrapolated from the pages. A woman appearing as "widow of" seems self-explanatory, but she might have been listed by her own name. Furthermore, she might

not have been a widow. A husband disappeared occasionally, and the wife continued to live at the same address. Nevertheless, it is a solid indication that the husband was no longer with her because of either death or abandonment. In some directories, husbands and wives are listed separately but are tied together by their names in parentheses beside the names of their respective spouses. If the person died, a time frame from which to seek death certificates is shortened. For common names, this can be a vital piece of information because death records may state where persons were born in Ireland.

County and Agricultural Directories

The opposite of the urban directory is the rural directory, familiar in the Midwest, Middle States, and into New England. The emphases were on rural addresses and farming. Farms on which people resided and their businesses contributed to the communities and so were of great importance. Biographical sketches of rural residents were generally provided, including birthplaces.

The rural directories are usually on a county basis and not indexed online in a database. However, because they are not abundant, searching them is not difficult even in an OCR capability. Some are alphabetical by surname, and others are by township or town, then alphabetical by surname within each. This type of a directory is on Archive.org and HathiTrust.org. They are also customarily held at state archives. Most date from the late 1800s and early 1900s and were

240   DIRECTORY OF McHENRY COUNTY.

RIORDEN, JOHN, Farmer, Sec. 8; Harvard P. O.; born in County of Kerry, Ireland, in 1830; came to this county in 1855; owns 80 acres of land. Married n 1862; no children.

RI   ; born in Kerry Co., Ireland, 1826; came to McHenry Co. in 1870. Married Catherine Sullivan in 1865; she was born in Cork Co., Ireland, in 1831; has six children.

SCHOFF, MICHAEL, Farmer, Sec. 34; Woodstock P. O.

SCULLY, JOHN, Farmer, Sec. 12; Woodstock P. O.

SCOTT, WILLIAM, Farmer, Sec. 18; Harvard P. O.

SCHWAMB, ANDREW, Lives on farm of O. W. Curtis, Sec. 34; Woodstock P. O.

SCHULTZ, CHARLES, Farmer, Sec. 8; Harvard P. O.; born in Germany, October 27, 1831; came to this county June 22, 1876; owns 120 acres of land. Married Wilimina Schmidt July 19, 1864, who was born in Germany June 11, 1859; has two children.

SHEAHAN, DENNIS, Farmer, Sec. 8; Harvard P. O.; born in Cork Co., Ireland, in 1826; came to this county in 1853; owns 80 acres of land. Married Mary McCarthy in 1858, who was born in Cork Co., Ireland, in 1836; has seven children living. ·

SHEAHAN, MICHAEL, Farmer, Sec. 7; Harvard P. O.; born in Cork Co., Ireland, in 1834; came to this county in 1853; owns 80 acres of land; married Margaret Barrett in 1864, who was born in Lockport, Ill., in 1842; has five children.

SHEAHAN, DANIEL, Farmer, Sec. 7; Harvard P. O.; born in Cork Co., Ireland, in 1816; came to this county in 1836; owns 80 acres of land. Married Margaret Moran in 1841, who was born in Kerry Co., Ireland, 1816; no children.

SPLAIN, DANIEL, Farmer, Sec. 7; Harvard P. O.; born in Cork Co., Ireland, 1824; came to this county in 1857; owns 30 acres of land. Married Eliza Barry in 1851, who was born in Cork Co., Ireland, 1824; no children.

STUPPEL, BENJAMIN, Lives on farm of D. Barry, Sec. 28; Woodstock P. O.

SULLIVAN, J. D., Farmer, Sec. 16; Harvard P. O.

SULLIVAN, C., Lives with father, Sec. 19; Harvard P. O.

SULLIVAN, DENNIS, Farmer, Sec. 13; Woodstock P. O.; born in Cork Co., Ireland, in 1829; came to McHenry Co. in 1865. Married Marry Hennessy in 1858, who was born in Cork Co., Ireland, 1833; has six children.

SULLIVAN, HENRY, Farmer, Sec. 16; Harvard P. O.; born in Hartland Township, McHenry Co., October 15, 1843; owns 200 acres of land. Married Elizabeth McCarthy, January 19, 1864, who was born in Buffalo, N. Y., 1843; has five children.

SULLIVAN, MAURICE, Farmer, Sec. 16; Harvard P. O.; born in Kerry Co., Ireland, 1813; came to McHenry Co. 1840; owns 120 acres of land. Married Ellen Sullivan in 1835, who was born in Kerry Co., Ireland, in 1813; has five children.

Figure 27: 1877 Biographical Directory of the Tax-Payers and Voters of McHenry County, Illinois… (This work is in the public domain in its country of origin and other countries and areas where the copyright term is the author's life plus 80 years or fewer.)

state]." Another foremost printer was the Standard Map Company, with titles such as "Atlas and Farm Directory of [county, state]." Still another was the Wilmer Atkinson Company that published "The Farm Journal Rural Directory of [county, state]," also printed as "The Farm Journal Illustrated Rural Directory of [county, state]." While these do not always have biographies with birthplaces, they do have sketches with details about land, spouses, and children, all of which can lead to other records.

Odd but equally fascinating directories are catch-all advertisements for counties, their histories, and their businesses, which can be more than simple farm directories. They do not have biographical material for everyone named in them, but they do certainly report birthplaces. An example is *Biographical Directory of the Tax-Payers and Voters of McHenry County [Illinois]* (Chicago, Illinois: C. Walker, 1877). A sketch from this directory is for Dennis Sheahan and reads:

published by companies that each customized all its publications to look alike. They can include pictures.

These companies included the Prairie Farmer Publishing Company, and the standardized titles were, for example, "Prairie Farmer's Directory of [county,

SHEAHAN, DENNIS, Farmer, Sec. 8; Harvard P.O.; born in Cork Co., Ireland, in 1826; came to this county in 1853; owns 80 acres of land. Married Mary McCarthy in 1858, who was born in Cork Co., Ireland, in 1836; has seven children living (p. 240).

Another such directory is the *Art Souvenir of Leading Citizens and Farmers' Directory of Sullivan County, Indiana* ([Sullivan, Indiana]: The Sullivan Times Company, 1896). One example from the "Business Directory" section has the following information:

McENENEY, PAT, born in Monaghan, Ireland, Sept. 9, 1838. Came to America, 1853. Came to Sullivan, 1859, engaged in the marble and granite business the same year and has since remained, operating the business successfully on a large scale. In June, 1862, married Miss Julia A., daughter of James Harris; four children born to the union (Image 120/288).

Many of these digitized editions are on various websites. They can be searched by words within the texts, and so other patterns can be explored, such as people with the same surname or everyone born in, for instance, County Westmeath. The latter investigation is to

find people from the same place in Ireland but with different surnames who might have known each other in Ireland or who were relatives. With other names to study in the Irish indexes, a pattern may emerge that, at some stage, could point to the county in Ireland where the ancestor was from.

Similar to farming directories are those that focused on a type of stock or agricultural pursuit. These directories documented registered owners of specific kinds of cattle, hogs, horses, or poultry and can be very detailed because the purity of livestock for its resale value was decisive for farmers. Important for potential buyers and sellers were registered growers with registered livestock who were in good standing with the associations. The associations established the criteria for the livestock, and in the case of cattle, the buying and selling of the registered animals for each year might have been printed in the directories. They look almost like land deeds!

The purpose of these kinds of directories is not biographies of the owners, although they do often supply the genealogies for animals. The intention is to set a standard. If an ancestor is discovered as having belonged to an association,

McENENEY, PAT, born in Monaghan, Ireland, Sept. 9, 1838. Came to America, 1853. Came to Sullivan, 1859, engaged in the marble and granite business the same year and has since remained, operating the business successfully on a large scale. In June, 1862, married Miss Julia, A., daughter of James Harris; four children born to the union.

Figure 28: Art Souvenir of Leading Citizens and Farmer's Directory of Sullivan County, Indiana, 1896. (This work is in the public domain in its country of origin and other countries and areas where the copyright term is the author's life plus 80 years or fewer.)

seek directories or convention reports with additional information about members. If he or she is not found, who else registered with the association from the same community or county? As with other research strategies, this might present a group from Ireland who had farms near one another and who bought and sold livestock among themselves. Unless a biographical sketch was published for a specific reason, the member's information usually consists of name, address, and registered livestock owned.

When searching for these directories online, such as on Archive.org or HathiTrust.org, "angus directory" or "livestock directory" or "dairy association" should produce some hits. Others are "poultry directory" or "pig almanac." Whatever combination of words brings up a potential list of published works is part of the research process.

A most unusual and seldom expected source is the "marks and brands" books, and when discovered, they make sense. From them, many research strategies can be developed. Each state, especially in the West, had a department that registered brands on cattle, horses, asses, goats, sheep, and less often, for pigs. The marks were often in ears as notches, and the brands could have been in designated places on the animals. The registered marks or brands and their locations on the animals were published in books, which were indexed by the names of the owners and with additional indexes for the marks or brands themselves. If an animal was lost or stolen, it could be linked through the books to a specific person within that state. A code embedded within each mark or brand enabled the creation of an index that tied it to the owner, for example, an E turned one way instead of another in relationship to a Z rotated at a certain angle. Letters, numbers, and figures were all arranged for distinct brands.

The marks and brands books are noteworthy and usually can be found from the 1840s until today. Whenever the period of the registration was completed, the owner had to register again to keep the mark or brand in his or her name. The huge cattle companies, prisons, orphanages, churches, and other institutions that had a reason to own cattle also are named in these books. Native Americans with the tribes to which they belonged are listed.

As with other agricultural directories, marks and brands books do not have birthplaces of the registrants. However, that is not the reason to consult them. Because of the nature of the frontiers and rough western areas of the country, livestock was vital, as was the protection of it. The business of doing so was serious, with the penalty for horse thieving or cattle rustling if convicted death by hanging, that is, if the offense ever proceeded past a vigilante mob made up of community ranchers. As immigrants went westward for farms and ranches, they often were not documented in the records in which they should have been. Marks and brands are a way of tracking their movements. Once the people are found, other sources can be examined that may have birthplaces in Ireland.

Marks and brands books are especially pertinent to women's studies. In the West, women often obtained and ran the homesteads. They were independent businesswomen. The number of women with registered brands is astounding.

Some state archives, such as Utah's, have indexed and digitized marks and brands books through their websites. A wide range of them are online at sites such as Archives.org and HathiTrust.org.

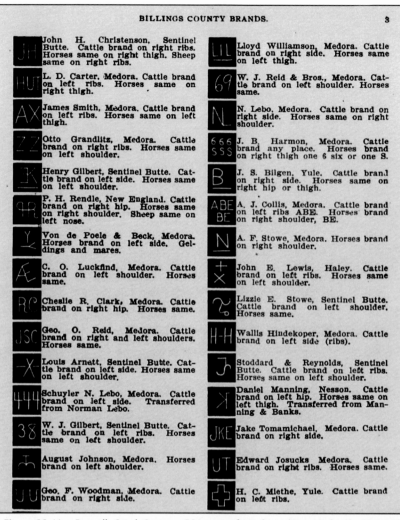

Figure 29: Van Dersal's Stock Growers Directory of Marks and Brands for the State of North Dakota, 1902. (This work is in the public domain in its country of origin and other countries and areas where the copyright term is the author's life plus 80 years or fewer.)

Religious Conventions

Almost all faiths had conventions or conferences, national, regional, or statewide. The business of the conventions and various motions and votes were typically contained in their convention reports. These are informative but not their true value. Their potential is records of missions and missionaries, new ministers being ordained, deaths, and even full biographical obituaries of deceased clergy. Many also have ministerial lists and residences for persons and where they pastored. The reports, published from the conferences, can document individuals who never attended conventions. Some denominations published them annually, while others were bi-annual or for other periods, depending on the customs of the faith groups.

When seeking this material online at websites such as Archive.org or HathiTrust.org, remember that the word "convention" may have a couple of definitions. Consider that many denominations are divided for internal governance into conferences that may or may not follow state boundaries. A "key word" search, for example, could bring up the Methodist Conference of [place] as the Methodist Church divided by geographical conferences. However, if the search is for a convention report for the Episcopal Church held in a particular year or span of years, the word convention may yield more Episcopal and fewer Methodist results. This is also complicated by the fact of there being historically the Methodist Episcopal Church (now the United Methodist Church) and two of the largest African American Methodist bodies, the African Methodist Episcopal Church and the African Methodist Episcopal Church Zion. All might come up in a general search when only the Episcopal Church was needed!

When biographies or obituaries are found in church reports, they can be magnificent assets. An example is a lengthy biography of deceased Methodist Episcopal Church worker Richard T. Wade published in the "Memoirs" section of the *Official Journal Troy Conference Minutes, 1893,* the year of the Sixty-First Session of the Troy, New York, Conference. It demonstrates what is produced in a regional level as opposed to material published at a national conference. Stated is that he was born in County Galway, Ireland, on 9 December 1815 and died in Amsterdam, New York, on 5 March 1893. The following is about his religious life:

He came from Westport, Ireland, to America in 1837, and for a few months was engaged in teaching in New Jersey. In 1838 he yielded to the call of the Divine Spirit and the Church, and began preaching on Bergen circuit. In 1840 he removed to New York State and was received on trial in Troy Conference in 1841, and into full connection in 1843. He was ordained deacon by Bishop Waugh in 1843 and elder by Bishop Hedding in 1845. January 19th, 1843, he was married to Eleanor W. Wakeman of Ballston, who died July 19th, 1859, leaving two children, who yet survive, a son, Edwin W. Wade, and a daughter, Mrs. Richard Peck, both residing in Amsterdam, N.Y. (pp. 121-123).

The sketch goes on to recount that he remarried and lived a long life, and "[h]is family life was exceptionally happy and beautiful."

Study religious directories or convention reports for an ancestor. Not all church members were listed, only those who had reasons to attend the conventions or had positions to fulfill, such as funding for churches. Ministers and missionaries are the main candidates for these published sources.

Chapter Six

Immigration Records

A first source researchers want to explore is the passenger arrival records. They are undeniably prized in genealogy because they establish the days ancestors entered the United States.

They are challenging. A principal consideration about them is that they might not be the primary source to consult, especially for common names. An example is Mary Kelly. Even more complicated is the circumstance of Mary Kelly arriving as a single young woman to meet someone already settled in America. Which Mary Kelly disembarking in New York City or any other port is the correct one? A reality in Irish research is that ages are not a determining factor because the Irish often did not know how old they were. Moreover, the place of origin on the passenger arrival papers for almost every one of the Irish people in the nineteenth century is simply Ireland or Great Britain, and so the country is not a guide.

In the case of Mary Kelly, without the name of a ship and a date, determining which one is the correct Mary is almost impossible.

On the other hand, if a name is rather uncommon and about when and where he or she landed has been indicated from another document, the passenger arrival record can be located. A family immigrating as a unit can be identified accurately as well.

From a genealogical perspective, some wonderful books or chapters in books have been written about how to use the records that are available. Among these, two are noteworthy:

Colletta, John Phillip. *They Came in Ships: Finding Your Immigrant Ancestor's Arrival Record.* 3rd ed., Orem, Utah: Ancestry.com, 2002.

Tepper, Michael. *American Passenger Arrival Records: A Guide to the Records of Immigrants Arriving at American Ports by Sail and Steam.* Rev. and enlarged ed., Baltimore, Maryland: Genealogical Publishing Company, 1999.

Several basic points need to be acknowledged about passenger arrival lists. Researchers assume that a year or an approximate one for immigration is already known. It might have come from a census, citizenship paper, or even personal letters. Nevertheless, immigrants frequently did not keep track of when they arrived, and so when they were asked questions for naturalization purposes or by the census enumerators in 1900, they were giving estimates. Sometimes, they are exact, but do not expect more than approximate years. Even so, the dates usually are somewhat close or, at least, within reason, and from them, the records can be examined.

Ports of Arrival

Researchers are inclined to assume that all immigrants came through the port of New York City. While perhaps that is the largest port of arrival, it was certainly not the only one. The main ports in the nineteenth century included:

- New York
- Boston
- Baltimore
- Philadelphia
- New Orleans

Smaller ports were all along the coasts of the Atlantic Ocean, the Gulf of Mexico, the Pacific Ocean, Alaska, and Hawaii. Many of them do not always have complete sets of records; however, the major five may not have complete ones either. Knowing where the gaps are can be ascertained through Michael Tepper's *American Passenger Arrival Records* (1993).

The port of Baltimore is a well-documented example. Many early Baltimore passenger arrival records were destroyed in a fire, but valuable information from other transcripts or abstracts has substituted for them. Even at this, what needs to be understood in trying to identify an Irish immigrant is that entire years, among which are 1842, 1844, 1846, 1847, 1851 to 1856, 1864, and 1867, are missing. The years were just before, during, and after peak Irish immigration. Some of this information is supplemented by

other sources such as City Lists or Quarterly Abstracts. Nevertheless, do not assume all information is duplicated. For Baltimore, supplements to the original lists (1820-1891) fall into three categories: State Department Transcripts (1820, 1822-1827, 1829); City Lists (1833-1866); and Quarterly Abstracts (1820-1869).

Major and minor ports of arrival lists are on Ancestry.com as well as on FamilySearch.org and several other websites. Access to them is not the issue. Finding the correct person in an overabundance of common names with little identifying information is continually the difficulty for researchers.

Any of the early port of entry records share the problem of common names as well as providing only the basic information. A good example is the seven-volume work *The Famine Immigrants: Lists of Irish Immigrants Arriving at the Port of New York, 1846-1851* (Baltimore, Maryland: Genealogical Publishing Company, 1983-1986), edited by Ira A. Glazier and Michael Tepper. Before the New York passengers' lists were digitized and available through several websites, such as Ancestry.com and FamilySearch.org, this was the go-to set for the famine era. The names of the people on the ships transporting mostly Irish people were extracted, but this needs explanation. The original lists sometimes have the nationalities as the places where the persons embarked. Under this practice, if an Irish person left from Liverpool, as countless ones did, he or she was designated English instead of Irish. With a source such as this, determining a country of origin is almost impossible for a single person with a common name. An exceptional name may be easier. If a family arrived together, the chance of finding the person is better because of the multiple names from which to work and study.

Continuing with this example, do not expect to find the ancestral Mary Kelly unless known ahead of time are the date she came and the ship on which she traveled. Even at that, several Mary Kellys might have been on the same ship. What does make the task simpler is that any results found from these monumental books can be compared with those in databases, for instance, "New York, Irish Immigrant Arrival Records, 1846-1851" on Ancestry.com. The database has a trouble-free method of viewing the documents from several perspectives, especially surname variations.

Passengers' Arrival Lists Post-1891

From 1820 through 1891, the information on the passengers' lists is basic. From 1891 forward, more details were recorded, and by 1906, birthplaces were given.

Part of the immigration strategy is to utilize all sources to help solve the research problem. One of these is the later arrival records to determine who might have gone to Ireland and returned. The records could include someone who had immigrated decades previously or someone from Ireland immigrating late or visiting a relative who had already immigrated. Either way, the later passengers' lists convey who they were intending to visit and who the contact persons were in the home countries. If these can be worked into an immigration strategy, they can identify Irish origins.

The more important questions to ask pertaining to this period that can assist with finding immigrant origins are:

- Whether having been in the United States before, and if so, when, where, and for how long.
- If joining a relative, who the person was, what his or her relationship was, and where he or she was living.
- If in possession of a train ticket to the final destination, who paid for the passage.

In 1906, not only was the place of birth reported but also the address of the closest living relative in the country of origin.

Passenger and Immigration Lists Index

Since the United States officially began recording passenger arrivals in 1820, the period before is the one that poses distinct challenges. That an arrival record does not exist cannot be concluded until what has been gathered has been explored.

The series *Passenger and Immigration Lists Index,* edited by P. William Filby and Mary K. Meyer, is an enormous index to already published passenger and immigration lists, probably the most extensive one for pre-1820 arrivals. Popular for decades in its printed form, it has been made into a comprehensive database on Ancestry.com as "U.S. and Canada, Passenger and Immigration Lists Index, 1500s-1900s." The Ancestry.com edition allows the information to be manipulated in a number of ways not possible with the books.   The work is so well known

Passenger Records Post-1820

Act of 1819

In 1819, federal legislation introduced regulations that outlined the responsibility of vessels wishing to disembark passengers in the United States and thus created formal Customs Passenger Lists. These lists began in 1820 and generally include:

- Name
- Age
- Sex
- Occupation
- Country to which allegiance was previously owed
- Country that the passenger intended to inhabit

The process was, thankfully, bureaucratic because it produced multiple copies that occasionally help with otherwise lost or damaged lists.

Step 1
- Ship captain or master
- Created and submitted actual list of passengers to collector of customs

Step 2
- Collector of Customs
- Reviewed and submitted quarterly abstract reports of passengers to Secretary of State

Step 3
- Secretary of State
- Submitted information from abstracts to congress

Step 4
- U.S. Congress
- Evaluated at will as necessary

Act of 1882

Actual passengers, rather than only the reporting of them, were brought under federal regulation in 1882, enacting a head tax and making immigration decisions more uniform from port to port. Additions to questions included:

- Country of citizenship
- Native country
- Specific intended destination

Not every port was able to immediately comply to these new lists, called Immigration Passenger Lists, but they were all successfully converted to the new standard forms by 1903:

Passenger Records Post-1820 (cont.)

Act of 1882

Dates that Ports Converted from Customs Passenger Lists to Immigration Passenger Lists	
1883	•Philadelphia
1891	•Boston
1891	•Baltimore
1897	•New York
1903	•New Orleans

Act of 1893

Lists turned over to the port authority were now "required" to have been generated at the port of embarkation instead of during the voyage. Added questions were:

- Married or single
- Whether can read or write
- Whether possessing a ticket to final destination
- Who paid for passage
- If passenger was in possession of more or less than $30.00
- Whether going to join a friend or relative
- If ever in the United States before, and if so, when and where
- If ever in prison
- If ever supported by charity
- If a polygamist
- If already under contract to perform labor in the United States
- Condition of physical and mental health, and whether deformed or crippled

*For pre-1820 details, see Chapter 10 in volume one of this series, Dwight A. Radford, *American Scots-Irish Research: Strategies and Sources in the Quest for Ulster-Scots Origins* (Orting, WA: Family Roots Publishing Co., LLC, 2020).

Passenger Records Post-1820 (cont.)

Act of 1903

Additional legislation was:

- Race identification
- Epileptics, anarchists, procurers, professional beggars, persons with two or more attacks of insanity, and previous deportees were among those excluded from admission into the United States

Act of 1906

This act coincided with the establishment of the Bureau of Immigration and Naturalization. It added:

- If passenger was in possession of more or less than $50.00
- Personal description of each passenger
  - Height
  - Weight
  - Color of hair
  - Color of eyes
  - Scars or deformities
- Specific birthplace for each immigrant

Act of 1907

The final congressional act worthy of note for ship passenger lists was passed in 1907.

- Asked for the name and address of the nearest living relative in the country from which the immigrant came

and consulted that in genealogical circles, it is simply nicknamed *Filby's* and is widely understood by that reference. The compass of the work is astounding because a quantity of varied and totally unrelated sources was gathered for it. Once an entry is found, the Ancestry.com version displays the published work that contains the entry with its page number. Whether using the published *Filby's* or the Ancestry.com database, remember that *Filby's* is just an index to the wider collections and is by no means the end of the search. The published book in which a record was originally printed still needs to be studied for further information, background, and names of people who might have been listed alongside the ancestor.

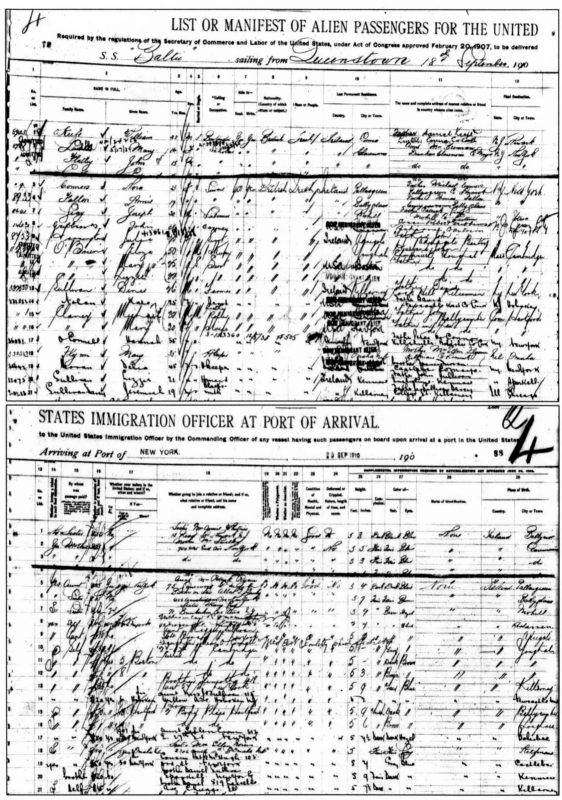

Figures 30a and 30b: Arrival of Jeremiah Sullivan-Darcy [line 21], dated 24 September 1910, at the Port of New York. Leaving behind his father, Jas., at College Street in Killarney, Ireland, he was traveling to meet his brother Daniel in Chicago, Illinois. Many additional details are shown, which can then be compared with others of the same surname and lead to other record sources such as Daniel's arrival, coordinating addresses of both together in city directories, and more. (Image courtesy of the National Archives and Records Adminsitration.)

Filby's can be valuable in tracing colonial ancestors and covers all periods in its over five million entries. For each individual, at least some of the following information can be found:

- Name and age
- Year and place of arrival
- Naturalization
- Source of the information
- Accompanying family members.

Even as mammoth as *Filby's* is, not finding an ancestor's arrival information is not unusual. It is common to discover several individuals with the same name in different lists, and whether any one of them is the ancestor can be uncertain.

Canadian Border Crossings

Ancestors frequently landed first in Canada and then proceeded to the United States, but an aspect people sometimes do not think about is that both Americans and Canadians went back and forth across the border for numerous reasons.

An Irish-American might have had family members who were Irish-Canadians, and over the decades, the visits generated records. The records of the trips introduce additional avenues of research in a viable immigration strategy because they identify the people with whom the immigrants intended to stay as well as birthplaces, invaluable discoveries.

This vast archive of records has been indexed and digitized in the database "U.S., Border Crossings from Canada to the U.S., 1895-1960" on Ancestry.com. It documents people returning to the United States from their travels. Do not let the records' late dates be a deterrent to research.

Remember that although main border crossings were at points of entry, both Americans and Canadians often had other routes that were undocumented. Rural areas could have been so remote that they seemed to have no borders. These passages were not uncommon

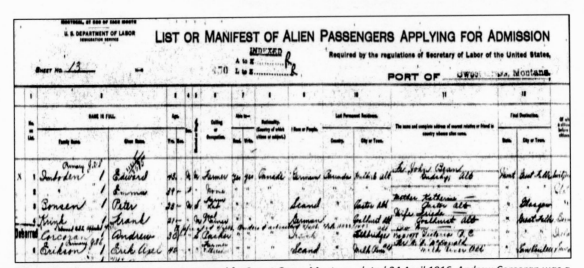

Figure 31a: Canadian Border Crossing record for Sweet Grass, Montana, dated 24 April 1916. Andrew Corcoran was a 30-year-old packer who was born in "Billina," Ireland, and originally immigrated through the Port of Quebec in June 1909. A variety of other details were shared as well. (Image courtesy of the National Archives and Records Adminisitration.)

and were not thought of as illegal crossings by either country. Not until 1908 did the International Boundary Commission properly survey and define the line of separation from the Atlantic to the Pacific. It was made permanent by treaty in 1925.

The records will provide name, residence, relatives, birthplace, age, and point of entry. The border crossings are chiefly, but not exclusively, places of entry across land. The entrance points and the years of records have been taken from the Ancestry.com database, but most of them remain in use today:

Idaho: Eastport (1924-1954); Porthill (1923-1954)

Maine: Bangor (1924-1952); Calais (1906-1952 [also includes a few arrivals from 1877 to 1905]); Eastport, Fort Kent, Lubec, and Madawaska (1906-1952 [also includes some departure records of United States citizens]); Fort Fairfield (1909-1953 [also includes a few arrivals at Easton, ME, Houlton, ME, Boston, MA, and Buffalo, NY, and a few alien departures]); Houlton (1906-1952 [also includes some Indian admissions, ca. 1941 to ca. 1953; "Records of Registry" documenting aliens' previous arrivals for which no records could be found; re-entry permits; persons admitted under the "Rule of Presumption"; land border departure records; war brides and their children]); Jackman (1909-1953); Van Buren (1906-1952); Vanceboro (1906-1952 [also includes a few arrivals from 1888 to 1905 and a few arrivals at Halifax, Nova Scotia, and St. John, New Brunswick])

Minnesota: International Falls, Baudette, Duluth, Mineral Center, Pigeon River, Pine Creek, Roseau, and Warroad (1907-1952 [also includes some departure records of United States citizens]); Noyes (1917-1929)

Montana: Babb (1928-1956); Chief Mountain, Cut Bank, Del Bonita, Gateway, Great Falls, and Roosville (1923-1956); Sweet Grass (1917-1954)

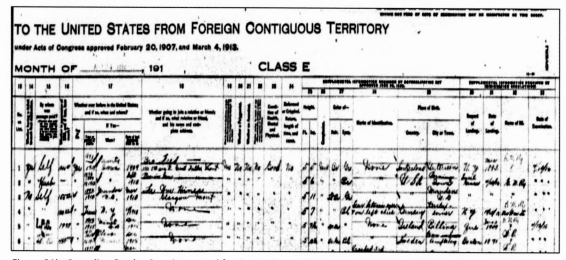

Figure 31b: Canadian Border Crossing record for Sweet Grass, Montana, dated 24 April 1916. Andrew Corcoran was a 30-year-old packer who was born in "Billina," Ireland, and originally immigrated through the Port of Quebec in June 1909. A variety of other details were shared as well. (Image courtesy of the National Archives and Records Administration.)

New York: Buffalo, Lewiston, Niagara Falls, and Rochester (1902-1954); Hogansburg, Malone, Morristown, Nyando, Ogdensburg, Rooseveltown, Waddington, Alexandria Bay, Cape Vincent, Champlain, Clayton, Fort Covington, Moers, Rouses Point, Thousands Island Bridge, and Trout River (1929-1956)

North Dakota: Northgate and St. John (1910-1921); Pembina and Walhalla (1917-1929); Portal (1915-1921)

Vermont: Newport (1906-1924); St. Albans (1895-1954)

Washington: Anacortes (1924-1953); Blaine (1905-1956); Danville (1931-1956); Ferry (1917-1956); Laurier and Marcus (1923-1951); Lynden (1923-1952); Metaline Falls (1924-1954); Northport (May 1923-1951); Oroville (1918-1954); Port Angeles (1929-1952); Sumas (1924-1956)

The Ancestry.com collection for people traveling from the United States to Canada may also be helpful. It comprises those who went to visit relatives in Canada, and the databases cited above should have records of them returning. The database for people entering Canada, with digitized images, is "Border Crossings: From U.S. to Canada, 1908-1935." Again, realize that many people crisscrossed in rural areas, over frozen rivers and lakes, without being documented. In some cities and towns on the border, immigration into Canada was customary, as easy as passing across a street, river, or bridge, and the travelers, either way, thought little about it.

Be Alert

Contrary to popular belief, ancestors did not change their names at Ellis Island or any other port of arrival. The list was already generated by the captain or master of the ship. Later on, it was recorded at the foreign port of departure during embarkation. Consequently, names later Anglicized are likely to be found in their original context in passenger lists.

For a more detailed explanation of why name variations, such as Eugene for Owen and Connor for Cornelius, should be considered when searching passenger lists, naturalization records and other sources, see "Chapter 19: Special Strategy—Names, Nicknames and Naming Patterns" in volume two of this series, Dwight A. Radford, *Discovering Irish Origins Using the Records of Ireland (Orting, WA: Family Roots Publishing Co., LLC, 2021).*

Chapter Seven

Institutional Records

Among the records most sought by family historians are those for institutions, usually orphanages and prisons. These do sometimes have birthplaces in Ireland, but they are not the only ones that do. Institutions and homes were properties of the states and counties, and each county had jails, orphanages, work farms, asylums, and poorhouses, whose records are typically at a state archive or digitized through Ancestry.com and FamilySearch.org. The present chapter is an introduction to solely state institutions that may provide or, at least, lead to more definite information on immigrant origins and includes:

- Asylums
- Industrial Schools
- Prisons

All three had their share of the Irish as residents or "inmates," the latter being the old term found in records. Although many institutions are worthy of discussion, a large majority of them, such as orphanages and hospitals, ordinarily noted in their registers only a country as the place of birth for almost every person.

Genealogists are fascinated with the topics of inmates and people who were in institutions, especially the unsavory ones. Infamous "black books" or "black sheep books" have been compiled by researchers who have scoured numerous and miscellaneous institution registers of, for instance, prisons, asylums, and the notorious industrial schools for "bad boys" and "bad girls." Some authors pore over newspapers for indictments for murders and other criminal activities for the periods of their studies. Unquestionably, these works are intriguing when discovered.

One is Robert Scott Davis Jr., Louise Moxley, and Colleen Elliott's *The Georgia Black Book: Morbid, Macabre, & Sometimes Disgusting Records of Genealogical Value* (Easley, South Carolina: Southern Historical Press, 1982, 1987). Unless the purpose of a work is to extract every lurid detail from a court case or registers of a facility, the books usually are indexes with basic information so that researchers can access the original records that have more particulars. These volumes are invaluable in learning about ancestors and where they were institutionalized. *The Georgia Black Book,* for instance, is in two volumes, with the subtitle to the second encompassing all its contents: "More morbid, macabre & sometimes disgusting records of genealogical value, just when you thought it was safe to get back into genealogy." The description is certainly not far removed from the truth.

The Asylum

Sometimes, someone not being with his or her family in the census schedules as would be expected is the first suggestion that he or she was committed to a mental health facility. With no evidence of a divorce or death, this absence of a name can be puzzling. In such an occurrence, expanding a search in the censuses for the ancestor living elsewhere is prudent. If he or she is found, determine whether the residence was an institution. The census takers normally labeled the facilities, and the inmates were enumerated accordingly. If an institution was not named in the census, a quick internet search of the town often mentions one located there. Many of these older institutions were later merged into modern mental health facilities. Each state has one or more of them. Termed state hospitals, they drew patients from throughout each state. Historically, they were simply "lunatic asylums" or "insane asylums." Counties also had smaller institutions to which the courts consigned the mentally ill.

To commit someone was a legal matter in the county court, resulting in a series of records, among which were the proof to a judge that the person needed to be committed, the admission to the facility, and the release, if the patient was ever released. The court actions are with other documents heard before a judge at the county level of government. If a court case has not been discovered, the admission books to the institution should cite the judge and court within a county that committed the individual.

When a court case or newspaper account has been located but the admission records have not been searched, the next step is to identify the institution. Was it a county or state facility? Large collections of court records for counties and even ones for county facilities are digitized on FamilySearch.org. Some for the state institutions are digitized on Ancestry.com and FamilySearch.org or filed at a state archive.

The records vary by period and institution. A number have, as a minimum, counties for the people born in Ireland, whereas others have no more than Ireland. Regardless, the history of the patient can be fascinating and offer insight into other family members.

Two examples of documents from the Ancestry.com collection of the "California, State Hospital Records, 1856-1923" are those for Michael Broderick and Mary Jane Robertson, both committed to the Stockton State Hospital.

10264 Michael Broderick Committed from San Mateo Co. by Hon. E. F. Head. Nov. 15, 1887 – Witness: Dr. A. E. Baldwin & others – Examining Physicians: Drs. Loveland & Ross – Age 33 – Nativity: Cork, Ireland – Civil condition: not stated – Sailor – Last from New York – One year in Cal. – Evidence of Insanity: General appearance and conversation. The principals are religious – Number and duration of attacks: unknown – Has not been intemperate nor addicted to narcotics – In fair physical condition – Cause of insanity:

unknown – Class: General insanity.
On Admission: In good physical condition but very crazy and excited
Admitted Nov. 17, 1887
Discharged: Jan. 2, 1889
No property

4186 Mary Jane Robertson Committed by Selden S. Wright Judge (Probate) of San Francisco May 12th 1870 aged 53 years; native of Londonderry Ireland; married; was last from Md. Has been in California 19 years; occupation housewife. The evidence of insanity is, she was first insane 3 years ago and recovered – became again insane and is now entirely so. She talks incessantly on all subjects in a very incoherent way – tears up her clothing has to be watched constantly to prevent her running off; will attack any person who crosses her; disease stationary no rational intervals for 12 months – no insane relations; has been temperate; has not suffered from disease or injury; class mania.
Admitted May 13th 1870 Husband pays
Discharged January 18th 1871

These entries are permeated with additional details that can advance research goals. Their parents' names are not given, and so a search of the indexes of church registers in Ireland cannot be undertaken without more information.

Michael Broderick was born in 1854 in County Cork, Ireland. His usual residence was in New York, and he had been in

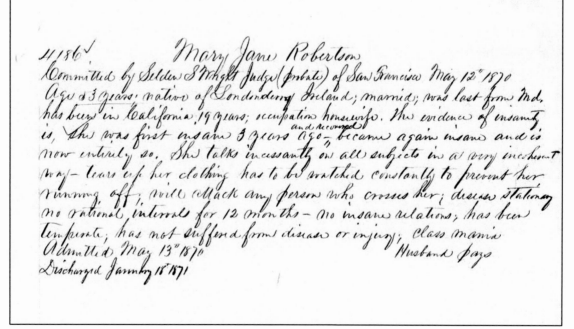

Figure 32: Mary Jane Robertson text abstracted from Stockton State Hospital, Commitment Registers, 1862-1870. (Image courtesy of California State Archives.)

California for one year. His occupation as a sailor might have brought him to San Mateo County, which was just south of the port of San Francisco. The San Mateo courts committed him on 15 November 1887. Exactly what "sailor" meant is a little vague. He might have been in the United States Navy or part of the American Merchant Marines, perhaps excellent clues, as are New York and San Mateo. The assumption is that if he had extended family in the United States, they were in New York. There was no intimation about whether he was married or returned to New York as a sailor. Other sources have to be consulted.

Essential evidence is present in Mary Jane Robertson's record. She was 54 in 1870, and thus she was born in 1817 in County Londonderry (Derry). She was married, and her husband was paying the bills. She had been in California for 19 years, placing her as an early resident of the state in 1851. The supposition is she came from Maryland, her last residence. Most importantly, she spent her previous 19 years in San Francisco, and so most of the civil records about her life were later destroyed in the 1906 earthquake and fire. Unless a church register for her in the city or a record in Maryland survived, there may be little to document her birthplace as County Londonderry (Derry) other than the Stockton State Hospital register. She was 89 at the time of the earthquake and fire, and so no other records about her life are in San Francisco.

These two California entries are but illustrations of the records. Even if the registers for the institution in question have nothing but countries for places of births, they have additional information. The advantage of these resources is that laws required facts. It may be a notation in a court case or a next of kin that is the key to solving immigrant origins. However, without looking first at the asylum registers, those priceless details are lost.

Industrial Schools

Countless stories in family history are about children being orphaned, and researchers assume that their parents cannot be identified. Certainly, that may be true in many situations, but it should not be the conclusion until all investigations are exhausted. One scenario often overlooked is that a child was sent by the parents or one parent to an industrial school because the family was too poor to care for him or her. There, the child, in theory, was supposed to acquire an education and a skill. In other circumstances, children were placed in these schools not necessarily because they were juvenile delinquents but because they were abandoned or neglected, and the local counties assigned them there for training, education, and moral guidance. Any of these reasons open the possibility that perhaps identifying the immigrant is not unattainable. What was left behind in the documents of the industrial schools that could disclose the parents?

Generally, the records for state institutions were preserved and are at state archives or digitized through FamilySearch.org. However, each state has a privacy policy in place about who can see all or only portions of records.

Because of the ages of the children, the hypothesis is that most were born in the

United States. This is not always correct. If they were born in America, the parents of the children were probably the immigrants. The child is the person being sought and most likely the person beyond whom an inquiry cannot progress. Therefore, researching an ancestor or the sibling of an ancestor sent to an industrial school is just one step away from the main goal of identifying immigrant origins. It is a holistic approach to solving the problem.

In developing an immigrant strategy, the records generated about the boys and girls are thorough enough that needed information is often inferred rather than stated outright. Most of the children sent to institutions went through processes, which had the potential of leaving a wealth of facts. Because the home was responsible for their well-being, the documents can include their health, habits, criminal activities, parentages, birthplaces, next-of-kin, and original residences.

One example of how these records can assist is the old Ohio Reform Farm. It was established in 1857 by the state and was the first in the country to be patterned after a family plan. Before this time, the various state reformatories were "Big House" models. Forty boys were overseen by an Elder Brother in each "family" setting. The children ranged from ten to eighteen years old. The home was set on 1,170 acres, five miles south of Lancaster in Fairfield County, Ohio. It ceased to function as a juvenile reformatory in 1980. Between 1857 and 1980, it was under several names: State Reform Farm (or School) from 1857 to 1884, the Boys'

Industrial School from 1884 to 1964, and the Fairfield School for Boys from 1964 to 1980. To demonstrate the abundance of clues that can be supplied about the children of Irish, two "inmate case records" are presented. William Holden's did have a birthplace in Ireland, but Thomas Dorty's did not (Book 1 [1858-1861]):

> *89*
> *Name and Parentage: William Holden, was born in Carloo [sic] County Ireland 1843*
> *Commitment: offence vicious & incorrigible conduct. Sentenced by Probate Court of Franklin County April 28th, 1859. Was never convicted of any crime.*
> *Education: [blank]*
> *Health Remarks: [blank]*
> *Employment: [blank]*
> *Miscellaneous: [blank]*

> *106*
> *Name and Parentage: Thomas Dorty, aged 16 yrs, born in 1843, father's name James Dorty (dead), mother's name Alice Dorty, mother is a washwoman lives in New York City*
> *Commitment: petit larceny, Police Court of the city of Cleveland*
> *Education: can read, write and cipher*
> *Health Remarks: health is quite good. Is near sighted.*
> *Employment: [blank]*
> *Miscellaneous: [blank]*

Little was noted about William Holden, perhaps because he was never convicted of a crime; he was a "vicious & incorrigible" young man. His parents' names were not given, but since he had to have immigrated with someone, the indication for research is the Probate Court of Franklin County, which committed him on 28 April 1859. William was 16 at the time. With a date and court, other records can be explored for his circumstances and perhaps closest relative involved. Depending on when he immigrated, he might have been in the 1850 census of Franklin County. Still, assuming he was Catholic and not Protestant, knowing County Carlow as his origin is not enough to find him in the Carlow Catholic register indexes without the names of parents. Thus, research is solidly in Franklin County records.

Thomas Dorty's case is loaded with hints. His exact date of committal is unknown, but chronologically, it must have been 1860 or 1861. He was born in 1843, but no birthplace is given. His father, James Dorty, was deceased, and his mother, Alice Dorty, was a washerwoman in New York City, implying that Thomas was born in either New York City or in Ireland. He was committed by the Police Court in Cleveland, Ohio, another excellent clue. However, at this point, it must be determined exactly what a "Police Court" was under nineteenth-century Ohio law. Were those records preserved by law? If so, are they with the police department, county courthouse, city hall, or on deposit at the state archive? Regardless of the state in which the institution was located, the questions are the same.

Reading between the lines in Dorty's report, the indication is that after his father died, his mother sent him to Cleveland to be with relatives because she could not afford to support him. Aside from any court records in Cleveland, the 1860 census of Cleveland and possibly the 1850 census of New York City can be studied. The names of his parents are known, and so finding a James and Alice Dorty with a son Thomas born around 1843 is possible. From there, whether Thomas was born in America or in Ireland can be determined. Nonetheless, the goal is to research James and Alice in New York City, and if they were the immigrants, the search is closer to solving immigrant origins.

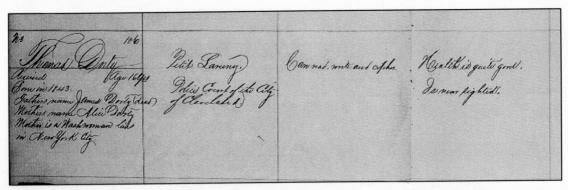

Figure 33: Thomas Dorty record, Fairfield School for Boys, Lancaster, Ohio, 1858-1861, abstracted from page 127. (Image courtesy of the Ohio History Connection.)

The counterpart of this institution, for girls, was in Scioto, Delaware County. Known as Scioto Village, it was formerly known as State Reform and Industrial School for Girls from 1869 to 1872, Girls' Industrial Home from 1878 to 1965, Girls' Industrial School from 1865, and Scioto Village currently. The registers' information mirrors that of the boys' school. The records for both institutions are indexed on the Ohio History Connection website, which is the state archive. Both are also digitized and on FamilySearch.org.

Begin the search for registers at the state archive websites and the ones on FamilySearch.org. Indexes may be online. When exploring institutional registers, always look for the clues from the time the child was committed.

Prison Records

Genealogists love records from prisons, which are state institutions, whereas jails are county or city facilities. Historical prison records can be a superb resource for the family historian and can usually be found at state archives. Also, large collections are on Ancestry.com and FamilySearch.org. These can range from minimal information to complete files with pictures, conviction reports, behavior in prison, and notations about next-of-kin. They have inestimable details. Even if an ancestor was never imprisoned, it was not uncommon for a relative to have been incarcerated. It may be within the prison record that the birthplace in Ireland is revealed as there was a reason to ask. If an individual was a habitual criminal, he or she may be found several times in the state penitentiary.

In developing an immigrant origins' strategy, these records are important because even if they only state the birthplace of the inmate as Ireland, the residence of the next of kin might have been in Ireland. Such a situation, from the digitized collection "Idaho, U.S., Old Penitentiary Prison Records, 1882-1961" on Ancestry.com, is for John Murphy (#239), who was received into the Boise, Idaho, prison on 8 June 1890 from Shoshone County for manslaughter. His sentence was seven years. He was 42 years old and a miner, born in Ireland. He was Catholic. The address of his nearest relative was his mother, Catherine Murphy, in Glengariff, County Cork.

Another report from the Idaho State Penitentiary is for Henry Lynch (#238), who was received on 28 June 1890, also from Shoshone County, for robbery. His sentence was five years. He was Catholic. The inmate file has only Ireland as his place of birth, but his nearest relative was a brother John Lynch, who was in Co. G, 1st Artillery, stationed at the Presidio Barracks in California. Research can turn to the brother, who might have left a record of his birth in Ireland in a military or pension paper.

Each state had its own record-keeping practices, and at times, birthplaces in Ireland were given. One such is in the Newgate State Prison, from the Ancestry.com online collection "New York, Prisoners Received at Newgate State Prison, 1797-1810." Newgate is recognized as the first state penitentiary in New York, opening in 1797 on the Hudson River in what is now Greenwich Village. It was originally modeled on the philosophy of reforming

U. S. PENITENTIARY, BOISE CITY, IDAHO.

Description of Convict.

Registered No. *207*   When Received *June 28th 1890*

Name *John Murphy*   Alias *none*

County *Shoshone*   Term *may 1890*

Crime *Manslaughter*

Sentence *7 years*

Age when received *42*   Born in *Ireland*

Legitimate occupation *Miner*   Served apprenticeship

Height *5* feet, *6¼* inches. Complexion *Dark* Weight *152*

Color of Hair *Dark Brown*   Color of Eyes *Blue*

* Conjugal Relations : Single. ~~Married. Separated. Widower. Has~~ Child.

* Domestic Relations : Father ~~living~~ Died when prisoner was (*38* years old

Mother living *yes* ~~Died when prisoner was~~ years old.

Prisoner left parents' home when *20* years old.

Religion : Has had religious instruction *yes* Attended Sunday School *yes*

In what Church *Catholic* Member of what Church now *Catholic*

* Education : ~~Illiterate. Can read.~~ Can read and write. Common school education.

~~Higher school and collegiate education~~ Attended school : *9* years.

° Habits of Life : Abstinent. ~~Moderate drinker.~~ Intemperate.

Former imprisonment : *none*

Name and address of nearest relative : *Catherine Murphy (Mother)*
Glengariff Cork Co Ireland

GENERAL REMARKS :

Peculiarity in build and feature :

Condition of teeth :

Beard worn when received :

Size of boot worn :

India ink marks, scars and deformities :

Property found on convict :

* Receiving officer will erase the items not answering the prisoner's description.

Figure 34: John Murphy record, Idaho State Penitentiary, Boise, Idaho, incarcerated 28 June 1890. (Image courtesy of Idaho State Archives and Historical Society. Permissions received.)

of the prison led to violent riots. It was closed in 1828, and the inmates were sent to Sing Sing Prison in Ossining, New York.

An example of a record from Newgate is for William Beatty, whose nativity was Wexford, Ireland. He was 28 years old, a weaver by trade, his residence New York (City), and he was sentenced for three years on 28 October 1797 for grand larceny but, at some point, was pardoned. His birth in County Wexford in 1769 is significant because the date is before that when almost all church registers began in Ireland. This may be the only document with his birthplace.

A notation about a second country, neither Ireland nor the United States, may solve the origins' question. An illustration is from the Sing Sing Prison in the digitized collection "New York, Sing Sing Prison Admission Registers, 1865-1939" on Ancestry.com

those charged with serious crimes other than murder and arson. Soon, it was overcrowded, and the communal nature for the inmate Francis Mills. He was committed to Sing Sing on 9 January 1866 (Register entry 19 January 1866) for manslaughter in the 4th degree and sentenced to two years by "Gilbert," being received from Kings County, New York. He was 36 years old, thus born in 1830, and he was born in Ireland. Some clues from his admission file are that he was single and at the time of his arrest was residing at 32 Fulton W., Brooklyn. He was Protestant, and his mother was living in England. Consequently, if no birthplace for him is found from an American record, research can shift to England. Perhaps Francis can be documented in the 1851 and 1861 censuses. Once his parents are identified, the investigation can proceed back to the Irish sources.

Similarly, also from Sing Sing Prison and from the same register page, is Thomas Hennessy, aged 22, which places his birth in 1844. He was committed on 13 January 1866 (Register entry 19 January 1866), from New York (City) for grand larceny for a five-year sentence. Thomas was single, a shoemaker, and at the time of his arrest, was living at 49 James W, New York City. In his admission record are two noteworthy pieces of information. One is that he had no relatives in the United States and second,

his parents were living in England. Can he be located somewhere in England with his parents in the 1851 or 1861 censuses? Once his parents, who were alive in 1866, are identified, then Irish research can proceed accordingly.

Figure 35: Old Idaho State Penitentiary in Boise, Idaho. (Images courtesy of Dwight A. Radford, April 2016.)

Chapter Eight

Internet Websites

In today's genealogy research, keeping up with new websites, let alone what they hold, is not possible. New indexing projects and databases are introduced every week. The largest and most accessed ones are Ancestry.com, FamilySearch.org, Findmypast.com, and MyHeritage.com, but they are by no means all of them. Every state archive and major public library has its own website, and regional genealogical societies and personal websites are regularly added for each one's own topic of interest. Sorting through them and understanding their value is worthwhile.

A mistake many researchers, especially novices, make is trusting that everything required is online. This is not true. The amount of data secluded in microfilm, books, and journal articles is almost inconceivable. Many sources will never be on the Internet because of copyright issues. Documents, books, and manuscripts belong to someone, and unless they are legally in the public domain, they cannot be duplicated in any form without the permissions of the copyright owners or the publishers.

This chapter concentrates on identifying the best websites that have some general and some specific information for United States research. Take into account that nobody knows what is really "out there" because of changes every day. Therefore, understanding a method for sorting through and determining what is good and what is not is essential.

Lineage-Linked Databases

The idea of a lineage-linked database is uncomplicated. A researcher places information online in a pedigree format with accompanying family group sheets. If the tree is for public view, it can be referenced on someone else's online tree, and you can reference theirs on yours, which is common on websites such as Ancestry.com. In its version, the tree has an owner, who can correspond with various researchers. The system has its advantages and its disadvantages.

Another version of the online Tree is the "Community Tree," where a person begins a new Tree and everyone else attaches it and works from it. It does not belong to any one person but is a group effort in which researchers can make changes. The resulting alterations can lead to battles of egos, unfortunate situations since all are frequently wrong in their assumptions. The Community Tree is on FamilySearch.org, and it also has its advantages and its disadvantages.

The point of these various concepts is to document a pedigree-linked family tree. Unfortunately, many do not cite sources for their material. The lack of documentation does not render the information useless but just limits valid research to examining the trees for clues only. Proof still must be added for the accuracy of the tree itself.

One problem with the pedigree-linked trees is that researchers often restrict themselves to the sources on the website on which they found or created it. For example, many Ancesty.com devotees fail to recognize the enormous collections on FamilySearch.org. Not everything is on Ancestry.com any more than it is on FamilySearch.org or any other single site. Websites have to be used in harmony, investigating all of them as if they were one.

Another major issue is people attaching sources to an online tree from the "Suggested Records" or "Helpful Hints," allowing the computer to determine whether the person being researched is the correct one. Too often, the hints have nothing to do with the person other than a similar name and birthplace. As a consequence, what may appear to be a well-documented tree may be nothing more than grabbing and attaching sources, involving no serious analysis. Yet, the erroneous information disseminates with its own force across the Internet. This is a principal problem.

Foremost to remember when using any of the popular websites is that the online trees need to be questioned. The websites themselves instruct users to document research. The advice most often evades acceptance.

Indexes to Websites

One fascinating way of getting around the explosion of valuable websites is the idea of a central website that acts as a catalog to all the others as they become available. Such a website does not consist of indexes but is an inventory of links. Two of the noteworthy and well-known ones are Cyndislist.com and USGenWeb.org.

Cyndislist.com is free and is constantly updated. It is arranged by category, whether by subject matter or geographically. Each topic is cataloged further by sub-topic, such as occupations or church records. Once the area of interest is found, it is a matter of browsing until a link is presented. This remarkably comprehensive website supplies access to innumerable subjects that might become lost on other sites.

The USGenWeb.org is also extraordinary in its own way, although it is not as straightforward as Cyndislist.com. The USGenWeb.org is part of a worldwide project that provides links and research extractions to geographical locations. With its presentation of record extractions along with links, it is useful from several perspectives.

The key to understanding the USGenWeb.org is that it is hosted by volunteers.

It is by state and then by county. Once on a county site, the task is to determine whether it is of value to present research goals or not. Some county sites have almost every pertinent link and primary extracted record anyone would want from the locality. The same principle applies to Louisiana, which has parishes, and Alaska, which has boroughs/census areas, not counties.

The information available is contingent on the volunteers. Most have links to county courthouses, public libraries, and genealogy and historical societies. Sometimes, one can be the discovery that leads to what is necessary to fully address the research goals. Some county sites have cemetery information, extractions from old history books, and information on churches, vital records, tax records, and maps that can be enormously beneficial in trying to understand where towns and townships are located.

Although Cyndislist.com and USGen-Web.org are integral parts of the modern research process, they are merely steps in its progress. Both have to be consistently visited every few weeks for added sites.

Major Genealogy Websites

A few websites have an enormous number of resources that can be accessed. All these also have the chief indexers of records, but it is important to understand that no website can digitize, let alone index, all the records of the world. For this reason, the larger websites, no matter if they are for profit or not, have been banding together to share indexing and images when copyrights allow. This has incalculably increased the speed of what is coming online.

The shared information and images may be free on FamilySearch.org, which is non-profit, whereas they are part of a subscription or membership on others. Although the same database may be on multiple websites, do not assume that because one site has a database of interest that it is a duplication of another's. On the contrary, the organizations at times are indexing the same source but with different indexers, to the advantage of genealogists. It is possible to discover something in one indexing program that was missed in another because of a more sophisticated search capability. Therefore, even if it is the same database, it may be that a specific website has a better way to search the data.

Although the websites below are not intended to reflect all that is online, they do represent the ones used every day in American genealogical research.

AmericanAncestors.org. The website is the New England Historic Genealogical Society's (NEHGS) in Boston, the oldest and perhaps the most prestigious genealogy society in the country. Even though it focuses on New England, it has a massive library in Boston and large collections for New York, Virginia, and the Maritimes in Canada as well as Ireland. This is a non-profit organization and funded through grants and membership.

The website has indexed and digitized images of the society periodicals, rich in genealogical material. This is not a website to be ignored. It shares some databases with FamilySearch.org and Ancestry.com. NEHGS is working with Ancestry.com to digitize and index the Catholic Archdiocese of Boston's registers. The NEHGS library also is a FamilySearch center of the Family History Library in Salt Lake City.

Ancestry.com. The website is the largest online genealogy collection available and is commercial. Many people confuse it with FamilySearch.org because the corporate headquarters of Ancestry.com is in Utah. However, the two are not connected. Ancestry.com also has a San Francisco office and European headquarters in Dublin, Ireland. Ancestry.com is subscription based with levels of individual membership, including a Worldwide Membership that includes all its collections. It also has Ancestryinstitution.com, to which the public and university libraries subscribe. Be aware that the institution version is different than an individual subscription and has fewer databases; it is a selection of the best of its collections but not everything.

Ancestry.com has many government documents, often with images attached to the indexes for births, marriages, and deaths. Many origins' problems for Irish immigration have been solved by viewing one of the online death certificates or marriage records. It has an arrangement with the AmericanAncestors.org

website and is indexing the Archdiocese of Boston Catholic registers. Ancestry.com and FamilySearch.org share certain databases. They also own Findagrave.com, Fold3.com, and Newspapers.com.

Ancestry.com is widely known for its DNA tests and the ability to connect DNA cousins, helping to solve many origins' questions also. The difficulty with the Irish is that even though an American family may connect with a DNA cousin in, for instance, Australia, Ireland, or Northern Ireland, the paper trail may not go back far enough to link to a common ancestor in historic Ireland. Ancestry.com does have Ancestry Trees owned by individuals and can be made public or private. They can be successfully used in conjunction with the Ancestry DNA results.

Archives.gov. Located in Washington, D.C., the National Archives and its regional archives across the country hold treasures from the nation's history. What it does not have are private records, such as those for churches. Major collections include documents for the military, Native Americans, land grants, the United States Congress, United States Supreme Court, passengers' lists, select agencies, and many more. It has digitization partnerships with Ancestry.com, FamilySearch.org, and Fold3.com, and its website has guides to specific record collections as well as digitized images.

FamilySearch.org. The website is the online genealogy arm of the Church of

Jesus Christ of Latter-day Saints. Its reason for existing is for its members to fulfill their genealogical obligations, but it is open to anyone worldwide. FamilySearch.org is constantly adding new collections and hosts databases from around the world, from where they have extracted records. It continues to scour the globe for new records, and its Family History Library in downtown Salt Lake City is the largest genealogy library in the world. Genealogy societies and individuals travel to it from all countries. It is non-profit and functions as such. No membership is required to use the database. It is helpful to set up a free FamilySearch.org account, which allows easier access to this immeasurable storehouse of material. It is digitizing its microfilm collections, where contracts allow, and with the new records, it is possible to conduct a great amount of personal research from home.

Findmypast.com. The website is by subscription and is adding new material continually. It is based in the United Kingdom and has sections for several world areas. It has a growing and often stunning array of United States records. For example, it has been signing contracts with various Catholic dioceses to digitize and index their records. Among these are the Archdioceses of New York, Baltimore, Cincinnati, Philadelphia, and others. Many Irish immigrant cases have been solved through these databases alone. Another is the immense "United States Marriages" with marriage records from throughout the United States, a truly impressive collection. It is also the largest collection of United States marriage records online. Findmypast.com and FamilySearch.org share some material. For instance, one has the images and the other, the indexers, and so the collection is on both websites. Their databases for the United Kingdom, Ireland, Canada, Australia, and New Zealand, among others, are outstanding. It can be used most effectively in conjunction with Ancestry.com and FamilySearch.org because of the international focus on the databases.

Findmypast.com also works in cooperation with the British Newspaper Library, which houses newspapers from throughout the Commonwealth. A level of subscription has those newspapers as part of a membership. Findmypast.com is an outstanding resource and a natural complement to Ancestry.com, FamilySearch.org, and MyHeritage.com.

Fold3.com. The website is for National Archive records and is owned by Ancestry.com. Because it focuses on United States military records from all wars and conflicts, it is a major contribution to American genealogy. It is a subscription-based membership complete with indexes and digitized images. The search feature allows collections to be limited to conflicts or states as well as names. Although the site is owned by Ancestry.com, the collections belong to the National Archives.

Genealogybank.com. The website has emerged as one of the major resources of digitized newspapers from around the United States, and its collections continue to grow. However, it offers more than newspapers. It hosts the Social Security Death Index, government publications, United States censuses, and an archive of historical books. The "Cultural Collections" category, which includes Irish American, African American, and Native American publications, is noteworthy.

MyHeritage.com. The online subscription-based website along with its MyHeritage DNA is headquartered in Israel with additional offices in California, Utah, and the Ukraine. It hosts many databases and images and is well known for its linked database programs that allow researchers a format from which to share information and contact one another. It has a working relationship with FamilySearch.org. This website has records from around the world and is most informative in conjunction with Ancestry.com and FamilySearch.org.

Chapter Nine

Land Records

People are pleasantly surprised when they learn that some types of land records contain birthplaces. Most property documents will not have them, especially for transactions registered with counties or for state grants. Even so, land books are extensively consulted in genealogy research, although not necessarily for immigration purposes. They can establish family relationships and position people in localities at precise times. Often, in county deeds, the first transaction for someone purchasing property will state where that person was previously residing. While not naming a birthplace, this information can lead to a record that will have it. Consequently, land records are essential to immigrant research.

Nevertheless, categories of land records did ask for birthplaces. Whether the country alone was noted by the Irish or they gave specific counties cannot be predicted. The point is that the question

was asked. In keeping with the theme of identifying Irish origins, this chapter centers on three distinct series of land records for which birthplaces were requested:

- New York Alien Residents (1825)
- Oregon and Washington Donation Lands (1855)
- Homestead Act (1862)

All these record types represent specific United States regions from coast to coast. Be aware, though, of other records that identified birthplaces, such as those by the Private Land Claims and the Desert Land Act (1877).

United States property record research is complicated. Reference books can be beneficial to anyone sorting through land laws and styles of registers. Solid works are:

Greenwood, Val D. *The Researcher's Guide to American Genealogy.* 4th ed., Baltimore, Maryland: Genealogical Publishing Co., 2017. (Four chapters are dedicated completely or in part to land records, including "Government Land: Colonial and American," pp. 469-494; "Local Land Records," pp. 495-528; "Abstracting Probate and Land Records," pp. 529-546; and "Property Rights of Women a Consideration," pp. 575-584.)

Hatcher, Patricia Law. *Locating Your Roots: Discovering Your Ancestors Using Land Records.* Genealogical Publishing Company, 2014.

Hansen, Holly T., James L. Tanner, and Arlene H. Eakle. *U.S. Land and Tax Records.* Morgan, Utah: Family History Expos, Inc., 2016.

Creative strategies in land research can:

- Produce an approximate date of immigration
- Social status in the town
- Occupation
- Identify a spouse and release of dower rights
- Unveil relatives through bordering properties/witnesses
- Reference naturalization information
- State places of previous origin
- Provide alternate residences
- Show date of death
- Include marriage information
- Allude to date of arrival into an area
- Allude to date of departure from an area
- Lead to other sources such as wills, etc.
- Reveal consistent association with others
- Enable segregation among common surnames

*For further land strategies, see "Chapter 5: Land Records" in volume one of this series, Dwight A. Radford, *American Scots-Irish Research: Strategies and Sources in the Quest for Ulster-Scots Origins* (Orting, Washington: Family Roots Publishing Co., LLC, 2020).

Hone, E. Wade. *Land & Property Research in the United States*. Salt Lake City, Utah: Ancestry, 1997.

Luebking, Sandra Hargreaves. "Land Records." *The Source: A Guidebook of American Genealogy*. 3rd ed., edited by Loretto Dennis Szucs and Sandra Hargreaves Luebking, Provo, Utah: Ancestry Publishing, 2006, pp. 431-498.

Although most are dated, being time bound by their publication dates, the records presented, and the strategies recommended are enduring.

New York Alien Residents (1825)

New York State had various laws, adjusted when needed, that allowed aliens to own land. The first series of records,

known as the "acts of the legislature," encompass 1790 through 1825, and although they are useful, they do not provide birthplaces of the applicants. In genealogy, they associate and locate people who are missing in the federal census schedules. While this law was in effect, an alien who was granted the right to land had no restrictions about what could be done with it. These records are not the subject of this section.

The focus of this discussion is the "depositions of resident aliens" from 1825 through 1913. Even though these also have their share of inferred information, they can state precise places in Ireland where the aliens were born. The records were made under the act of 21 April 1825, through which aliens were allowed to own lands but with certain stipulations. One required the aliens to apply for citizenship at the same time the land ownership depositions were filed. This at least meant the declarations of intention had to have been submitted to the courts. Another restraint was that until they were fully naturalized, aliens could not lease their lands.

This group of records, known as the "Alien Depositions of Intent to Become U.S. Citizens, 1825-1913" is housed at the New York State Archives (A1869, 95

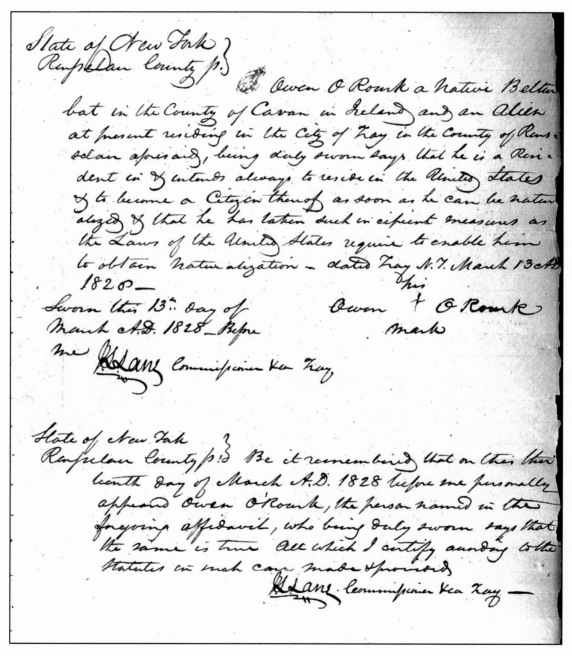

Figure 36: The alien registration record for Owen O'Rourk in Rensselaer County, New York, dated 13 March 1828. Owen was shown as a native of Belturbat (Belturbet), County Cavan, Ireland. (Image courtesy of New York State Archives.)

volumes). Also at the archive are "Abstracts of Alien Depositions, 1825-1913" (A1870, 33 volumes) and "Index to Alien Depositions of Intent to Become U.S. Citizens, 1825-1913" (A1898, 3 volumes).

The published index *New York Alien Residents, 1825-1848* (Baltimore, Maryland: Clearfield Company, 1991) by Kenneth Scott and Rosanne Conway is for the first four volumes and is digitized as an Ancestry.com database "New York Alien Residents, 1825-1848," which includes 4,260 alien residents. The years are limited, but its advantage is the various keywords that can bring results, if only the keyword Ireland or a county in Ireland. Thus, many different approaches to manipulating the data are permitted. However, these files are the same as the ones in the Ancestry.com database covering 1825 to 1913 except Ancestry.com has digitized images from the papers themselves. The search capability is not as comprehensive though.

Volumes 1 through 50 of the deposition volumes themselves are digitized on the Ancestry.com database "New York, Alien Depositions of Intent to Become U.S. Citizens, 1825-1871," containing 27,000 depositions of intents to naturalize. The depositions gave the aliens six years to complete the naturalization process.

These depositions are also a resource in women's studies. Before 1848, women lost control over the property they owned when they married, and any property that wives might have received went to their husbands. Women did not have the right to acquire property after marriage. The "Married Women's Property Act of April 7, 1848" permitted women to buy, sell, and receive property that was protected by law. By 1848, about one-third of the depositions in this collection were filed by women.

The registrations are typically two pages, handwritten on the fronts and backs, and other than personal data, they have the same information for all applicants. Still, it is wise to check both Ancestry.com databases because the Scott and Conway book is a scan of the volume, not an indexing of it. More information is in the digitized papers than is in the published book. Samples of alien depositions adapted from the digitized images on the Ancestry.com database "New York, Alien Depositions of Intent to Become U.S. Citizens, 1825-1871" are:

> *256: Owen O'Rourk a native of Belturbat in the County of Cavan in Ireland and an alien residing in the city of Troy, Rensselaer County, intends always to reside in the United States and become a citizen as soon as he can be naturalized. Dated 13 March 1828, Registered 14 March 1828.*

> *1878: James McMeekan, late of the County of Antrim in Ireland now of the city of Buffalo, Erie County, always intends to reside in the United States and to become a citizen as soon as he can be naturalized. Dated 15 March 1836, Received 21 March 1836.*

> *1899: Patrick McLaughlin of the city of Troy, Rensselaer County, always intends to reside in the*

United States and become a citizen as soon as he can be naturalized. He was born in the county of Roscommon in the parish of Killronan in Ireland. He has been a resident of the city of Troy since November 1835. Dated March 1836, Received 5 April 1836.

2306: Charles Moorhead a native of Ulster in Ireland swears that he is a resident of the city of Troy, Rensselaer County. He intends to always reside in the United States and to become a citizen as soon as he can be naturalized. Dated and Received 10 July 1837.

3556: Ann Mulligan, an alien, a native of the town of Mullebreck, County Down, Ireland, now resident of the town of Canajoharie in Montgomery County, New York, and wife of Robert Millegan of said place. I came to the United States in the year 1831, and I am aged 56 years, and it is my intention to become a naturalized citizen of the United States. Dated: 27 December 1844, Received 25 January 1845.

4140: Thomas Murray of Buffalo in the county of Erie says that he is an alien by birth and that he was born in the county of Roscommon in Ireland. He now is a resident of the United States and intends to always reside in the United States and to become a

citizen. Dated 11 October 1847, Received 14 October 1847.

4141: Timothy Murray of Buffalo in the county of Erie says he is an alien by birth, that he was born in the county of Roscommon in Ireland, that he now is a resident of the United States and intends always to reside in the United States and be a citizen. Dated 11 October 1847, Received 14 October 1847.

All had taken "incipient measures" by that point, which means the citizenship process had begun, most likely with the declaration of intention filed. A few necessitate follow-up questions.

The case of Patrick McLaughlin (1899) of Troy, Rensselaer County, is most interesting and illustrates how Irish place names are confusing. Scott and Conway's book cites the deposition correctly but then adds the editorial comment that the birthplace of Killronan is in County Galway. They are correct about the Roman Catholic parish being in Galway, and it is on the border with Roscommon. However, a civil parish by that name is also in northern Roscommon. Even if Patrick McLaughlin was Catholic, which is not mentioned in the deposition, his reference was probably to the civil parish in Roscommon, not to the Catholic parish in Galway. Do not hesitate to question editorial comments or corrections by authors.

The place of birth of Ann Milligan (3556), Mullebreck, County Down, was given, but it is not enough to follow her within

Ireland. She was 56 years old in 1844 and so was born in 1788. Church registers likely do not go back that far to document her birth, and her maiden name is not known. Hence, she and her husband, Robert Milligan, have to be traced to learn more about them. She immigrated in 1831, at 43 years old. The assumption is she married in County Down, although that cannot be proved. In short, even with a locality in Ireland known, research still must begin in Canajoharie, Montgomery County, New York.

The conjecture is that Thomas Murray (4140) and Timothy Murray (4141) were brothers, cousins, or perhaps father and son because both were in Buffalo, born in County Roscommon, and filed their alien depositions on the same day. Therefore, the Buffalo records for the two men and other Murrays from Roscommon need to be searched to determine ages and relationships with the goal of approaching the County Roscommon records.

Oregon and Washington Donation Lands (1855)

If ancestors or their relatives settled in the Pacific Northwest before 1855, they might have been documented in the Donation Land papers. The Donation Lands of Oregon and Washington Territories had one of the most descriptive application processes in the United States during this era. There were over 7,500 applications. The claims for Washington Territory were separated from those of Oregon Territory in 1853, but the procedures for claiming lands was the same. Oregon became a state in 1859, and Washington, in 1889.

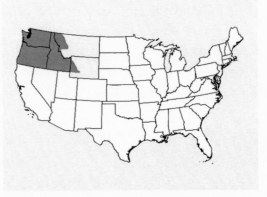

Figure 37: Oregon Territory, 1848-1853. This was divided into Oregon and Washington Territories in 1853.

The land applications for the Irish are second in number only to those filed by American-born citizens. Because the records often have exact birthplaces, the Donation Lands are a primary source. Even if an ancestor did not settle in the Pacific Northwest, accessing the submissions to document relatives who did is prudent. Understandably, if a brother or sister went to the Northwest on the Oregon Trail or by sea while the direct ancestor stayed back East, the papers of the Donation Lands may hold the birthplace in Ireland.

As with all records, some are more descriptive than others. A number have Ireland for birthplaces while others have more specific places, such as counties in Ireland. Consider that these were the original settlers, the founders of their communities. That, by default, made them noteworthy people and, hopefully, pillars of their towns or counties. This also separated them from the settlers who came later, who might never have received Donation Lands and who never had a reason to leave records of where they were from in Ireland.

Even if claims do not supply as much information as desired, what they do offer can be equally as valuable. For example, part of the process was a question regarding citizenship status, and if the person was a citizen, where the naturalization took place. It may solve the mystery of immigrant origins because someone in the Pacific Northwest might have been naturalized in the East, two or three thousand miles away. Remember, the distance from Boston, Massachusetts, to Portland, Oregon, is around 3,000 miles. It was a long journey from one end of the continent to the other, with much happening in between. The answer to the Irish birthplace may be in a record in Boston and not Portland, as easily as it can be the other way around.

Oregon Territory was established in 1848 from regions that are now Oregon, Washington, Idaho, and a small portion of Wyoming. Most applications involved present-day Oregon and Washington. Donation Land applications began in 1850 and provided free land to white and mixed-blood settlers who arrived in the territories before 1 December 1855. Each arrangement was in exchange for four years of residence and cultivation. Applicants were given up to 640 acres. Sometimes, the claims for land continued for decades. The original point of the Donation Lands was to produce a buffer of American settlers from the British claims in what became British Columbia, Canada, although the Pacific Northwest had been divided by agreement between the two countries in 1846.

The original files are at the National Archives with digitized copies at FamilySearch.org. The Washington State Library and the Oregon State Archives, as expected, also have a great deal of information on the Donation Lands because they can so successfully trace Pacific Northwest families. The collection is known as "Oregon and Washington Donation Land Files, 1851-1903" and contains the records from the following land offices:

Oregon
- La Grande Land Office
- Oregon City Land Office
- Winchester-Roseburg Land Office
- The Dalles Land Office

Washington
- Colfax-Spokane Falls Land Office
- Walla Walla Land Office
- Vancouver Land Office

The original claims' files are alphabetical by state and land office. Within each land office, the claims are typically but not always arranged by final certificate numbers. Documents are assembled as chronologically as possible in the files. If a claim was canceled or rejected, not all the documentation is as available as it is for a completed claim.

Years were restricted to when settlers entered the territory, which were extended three times: before 1 December 1853; between 1 December 1850 and 1 December 1853; and finally, before 1 December 1855. No limits were on the dates for applications, and so someone arriving as a child before 1 December 1855 could apply for land upon turning 21 years of age. For the application process, questions were asked, one being where the person was born.

The records for the Pacific Northwest are so valuable that material about them and regional genealogy societies' extracts from them are abundant. The database "Genealogical Material in Oregon Donation Land Claims" is on Ancestry.com, and thus a large amount of the material and indexes is easily obtainable. Comparing one database against another to make sure nothing is missed is always wise. In this case, the online index at Genealogical Forum of Oregon and the Bureau of Land Management database on Glorecords.blm.gov afford that holistic balance.

Three document examples from the Donation Lands that can reveal or indicate Irish origins are for John Gearin, Bartholomew Soden, and John Flinn. All were abstracted from the Oregon City Land Office and taken from the Ancestry.com database "Genealogical Material in Oregon Donation Land Claims":

> *John Gearin (#2058), in Marion County, Oregon. He was born November 1812 in Ireland, arrived in Oregon 8 September 1851, and settled his claim on 25 December 1851. He married Ellen in Fort Wayne, Indiana. His application for citizenship was made in the 8th Judicial Circuit Court of Indiana on 8 June 1838 and awarded by the 12th Judicial Circuit Court of Indiana on 22 August 1842. His citizenship papers stated he had migrated from Cork, Ireland, 15*

> *April 1834 and arrived in Boston 6 July 1834.*

> *Bartholomew Soden (#2059), in Polk County, Oregon. He was born in Athlone, [Roscommon], Ireland, in 1807. He was in Oregon 2 June 1851 and settled his claim on 20 November 1853. He married Ann Goodale on 4 August 1836 in Lancaster, Australia. He was awarded his land on 6 September 1858 in the 1st Judicial District Court of Oregon, Marion County.*

> *John Flinn (#1735), in Benton County, Oregon. His land was T10S R4W S6,7, consisting of 320 acres. His papers showed he was born in 1817 in Ireland. He arrived in Oregon before December 1850 and settled his claim 7 December 1852. His declaration of intention to become a citizen had been filed earlier, on 8 March 1850, in Cumberland, Western District Court, Maine, the document stating he was living in Kennebunk, York County, Maine. The declaration noted he was born in Rosenallis, Queens County, Ireland, in 1817, came to the United States in 1840, arrived in New York and then went to St. Johns, New Brunswick, then to Portland, and next to Kennebunk, where he lived until 1848.*

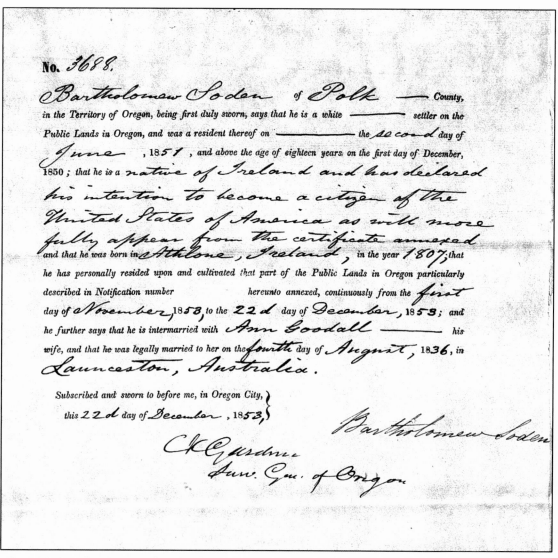

Figure 38: One of many papers found in the Oregon Donation Land file for Bartholomew Soden of Polk County, Oregon. Refer to additional abstracts on the previous page. (Image courtesy of National Archives and Records Administration.)

A birthplace was not given for John Gearin (#2058) of Marion County, Oregon, only that he had left from County Cork, Ireland. Nonetheless, his departure from County Cork does at least place him in an area of the island. His landing in Boston may or may not be useful, other than perhaps finding a passenger arrival record for him. The important clue was his settlement in Fort Wayne, Indiana. Why was he there? Who was he joining, possibly another relative from Ireland?

The question is logical in trying to learn where in Ireland John Gearin was from. To find whom he intended to meet in Fort Wayne may be to solve the immigrant origins' question.

Bartholomew Soden (#2059) of Polk County, Oregon, was born in Athlone, County Roscommon, Ireland, in 1807, but, likely, no record to document his birth that early has survived. An amazing clue for him is his journey from Lancaster,

Australia, eastward, not from the eastern United States westward. In Lancaster, he married Ann Goodale on 4 August 1836. The possibility of more details in an Australian document for Bartholomew Soden is far greater than what the average American one could state. The secondary questions are how he arrived in Australia and whether he was a convict or a free settler. Either way, his records are in Australia.

The Irish birthplace of John Flinn (#1735) of Benton County, Oregon, was not revealed in the Donation Lands papers, but it is in the naturalization papers included as part of the claim process. According to his Maine Declaration of Intention, he was born in Rosenallis, Queens County, Ireland, in 1817. Also significant is that he immigrated in 1840 to the United States, but his destination was St. Johns, New Brunswick, or, at least, he landed there. He probably had family in the Maritimes.

At some point, John Flinn went to Maine. This information not only directs the investigation to the Maritime records in Canada and perhaps more specifically to St. Johns, New Brunswick, but also to the Maine records. Why was he in either place? Who did he know there from Rosenallis? All are tantalizing areas of exploration. It must be considered that the Rosenallis Catholic registers (assuming he was Catholic) do go back to the 1817

Figure 39: On the Kansas-Nebraska border, south of Red Cloud, Webster County, Nebraska. The photograph represents the typical homestead opportunities in the Midwest. (Image courtesy of Dwight A. Radford, 2019.)

period, but with a common name such as John Flinn (or Flynn), several men with the name might have been there. Consequently, more American and Canadian sources may be needed to positively identify him.

Homestead Act (1862)

The series of Homestead Laws began with the Act of 20 May 1862. Their purpose was merely to place public lands in the hands of people who were without lands. Although large-scale immigration necessitated the Homestead Act (1862), the Civil War also played its part. It encouraged citizens loyal to the Union to settle in less developed areas of the frontiers. Under this law, about 783,000 citizens or intended citizens became patented landowners, completing the process. Almost 2 million entries were made, but about 60% were cancelled. Still, whether applications were cancelled or not, one of the largest archives of land-related records in the world was created. Claims were filed mainly between 1863 and 1917. The law was completely abolished in 1976. The portion of the granted land concerning homesteads encompassed 285 million acres, almost one-eighth of the United States.

Under the Homestead Act and subsequent acts, persons applying for lands had to be naturalized citizens and had to improve the properties. The processes, from filing for the claims to receiving the final certificates, stretched over several years, and many questionnaires were filled out along the way. Birthplaces were requested. As with any records, answers from the Irish could have been only Ireland or exact counties in Ireland.

The Homestead Act (1862) applied to the federal-land states. An index to those who went to the final proceedings is on the Bureau of Land Management (BLM) website Glorecords.blm.gov. The GLO stands for General Land Office and is today the BLM. The website's material is appreciable even though the search is basic. Therefore, each potential spelling variation must be searched separately and perhaps creatively.

One strong point of the site is that all homesteads can be viewed by county or by surname within a state. It is important to know that for each county, the Township, Section, and Range of the property is also listed, and so even if the county boundaries change, the county is presented in the database by the coordinates corresponding to the boundaries of the modern one. This index also allows a search of the "neighborhood" by the coordinates for studying potential common settlement patterns. Perhaps a group of people emigrated from one place and settled together, leading to the logical question in developing an immigration strategy: Were some in the group from the same place in Ireland?

Another index helpful for many states is "U.S. General Land Office Records, 1776-2015" on Ancestry.com. The index permits a more expanded search of surname spellings and variations. It is linked to the Glorecords.blm.gov website.

When consulting indexes for the BLM (GLO) records, remember that the emphasis is on those who completed the process. If someone did not or left the land before finishing the requirements

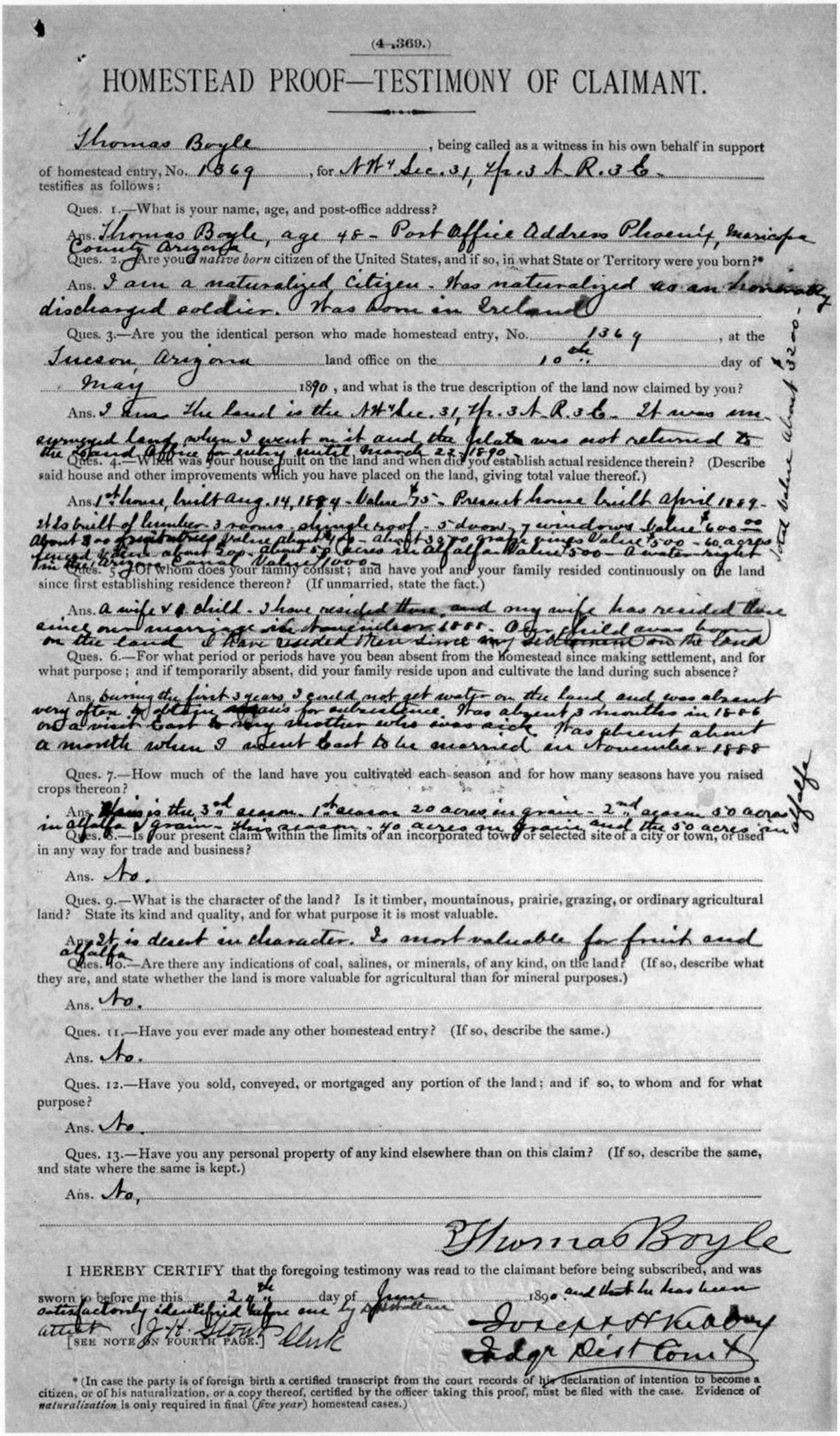

Figure 40: Page from the Homestead File of Thomas Boyle. For more details, see his abstract on the following page. (Image courtesy of National Archives and Records Administration. This work is in the public domain in the United States because it is a work prepared by an officer or employee of the United States Government as part of that person's official duties under the terms of Title 17, Chapter 1, Section 105 of the U.S. Code.)

for ownership, the acreage was restored to the system and someone else could file for it. Never forget that many Missouri settlers went to Montana, only to make it through the first winter and then abandon their claims, returning to Missouri. This often accounts for the birthplaces in the United States census reports that do not make sense, such as those in a Missouri census for one child born in Montana and the ones before and after born in Missouri.

Even if a desired homestead record is found, the documents digitized are only the basic ones. Case files accompany the coordinates and land offices corresponding to lands, detailing the actions from applications to final certificates. The birthplace and naturalization questions are noted in the case files, and so the index is only the beginning of the search and not the end.

The case files, housed at the National Archives, are part of RG 49. These are being digitized and indexed on the Ancestry.com database "U.S., Homestead Records, 1863-1908." Two from the database are examples of what this record source may contain. One lists solely Ireland as a place of birth while the other has a county of birth:

> *Application 1369: Thomas Boyle, Tucson, Arizona, Land Office on 6 September 1890 received his final certificate 155 36/100 acres. He was a resident of Phoenix, Maricopa County. He declared that he was a discharged private from the 3rd Battery Wisconsin*

Light Artillery, and he was mustered for military service on 4 October 1861 and was honorably discharged 10 October 1864. He was filing for his homestead under the "Act of June 8, 1872 giving homesteads to honorably discharged soldiers and sailors, their widows and orphan children." His affidavit for the "Soldiers' and Sailors' Homesteads under Act June 8, 1872" was filed 1 May 1890 with the 2nd Judicial District of Arizona in Phoenix. In the file were papers for his military service.

Several documents in the case file stated he was born in Ireland but specified no other place. His "Homestead Proof – Testimony of Claimant" papers stated he was 48 years old (as of 1890), lived in Phoenix, Maricopa County, was a naturalized citizen, born in Ireland, improved his land, and built his first house in 1884 and his second home in 1889. He and his wife had resided on the property since their marriage in November 1888, but he had resided on the land since settling there. They had one child.

When asked if he had been absent from the land, he stated that he was absent for three months in 1886, when he visited his sick mother in the East. He was also absent for a month when he was in the East to be married, in November 1888. In his 1864 papers about his military service, he was listed as a farmer and discharged in Milwaukee. Reports of his naturalization were dated 16 October 1876 in the 19th Judicial District Court of San Francisco.

Application 281: John Broderick, Carson City, Nevada Land Office, 15 September 1897, received his final certificate for 141.83 acres. The original homestead (Application 281) was begun on 14 December 1891 at the Eureka, Nevada, Land Office. At that time, John Broderick was living in Fort Halleck, Elko County, Nevada. The "Notice for Publication" concerning the filing was in the newspaper first on 10 July 1897, and it was officially filed with the County Clerk of Elko County on 18 August 1897. The witnesses who attested to his continuous residence and cultivation of the land were: Archie Wilson of Fort Halleck, Nevada; Edward C. Murphy of Fort Halleck, Nevada; Patrick Sheridan of Fort Halleck, Nevada; and James Murphy of Fort Halleck, Nevada.

Included in the file was John Broderick's naturalization certificate from the Court of Common Pleas, held in Williamsport,

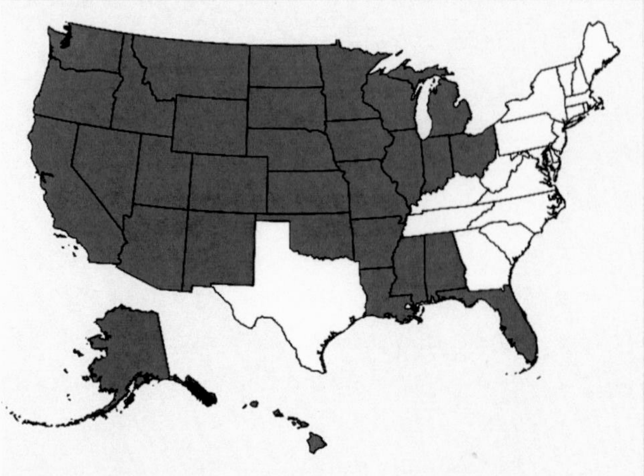

Figure 41: Map showing federal-land states where homesteads might be found for one's ancestors.

Lycoming County, Pennsylvania, 28 November 1877. The key document was the "Homestead Affidavit" from the Clerk of the Court for Elko County, Nevada, dated 9 January 1892, stating John was naturalized, born in Galway, Ireland, was 43 years old and was not the head of a family. He was a single man. His witness affidavits were also included in the file.

The case file for Thomas Boyle in Arizona has only Ireland as his birthplace, but additional clues to pursue are not scarce, such as military records and Wisconsin records. His naturalization in San Francisco is less helpful because of the 1906 earthquake and fire. The report also reveals he was married in the East in 1888, and his sick mother lived in the East in 1886, although a place was not named. The deduction, albeit not confirmed, is that Wisconsin counted as East.

John Broderick was a single man when he obtained his homestead in Elko County, Nevada, in 1897, but the file asserts he was naturalized in Lycoming County, Pennsylvania, in 1877, and he was in Elko County by at least 1891, when he applied originally. His migration trail is thereby left. That he was from County Galway is significant. The assumption is he had family in Lycoming County, Pennsylvania, who also might or might not have gone to Nevada. If the Broderick Irish origins cannot be found in a Pennsylvania document among those who stayed, certainly the life and homestead records of the single man John Broderick, who went to the West, are of immediate interest.

Chapter Ten

Military Records

American military records are some of the most valued resources in developing a research strategy for Irish immigration. Within muster rolls and pension records, soldiers' or veterans' birthplaces might have been noted, from no more than Ireland, which was sometimes designated as Britain, to specific counties, towns, or parishes in Ireland.

The early conflicts in which the Irish were primarily involved, particularly the Scots-Irish immigrants from Ulster and their descendants, were:

- Colonial Period (1718-1776)
- Revolutionary War (1775-1783)
- War of 1812 (1812-1815)

The Scots-Irish Protestants and their participation in these three periods have been summarized and inventoried in Dwight A. Radford's chapter "Military Records" in *American Scots-Irish*

Research: Strategies and Sources in the Quest for Ulster-Scots Origins (Orting, Washington: Family Roots Publishing, 2020). Because 1718 was the year of the immense influx of Ulster-Scots to colonial America, the years through 1776 were chosen to represent the colonial period. The focus of the present chapter is on sources that encompass the Irish Catholics and Irish Protestants in the following wars:

- Mexican-American War (1846-1848)
- American Civil War (1861-1865)
- Spanish-American War (1898)
- World War I (1917-1918)

Even though other conflicts are worthy of discussion, these four are a solid foundation from which to continue the search for Irish origins in American military records.

All these wars were fought by the United States Army, not by the state and local units, and the two should not be confused. The men from Ireland enlisting in federal regiments often did give exact birthplaces, such as counties or places within counties. These invaluable records have been indexed and digitized on the major websites Ancestry.com, FamilySearch.org, and Fold3.com. The database on Ancestry.com is titled "U.S. Army, Register of Enlistments, 1798-1914," and on FamilySearch.org, it is "United States Register of Enlistments in the U.S. Army, 1798-1914." Both are from one source but are dissimilar sets of indexing.

Associated with the United States military and its soldiers is a rich body of documents. They are subjects of complete volumes as well as important chapters in instruction books. Although the works are dated, the records themselves remain the same. Only changed are where they are located and whether they have been digitized, microfilmed, or indexed online. Standard references on the market include:

Bockstruck, Lloyd DeWitt and Sandra Hargreaves Luebking. "Military Records." *The Source: A Guidebook of American Genealogy.* 3rd ed., edited by Loretto Dennis Szucs and Sandra Hargreaves Luebking, Provo, Utah: Ancestry Publishing, 2006, pp. 431-498.

Greenwood, Val D. *The Researcher's Guide to American Genealogy.* 4th ed., Baltimore, Maryland: Genealogical Publishing Co., 2017, pp. 653-688 and 689-726.

Neagles, James C. *U.S. Military Records: A Guide to Federal & State Sources, Colonial America to the Present.* Provo, Utah: Ancestry Publishing, 1994.

Mexican-American War (1846-1848)

The Mexican-American War, also referred to as the Mexican War, is complex, but when it was over, the United States annexed former Mexican lands from Texas to California. The regiments were raised from the states and territories of the period, and 73,532 regular and volunteer American soldiers served.

As a result of the war, residents who had originally received their land grants under Spanish or Mexican governments were brought into the country. Many were Irish and Scots-Irish who left the United States years before, becoming subjects of Spain and later Mexico. Included were those who had settled in Mexico from the United States and established the Republic of Texas as well as families who had been in California and New Mexico for hundreds of years. The war had distinct repercussions for the residents and their foreign-granted lands as they sought to integrate into the United States, effects that lasted into the early twentieth century.

The root of the war with Mexico was the annexation of the Republic of Texas by the United States, but it was only where the complication began. The vision of American Manifest Destiny, land claims, the right to expand to the Pacific, and whether these new territories, later states, would enter with slaves were tied to the hostility.

The Republic of Texas existed from 1836 to 1846. It came into being during the Texas Revolution (1835-1836), when it declared its independence from Mexico. However, Mexico never recognized the Republic of Texas as anything other than Mexican Texas. Conflicts between Texas and Mexico continued, but the United States acknowledged Texas as an independent and free country in 1837. While perhaps most of the residents of the Republic of Texas wanted the Americans to take possession of the territory, the government initially did not do so until 29 December 1845. It was admitted as a state on 19 February 1846, and as a slave state.

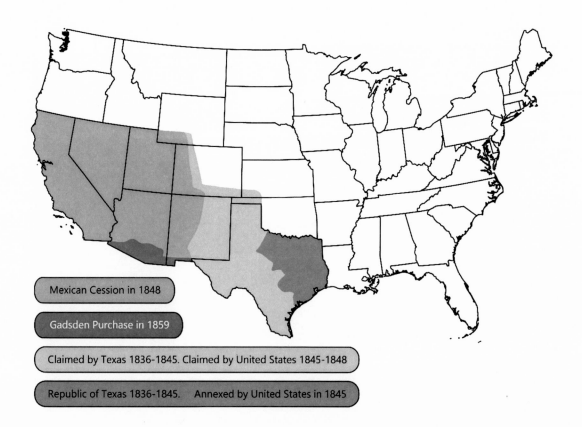

Mexican Cession in 1848

Gadsden Purchase in 1859

Claimed by Texas 1836-1845. Claimed by United States 1845-1848

Republic of Texas 1836-1845.   Annexed by United States in 1845

Figure 42: Map illustrating the regions involved in the Mexican War along with the subsequent purchases that helped shape the United States and its present-day boundaries.

Part of the vision of expanding the United States was to bring Oregon into the country. Sending the American Army and stationing it in Texas was considered an act of war by Mexico. The United States government luring Mexico into a war allowed more troops to be sent and Mexican territory secured. By the end of the war, an American victory, the United States stretched across the continent, and the Rio Grande River, separating Texas from Mexico, was the accepted boundary between the two countries.

Records for the Mexican-American War can be found digitized on Ancestry.com, FamilySearch.org, and Fold3.com. One of the first records family historians seek is the indexes to soldiers to ascertain whether a soldier was involved in the conflict. One database is "U.S., Compiled Military Service Records for American Volunteer Soldiers, Mexican War, 1845-1848" on Ancestry.com. The digitized index is basic but provides enough information to determine whether a soldier was the ancestor or not, which can be an issue with common Irish names. The details can include name, age, regiment, rank, enlistment location, payments, and dates of mustering in and out.

A large collection of card pension indexes for veterans of the Mexican War has been digitized through FamilySearch.org in the database "Mexican

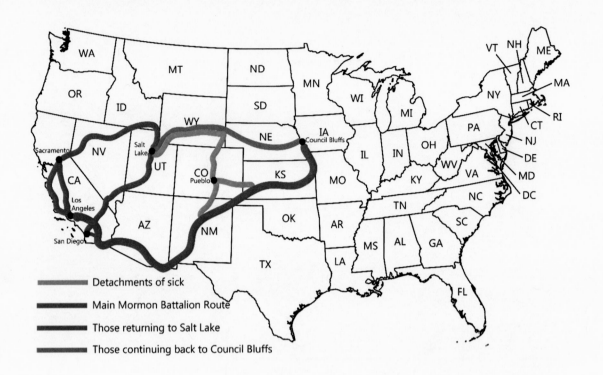

Figure 43: Mormon Battalion March, considered the longest march in military history. Along the way, detachments of sick were rerouted to Salt Lake City. (Map adapted from a version by Brian Cole.)

War Pension Index, 1887-1926." They have minimal information, including widows' names, but enough to order the correct pension file from the National Archives. A noteworthy, published index and abstract is Virgil D. White's *Index to Mexican War Pension Files* (Waynesboro, Tennessee: National Historical, 1989), which is a substantial work. The pension files are at the National Archives.

One stand-alone, extensively accessed collection from this period in the West and especially for Mormon research is "United States, Mormon Battalion Pension Applications, 1846-1923" on FamilySearch.org and Fold3.com. It consists of the pensions from the famous Mormon Battalion, the only religious-based unit in the war. The regiment comprised

over 500 Mormon men who had gathered at Council Bluffs, Iowa, to join the United States Army. Most enlisted for one year, but several continued for another eight months. The resulting pensions were claimed by veterans, widows, or dependents and are from the National Archives collections. During this period, when the main body of the church was heading across the prairie to the deserts of the Salt Lake Valley, these men were on a southward journey into unknown Mexican territory. They traveled some 2,100 miles from Council Bluffs, Iowa, to San Diego, California, opening a new, southern trail into California and assisting in securing the Southwest for the Americans. Their role in the settlement of Arizona, California, and Utah was significant.

From the local native tribes around Tucson, Arizona, in 1846, the Mormon Battalion learned how to irrigate the desert. The men brought those skills back to Utah after the war, and the West was transformed from arid barren land into fertile farmland.

A regionally produced compilation is the Ancestry.com database "Members of the Mormon Battalion," which was derived from Susan Easton Black's *Members of the Mormon Battalion: A Sesquicentennial Remembrance* (Provo, Utah: Brigham Young University, 1980). Black's work presents records for John Steele and William J. Robinson, exhibiting unequal amounts of information:

> *Name: John Steele*
> *Gender: Male*
> *Birth Date: 21 March 1821*
> *Birth Place: Hollywood, Down, Ireland*
> *Marriage Date: 1 January 1840*
> *Death Date: 31 December 1904*
> *Death Place: Kanarraville, Iron, Utah*
> *Spouse's Name: Catherine Campbell*
> *Father's Name: John Steele*
> *Mother's Name: Nancy Kennedy*
> *Rank: Private*
> *Company: D*

> *Name: William J. Robinson*
> *Gender: Male*
> *Birth Date: 28 February 1828*
> *Birth Place: Dublin, Ireland*
> *Death Date: 27 April 1898*
> *Death Place: Fayette, Utah*
> *Rank: Private*
> *Company: D*

The families of most converts from Ireland did not join the new religion and might or might not have emigrated. If they did, they almost never settled in the Mormon colonies. Regardless, the birthplace in Ireland for the family may be within the church records of the convert and in sources such as those for the Mormon Battalion. The Mormon Battalion was so famous in the history of westward expansion that its members are subjects of books, articles, genealogies, and databases.

Many compilations are about soldiers in the war who lived in a particular state. These are regionally produced works and should not be ignored. Sometimes written by historians or a genealogy society, they focus on veterans living in a specific county, and whether the state or county is in the subject, they can be biographical in nature. As is the above-cited source for the Mormon Battalion, they are excellent secondary sources to consult. A large collection is at the Family History Library, state libraries, or public libraries with an emphasis on genealogy. Ancestry.com should also be consulted.

American Civil War (1861-1865)
The American Civil War was brutal. Not only did it rip the country apart but also the repercussions are still felt in today's culture in countless ways. The process of both sides enlisting troops, burying troops, pensioning veterans, and taking care of aged ones has resulted in

unimaginable archives of records. Not all have birthplaces in Ireland, but some have the potential for discovering them, a few of which are presented in this section.

The time frame, history, and some logic are helpful in determining whether an ancestor fought in the war. Consider that one of the great cultural divides in the United States was the North holding most of the population and industry while the South controlled most of the agricultural pursuits and accompanying slave labor. They were two extremely different worlds.

The North could furnish more troops and younger ones than the South could. The South had limited resources and industry and had to rely often on whomever it could enlist. In consequence, perhaps a Union soldier was in his 20s or maybe 30s, whereas a Confederate soldier was younger than 20 or older than 30. Not every man fought in the war, and so if an ancestor did not, direct research to the ancestor's brother or cousin who did. The theory is that they were all born in the same place in Ireland, and so finding where one was born will identify the rest in Ireland.

Another consideration is that loyalties within a family might have been split. Many states almost had their own civil wars. For example, the East Tennessee counties backed the Union, being heavily white Scots-Irish with small, individual farms and few plantations and slaves. Middle Tennessee and West Tennessee kept plantations and large slave populations. Memphis, in the west on the

Mississippi River, was a major port of slave trading. Middle and West Tennessee were not less Scots-Irish, but their economics were not alike. In the end, Tennessee sided with the Confederate States of America, although the pro-Union sentiments in East Tennessee did not dissipate.

Kentucky enlisted both Union and Confederate units, but the state itself was with the North. Virginia split in 1863, creating West Virginia, which was with the Union. Again, the population was composed of small farmers in a mountainous terrain who were predominantly Scots-Irish. The plantations and large slave populations were eastward in Virginia, a Confederate state. Researchers need to be broadminded about who did what in these obvious and well-known internal conflicts.

When the nation of the Confederate States of America was created in 1861 and war broke out, it consisted of eleven states, Alabama, Arkansas, Florida, Georgia, Louisiana, Mississippi, North Carolina, South Carolina, Tennessee, Texas, and Virginia. The United States government did not recognize the new country.

Records for the Civil War can be found on most of the leading commercial and non-commercial websites, Ancestry.com, FamilySearch.org, and Fold3.com. Because the Civil War has been a popular topic of interest, its history and soldiers are documented on no shortage of websites, either private or institutional. These are usually non-commercial, and a simple search on the Internet or a website of links such as USGenWeb.org or

Cindislist.com displays sites as they are added online.

The first task is determining whether an ancestor served. In the Union areas, a draft was instituted, which is an excellent place to start. The Ancestry.com database "U.S., Civil War Draft Registrations Records, 1863-1865" names men who registered for the draft. They might not have served, but they registered. This registration did ask for birthplaces and depending on the forms, may provide more than simply the country for the Irish.

Between 1863 and 1865 were four drafts that included about 3 million men. The draft registrations are divided into two classes. Class I included men aged 20 to 35 and 36 to 45, all unmarried. Class II was for everyone else. The forms, by Congressional District, list name, age, and physical description. Birthplaces in Ireland were given as "State or Kingdom" and more exactly, "Town or County." If an ancestor was registered, look for other forms for men from the same place in Ireland residing in that Congressional District or town. The men could have been relatives or friends from the same place in Ireland, a clue indicating that a group of Irish settled together.

Most researchers begin their searches on a composite database such as the Ancestry.com edition "U.S. Civil War Soldiers, 1861-1865," consisting of those who served in the Union and the Confederacy. It is massive, with 6.3 million entries, but

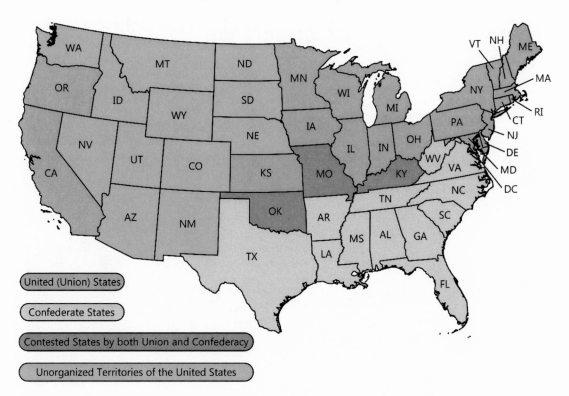

Figure 44: Map of the present-day United States and its Civil War divisions based on modern-day state boundaries. Most territories tried to remain neutral. As depicted, Oklahoma, Missouri, and Kentucky were claimed by both sides and held slave and non-slave supporters. West Virginia ceded from the Confederacy and joined the Union in 1863.

WIDOW'S APPLICATION FOR PENSION. Printed and Sold by Benton & Andrews, Rochester, N. Y.

State of New York, } ss.
COUNTY OF Steuben }

On this 2d day of September A. D. 1864, personally appeared before the undersigned a Justice of the Supreme Court in & for County and State aforesaid Catharine Riordon a resident of Corning in the County of Steuben and State of New York, aged thirty years, who, being first duly sworn according to law, doth on her oath make the following declaration, in order to obtain the benefit of the provision made by the Act of Congress, approved July 14, 1862: That she is the widow of Thomas Riordon who was a Private in company C commanded by Capt Fox in the 107th regiment of N. Y. State volunteers in the war of 1861, who died at Potterville in the State of Pennsylvania on the 26th day of August 1864, while in the service of the United States, and in the line of duty. That her said husband left only one child under sixteen years of age him surviving, named Anne Riordon born on the 16 day of April 1854 who now lives with George McGuigan her grandfather in the Parish of Killevy Ireland – And deponent says that previous to his death the said soldier was on the [illegible] of June duly transferred to the 2d Co 1st Battallion of the Invalid Corps (now V.R.C.) in which Company & Battallion he was serving at time of his death.

She further declares that she was married to the said Thomas Riordon on the 18th day of May in the year 1853, by the Curate in Charge of the parish of Killevy Ireland – as will appear by certificate duly authenticated annexed, and that her name before her marriage was Catharine McGuigan and that there is no record of her said marriage except in said Parish and that her husband, the aforesaid Thomas Riordon died on the day above mentioned, and that she has remained a widow ever since that period, as will more fully appear by reference to the proof hereto annexed. She also declares that she has not in any manner been engaged in, or aided or abetted, the rebellion in the United States; that she resides at Corning Steuben County State of New York and that her Post Office address is Corning Steuben Co N.Y.

And she hereby constitutes and appoints Sherwood & Payne of Corning N.Y. her true and lawful Attorneys with full power of substitution, to prosecute this her claim, and to receive and to receipt for any certificate, draft or money which may be due to this deponent.

Catharine (her X mark) Riordon

Also personally appeared Margaret Sheehan and James Sheehan residents of Corning persons whom I certify to be respectable and entitled to credit, and who, being by me duly sworn, say that they were present and saw Catharine Riordon make her mark to the foregoing declaration; and they further swear that they have every reason to believe, from the appearance of the applicant and their acquaintance with her, that she is the identical persons she represents herself to be, and that they have no interest in the prosecution of this claim.

Margaret Sheehan
James Sheehan

Figure 45: Details of Thomas Riordon (indexed as Reardon) from his widow's pension application for the Civil War. Among the statements are that he was married to Catharine McGuigan on 18 May 1853 in the parish of Killevy, [County Armagh], Ireland; their only daughter, Anne, was born on 16 April 1854 and now lives with her grandfather, George McGuigan, in Killevy; and the soldier died on 26 August 1864 in Pottersville, Pennsylvania. The widow of Thomas Riordon resided in Corning, Steuben County, New York, at the time of filing. (Image courtesy of the National Archives and Records Administration.)

each includes the side for which the soldier fought, regiment name, company, rank, alternative name, and the National Archives' reference from which the information was obtained.

Because the details are minimal, distinguishing one man, for example, John Kelly in Pennsylvania, from another is challenging. However, if an old county history or database specifies the regiments recruited from the county where the ancestral John Kelly was known to have lived, this database begins to make sense. All men serving in that regiment or company within the regiment can be called up by leaving the personal name fields blank. Were other Kelly men in that regiment? If so, they could have been relatives from Ireland, which automatically broadens the search to other men while limiting the common Kelly name to one specific unit.

Consulting individual databases for more information is another angle. One is the Ancestry.com databases "U.S., Union Soldiers Compiled Service Records, 1861-1865" and "U.S., Confederate Soldiers Compiled Service Records, 1861-1865." Both supply the place where the soldier enlisted as well as the unit name. Keep in mind that where a man enlisted might not have been his county of residence but was likely close to it, if not exact. With a geographical area targeted, additional sources such as the 1860 census can fill in the gaps. Once the name of the regiment is identified, other records can be explored as a method of sorting through the myriad of John Kellys in Pennsylvania.

The goal is locating a pension file for the veteran or his widow at some point. The pension indexes for Union veterans are on all the major genealogy websites. The Ancestry.com edition is "U.S., Civil War Pension Index: General Index to Pension Files, 1861-1934" and is a standard National Archives creation to the ones in its collection. It contains 2.5 million cards.

If a regiment and state from where the veteran or widow applied are already identified, it is relatively easy to position the common names. Remember that not all veterans or widows applied, but when they did, page after page of questionnaires and testimonies can stretch over years before the pension was granted or denied. The widows' pensions can be the most interesting because they had to prove they were wives of soldiers. Whether the veteran or his widow filed, both commonly reported birthplaces, and those for Ireland were precise. The pension files are not uniform because requirements varied at different times. The case files, the card index references, are at the National Archives, and until they are ordered and read, their contents cannot be foreseen.

Other indexes to Civil War pension materials are at the National Archives. Another is the Ancestry.com database "U.S., Civil War and Later Wars Index to Remarried Widow Pension Applications, 1848-1934." Fold3.com should always be consulted to see what it has scanned as part of its databases.

The last years of soldiers' lives were often at Soldiers' Homes, institutions set up after the Civil War so that veterans would

Select "U.S. National Homes for Disabled Volunteer Soldiers, 1866-1938."

Home	Town	State	Records
Bath Branch	Bath	New York	1876-1934
Battle Mountain Sanitarium	Hot Springs	South Dakota	1907-1934
Central Branch	Dayton	Ohio	1867-1935
Danville Branch	Danville	Illinois	1898-1934
Eastern Branch	Togus	Maine	1866-1934
Marion Branch	Marion	Indiana	1890-1931
Mountain Branch	Johnson City	Tennessee	1903-1932
Northwestern Branch	Milwaukee	Wisconsin	1867-1934
Pacific Branch	Los Angeles	California	1888-1934
Roseburg Branch	Roseburg	Oregon	1894-1937
Southern Branch	Hampton	Virginia	1871-1933
Western Branch	Leavenworth	Kansas	1885-1934

be cared for. They were scattered across the country, and veterans were sent to them from their last residences. The records have been indexed and digitized in the Ancestry.com database "U.S. National Homes for Disabled Volunteer Soldiers, 1866-1938." The homes and the years covered in the online registers are shown in the table above.

The "fill in the blank" register forms have military and personal information, as is expected. However, birthplaces for the Irish can be just the country or a more exact place, such as county.

One group of records, the Southern Claims Commission, although technically not military, arose from the destructions of the Civil War. Because of their value, they have been added to this section. Within them, researchers may find new clues for documents for families in the South just a few years after the war ended, when their lives were in shambles.

They do not list birthplaces, but they are good for locating people.

The Southern Claims Commission was established in 1871 and was dissolved in 1880. Its purpose was to review property loss claims by Southerners who remained loyal to the Union during the Civil War or said they did. Of the 22,298 claims received, only 7,092 were approved. While most of the claims (accepted and rejected) were for white citizens, a significant number were for Blacks. Importantly, the claims listed witnesses, usually family members and friends. About 222,000 witnesses with their personal information were recorded.

Each of the documents has approximately 80 questions that required answers from the applicants and the witnesses. The Southern Claims Commission records (1871 to 1880) are a colossal treasure of insight into Southern families during the Reconstruction Era. They are digitized and on Ancestry.com in three indexes: "U.S. Southern Claims Commission Master Index, 1871-1880"; "U.S., Southern Claims Commission Allowed Claims, 1871-1880"; and "U.S. Southern Claims Commission, Disallowed and Barred Claims, 1871-1880." When studying the indexes to the digitized records, do not insert a name but only the county into the search so that it is possible to see who else was filing a claim from the county. This is advantageous if the other people are connected to the ancestor.

This tactic also is applicable when an ancestor cannot be found and a transcription or spelling error is suspected as the cause. By examining the names of everyone in a particular county who filed a claim, what looks like the family can be recognized in the index. A source such as the Southern Claims Commission is indeed problematic because of the amount of marginally literate people who were maneuvering through the government paperwork and dealing with officials while trying to file claims. For example, can an index search translate Candy or Cannie for Kennedy? If not, scanning a list of all claimants from a county may reveal the Candy or Cannie entries, and further searches can be pursued from that point.

Spanish-American War (1898)

The Spanish-American War was between the United States and Spain. It was declared on 21 April 1898, lasted until 10 December 1898, and took place in Cuba,

Figure 46: Primary battlefields of the Spanish-American War, 1898. This conflict represented the first occurrence of the United States overseeing foreign interests.

Guam, the Philippines, and Puerto Rico. The short conflict saw 72,339 American troops serving, with 385 killed, 1,662 wounded, and 2,061 dying from disease.

It began with a mysterious explosion of the *USS Maine*, which sank in Havana Harbor, leading to the United States intervening in the Cuban War of Independence. The Americans demanded the Spanish withdraw from Cuba. On 21 April, the United States Navy began a blockade of Cuba, and each country declared war on the other. Neither had allies. The main issue of the war was rooted in Cuban independence from Spain.

The Treaty of Paris (1898) ended the struggle in favor of the United States. Because of the negotiation, temporary American control over Cuba was allowed, and ownership of Guam, the Philippine Islands, and Puerto Rico was ceded from Spain to the United States. With this defeat, Spain lost its remaining empire, and the United States suddenly expanded across the globe. It also resulted in the Philippine-American War (1899 to 1902).

A wide selection of the records for the Spanish-American War and the resulting Philippine-American War (also called the Philippine Insurrection) can be found digitized and indexed at Ancestry.com, FamilySearch.org, and Fold3.com. Manuscripts are typically by states and the men who volunteered from that state. Other sources, such as lists of soldiers, have been published in books by state. Keep in mind that records filed at the federal level with the National Archives

can be on any of the major websites, whereas state compilations and indexes are mainly at state archives, Ancestry.com, or FamilySearch.org.

One nationwide index is the Ancestry.com database "U.S., Spanish American War Volunteers Index to Compiled Military Service Records, 1898." The information on the cards has merely the names of the volunteers, the companies in which they served, and ranks. However, it is the first clue, if the name is not too common, that a man served in the war, from which knowledge other records can be sought.

A notable example of papers filed at the time of enlistment is in the Ancestry.com database "New York, Spanish-American War Military and Naval Service Records, 1898-1902." The database covers the Army, Cavalry, Marine Corp, National Guard, Naval Militia, and Navy. Although the title of the database may give the impression it is solely for the Spanish-American War, the years encompassed include New York serving in the Philippine-American War and the "Boxer Rebellion" in China. The registers were created by the New York Adjutant General. Aside from the expected information is also a birthplace question. The answer, again as anticipated, from an Irishman was Ireland, perhaps a county in Ireland, and sometimes even a place within the county. In any database, be aware that the indexers might not have been familiar with Irish place names, and, therefore, a percentage will be wrong. It is not rare to see Longford as Dongford or Lought for Louth.

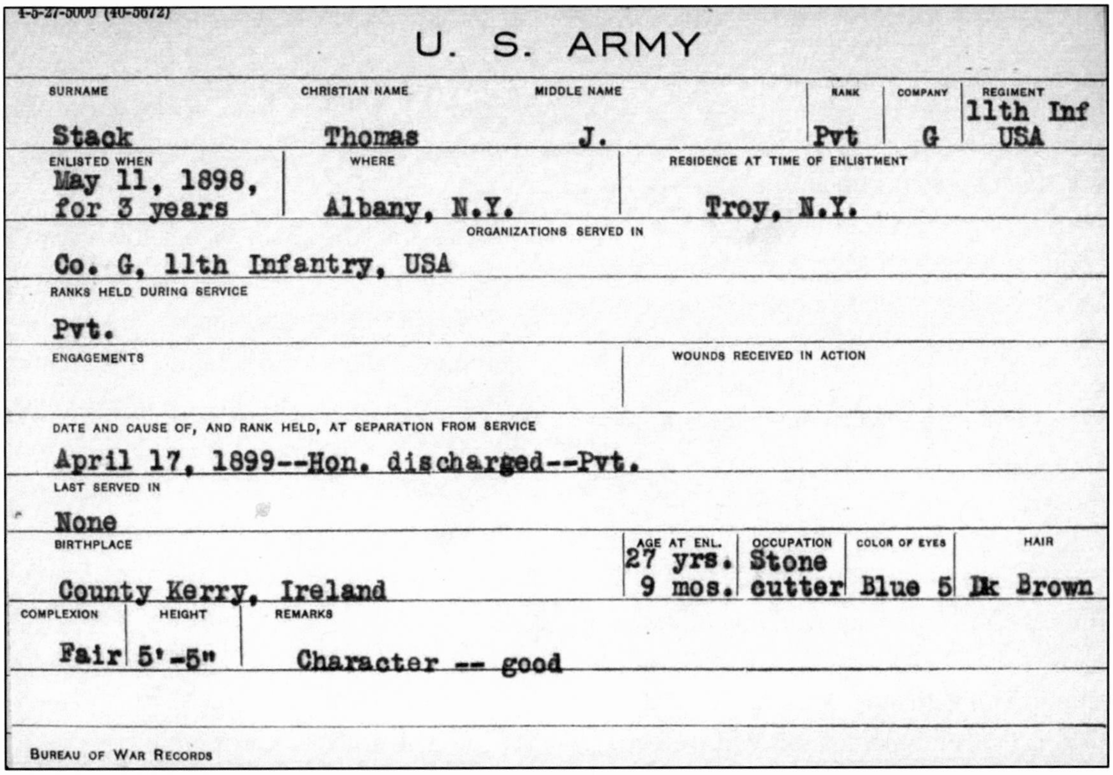

U. S. ARMY						
4-5-27-5000 (40-5672)						
SURNAME	CHRISTIAN NAME	MIDDLE NAME		RANK	COMPANY	REGIMENT
						11th Inf
Stack	Thomas	J.		Pvt	G	USA
ENLISTED WHEN	WHERE		RESIDENCE AT TIME OF ENLISTMENT			
May 11, 1898, for 3 years	Albany, N.Y.		Troy, N.Y.			

ORGANIZATIONS SERVED IN

Co. G, 11th Infantry, USA

RANKS HELD DURING SERVICE

Pvt.

ENGAGEMENTS	WOUNDS RECEIVED IN ACTION

DATE AND CAUSE OF, AND RANK HELD, AT SEPARATION FROM SERVICE

April 17, 1899--Hon. discharged--Pvt.

LAST SERVED IN

None

BIRTHPLACE	AGE AT ENL.	OCCUPATION	COLOR OF EYES	HAIR
County Kerry, Ireland	27 yrs. 9 mos.	Stone cutter	Blue 5	Dk Brown

COMPLEXION	HEIGHT	REMARKS
Fair	5'-5"	Character -- good

BUREAU OF WAR RECORDS

Figure 47: Service record card for Thomas J. Stack, a soldier in the U.S. Army during the Spanish-American War. (Image courtesy of New York State Archives.)

Reasonably, any soldier fighting around 1898 was born in the 1870s, but some older men also fought. Some men reenlisted several times, and all of them were tallied on the cards in this New York collection. A typical card from the New York database is for Thomas J. Stack from Troy, New York. He enlisted in the United States Army as a private in G Company, 11th Infantry, on 11 May 1898 for three years at Albany. He was honorably discharged on 17 April 1899. He answered the "Last served in" question as none. Most noteworthy was that he was born in County Kerry, Ireland. He was 27 years and 9 months old and a stone cutter by trade. His character was listed as good.

The cards from the state of Florida do not look like those of New York and are in the Ancestry.com database "Florida, Spanish American War Compiled Service Records, 1898." One is for Edward J. Lynch, private in Company L, 1st Regiment, Florida Infantry. He was part of the Field, Staff and Band Muster-in Roll, mustered at Tampa on 25 May 1898 at the age of 28 for two years. His residence was Tampa. Several cards about his service at various places in the southern United States and medical examinations are on file, but only two have his birthplace as Cork, Ireland. He was recorded as a principal musician. One card stated he was a printer and another, a journalist. Edward was mustered out in Huntsville, Alabama, on 27 January 1899.

If the index to the soldier's records does not note a birthplace in the state-related databases, one could be listed in the papers themselves. Some databases are indexes, and others have the digitized records.

Another source for tracing veterans is the pension records. The older ones for the Spanish-American War are at the National Archives and indexed together with other wars. For example, the database "United States General Index to Pension Files, 1861-1934" digitized on FamilySearch.org explains that while most of the files indexed are for those who fought for the Union in the Civil War, included are those who fought in the Spanish-American War, Philippine Insurrection, Boxer Rebellion, and Regular United States military forces. The card index lists the veterans or widows and enough identifying information from which to order pension files.

World War I (United States, 1917-1918)

World War I began on 28 July 1914 and lasted until 11 November 1918. Although the war had been raging, the United States did not enter until 2 April 1917, when President Wilson called for war against Germany. Congress declared war four days later. Through the Selective Service Act, the government drafted 2.8 million men, and so many records were created from which to pursue an Irish immigrant research strategy. Although some may consider this a late war for developing a research plan, it is not. A young soldier would have been born in the 1890s, and so he might have been one of the younger children of an immigrant family or even the only one who immigrated, tying the family to this

soldier. Furthermore, records such as the draft registrations expand the pool of potential soldiers back to men born as early as 1872.

In this war, the main Allied Powers were the British Empire (1914-1918), Italy (1915-1918), France, Japan, the Russian Empire (1914-1917), and the United States (1917-1918). Other nations joined at separate times. The Central Powers they were fighting, and would ultimately defeat, were the Austria-Hungary Empire, Bulgaria, and the German Empire, with others. After the war, the map of Europe and Africa was not the same as before because the Central Powers lost territories as their empires were broken up. By the time World War I was over, the horrors of it were so evident that it was dubbed the "War to end all wars."

Records from the American side can be found on the foremost websites Ancestry.com, FamilySearch.org, and Fold3.com. Some of the databases overlap between the websites. Of the various records made by the government and the states, one set stands out for immigration purposes, the WW I Draft Registration Cards.

The draft cards are certainly the primary source when constructing an origins' strategy. The most prominent indexed and digitized version of this is the Ancestry.com database "U.S., World War I Draft Registration Cards, 1917-1918," although it is not the only website where the cards are located and indexed. Context to this amazing resource is necessary to understand and manipulate the database.

During 1917 and 1918, about 24 million men in the United States registered for the draft. Their data is on the fronts and backs of cards, which are important in immigrant research because they account for 98% of men living in the country born between 1872 and 1900. The total population was 100 million, and thus about 25% of the population is represented in this set of records. They all might not have served but merely registered to serve.

Each of the three programs through which men registered asked slightly dissimilar questions. The most useful are for age, birthplace, citizenship, and nearest relative. Other information includes occupation, employer, military service, and home address. Understanding the three is the key to an immigrant research tactic. The qualifications are adapted from the Ancestry.com explanation of the database:

First Registration. Held on 5 June 1917 for men aged 21 to 31, that is, men born between 6 June 1886 and 5 June 1896.

Second Registration. Held on 5 June 1918 for men who had turned 21 since the first registration, or men born between 6 June 1896 and 5 June 1897. If men had not previously registered or were not already in the military, they also registered at this time. In a supplemental registration, men who had turned 21 as of 24 August 1918 were included.

Third Registration. Held on 12 September 1918 was the largest one and was for men aged 18 to 21 and 31 to 45, thus born between 11 September 1872 and 12 September 1900.

The original registrations were by state, county, and local draft board, and so people with the same surname registering within the same local board might have been relatives. The approach can work well in areas without multiple draft boards, mostly urban ones. In some cases, where the registration did not ask for birthplace, a loose term such as British might have been used for someone born in Ireland.

The first two registrations asked for birthplace, but the third did not. Each of the three is valuable in its own way, and if several family members can be found among them, a more complete picture of the family can emerge. The goal is a listing of a place of birth in Ireland or enough information to lead to another record that will have it. Because every man was directed to sign his card, the ancestor's literacy can be surmised. If he was not literate, he signed with an X or had someone sign for him.

The draft cards can also reveal facts about a family or individual long forgotten or not talked about. Their migrations can be traced, such as someone who should have been living in Gary, Indiana, being found in Seattle, Washington. That can be a surprise while raising an entirely new set of questions.

Figure 48: Men holding draft cards after successfully registering for the first draft of World War I, 5 June 1917. The location was next to Bahnsen & Roeloffs grocery store in New York City. (Image courtesy of George Grantham Bain Collection, Library of Congress, Prints and Photographs Division. Reproduction number: LC-DIG-ggbain-24573. Permissions received.)

The listing for the spouse may be startling as well. The draft cards are a definite means of identifying the first or second families nobody ever talked about or perhaps even a third or fourth marriage. This was not uncommon because finding someone during the time was not as simple as it is today.

If a man changed his name and not his birth date or birthplace, a search of information other than the name can be performed in the nationwide database of draft registrations. It could raise any number of secondary "why" questions.

Examples of some draft cards showing birthplaces in Ireland are adapted as follows:

Name in full: John Francis Cahill
Age: 25
Home Address: Parnell Street, Medfield, Massachusetts
Date of Birth: 4 August 1892
Citizenship? Alien
Where were you born? Kerrick, Waterford, Ireland
Occupation? carpenter
By whom employed? E. F. Hodgeson Co.
Where Employed? Dover, Massachusetts
Dependents? no
Married or single? single
Race? Caucasian
Military Service? None
Claim exemption? No
Tall, medium short? Medium
Slender, medium or stout? Medium

Color of eyes? Brown
Color of hair? Brown
Bald? No
Registrar: Walter E. Morris
City or County: Medfield, Massachusetts
Registration: 5 June 1917

Name in full: John Joseph Murray
Age: 28
Home Address: 118 East 52nd Street, New York, New York
Date of Birth: 7 May 1889
Citizenship? naturalized
Where were you born? County of Louth, Island Ireland
Occupation? chauffeur
By whom employed? Mrs. James A. Burdn
Where Employed? Hotel St. Regis
Dependents? mother
Married or single? single
Race? white
Military Service? no
Claim exemption? Yes, supports mother.
Tall, medium short? 5 ft. 9 in.
Slender, medium or stout? medium
Color of eyes? blue
Color of hair? brown
Bald? no
Registrar: Wm. I. Vanderhoof
Precinct: 21-27
City or County: New York
State: New York
Registration: 5 June 1917

John Francis Cahill was single and had no dependents. He was an alien. If no knowledge of other family members is in

the United States, he might have emigrated as a young man on his own or with some of his close friends from County Waterford. A place within County Waterford was listed. With the birth date and a locality, the Irish Civil Registration of births and the Irish church records' indexes can be searched.

The papers for John Joseph Murray in Manhattan hold solid information even though only County Louth is reported as his birthplace. He was a naturalized citizen, and he was supporting his mother. The assumption, although not stated, is that his mother's residence was Manhattan. The implication is that he lived with her and supported her. Because his address in Manhattan is known, the city directories can be read for all Murray entries at that address around 1917. Perhaps siblings or his mother (assumed to be a widow) were named in the directories, and so the 1920 census can be consulted for the family if it remained at that address. Once a family unit has been reconstructed, the indexes of Irish church records and the Irish Civil Registrations of birth indexes can be explored.

For an example of a World War I Draft Registration Card, see page 170.

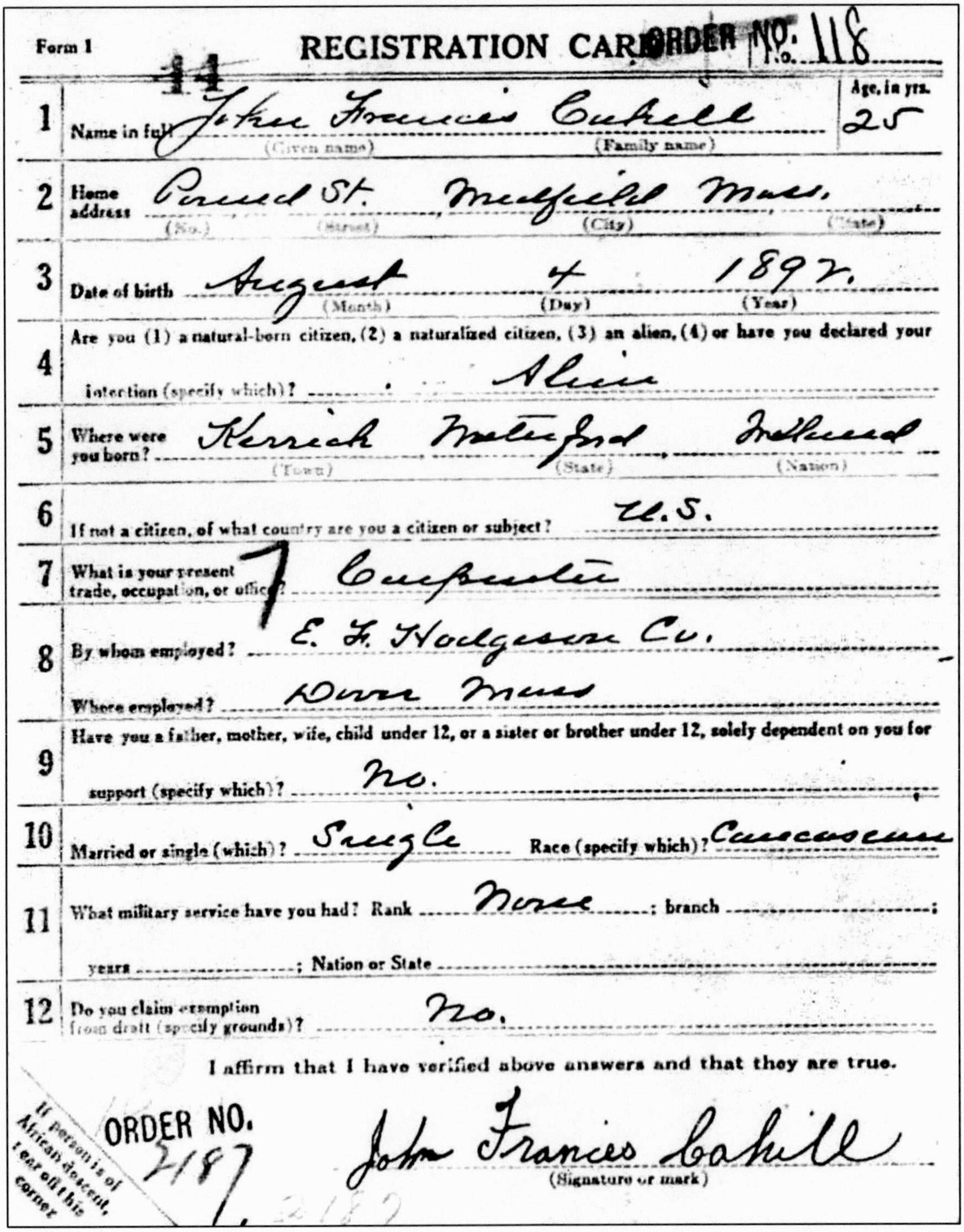

Form 1 — REGISTRATION CARD — ORDER NO. 118

44

1 Name in full John Francis Cahill (Given name) (Family name) — Age, in yrs. 25

2 Home address Pond St. Medfield Mass. (No.) (Street) (City) (State)

3 Date of birth August 4 1892. (Month) (Day) (Year)

4 Are you (1) a natural-born citizen, (2) a naturalized citizen, (3) an alien, (4) or have you declared your intention (specify which)? Alien

5 Where were you born? Kerrick Waterford Ireland (Town) (State) (Nation)

6 If not a citizen, of what country are you a citizen or subject? U.S.

7 What is your present trade, occupation, or office? Carpenter

8 By whom employed? E. F. Hodgson Co. Where employed? Dover Mass

9 Have you a father, mother, wife, child under 12, or a sister or brother under 12, solely dependent on you for support (specify which)? No.

10 Married or single (which)? Single Race (specify which)? Caucasian

11 What military service have you had? Rank None; branch ; years ; Nation or State

12 Do you claim exemption from draft (specify grounds)? No.

I affirm that I have verified above answers and that they are true.

ORDER NO. 2187

John Francis Cahill (Signature or mark)

If person is of African descent, tear off this corner

Figure 49: World War I Draft Registration Card for John Francis Cahill. For further details and assessment, see the abstracts of this card beginning on page 168. (Image courtesy of the National Archives and Records Administration.)

Chapter Eleven

Naturalization and Citizenship Records

The process of becoming a citizen of the United States generates records at every step. This chapter does not concern the earliest records. For that discussion, refer to Dwight A. Radford's chapter "Naturalization and Citizenship" in *American Scots-Irish Research: Strategies and Sources in the Quest for Ulster-Scots Origins* (Orting, Washington: Family Roots Publishing Co., LLC, 2020). The book concentrates on the Scots-Irish, but the principles outlined can easily be tailored to other Irish who arrived in the country early.

When consulting citizenship records as part of an immigrant origins' strategy, remember that since the 1840s and the Potato Famine, the commonness of names exploded even though they were abundantly ordinary before that time. They are a problem when dealing with indexes to citizenship records. As with any other document, distinguishing which Patrick Callaghan, for instance, is the ancestor among innumerable ones is a feat. And how many ways can Callaghan be spelled? When tracking these citizenship papers, one wrong assumption can easily connect to a wrong family with the right name. However, care and knowledge can circumvent many pitfalls.

An alien could file various papers in diverse courts in the citizenship process. These courts could include chancery, criminal, marine, municipal, police, probate, and surrogate. It can be prudent to check all available courts in an area, which can include a region or just a county. A county in Ireland as the birthplace could be in one of the records.

Citizenship papers are so valuable to the family historian that the subject always requires a chapter in genealogy reference guides, if not entire books. Many of the standard works are dated, but the discussions about the records, most of which have been digitized and are now online at Ancestry.com and FamilySearch.org, do not change. Some of the standard works recommended are:

Greenwood, Val D. "Court Records and Family History." *The Researcher's Guide to American Genealogy.* 4th ed., Baltimore, Maryland: Genealogical Publishing Co., 2017, pp. 560-567.

Luebking, Sandra Hargreaves. "Immigration Records." *The Source: A Guidebook of American Genealogy.* 3rd ed., edited by Loretto Dennis Szucs and Sandra Hargreaves Luebking, Provo, Utah: Ancestry Publishing, 2006, pp. 399-408.

Newman, John J. *American Naturalization Records 1790-1990*. Bountiful, Utah: Heritage Quest, 1998.

Schaefer, Christina K. *Guide to Naturalization Records of the United States*. Baltimore, Maryland: Genealogical Publishing Co., 1997.

Szucs, Loretto Dennis. *They Became Americans: Finding Naturalization Records and Ethnic Origins*. Salt Lake City, Utah: Ancestry Publishing, 1998.

Many laws continue to regulate who can become a citizen and who cannot. These laws and the documents created under them are addressed in the aforementioned books. Citizenship laws began in 1790, and for the purpose of this work's subject, they are listed through 1965, not including those preventing Chinese and other Asians from entering the United States. The laws below are adapted from the online chart "Major United States Laws Relating to Immigration and Naturalization: 1790-2005" of the National Archives at Archives.gov:

Major Laws Relating to Naturalization: 1790-2005

Date	Provision
26 Mar 1790	One visit to court; two-year residency; free white alien; children of naturalized citizen are to be considered citizens.
29 Jan 1795	Free white aliens of good moral character; five-year residency with one year in state; declaration of intention filed after two years; petition filed three years after declaration.
18 Jun 1798	14-year residency; declaration of intention filed 5 years before granting of citizenship.
14 Apr 1802	Reasserted residence requirements of 1795 act; children of naturalized citizens considered to be citizens.
26 May 1824	Alien minors naturalized upon reaching 21 years of age if alien had lived in U.S. for five years.
10 Feb 1855	Alien women married to U.S. citizens considered to be citizens.
17 Jul 1862	Aliens who received honorable discharges from U.S. Army were not required to file declaration.
03 Mar 1891	The office of superintendent of immigration was established. Classes of people denied the right to immigrate were defined as: insane, paupers, people with contagious diseases, those convicted of felonies or misdemeanors of moral turpitude, and polygamists.

Major Laws Relating to Naturalization: 1790-2005

Date	Provision
26 Jul 1894	Aliens who had received an honorable discharge from the U.S. Navy and Marines were not required to file a declaration.
29 Jun 1906	The Bureau of Immigration and Naturalization was established, and naturalization papers became standardized. Any court having common law jurisdiction could naturalize aliens.
2 Mar 1907	American-born women married to foreign-born men took the citizenship status of their husbands. If the marriages were terminated, the women regained their American citizenship. However, no process for regaining citizenship was defined.
09 May 1918	Aliens in the U.S. military were permitted to file for citizenship after serving three years.
19 May 1921	The Quota Act of 1921 established annual immigrant admissions per country using a formula based on the 1910 federal census.
22 Sep 1922	Alien wives of U.S. citizens could file for citizenship after one year of residency. It also stopped removals of citizenship status from native-born American women who had married aliens not eligible for U.S. citizenship.
26 May 1924	A limit was placed on the number of immigrants in permanent status. Aliens were to obtain visas in advance from a U.S. embassy. Courts were no longer allowed to determine naturalization eligibility. This law was aimed at further restricting the large-scale immigration of Southern and Eastern Europeans and prohibiting Middle Easterners, East Asians, and Asian Indians.
02 June 1924	Native Americans and persons born in the United States were granted full U.S. citizenship.
02 Mar 1929	Certificates of arrival with the dates and places of arrival were to be issued to immigrants. Persons who wished to become citizens were required to file certificates upon arrival with declarations of intention. If they arrived before certificates of arrival were required, they had to be listed on a passenger arrival manifest, at which point retroactive certificates were issued.
25 Jun 1936	American women who had lost their citizenships by marrying aliens could regain citizenships by taking oaths of allegiance to the United States.

Major Laws Relating to Naturalization: 1790-2005

Date	Provision
25 Jun 1952	Established national origins minimum quota of 100 persons per country and lowered the age requirements of naturalization to 18 years.
03 Oct 1965	National quotas were replaced with annual ceilings for the number of immigrants. Imposed on the Western Hemisphere was an immigration limitation (120,000 per year), with the Eastern Hemisphere limited to 170,000. Because of the family preference, immigration was mainly through "chain migration," in which recent immigrants already in the United States sponsored relatives.

Some matters are of importance for genealogical purposes. First, in the early years, only men tended to be naturalized. Second, not all who started the process finished it, explaining why declarations of intention were filed but naturalization certificates cannot be found. The third is that the steps in the process can take place in different courts within a state, or someone can move to another state to complete them. A fourth consideration is that no laws required an immigrant to become a citizen.

One fascinating source as an excellent model of tying many of these principles together is the Great Voter Registers of California. These are printed books of registered voters and can have exceptional details. Thomas Fitzpatrick of Salinas, Monterey County, is an illustration of their value. He was registered to vote in the 4th Precinct of Salinas on 7 October 1898, and Salinas was his post office. He was a laborer, 53 years old (born in 1845), and born in Ireland. Included with his physical description were the questions employed to disenfranchise voting rights for certain groups, such as: able to read Constitution in English; able to write name; and physically able to mark ballot. He passed all the requirements. Perhaps the principal point of the example is that he was naturalized on 16 October 1868 in the District Court in Rensselaer County, New York. If the California records do not reveal where Thomas Fitzpatrick was born in Ireland, research should turn to the Rensselaer County, New York, records, beginning with the naturalization papers. (See pp. 176-177.)

The Great Voter Registers of California are on Ancestry.com as well as many other websites because of their universally recognized value within the genealogy community. The Ancestry.com databases are "California, Voter Registers, 1866-1898," and "California, Voter Registers, 1900-1968." This simple voter list with all its additional information can significantly advance resolving an Irish immigrant origins' problem even when the Great Voter Registers itself states only Ireland as a birthplace. If the researcher did not know Thomas was in

New York, let alone in Rensselaer County, a record such as the Great Voter Registers can be the link between California and New York.

While the various papers filed to become a citizen may yield the Irish birthplace, many will not. What is contained in the papers cannot be known until they are searched. They can be a mine of information or a huge disappointment, but they are part of the holistic approach to immigrant research and must be examined.

Women did not have the right to vote until 1920, and so they had no real need to go through the process, although many did. Laws were also enacted that discouraged women from seeking citizenship. An excellent article by Marian L. Smith "'Any woman who is now or may hereafter be married...' Women and Naturalization, ca. 1802-1940" can be found on the National Archives website, Archives.gov, and provides background about women and the naturalization process.

The Naturalization Process
Before 1906, citizenship records were not standardized. Each court kept its own documents that varied widely from minimal to detailed entries, which thus raise difficulties when studying them. However, some facts were always given:

- Name of immigrant
- Residence of immigrant
- Country of origin or allegiance

The researcher is seeking more than the basics. Additional information, which may or may not be customary, depending on the court, can have some of the following:

- Port of arrival
- Date of arrival
- Age of immigrant
- Residence of immigrant
- Birthplace of immigrant

These records do not have parents' names. When more details are found, if the name is common, they are a method of sorting through who is who. One certainly is an address for the person submitting the papers, after which other records can continue the sorting process in, for instance, city directories in large urban cities. If the records note a port of departure, it may help. Often, it is Liverpool, England, which is less than beneficial, but Queenstown (Cobh) in the south of Ireland versus Londonderry (Derry) or Belfast in the north can be significant. If ancestors were Protestant and Presbyterian, they usually sailed from Londonderry (Derry) or Belfast and not Queenstown (Cobh) because the Scots-Irish (Ulster-Scots) Presbyterians were mainly concentrated in Ulster Province. However, since the citizenship papers do not list religion, caution is needed with this strategy.

The citizenship process typically involved Declarations of Intention, called "first papers." Questions were asked at that time, and often within these declarations to become citizens, birthplaces were recorded. The Petitions were filed two or three years after the declarations were. These were the "second or final papers." At that time, Oaths of Allegiance to the

SALINAS No. 4 PRECINCT—ADI

Voting No.	Voted	Ballot No.	Reg. No.	NAME.	Business or Occupation.	Age.	Height Ft.	In.	Complexion.	Color of Eyes.	Color of Hair.	Visible Marks or Scars, if any, and their locality.	Country of Nativity.
6861			5354	Arellanes, Uldarico L	Laborer	28	5	10	Brown	Brown	Dark		California
6862			4899	Acker, Fred	Upholsterer	34	5	9	Light	Gray	Brown		California
6863			4903	Antrim, George W	Brickmason	40	5	4	Dark	Gray	Brown		Pennsylvania
6864			4909	Arellanes, Arnulfo	Laborer	21	5	9	Dark	Dark	Dark		California
6865			6968	Abbott, Elmer L	Laborer	30	6	5¾	Medium	Brown	Dark		Iowa
6866			5674	Burton, Frank	Laborer	63	5	7	Medium	Blue	Brown		New York
6867			5675	Button, Thomas	None	79	5	9	Fair	Gray	Gray		Kentucky
6868			5664	Bland, William A	Laborer	30	5	6	Light	Blue	Brown		California
6869			5350	Breschini, Domingo	Saloonkeeper	45	5	9	Brown	Gray	Brown		Switzerland
6870			5206	Beiersdorff, John	Laborer	50	5	3	Brown	Blue	Brown	Scar or lump on middle finger of right hand.	Germany
6871			4918	Bailey, James F	Farmer	42	5	7	Dark	Blue	Dark		Pennsylvania
6872			6294	Burke, Robert	Plasterer	49	5	11¾	Medium	Brown	Dark		Scotland
6873			6353	Bourge, Pierre	None	75	5	3	Light	Blue	Gray		France
6874			6535	Breyer, Joseph L	Merchant	44	5	4	Medium	Brown	Dark		Roumania
6875			7009	Brousse, Jas Henry	Laborer	38	5	4½	Dark	Gray	Dark		Louisiana
6876			7049	Boudour, Chas	Farmer	25	5	7	Dark	Brown	Black		California
6877			5687	Crow, George M	None	76	5	8	Light	Blue	Light		Virginia
6878			5677	Castro, Manuel A	None	70	6	1	Dark	Brown	Gray		California
6879			5585	Castro, Rafael	Laborer	61	6		Brown	Brown	Brown		California
6880			5214	Cleland, William T	Surveyor	31	6		Light	Gray	Light		Kansas
6881			4915	Callaghan, Patrick	Laborer	53	5	8	Medium	Blue	Gray		Ireland
6882			4941	Colburn, Charles H	Painter	35	5	7	Light	Gray	Brown		Massachusetts
6883			4942	Cook, Peter	Laborer	38	5	10	Light	Blue	Light		Missouri
6884			4945	Curtin, Daniel F	Laborer	23	5	11	Medium	Blue	Light		California
6885			6054	Chanteloup, Eugene	Laborer	25	5	3	Medium	Brown	Brown		France
6886			6762	Curran, Mart E	Carpenter	26	5	10½	Light	Blue	Brown		Illinois
6887			6164	Cunningham, Elmer L	Laborer	29	5	7½	Medium	Blue	Brown		Kansas
6888			6415	Callihan, Charles J	Laborer	22	5	8	Sandy	Gray	Auburn		West Virginia
6889			6471	Curran, James S	Laborer	44	5	7	Fair	Brown	Brown		Michigan
6890			6568	Comerford, Thomas R	Porter	21	5	5	Light	Blue	Dark		California
6891			5690	Donner, Louis	Laborer	50	5	6½	Light	Blue	Light		Prussia
6892			5590	Downie, Moses M	Teamster	58	5	6	Light	Blue	Brown		New York
6893			5219	Daly, Patrick	Carpenter	34	5	8	Light	Blue	Brown		Ireland
6894			5221	Decarli, Frank	Laborer	27	5	9½	Light	Blue	Brown		Switzerland
6895			4952	Delaney, Henry W	Horse trainer	33	5	7¾	Light	Blue	Brown		New York
6896			4953	Deutsch, E. Manuel	Painter	44	5	4	Dark	Brown	Gray		Hungary
6897			4965	Donnelly, Andrew J	Laborer	54	5	8	Light	Blue	Gray	Scar on left wrist.	Canada
6898			4955	Duckworth, Samuel	Laborer	27	5	9½	Dark	Brown	Dark		California
6899			6172	Debernardi, Silvio	Farmer	25	5	8½	Medium	Blue	Dark		Switzerland
6900			6579	Donohue, Jerry T	Machinist	23	5	4¾	Fair	Blue	Brown	Scar on back of head	Illinois
6901			6912	Duffy, James F	Machinist	48	5	4	Fair	Brown	Gray		Pennsylvania
6902			7024	DeFrees, John Mc	Conductor	49	5	8	Fair	Blue	Brown		Indiana
6903			7057	Daniels, Albert	Laborer	54	5	7	Medium	Gray	Gray		England
6904			5694	Enos, Joseph	Laborer	67	5	6	Fair	Brown	Gray	Scar inside finger right hand.	Western Isles
6905			5227	Estabrook, Clarence R	R. R. Agent	42	5	6½	Light	Gray	Brown		N. Brunswick
6906			4957	Eade, Sherman T	Butcher	27	5	8	Fair	Blue	Dark	Scar on back of left hand.	Illinois
6907			7026	Edwards, Burt E	Carpenter	26	6	3	Fair	Blue	Brown		Illinois
6908			6974	English, William	Laborer	45	5	7	Light	Blue	Gray		Ireland
6909			4966	Fogarty, Frank J	Laborer	34	5	9½	Dark	Brown	Brown		California
5899			4961	Fitzgerald, James	Laborer	59	5	10½	Sandy	Gray	Gray		New York
6911			5899	Forbes, Robert	Laborer	27	5	11	Dark	Brown	Black		California
6912			6308	Felt, Benjamin F	Carpenter	58	5	11½	Medium	Brown	Dark		New York
6913			6978	Foster, Luke Wilber	Laborer	24	5	11	Dark	Brown	Black	Scar on inside left hand.	Kansas
6914			7019	Fitzpatrick, Thomas	Laborer	53	6		Light	Blue	Gray		Ireland
6915			5601	George, James G	Laborer	[illegible]	5	11	[illegible]	[illegible]	[illegible]		[illegible]
6916			5702	Greenwood, Frank	Machinist	68	5	4	Light	Hazel	Gray	Right hand and fingers stiff.	Pennsylvania
6917			5600	Gambetta, Faustino	Saloonkeeper	30	5	4	Light	Hazel	Brown		Switzerland

Figure 50a-b: Great Voter Register for the State of California, 1898. Thomas Fitzpatrick links to naturalization in New York and other details. See descriptions on pages 174-175. (Image courtesy of California State Library.)

United States were signed. The Naturalization Certificates for citizenship, from the same courts as those in which the Petitions were filed, were presented when the immigrants were sworn in.

The easiest way to look at all documentation is through Ancestry.com and FamilySearch.org. Both may have some of the same records, but they also have their own collections. The two sites are the largest ones online for these records. The FamilySearch.org compilation is under the state, county, or city level in the FamilySearch Catalog in the category "Naturalization and Citizenship."

Indexes to Records

Indexes can be demanding to use because they are likely to have only basic information. Often, they are the old card indexes from the National Archives that are being digitized and indexed on Ancestry.com and FamilySearch.org. The first clue about a year of naturalization generally is from either a voters' list or a census that has citizenship questions.

DITIONS—MONTEREY COUNTY.   105

Place of Residence. Precinct.	NATURALIZED. Date.	By What Court.	Place.	Date of Registration	Post-office Address.	Able to read...	Able to write...	Physically...	Nature of Disability
Salinas No. 4				Mar. 14, 1898	Salinas	Yes	Yes	Yes	
Salinas No. 4				Feb. 6, 1897	Salinas	Yes	Yes	Yes	
Salinas No. 4				Dec. 15, 1896	Salinas	Yes	Yes	Yes	
Salinas No. 4				Feb. 24, 1897	Salinas	Yes	Yes	Yes	
Salinas No. 4				Oct. 19, 1898	Salinas	Yes	Yes	Yes	
Salinas No. 4				July 30, 1898	Salinas	Yes	Yes	Yes	
Salinas No. 4				July 30, 1898	Salinas	Not	Not	Not	Blindness
Salinas No. 4				July 30, 1898	Salinas	Yes	Yes	Yes	
Salinas No. 4	Sept. 17, 1874	County	Monterey	Mar. 16, 1898	Salinas	Yes	Yes	Yes	
Salinas No. 4	Sept. 22, 1886	City	Albany, N. Y.	Mar. 7, 1898	Salinas	Yes	Yes	Yes	
Salinas No. 4				Jan. 27, 1897	Salinas	Yes	Yes	Yes	
Salinas No. 4	1872	Com Pleas	New York	Aug. 10, 1898	Salinas	Not	Not	Yes	
Salinas No. 4	Sept. 6, 1879	County	Tehama	Aug. 12, 1898	Salinas	Yes	Yes	Yes	
Salinas No. 4	Oct. 1876	U. S. Dist.	Ohio	Aug. 16, 1898	Salinas	Yes	Yes	Yes	
Salinas No. 4				Oct. 13, 1898	Salinas	Yes	Yes	Yes	
Salinas No. 4				Oct. 11, 1898	Salinas	Yes	Yes	Yes	
Salinas No. 4				July 30, 1898	Salinas	Yes	Yes	Yes	
Salinas No. 4				July 27, 1898	Salinas	Yes	Yes	Yes	
Salinas No. 4				June 23, 1898	Salinas	Yes	Yes	Yes	
Salinas No. 4				Feb. 12, 1898	Salinas	Yes	Yes	Yes	
Salinas No. 4	Jan. 27, 1897	Superior	Monterey Co	Jan. 27, 1898	Salinas	Yes	Yes	Yes	
Salinas No. 4				Feb. 11, 1898	Salinas	Yes	Yes	Yes	
Salinas No. 4				Feb. 6, 1898	Salinas	Yes	Yes	Yes	
Salinas No. 4				Feb. 6, 1897	Salinas	Yes	Yes	Yes	
Salinas No. 4	Aug. 8, 1898	Superior	Monterey	Aug. 8, 1898	Salinas	Yes	Yes	Yes	
Salinas No. 4				Aug. 10, 1898	Salinas	Yes	Yes	Yes	
Salinas No. 4				Aug. 8, 1898	Salinas	Yes	Yes	Yes	
Salinas No. 4				Aug. 9, 1898	Salinas	Yes	Yes	Yes	
Salinas No. 4			Superior	Aug. 13, 1898	Salinas	Yes	Yes	Yes	
Salinas No. 4			Monterey	Aug. 15, 1898	Salinas	Yes	Yes	Yes	
Salinas No. 4	June 15, 1882	Superior		July 30, 1898	Salinas	Yes	Yes	Yes	
Salinas No. 4				July 22, 1898	Salinas	Yes	Yes	Yes	
Salinas No. 4	Nov. 20, 1895	Superior	San Francisco	Mar. 7, 1898	Salinas	Yes	Yes	Yes	
Salinas No. 4	March 2, 1898	Superior	Monterey	Mar. 2, 1898	Salinas	Yes	Yes	Yes	
Salinas No. 4				Jan. 11, 1898	Salinas	Yes	Yes	Yes	
Salinas No. 4	June 22, 1892	Superior	Fresno	Mar. 4, 1897	Salinas	Yes	Yes	Yes	
Salinas No. 4	Aug. 17, 1877	County	San Mateo	Jan. 25, 1897	Salinas	Yes	Yes	Yes	
Salinas No. 4				Feb. 17, 1897	Salinas	Yes	Yes	Yes	
Salinas No. 4	March 21, 1896	Superior	Del Norte Co	Aug. 10, 1898	Salinas	Yes	Yes	Yes	
Salinas No. 4				Aug. 13, 1898	Salinas	Yes	Yes	Yes	
Salinas No. 4				Oct. 6, 1898	Salinas	Yes	Yes	Yes	
Salinas No. 4				Oct. 6, 1898	Salinas	Yes	Yes	Yes	
Salinas No. 4	Aug. 29, 1877	County	Monterey Co	Oct. 11, 1898	Salinas	Yes	Yes	Yes	
Salinas No. 4	Oct. 5, 1888	Superior	Monterey	July 30, 1898	Salinas	Not	Not	Yes	
Salinas No. 4	Father a citizen			Feb. 14, 1898	Salinas	Yes	Yes	Yes	
Salinas No. 4				Feb. 8, 1897	Salinas	Yes	Yes	Yes	
Salinas No. 4				Oct. 7, 1898	Salinas	Yes	Yes	Yes	
Salinas No. 4	Father a Citizen			Oct. 7, 1898	Salinas	Yes	Yes	Yes	
Salinas No. 4				Feb. 26, 1897	Salinas	Yes	Yes	Yes	
Salinas No. 4				Jan. 20, 1897	Salinas	Yes	Yes	Yes	
Salinas No. 4				Aug. 4, 1898	Salinas	Yes	Yes	Yes	
Salinas No. 4				Aug. 10, 1898	Salinas	Yes	Yes	Yes	
Salinas No.				Oct. 8, 1898	Salinas	Yes	Yes	Yes	
Salinas No. 4	Oct. 16, 1868	District	Rensaler Co., N. Y	Oct. 7, 1898	Salinas	Yes	Yes	Yes	
Salinas No. 4									
Salinas No. 4				July 25, 1898	Salinas	Yes	Not	Yes	
Salinas No. 4	July 28, 1890	Superior	Monterey	June 14, 1898	Salinas	Yes	Yes	Yes	

Figure 50a-b: Great Voter Register for the State of California, 1898. Thomas Fitzpatrick links to naturalization in New York and other details. See descriptions on pages 174-175. (Image courtesy of California State Library.)

Otherwise, it is conjecture since researchers do not know a year of naturalization or the court. With common names, unless an index is precise enough so that a county of residence can be used as a guide or a range of years can be searched, it is nearly impossible to know which John Collins, for example, if any, was the ancestor. This is a problem with state courts or in larger collections that have indexed numerous records from numerous courts and counties.

Begin the search in the county where the ancestor is known to have lived. Typically, this is a certain piece of information gathered from a census report or other record. It also demonstrates the successful genealogical principle of "Start with the known and go to the unknown." If a database does not allow a search to be limited by county, or whether it does is uncertain, look specifically under that county in the FamilySearch Catalog on FamilySearch.org. The catalog states which court records were digitized or microfilmed. Search all for the correct period. Many naturalization registers have indexes in the fronts. If they do not, a local genealogical society may have compiled one online, and USGen-Web.org is a place to start. If none is still displayed and the county is rural with limited numbers of naturalizations, read the digitized images.

Do not ignore others by the correct surname in the targeted time. They could be relatives from the same place in Ireland. If an ancestor who is known to have been naturalized is not found, the search may need to extend to a higher-level court. For records, the Ancestry.com and FamilySearch.org indexes should assist. However, there, the pool of possible entries of common names is encountered from an area covering several counties. Keep in mind that neither website has images and indexes of all citizenship papers, and so contacting a county courthouse or state archives may be necessary. Nevertheless, the two websites are a solid beginning.

Strategies for Using Citizenship Records

When additional information is in the records, it may not be specific enough to further the research goals. A birthplace in Ireland may be discovered by expanding the search to all the ancestor's papers, from declaration through naturalization. For example, because the pre-1906 records were not standardized, the record may state only Ireland as a birthplace. If so, all possible relatives with the same surname should be studied for the period in question. One of their records may have a county or town in Ireland.

Another strategy for exploring a rural county is to make an inventory of those places within the targeted time if it is found and if most of the declarations or naturalizations do provide a county in Ireland. If the majority of the people gave a particular county as the birthplace, a migration into that specific American county might have occurred, pointing to the ancestor as also being from the one county in Ireland. It is not positive, but it is a place from which to further test the theory. Witnesses for the person to be naturalized can also be a good clue. Were they friends or family from the same place in Ireland? These are logical questions.

If a county of birth in Ireland has been determined from another record and the Irish church records are incomplete or do not go back far enough, look in the citizenship papers for all people regardless of surname who originated from that Irish county and pursue their lives. In rural farming areas especially, the theory is that the ancestor was there for some reason. After all, why settle in rural Kansas as opposed to Chicago? Usually, he or she was joining family or friends from Ireland. Identifying the residence in Ireland of friends and family who were living in the ancestor's county in America will find where the ancestor originated as well.

The post-1906 records were standardized, and within them, birthplaces were frequently listed. The strategy changes with them. Beginning on 27 September 1906, the process of naturalization became part of the federal courts. Also, at this point, copies of the naturalization papers were kept by the Immigration and Naturalization Services (INS) and by

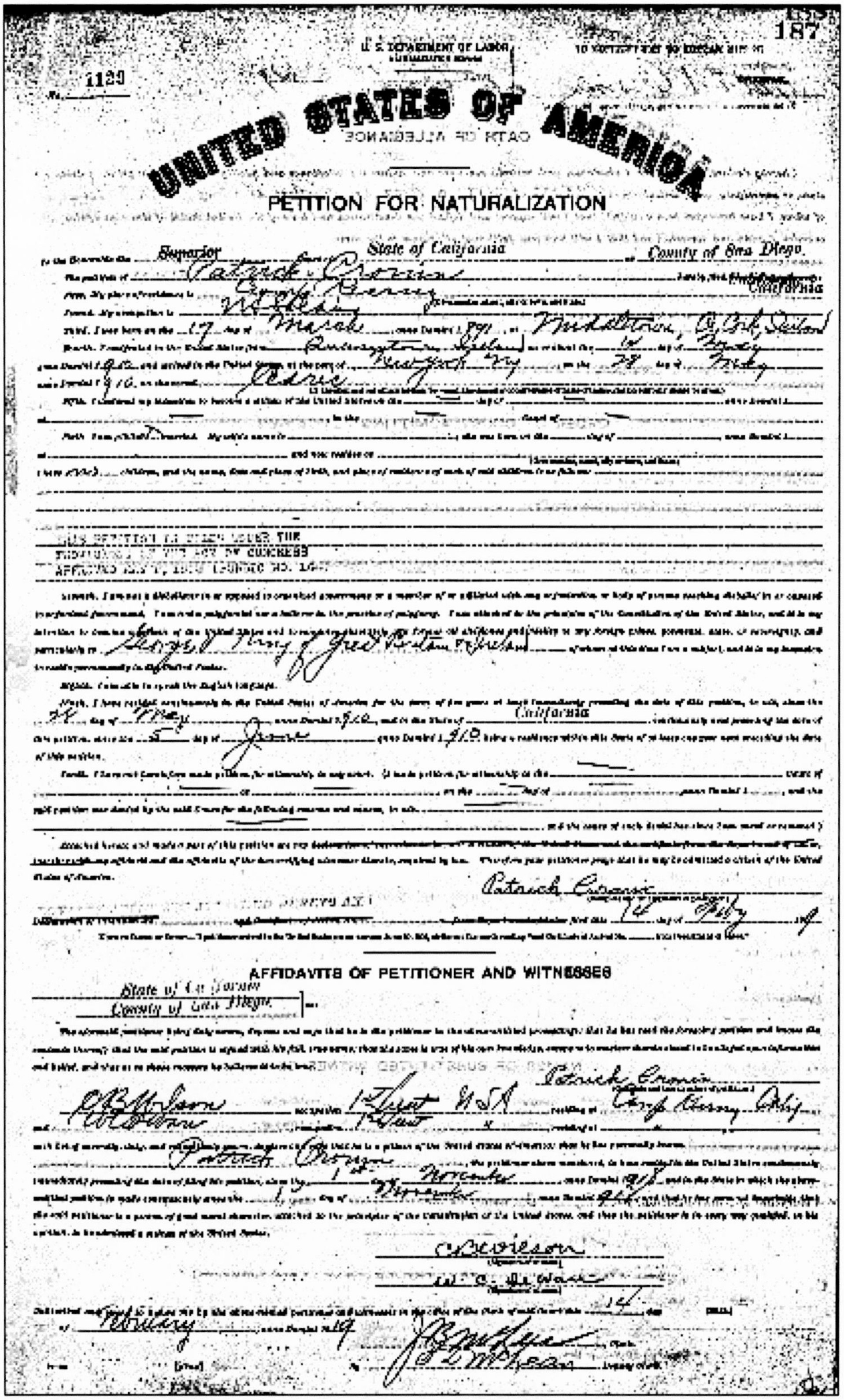
1187

U. S. DEPARTMENT OF LABOR

No. 1129

UNITED STATES OF AMERICA

PETITION FOR NATURALIZATION

Superior State of California County of San Diego

AFFIDAVITS OF PETITIONER AND WITNESSES

State of California

County of San Diego

Figure 51: Petition for Naturalization by Patrick Cronin. He was born 17 March 1891 in Middletown, County Cork, Ireland, according to this document finalized on 14 February 1919. It also conveys that Patrick arrived in the United States aboard the vessel Cedric on 28 May 1910. (Image courtesy of National Archives and Records Administration.)

the courts. After 1906, naturalization records may contain the following:

- Birth date and place of birth
- Marital status
- Spouse and children
- Birth dates and birthplaces for spouse and children
- Port of arrival
- Date of arrival
- Vessel of arrival
- Occupation
- Physical description
- Marriage date
- Age
- Residence
- Last foreign address

Of course, information asked was dependent upon the laws and years, but the above were possible questions.

Many of the post-1906 naturalization forms are being digitized through Ancestry.com and FamilySearch.org. Be aware that with any indexing of these records, what is indexed and what the actual records state may be quite different. For instance, did the indexers extract the birthplaces in Ireland, which are on the forms, or just Ireland? An index search can be the beginning and not the end of the investigation process.

Birthplaces on the post-1906 fill-in-the-blank forms vary in information; however, each consistently gives more than merely Ireland as a place of origin. Also, the indexes for Ancestry.com and FamilySearch.org may not be alike for the same records.

Chapter Twelve

Newspapers and Obituaries

Newspapers, a rich resource for any family historian, are being digitized in unimaginable quantities of pages by several commercial websites and to the extent that some have calculators displaying how many pages have been added daily. The major commercial ones, Genealogybank.com, Newspaperarchive.com, and Newspapers.com, have OCR technology for scanning the papers for keywords, although they are not indexes created under human supervision. They can be cumbersome to search because they either do not always detect words or disclose too many items to read in any reasonable amount of time. Yet, the information they can produce is unparalleled.

Because quite a few websites are available, some with the same newspapers, keywords not picked up on one website may be on another through an identical search. Sometimes, the quality of the digitized newspapers explains the difference, especially if images are faded or smudged. All the commercial websites are constantly adding new material, and so reviewing them periodically is wise.

Websites such as the Library of Congress's "National Digital Newspaper Program" at Loc.gov/ndnp and "Chronicling America" at Chroniclingamerica.loc.gov are preserving the nation's newspaper heritage. Many state, historical, and genealogical societies also have programs that digitize and host various collections, and some public libraries with scanning technology digitize newspapers from their areas. To locate regional or state links, consult the USGenWeb.org for the state or simply search the Internet with a combination of words such as "Alabama newspaper database" or "Nebraska historic newspapers online."

Problems can occur when consulting an inventory of the commercial websites. A community never having a newspaper or its not being online is frustrating. In such a circumstance, efforts need to be expanded. If an ancestor had a farm in rural America, the main newspaper was probably in the county seat or in a nearby large city. A general search of the state may reveal that a birth, marriage, death, or some other article was published miles from where an ancestor lived.

A crime, especially a gruesome homicide, can be expected to be in several papers and even syndicated nationwide. If there

OBITUARY.

Daniel Toomey of Dunkirk, a Former Employee of the Erie Road.

DUNKIRK, Dec. 19. — [*Special.*] — Daniel Toomey died at his home on Robin Street this morning, aged 80 years.

The deceased was born in Brandon, County of Cork, Ireland, and came to this country in 1849. He had been in the employ of the Erie railway company since that date until five yeas ago. While in Ireland he married Miss Catherine Buckley, who died in Dunkirk in 1861. In 1864 he married Mrs. Mary Murphy, who survives him. Three children by his first marriage are living: Miss Nora Toomey, Daniel F. Toomey, and Michael P. Toomey. He also leaves one daughter by his second marriage, Miss Lizzie Toomey. Mr. Toomey was the fifth of a family of 10 brothers and three sisters, only three of whom are now living: Capt. William Toomey, Erie, Pa.; Thomas Toomey, foreman of the Erie freight house, Dunkirk, and Mrs. Jeremiah Long, whose husband is yardmaster of the Erie at Dunkirk. The funeral will be held Wednesday at 8:30 A. M. at the house and at St. Mary's Church at 9 o'clock.

Mrs. George M. Abell is in Chicago, the guest of her sister-in-law, Mrs. Blanchard.

Figure 52: Obituary of Daniel Toomey of Dunkirk, New York, published 20 December 1892. It describes his birth in Brandon [Bandon], County Cork, Ireland, his immigration to the United States in 1849, his marriage to two women (the first while still in Ireland), and his death on 19 December 1892. Additionally, a host of descendants were presented. (Image courtesy of Buffalo Courier.)

and unexpected results. Previous marriages, divorces, anniversaries, criminal acts, court cases, visits from out-of-town relatives, social engagements, disputes, and just about anything else about ancestors can appear in newspaper articles. In smaller towns, where any news was interesting, the "gossip columns" can be a boon for the family historian. People came and went. Any visits by out-of-town relatives and locals traveling for vacations or funerals were newsworthy in American small towns. These columns have personal information that could have been unfamiliar previously, such as divorce cases or a daughter no one knew existed until she visited her parents. The amount of detail is entertaining and stunning!

was a murder in the family, do a nationwide search in the databases for another newspaper carrying the story, which will replace the missing local newspaper not online.

Strangely enough, some of the best discoveries are the ones found by trial and error. Occasionally, simply the name of an ancestor in the search engine in one of the newspaper databases for a city for an exact time frame can yield fascinating

The Obituary

Most people are seeking a newspaper obituary or a death notice, which can be detailed or confined to a few lines. Even though death notices are one or two lines, they can be enlightening. Where the funerals were being held, the officiating ministers' names, and the cemeteries can be in the notices. Obituaries may or may not provide more information. Newspapers from the same city might have published two versions of an obituary on the same or different days.

Obituaries just as often relay where someone was born as they do not. Regardless, presented in obituaries can be previous marriages, parents' names, birthplaces, children (living and deceased), the churches or parishes of attendance, and society memberships, all of which are avenues to new records for research. One of the most worthwhile pieces of information could be the names and residences of the siblings of the deceased.

Siblings' names are indispensable when the obituary or any other record does not disclose where the deceased was born in Ireland. Research should then be diverted to the siblings. A typical obituary states where the siblings reside, opening many possibilities from which to continue the investigation. Also, if the children of the deceased have scattered, the obituary usually notes where they are living. Even if the children or the siblings of the deceased were born in the United States, their parents' birthplaces in Ireland should be on their death certificates.

A name can be so ordinary that finding an obituary is almost impossible, especially when the date of death is unknown. For example, if the person with a common name was alive in New Orleans in the 1880 census but dead by 1900, 20 years need to be examined for him or her. It may be necessary to take what is known, such as Mary, the widow of Thomas Cullen in Baltimore, and look for that information in the 1880 to 1900 city directories. The database "U.S. City Directories, 1822-1995" on Ancestry.com allows a keyword search, such as an address or in this case, the second name of Thomas that designates when Mary first appeared as a widow instead of the wife of Thomas. With that one- or two-year range, the death certificate indexes can be read to further restrict the death to a day, month, and year, after which the newspaper databases can be explored for either an obituary or a death notice.

Want Ads Published in Newspapers

One aspect of Irish culture that fascinates family historians is the "want ads" in newspapers to find long-lost relatives and friends. While the idea of a "want ad" is not uniquely Irish, it did assume its own significance among the Irish. The *Boston Pilot*, a Jesuit newspaper, had such wide coverage that an advertisement increased the chances of finding lost people. While it might be expected that only Catholics placed ads, former Catholics also did so. Therefore, if an Irish Catholic ancestor became a Methodist, do not assume he or she did not advertise for a missing person or that someone might not have been looking for him or her.

The newspaper ads have been made into the Ancestry.com database "Searching for Missing Friends: Irish Immigrant Advertisements Placed in 'The Boston Pilot,' 1831-1920." The original source is the digitized books by the same name by Ruth-Ann Harris, Donald M. Jacobs, and B. Emer O'Keeffe, published by the New England Historic Genealogical Society in 1989. They are an impressive set that attempt to clarify confusing parts of ads through research and are exceptionally helpful when the ads have the names of towns in Ireland but not the counties. Typical ads from these books are similar to the ones for Edward Tierney and Thomas Foley published in the 4 January 1851 edition:

> *Of EDWARD TIERNEY, native of Newtown, parish of Burriscarra, co. Mayo, who landed in Boston in the Spring of 1848. He left Boston in May, 1849, for Vermont in company with Martin Foy and Patrick Coulter, and not heard from since. Any information respecting him will be thankfully received by his brother, THOMAS TIERNEY, Hopkinton, Massachusetts.*

> *OF THOMAS FOLEY, aged 26 years, a native of parish of Portlaw, co. Waterford. He has not been heard from since October 11th, 1848; he was then in Rockingham, Vermont. Any information respecting him will be thankfully received by his brother, EDMOND FOLEY, Meckanickville, Saratoga County, N.Y., care of Mr. Michael Butler.*

Edward Tierney's town and parish in County Mayo were specified along with the name of his brother Thomas Tierney. Their ages were not reported. If the parish registers go back far enough and are reasonably complete, the Irish Catholic indexes, such as those on Ancestry.com, Findmypast.com, and RootsIreland.ie, should solve the immigrant origins' question. If not, other clues are available,

as in this one ad. For example, Edward was travelling with, or at least associated with, Martin Foy and Patrick Coulter. Were they all from the same place in Ireland? What was going on in Vermont in 1849 that attracted three young Irish men? Both questions are logical. Tracing the brother Thomas in Hopkinton, Massachusetts, also is a valid strategy.

Thomas Foley's age was given in 1851 as 26, or born in 1825, in presumably Portlaw Parish, County Waterford. His port of arrival or immigration date was not listed, but his destination of Rockingham, Vermont, is good evidence. What drew him there? The assumption is a job, and he had to have learned about the job from someone, perhaps a friend. If he heard about it from a relative, reasonably it was his brother Edmond Foley who contacted the relative, who was perhaps a friend from the home parish in Waterford. With the two names and Thomas's age, the family should be found in the parish register indexes online. If not, research should proceed to the brother Edmond in *Meckanickville*, Saratoga County, New York.

Direct finds such as these are not the only use for this invaluable database. When the person is found, numerous research sources are disclosed. When the ancestor is not listed, though, delving deeper into the database itself is necessary. Among the strategies that can be employed are:

Place Names. If it is not known where a person was from in Ireland, concentrate a search on where he or she settled. The Boston Pilot is applicable to all North

256   *Missing Friends*

OF FRANCIS HYNES, (or Haynes), son to the late Mr William Hynes, farmer, of Ballyeddy, Ballinhassig, near the city of Cork, Ireland; when last heard from was living in Sherbrook, Montreal, Lower Canada, about nine years ago, and was at that time preparing to leave for some part of the United States. If this comes to his notice, he is earnestly requested (as he will hear of something to his advantage) to write at once, or any information given about his whereabouts will be most thankfully received by Mr Francis J Grant, Post-office, Lafayette, Indiana.

OF JAMES and DAVID POWER, formerly of Ballyhall, county Kilkenny. James lived in St Louis, Missouri, and David when last heard from was known to be in New Orleans, and between New Orleans and St Louis or New York. Any information of them, or any of James's three sons, will be thankfully received by their brother, John Power, Ludlow, Vermont, who lately came to this country.
 - St Louis and New Orleans papers please copy.
(ad. of 12/5/63 changes: "of Ballyhale, county Kilkenny")

OF JAMES SHEAHEN, native of Guarrane, parish of Newcastle West, county Limerick; when last heard from, about six years ago, he was in Chicago, Illinois. Any information concerning him will be thankfully received by his daughter, Catherine Sheahen, 425 Washington street, East Louisville, Kentucky.

OF JAMES CRIMONS, native of Port William, of the parish of Rathkeale, county Limerick, Ireland; when last heard from, eight years ago, was in Chicago, Illinois. Any information of him will be thankfully received by his sister, Mrs Mary McNamara, corner of 4 1/2 and Maryland Avenue, Washington, DC.

OF PATRICK, Edward and Bridget FITZGERALD, of the parish of Pallasgrene, county Limerick; the last heard of Patrick and Edward, they were in the Barrens, ten miles of Elgin, Cain county, Illinois; the last heard of Bridget she was in Westport, Kennent (or Kentucky), 12 years ago. Any information will be thankfully received by James Fitzgerald, West Charleston, Marion county, Ohio.
(ad. of 12/12/63 changes: "Miami county, Ohio.")

OF MICHAEL and MARY MURRAY, (otherwise Deaveny), of the parish of Kilteely, county Limerick; when last heard from, was in Dubora [sic], Iowa. Any information concerning them will be thankfully received by addressing Bridget Sheahen, care of Wm Collins, on H street, between 6th and 7th streets, Island, Washington, D C.
 - Iowa papers please copy.

Figure 53: A page from the collections of "Missing Friends" in the Boston Pilot. (Image courtesy of Searching for Missing Friends: Irish Advertisements Placed in "The Boston Pilot," 1831-1920, *by Ruth-Ann Harris, et. al. 1989)*

American research. Use the search feature to identify all Irish who settled in a locality. Who was looking for people who resided in a particular state or city or with that surname? Once the results are studied, determine if a pattern emerges. For example, are most of the ads seeking people from County Tipperary? If so, the place in Ireland where the ancestor was from may have been stumbled upon.

This strategy can be used in reverse when the county in Ireland is known but a parish is not. Who from that county placed ads for people living where the ancestor settled? Does a pattern appear?

Searching geographically works best for areas other than urban ones.

Associate Names. Because the godparents at children's christenings were always assumed to have been friends and family of the parents, they might have known the ancestors in Ireland before immigrating. Using this logic, run the names of the godparents as found in the immigrant parish through the *Boston Pilot* databases for a pattern. Who is looking for them, or are they looking for someone?

With these extra strategies, the *Boston Pilot* database may divulge where the ancestors originated even if the ancestor is not listed. The tactics are not straightforward, but they can work.

As important as the *Boston Pilot* is, keep in mind it is not the only newspaper that accepted want ads. The ads in the *Irish-American* were reprinted for a book, now an Ancestry.com database "Irish Relatives and Friends," by Laura Murphy DeGrazia, *Irish Relative and Friends: From "Information Wanted" Ads in the Irish-American, 1850-1871* (Baltimore, Maryland: Genealogical Publishing Co., 2001). This newspaper was aimed at the Irish immigrant community. While not nearly as widely distributed as the *Boston Pilot*, it is a major resource for the New York City area. The Ancestry.com search capability is not as sophisticated as that of the *Boston Pilot* database. In the latter, the scanned images of the digitized book with a keyword or surname search are presented. If the location is not found, try the keyword.

Even as wonderful as these two databases are, they are still not the only sources. The want ads for people were placed in city newspapers everywhere. With the large commercial newspaper databases, it is now possible to find the notices. Keywords along with the name of the person can be "wanted Ireland" or similar ones. Although "wanted" is typical for any want ad, combining it with "Ireland" does reduce the number of results.

Newspapers and the Irish Repeal Societies

It is not uncommon for newspapers to have articles featuring the meetings of various societies. Most were simply reporting on the social activities being discussed or promoted in meetings, but others listed members and their birthplaces, as did the Irish Repeal Societies. For many Irish, leaving Ireland behind emotionally was not an option. They continued to be interested and invested in what was going on in the old country. For many immigrant-ethnic groups as well as for many people born in Ireland, becoming American far outweighed politics back home. However, it was not a unanimous feeling among the Irish, which opens research possibilities that might not be possible for another ethnic group. The Irish Repeal Societies are the perfect example of this principle.

The concept of the Repeal Society dates to the Act of Union in 1801 that united Great Britain and Ireland as the United Kingdom. This union was not universally accepted by those in Ireland and those who had already immigrated, eventually leading to organized societies to continue to contest it. The common names for this opposition movement were "repeal societies" or "Friends of Ireland," both terms denoting this organization of like-minded political thinkers. While officially organized in 1840 in North America, the Repeal Society was particularly active from 1841 to 1845 and had died out by the late 1840s. Although most belonging to the society were Catholics, some were Protestants.

The Repeal Societies were also active in Canada. Their activities were carried in American newspapers. Religious newspapers, such as the *Boston Pilot* (a Jesuit newspaper), and city newspapers, such as the *Missouri Republican,* reported on the meetings. The value of published articles about these societies is immense because they name those in attendance and often where they were born in Ireland.

The columns have not escaped the attention of genealogists. For example, Marie E. Daly's table "Repeal Society Meeting Reports in which members' origins are listed in the *Boston Pilot,* January 1842-December 1845" lists the issues of the *Boston Pilot* in which these types of articles appeared. Her table is in "Sources of Irish-American Genealogy in New England" in *The Irish in New England* (Boston, Massachusetts: New England Historic Genealogical Society, 1985), pp. 19-21, and has been reprinted in Kyle J. Betit's "Irish Repeal Societies in North America" in *The Irish at Home and Abroad,* Vol. 5, No. 1 (1st Quarter 1998),

pp. 23-25. In the *Boston Pilot,* meetings in a variety of locations were reported. They can be found on the following page.

If an ancestor lived in one of these areas from 1842 to 1845, he or she might have supported a local Friends of Ireland society, and the *Boston Pilot* is a logical newspaper to consult for Irish origins. The newspaper is digitized from 1838 to 1857 on the website of the Boston College Libraries, Newspapers.bc.edu. A word of caution is warranted. Even though this is an extensive reporting, it did not include all places or meetings of these societies.

Some of the newspaper articles from the city papers have been extracted and published in genealogical society journals or online. One example is "Repeal Association of the Friends of Ireland, 1842" from the St. Louis Genealogical Society website Stlgs.org. The society enhanced the original article, which named 172 individuals in the *Missouri Republican* of 10 May 1842, with information from the 1850 St. Louis census, St. Louis Marriage Index, and the 1840/41 city directory.

With the advent of the commercial newspaper websites, finding new societies should be easier than ever before. A search must be limited to, for instance, 1840 to 1850, with terms "repeal society" or "Friends of Ireland" to further confine articles to a specific city newspaper.

One way to access already extracted and published newspaper materials that are locked away in genealogical journals is through the Periodical Source Index (PerSI). This is the creation of the Allen County Public Library in Fort Wayne, Indiana, which houses the largest collection of genealogical periodicals in the world. The PerSI database inventories article titles and then indexes them by subject, and it is practically the only way to access obscure articles published worldwide. The searchable database is on Findmypast.com, and keywords "repeal society," "repeal societies," or "Friends of Ireland" will sort through the millions of entries.

Newspapers are known for publishing birthplaces in Ireland, but like any other source, sometimes they do not. Often, the articles consist of the names of those attending social events, including unknown relatives, or the amounts they contributed to causes. Consequently, even if the articles do not have birthplaces, they are quite serviceable because the number of potential family members to study is increased. For those whose birthplaces were recorded, determine whether they indicate a chain migration into a community from a particular county in Ireland, a valuable research prospect.

Irish Repeal Societies in North America

State/Province	Town
Connecticut	Hartford, Hitchcockville, Middleton, New Haven, Stonington, Waterbury
Louisiana	New Orleans
Maine	Bangor, Portland
Maryland	Baltimore
Massachusetts	Billerica, Boston, Boston (East), Boston (South), Boston (*USS Ohio*), Bridgewater (North), Brighton, Cabotsville, Cambridge (East), Charlestown, Chelsea, Danvers, Dorchester & Milton, Fall River, Hinsdale, Lowell, New Bedford, Northampton, Norton, Pittsfield, Quincy, Randolph, Roxbury, Salem, Sandwich, Saxonville, Springfield, Southbridge, Stockbridge, Taunton, Waltham, Westfield, Worcester
Missouri	St. Louis
New Brunswick	St. John, St. Stephen
New Hampshire	Dove
Rhode Island	Cranston, Newport, Pawtucket, Providence, Warwick, Woonsocket & Waterford
Vermont	Northfield, St. Albans
Virginia	Harper's Ferry

Chapter Thirteen

Published Biographical Books and Who's Who

Many published books are presented as "who's who" or are labeled as such. They range from multi-volume works to a dedicated appendix in a convention report. These sources are worth considering in the quest for immigrant origins. Although many of the subjects of biographies were prominent people, do not assume they all were. The matters in which the people might have been involved were political, religious, or occupational. However, most researchers are already acquainted with the biographical materials in old county histories, which can be exceptional in their detail. These local publications feature farmers, business people, church workers, and anyone else who wanted a biography and perhaps a portrait and could afford the fee.

Biographical sketches are almost limitless and are being digitized on several websites. Renowned ones are Archive.org and HathiTrust.org. Another program is currently being undertaken by FamilySearch.org under the "Books" category to partner with major repositories to digitize copyrighted material. Old county histories themselves, whether digitized or not, can be found at the Family History Library, at state archives, local public libraries, and, of course, at the Library of Congress. Any large library with a dedicated genealogy section knows the value of the county histories. It is not uncommon for the biographical material from these works to be extracted and placed online, such as on USGenWeb.org, or on state and county sites.

Although many types of publications function as a who's who for an area, profession, or organization, the ones offered as examples include only:

- Location-specific biographies
- Political biographies
- Women's biographies

Biographies and county histories are not books of the past. During the 1976 Bicentennial period, scores were published, usually focused on counties. The emphasis in this chapter is the late nineteenth and early twentieth centuries' creations because these were often written when the subjects of the biographies were still living. These are no longer protected by copyright and are constantly appearing on various websites in search-able digital formats.

Location-Specific Biographies

Many biographical works were published by states or counties. The attention of state books was most likely on promi-nent members of the business, legal, re-ligious, or political arenas. One example from the Minnesota volume of the na-tionally produced series *Biographical Dictionary and Portrait Gallery of Emi-nent and Self-Made Men* (New York and Chicago: American Biographical Publish-ing Company, 1879) is for Michael Doran, a state senator from Le Sueur County:

> MICHAEL DORAN, state senator from Le Sueur county, and one of the most successful business men in the county, was the son of James Doran and Bridget McGuire, and was born in the county of Meath, Ireland, on the 1st November 1829. He received very little education before com-ing to this country; left his native land in 1850, landed in New York city, and after remaining in the Empire State about one year, working on a farm, he removed to Norwalk, Ohio. He attended a country school about two years while in Huron county, farmed some, and subsequently kept a grocery store.

> In 1856 Mr. Doran pushed west-ward once more, crossing the Mississippi river, settling in Le Sueur, and engaged in tilling land. Four years afterward he

was elected county treasurer, and by repeated re-elections held that office eight years, deal-ing, meanwhile, quite success-fully, in real estate, and estab-lishing a reputation for shrewd business management, as well as for official faithfulness.

Since 1870 Mr. Doran has been in the banking business, at first in partnership with the late George D. Snow, and since the 1st of August, 1878, with Edson R. Smith. The Bank of Le Sueur, under their management, is a prosperous institution. They also own the steam flouring mill and the elevator at Le Sueur.

Mr. Doran has three farms under improvement, and about two thousand acres of wild, all in Le Sueur county. Besides his build-ings, etc., in the village of Le Sueur, he has property in and near Saint Paul, and is a marked example of energy well ex-pended.

Mr. Doran was a member of the state senate in 1872, 1873, 1874, 1875, and again in 1877 and 1878, and in the last-named year was chairman of the special com-mittee appointed to investigate the management of the Institu-tion for the Insane, at Saint Peter.

He is a life-long democrat, and a very influential man in his part.

In 1864 and 1876 he was a delegate to the national democratic convention which nominated General George B. McClennan and Samuel J. Tilden for the Presidency, and in the autumn of 1875 was nominated by his party as a candidate for state auditor, but declined to run.

Senator Doran has had two wives. The first was Miss Ellen Brady, of Norwalk, Ohio; married in May, 1855. She died on the 11th of March 1863, leaving five children, four of them yet living. His present wife was Miss Catherine J. Grady, of Le Sueur; chosen on the 10th of February, 1864. He has seven children by her. (pp. 18-19).

A few points stand out about Michael Doran that summarize how self-made men were perceived. First, he was one of the most successful businessmen of Le Sueur County; second, he received very little education in Ireland; and third, he "is a marked example of energy well expended."

Perhaps most revealing is that only one paragraph was dedicated to his family, and at that, his second wife, Catherine J. Grady, was "chosen on the 10th of February, 1864." She was not courted or married, but chosen. While the assumption is the family was Catholic, that was not mentioned, but his association with the Democratic Party was. Sometimes, what

is not in these sketches can be just as noteworthy as what is.

Reasonably, the descendants of Michael Doran who are conducting family research already know from any number of sources where he was from in County Meath, Ireland. However, to reiterate a more holistic approach, Michael must have had siblings who attained no wealth or eminence. Upon immigrating, they might have experienced simple lives, never appearing in biographies, obituaries, or any other records noting birthplaces. It may be the information is preserved only within the profile of their sibling Michael Doran.

The sketches for the common persons were published in county or regional works for small fees. One, from the 1899 work *Memorial and Biographical Record and Illustrated Compendium of Biography...Including Biographical Sketches of Hundreds of Prominent Old Settlers and Representative Citizens of Butler, Polk, Seward, York and Fillmore Counties, Nebraska* (Chicago, Illinois: Geo. A. Ogle & Co., 1899), is for Joseph Neville of York County, Nebraska:

JOSEPH NEVILLE – Among the sturdy, energetic and successful farmers of York county, who thoroughly understand the vocation which they follow, and are consequently enabled to carry on their calling with profit to themselves, is the subject of this sketch. He is actively engaged in agricultural pursuits on section

Her parents, David and Mary (Comer) Denney, are natives of Ohio and Indiana, respectively, and in 1851 emigrated to Iowa, where they still continue to reside. The children born to Mr. and Mrs. Price are as follows: Nettie A., deceased; Clyde B., Harry C., Iva L., Homer O. and Rolland D. The mother and children are connected with the Methodist Protestant church, and the family is one of social prominence in the community. Politically Mr. Price is a stalwart Republican, and socially is a worth member of the Modern Woodmen of America, and the Modern Brotherhood of America.

JOSEPH NEVILLE.—Among the sturdy, energetic and successful farmers of York county, who thoroughly understand the vocation which they follow, and are consequently enabled to carry on their calling with profit to themselves, is the subject of this sketch. He is actively engaged in agricultural pursuits on section 35, Leroy township, where he owns a fine farm of one hundred and sixty acres.

Mr. Neville is a native of the Emerald Island, born May 4, 1847, in Kings county, Ireland, and in 1855 was brought to America by his parents, Abraham and Margaret (Maloy) Neville, who first settled in Albany, New York, but a few years later removed to Quebec, Canada, where the father died. The mother is still living and now makes her home in York county, Nebraska.

Coming to this country at the age of eight years, Joseph Neville grew to manhood on this side of the Atlantic, and received a common school education, as he says "very common at that." He accompanied his parents on their removal to Canada, but when about twenty-two years of age he returned to the United States, and lived for a time in Vermont. Subsequently for several years he resided in Michigan, where he engaged in farming, teaming and lumbering. It was in March, 1875, that he arrived in Nebraska and bought one hundred and sixty acres of railroad land in York county, on which he still resides. To the cultivation and improvement of the wild tract he at once turned his attention, erecting thereon a small frame house with a large sod addition, and also a sod stable. As the years have passed he has placed acre after acre under the plow, has built a more comfortable and modern residence, good barns and other outbuildings, and now has one of the most desirable farms of its size in the township. As a result of hard work, economy and good management he has secured a comfortable competence which ranks him among the well-to-do citizens of the locality.

November 25, 1879, was celebrated the marriage of Mr. Neville and Miss Elizabeth Foley, who was born in Peoria, Illinois, a daughter of John and Ellen (Donevan) Foley, natives of Ireland. One daughter, Mary, graces this union. The family are communicants of the Catholic church at York, and in the social circles of their community occupy an enviable position. Mr. Neville casts his ballot with the Democracy, and has acceptably served his fellow citizens in the capacity of town treasurer.

LIEUT. JOSEPH MILLER, whose home is on section 32, township 15, range 2, Platte precinct, is one of the prominent and representative citizens of Polk county, who as a Union soldier during the dark days of the Rebellion made for himself a war record both honorable and glorious. He was born July 29, 1842, in Fayette county, Pennsylvania, a son of Peter and Nancy (Bradman) Miller, also natives of the Keystone state, and the former of Quaker stock. The father died in 18—, the mother in 1875. Both were lifelong members of the Methodist church, took an active part in its work,

Figure 54: Biographical sketch of Joseph Neville of York County, Nebraska, as found in "Memorial and Biographical Record and Illustrated Compendium of Biography…Including Biographical Sketches of Hundreds of Prominent Old Settlers and Representative Citizens of Butler, Polk, Seward, York and Fillmore Counties, Nebraska…" by G.A. Ogle & Co., Chicago, 1899.

35, Leroy township, where he owns a fine farm of one hundred and sixty acres.

Mr. Neville is a native of the Emerald Island, born May 4, 1847, in Kings county, Ireland, and in 1855 was brought to America by his parents, Abraham and Margaret (Maloy) Neville, who first settled in Albany, New York, but a few years later removed to Quebec, Canada, where the father died. The mother is still living and now makes her home in York county, Nebraska.

Coming to this country at the age of eight years, Joseph Neville grew to manhood on this side of the Atlantic, and received a common school education, as he says "very common at that." He accompanied his parents on their removal to Canada, but when about twenty-two years of age he returned to the United States, and lived for a time in Vermont. Subsequently for several years he resided in Michigan, where he engaged in farming, teaming and lumbering. It was in March, 1875, that he arrived in Nebraska and bought one hundred and sixty acres of railroad land in York county, on which he still resides. To the cultivation and improvement of the wild tract he at once turned his attention, erecting thereon a small frame house with a large

sod addition, and also a sod stable. As the years have passed he has placed acre after acre under the plow, has built a more comfortable and modern residence, good barns and other outbuildings, and now has one of the most desirable farms of its size in the township. As a result of hard work, economy and good management he has secured a comfortable competence which ranks him among the well-to-do citizens of the locality.

November 25, 1879, was celebrated the marriage of Mr. Neville and Miss Elizabeth Foley, who was born in Peoria, Illinois, a daughter of John and Ellen (Donevan) Foley, natives of Ireland. One daughter, Mary, graces this union. The family are communicants of the Catholic church at York, and in the social circles of their community occupy an enviable position. Mr. Neville casts his ballot with the Democracy, and has acceptably served his fellow citizens in the capacity of town treasurer (p. 432).

Most short biographies published on the county level followed the same format as this regional one for Joseph Neville, and personal details can be astounding.

Remember that biographical sketches about rural residents may contain the only evidence of places of births in

Ireland. Joseph Neville's was Kings County, Ireland (modern County Offaly). Moreover, what is not in the synopsis is significant. The assumption is that he had siblings who also might have emigrated from Quebec to Nebraska at some point because his mother, who was living in 1899, had relocated to York County. With whom did she move, since Joseph had been in Nebraska since 1875? This is where a second search of the same book or others specifically dedicated to York County may be warranted. A key word search of any digitized online book can be undertaken for "Kings County," "Neville," "Albany, New York," and "Quebec," or narrow it to where Joseph was living in "Leroy township." Family members may still be in Quebec, or they might have migrated. Once the Neville family is reconstructed with American records, it can be compared with the Catholic records of County Offaly.

Political Biographies

Books specific to politics were written. They can be biographical in nature even if the information mainly is about the subjects' involvement with politics.

To develop an immigration strategy, first identify the party with which an ancestor was associated during his or her life. For example, were ancestors Democrat, Independent, Prohibition, Republican, or Socialist? Some works were published on a national or even international basis (as with the Socialist Party), whereas others were limited to states. They can be strictly biographical or attached to an event, such as a state Constitutional Convention. Regardless, they can hold a wealth of personal details.

Political parties historically were not the same as they are today. In past years, the Republican Party was viewed as progressive (like "the party of Lincoln") and the Democrats, conservatives (such as segregationists). The Socialist Party was not the pariah it has been touted to be since the Cold War. To complicate this, most people today are unaware that there was a Prohibition Party with a distinct platform and conventions. To understand an ancestor and identify the published works in which he or she might have been documented, judgment must be suspended and historical context considered, usually explaining why people did what they did.

An example of what the modern American may not expect to find in research is Socialism. In the early twentieth century, Socialism was an active and viable political party in the United States. It declined in the 1930s. All one has to do is look at the California Great Voter Registers for political parties, where a voter could have been registered as an "S" for Socialist as easily as he could have been for another party. A fascinating work is the 1913 directory *Who's Who in Socialist America* (Girard, Kansas: Arsenel of Facts, 1913) with biographical sketches of Socialists and histories of their associations with the party. Most importantly, it demonstrates the odd and forgotten kinds of published material now available online. Two examples from HathiTrust.org are for Matthew Semple and Michael Sullivan:

SEMPLE, Matthew, paper hanger and decorator, Ottawa, Kan. Born, Larne, Ireland, Oct. 14, 1848; formerly greenbacker; converted to Socialism through the oppression of the Irish landlordism, 1880; joined Socialist party at St. Joseph, Mo., May, 1880; helped organize local at Princeton, Kan.; distributed many pieces of Socialist literature, walking many miles to do so (p. 86).

SULLIVAN, Michael, retired policeman, Detroit, Mich. Born, Ireland, 1832; formerly democrat; converted to Socialism through

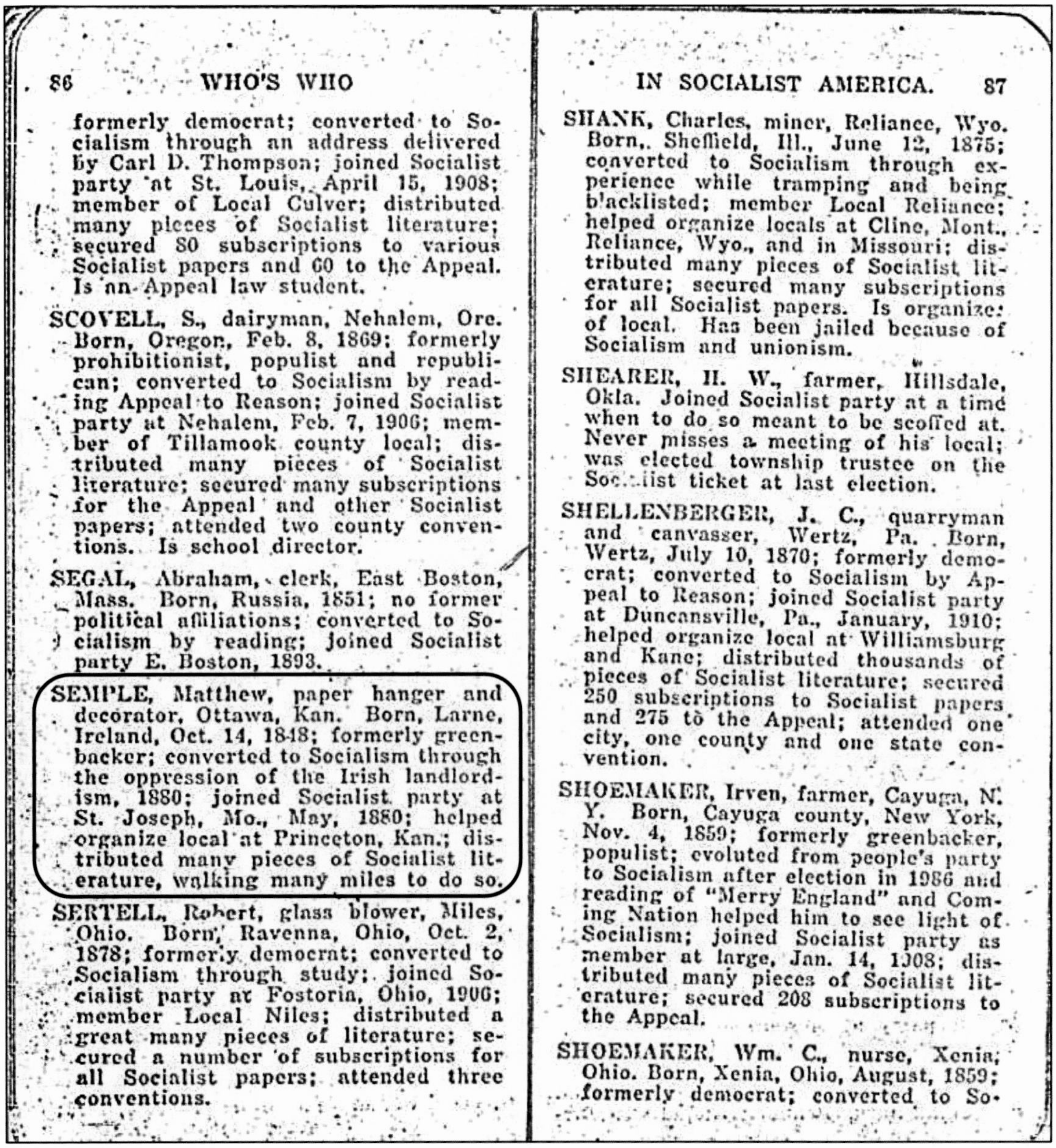

86 WHO'S WHO

formerly democrat; converted to Socialism through an address delivered by Carl D. Thompson; joined Socialist party at St. Louis, April 15, 1908; member of Local Culver; distributed many pieces of Socialist literature; secured 80 subscriptions to various Socialist papers and 60 to the Appeal. Is an Appeal law student.

SCOVELL, S., dairyman, Nehalem, Ore. Born, Oregon, Feb. 8, 1869; formerly prohibitionist, populist and republican; converted to Socialism by reading Appeal to Reason; joined Socialist party at Nehalem, Feb. 7, 1906; member of Tillamook county local; distributed many pieces of Socialist literature; secured many subscriptions for the Appeal and other Socialist papers; attended two county conventions. Is school director.

SEGAL, Abraham, clerk, East Boston, Mass. Born, Russia, 1851; no former political affiliations; converted to Socialism by reading; joined Socialist party E. Boston, 1893.

SEMPLE, Matthew, paper hanger and decorator, Ottawa, Kan. Born, Larne, Ireland, Oct. 14, 1848; formerly greenbacker; converted to Socialism through the oppression of the Irish landlordism, 1880; joined Socialist party at St. Joseph, Mo., May, 1880; helped organize local at Princeton, Kan.; distributed many pieces of Socialist literature, walking many miles to do so.

SERTELL, Robert, glass blower, Miles, Ohio. Born, Ravenna, Ohio, Oct. 2, 1878; formerly democrat; converted to Socialism through study; joined Socialist party at Fostoria, Ohio, 1906; member Local Niles; distributed a great many pieces of literature; secured a number of subscriptions for all Socialist papers; attended three conventions.

IN SOCIALIST AMERICA. 87

SHANK, Charles, miner, Reliance, Wyo. Born, Sheffield, Ill., June 12, 1875; converted to Socialism through experience while tramping and being blacklisted; member Local Reliance; helped organize locals at Cline, Mont., Reliance, Wyo., and in Missouri; distributed many pieces of Socialist literature; secured many subscriptions for all Socialist papers. Is organizer of local. Has been jailed because of Socialism and unionism.

SHEARER, H. W., farmer, Hillsdale, Okla. Joined Socialist party at a time when to do so meant to be scoffed at. Never misses a meeting of his local; was elected township trustee on the Socialist ticket at last election.

SHELLENBERGER, J. C., quarryman and canvasser, Wertz, Pa. Born, Wertz, July 10, 1870; formerly democrat; converted to Socialism by Appeal to Reason; joined Socialist party at Duncansville, Pa., January, 1910; helped organize local at Williamsburg and Kane; distributed thousands of pieces of Socialist literature; secured 250 subscriptions to Socialist papers and 275 to the Appeal; attended one city, one county and one state convention.

SHOEMAKER, Irven, farmer, Cayuga, N. Y. Born, Cayuga county, New York, Nov. 4, 1859; formerly greenbacker, populist; evoluted from people's party to Socialism after election in 1986 and reading of "Merry England" and Coming Nation helped him to see light of Socialism; joined Socialist party as member at large, Jan. 14, 1908; distributed many pieces of Socialist literature; secured 208 subscriptions to the Appeal.

SHOEMAKER, Wm. C., nurse, Xenia, Ohio. Born, Xenia, Ohio, August, 1859; formerly democrat; converted to So-

Figure 55: Matthew Semple, as found in "Who's Who in Socialist America," by Arsenel [sic] of Fact, Girard, Kansas, 1913.

the Appeal; joined Socialist party in 1898; distributed hundreds of pieces of Socialist literature and secured many hundred subscriptions for the Appeal and other Socialist papers (p. 95).

In 1913, Michael Semple was living in Ottawa, Franklin County, Kansas. He was born in Larne, County Antrim, Ireland, in what is today Northern Ireland, on 14 October 1848. While solving the immigrant origins' question, his short entry is brimming with additional clues. He was a "greenbacker," a reference to the Greenback Party, which was later known as the Independent Party, the National Independent Party, and the Greenback Labor Party. It was an anti-monopoly American political party whose candidates ran in elections in 1876, 1880, and 1884, when it declined. It was originally an agrarian organization active from 1874 to 1889.

His conversion "to Socialism through the oppression of the Irish landlordism, 1880" is a reference to Irish politics and the Irish National Land League, active during that year. This does not mean he was living in Ireland but, rather, a supporter of the cause to put land in the hands of the tenants. What is stated is that he immigrated before 1880 because he joined the Socialist Party in 1880 in St. Joseph, Missouri. In addition, he was active in organizing socialists in Princeton, Kansas, which is also in Franklin County, where he was living in 1913. Therefore, some extra evidence exists about his migration pattern, political activity, and even Irish politics.

The sketch about Michael Sullivan is more basic and has only Ireland as his birthplace. Additional evidence was given that can assist research. He was a retired policeman in 1913, and it is assumed, although not stated, that he worked in Detroit. That is a good clue. He joined the Socialist Party in 1898, again supposedly in Detroit, after reading the Socialist periodical *Appeal*, for which he seemed to have worked in some capacity. Although his biography is brief, it is useful as a comparison to census reports, citizenship papers, police records, and, of course, various Socialist periodicals.

Another type of convention report was for state conventions, at which time delegates made up of lawmakers, public officials, and judges assembled to work on constitutional matters, for instance, a state holding a Constitutional Convention whereby laws were updated. One example is the 1875 Constitutional Convention, published as *Journal Missouri Constitutional Convention of 1875* (Columbia, Missouri: The State Historical Society of Missouri, 1920), which had profiles of each delegate. One was for Nicholas A. Mortell:

NICHOLAS A. MORTELL (Democrat) was born in the County of Cork, Ireland, in 1843. When nine years old he came to the United States and for three years worked as a newsboy in New York. In 1855 he set out for the West, and located in Alton, Illinois, where he began to learn the trade of a coppersmith.

There he attracted the attention of Col. George B. Ingersoll of Shipman, Illinois, who sent him to St. Paul's College at Palmyra, Missouri. He was graduated from that institution in 1861. For a year following he had charge of the Cathedral school at Alton, Illinois, and then took up the study of law in the office of Judge Krum of St. Louis, and was admitted to the bar. In 1866 he was a delegate to the Great Fenian Convention held in New York. He was a member of the 1871 General Assembly. In the same year he was elected city attorney of St. Louis. He died in St. Louis, March 1, 1876 (p. 96).

The people mentioned in this convention report were well educated and well connected, and so birthplaces might have been preserved in numerous other sources. If researching the sibling or another relative of one of these delegates, the answer to immigrant origins may lie solely with the prominent person and not the farmer sibling. The biographies of the more renowned people are exceptional examples of why researching relatives is essential. A farmer in rural South Dakota might never have had a reason to appear in any biography whatsoever, but his or her attorney brother would have! Remember, all siblings born in Ireland were most likely born in the same place, whether they were common farmers or attorneys.

Women and Biographies

Even though women before 1920 were denied the vote and had enormous social constraints placed upon them, thinking that women were not socially active in any number of causes is a mistake. The chances of finding well-educated women active in the Temperance Society, labor reform, suffrage, charity causes, child-labor issues, and religious movements such as Liberal Protestantism, Spiritualism, Theosophy, New Thought, and Christian Science are quite likely. Educated and progressive women's names may appear in any number of period biographical books, dictionaries, or encyclopedias (cyclopedias). One is the serial *Biographical Cyclopedia of American Women* (New York, New York: The Halvord Publishing Company, Inc., 1924-[-]), which contains life stories running for pages in excruciating detail. This publication alone is filled with Irish-born women and daughters of immigrants.

The key to finding these publications online is the word "women" somewhere in the search. "Women biographies," "women cyclopedia," "women dictionaries," "women temperance," "women teachers," or any other combination should identify what is being digitized on various websites. To further separate these works from those published in Canada or the United Kingdom, add the word American.

The details in female biographies, often extremely personal, are not like those of men. An illustration is from Frances E. Willard and Mary A. Livermore's 1897

Figure 56: Mrs. Myra Clark Gaines, as found in a biographical compilation for women: "American Women: Fifteen Hundred Biographies with over 1,400 Portraits; A Comprehensive Encyclopedia of the Lives and Achievements of American Women During the Nineteenth Century," by Frances E. Willard, published by Mast, Crowell & Kirkpatrick of New York, 1897. See detailed abstract on this page.

GAINES, MRS. MYRA CLARK, heiress, born in New Orleans, La., in 1805, and died in that city, 9th January 1885. She was the daughter of Daniel Clark, a native of Sligo, Ireland. He emigrated from Ireland and settled in New Orleans. In 1796 he inherited a large property from an uncle. He died in New Orleans, 16th August, 1813, and his estate was disposed of under his will dated 20th May, 1811, giving the property to his mother, Mary Clark, then living in Germantown, Pa. Myra Clark was his child by a secret marriage and was reared in a family by the name of Davis. After her marriage in 1832 to W. W. Whitney, of New York City she learned of her true parentage, and tried to regain the estate. Through a long period of litigation, extending over forty-two years, she recovered six million dollars of the thirty-five million, the valuation of the estate. She showed great magnanimity in refusing to dispossess four-hundred families occupying her lands. Mrs. Whitney became a widow and in 1839 was married to Gen. Edmund Pendleton Gaines (p. 309).

work *American Women: Fifteen Hundred Biographies with over 1,400 Portraits*, 2 vols. (New York, Chicago, Springfield, Ohio: Mast, Crowell & Kirkpatrick, 1897) about the life of Mrs. Myra Clark Gaines, a possible illegitimate daughter of Daniel Clark:

The amount of intrigue and suggestion embedded in this one paragraph alone is staggering. The additional paperwork generated over the 42-year litigation of the estate must be mind-boggling. While Myra Clark Gaines (or Myra Davis Gaines) was the daughter of the immigrant from County Sligo, it may be within all the court cases that her father's birthplace was preserved and thus available.

In 1796, when Daniel Clark, the father, was in New Orleans, the city did not belong to the United States but was part of France (1718-1763), of Spain (1763-1802), and of France again (1802-1803). In 1803, it was part of the Louisiana Purchase sold to the United States, which leads to both French and Spanish colonial records in addition to American records. The indication from the sketch is that Daniel Clark and his family went to Pennsylvania first and traveled to New Orleans, where he settled by at least the 1790s. Another assumption is that the family was in Philadelphia because it was a major port and commercial center, as was New Orleans.

Not defined are what a "secret marriage" meant in this summary and how the Davis family was connected to Daniel Clark, if any explanation exists. Was the "secret marriage" a common-law marriage? Who was the Davis family, and was the wife of a Mr. Davis in New Orleans the presumed one-time common-law wife of Daniel Clark? All are points to consider. Even with all the drama, the birthplace of the Clarks in Ireland was County Sligo.

Biographical reports without the glamour can still have amazing details. One

from the 1914-1915 edition of John William Leonard's *Women's Who's Who of America: A Biographical Dictionary of Contemporary Women of the United States and Canada* (New York, New York: The American Commonwealth Company, 1914) is for Margaret Belle Edgar, a Reformed Presbyterian missionary in Latakia, Syria:

> *EDGAR, Margaret Belle, Latakia, Syria, Turkey.*
>
> *Missionary; b. Belfast, Ireland, June 25, 1861; reared at Cincinnati and Rushsylvania, Ohio; ed. Geneva Coll., class of '81. Teacher at Cedarville, Ohio, 1881-83; Bellefontaine, Ohio, 1883-86. Missionary of the Reformed Presbyterian Church at Latakia, Syria, since 1886 (p. 268).*

Margaret's abbreviated biography has enough information to link her to her family. The assumption is that Edgar was her birth name. A profile such as this has enough facts to open Ohio documents as well as Presbyterian ones about her missionary work. Of course, before searching any Irish records, determine if Edgar was Margaret's maiden or married name.

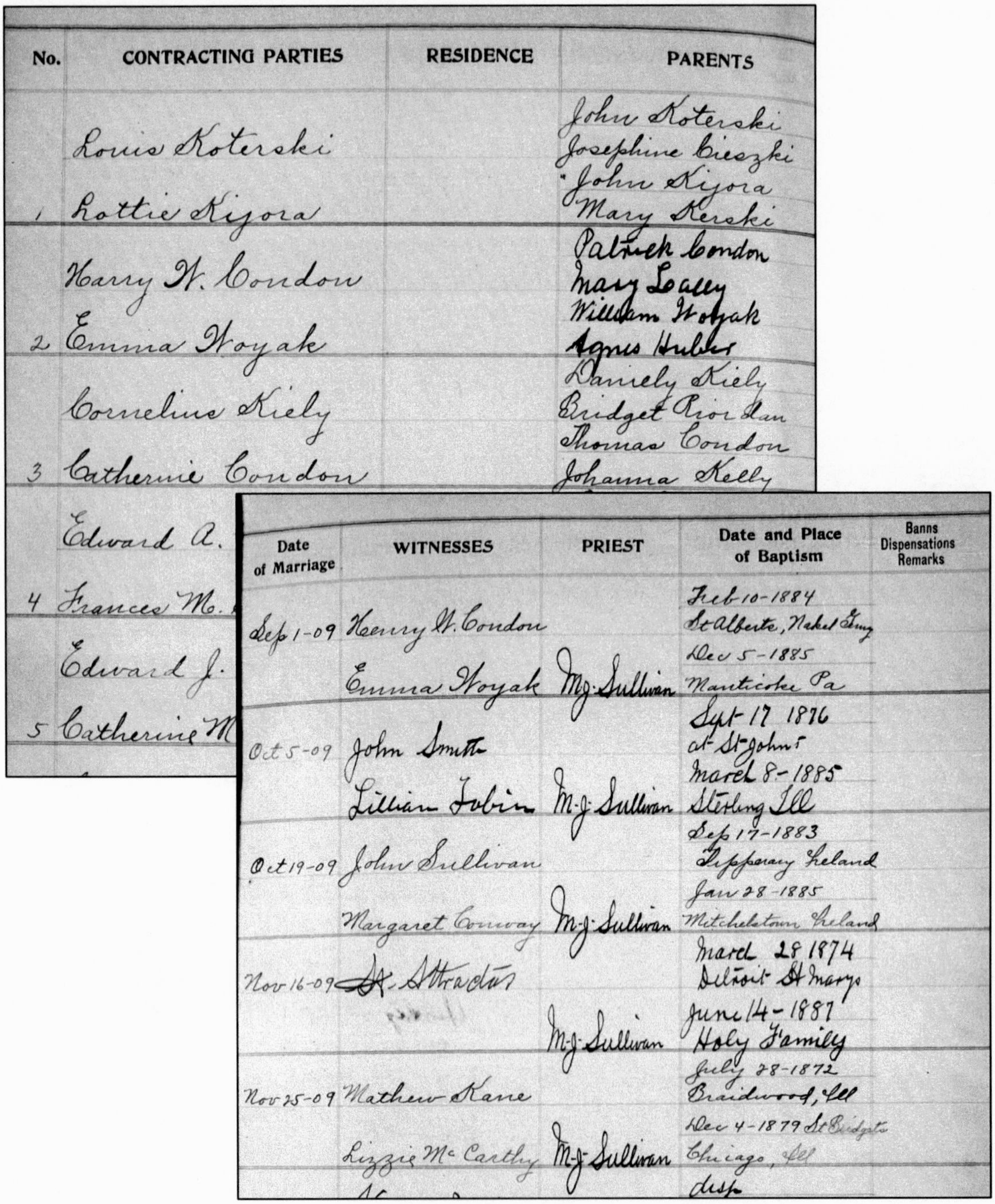

No.	CONTRACTING PARTIES	RESIDENCE	PARENTS
	Louis Koterski		John Koterski
Josephine Cieszki
1	Lottie Kijora		John Kijora
Mary Kerski
	Harry W. Condon		Patrick Condon
Mary Lealey
2	Emma Woyak		William Wohak
Agnes Huber
	Cornelius Kiely		Daniely Kiely
Bridget Riordan
3	Catherine Condon		Thomas Condon
Johanna Kelly
4	Edward A.
Frances M.		
5	Edward J.
Catherine M.		

Date of Marriage	WITNESSES	PRIEST	Date and Place of Baptism	Banns Dispensations Remarks
Sep 1-09	Henry W. Condon
Emma Woyak	M.J. Sullivan	Feb 10-1884
So Alberte, Nekel Frmy
Dec 5-1885
Nanticoke Pa	
Oct 5-09	John Smith
Lillian Tobin	M.J. Sullivan	Sept 17 1876
at St John's
March 8-1885
Sterling Ill	
Oct 19-09	John Sullivan
Margaret Conway	M.J. Sullivan	Sep 17-1883
Tipperary Ireland
Jan 28-1885
Mitchelstown Ireland	
Nov 16-09	A. Attracta	M.J. Sullivan	March 28 1874
Detroit St Marys
June 14-1887
Holy Family	
Nov 25-09	Mathew Kane
Lizzie McCarthy	M.J. Sullivan	July 28-1872
Braidwood, Ill
Dec 4-1879 St Bridgets
Chicago, Ill
disp	

Figure 57: Cornelius Kiely and Catherine Condon ecclesiastical marriage record, 19 October 1909, St. Patrick Catholic Church, Chicago, Cook County, Illinois. Since Chicago preserved primarily marriage certificates, which contain minimal information and not the applications and other parts of the marriage process, turning to church records supplies many more details. For example, Cornelius was baptised in Tipperary, Ireland, while his wife was baptised in Mitchelstown, Ireland. Parents of each are also included. (Images courtesy of St. Patrick Church.)

Chapter Fourteen

Vital Records

Documents for births, marriages, and deaths are termed vital records in the United States and civil registrations in other countries. Although alternative evidence can substitute as vital records in research, the present discussion is about legal certificates of births, marriages, and deaths for states.

The novice researcher often expects vital information to have been registered for an ancestor. This is not always the case. In fact, each state began recording vital events at different times. Some states have excellent registrations, such as those of Massachusetts that began in 1840 for births and marriages and in 1841 for deaths. South Carolina, though, did not register births and deaths on a state level until 1915 and marriages until 1911. In Pennsylvania, statewide registration of births and deaths started in

1906, and marriages were county matters. In New York, the deaths were recorded beginning in 1880, and births and marriages, in 1881. Knowing the year of the commencement of each state registration minimizes frustration while researching. The dates are readily obtainable on various websites, including FamilySearch.org/wiki, as well as in the chart on page 210 of this book.

Collections of vital records are becoming prevalent on websites such as Ancestry.com and FamilySearch.org. What is hosted or allowed to be hosted on these websites depends on state laws and right-of-privacy issues, also explaining why some states do not allow their vital records to enter the public domain. If the desired records are not online or periods in question are not, certificates have to be ordered from the states' departments of vital statistics.

When a Record Exists
While earliest records may differ slightly in content, vital records contain key information for genealogists. One can anticipate the following to possibly be available:

Birth Records
- Name
- Sex
- Place of birth
- Sequence of child born to mother
- Parents' names
- Ages of parents
- Residence
- Occupation of father

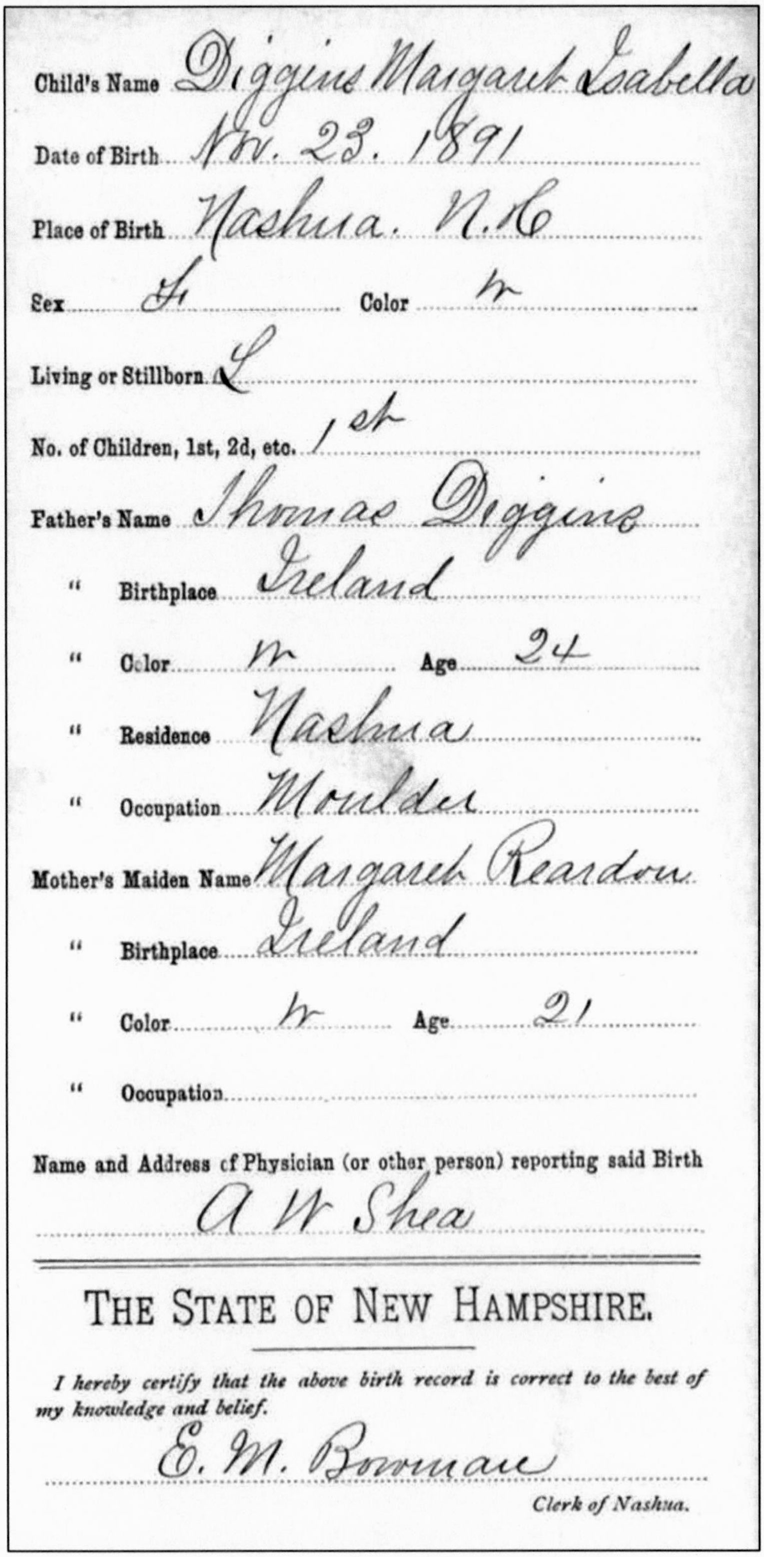

Child's Name Diggins Margaret Isabella

Date of Birth Nov. 23. 1891

Place of Birth Nashua. N.H.

Sex F Color W

Living or Stillborn L

No. of Children, 1st, 2d, etc. 1st

Father's Name Thomas Diggins

" Birthplace Ireland

" Color W Age 24

" Residence Nashua

" Occupation Moulder

Mother's Maiden Name Margaret Reardon

" Birthplace Ireland

" Color W Age 21

" Occupation

Name and Address of Physician (or other person) reporting said Birth

A W Shea

THE STATE OF NEW HAMPSHIRE.

I hereby certify that the above birth record is correct to the best of my knowledge and belief.

E. M. Bowman

Clerk of Nashua.

Figure 58: Birth card for Margaret Isabella Diggins, 23 November 1891, Nashua, New Hampshire. She was the first child of Thomas Diggins and Margaret Reardon, both natives of Ireland. (Image courtesy of New Hampshire Registrar of Vital Statistics.)

In some cases, individuals registered births much later than they occurred. These are called delayed certificates or reconstructed certificates, and they can predate the beginning of vital records for an area. These were most common when individuals began filing for Social Security in the 1930s and 1940s. The people for whom births had not been recorded found themselves frantically filing delayed certificate requests with their states. These certificates provide witnesses and attestations, and the forms expected more details than did the original ones required at births.

Carefully search for the entire family in birth records, not for only the ancestor. The image at left reveals that Margaret Isabella Diggins was born in Nashua, New Hampshire, in 1891. A sibling was noted in 1895 as born in Ireland, though registered in New Hampshire. Although it might have been a clerical error, further research may also disclose that the family returned to Ireland for a brief time.

Especially with ethnic groups, such as the Irish, names can be common, and if a mother's maiden name is not listed on the birth certificate of her child, it can be difficult to differentiate one Patrick & Catherine O'Riley from the others in each locality. This is a problem in large urban areas, such as Manhattan. If the address for the family is listed on the birth certificate for a child, and the family remained somewhat stable for a few years in a tenement apartment, such a circumstance can separate families with the same names. An unusual occupation for the father can serve the same purpose. The only prerequisite for this strategy to work is that the home address or the father's occupation must be listed, and a definite address for the family for at least one year must have already been identified.

Even when families moved, as they constantly did in urban areas, if they can be tracked through the city directories for the period during which children were born, a series of addresses will be known. The birth certificates for the various Patrick & Catherine O'Riley's then can be separated and the correct one recognized.

Church records can also substitute for missing vital records, especially baptism documents for missing birth registers. These were not state generated, but in some areas, entire collections were submitted with the information being accepted by the state for the creation of birth certificates. Again, most were for other legal purposes, such as Social Security and pension. One well-known example is the state of Alaska, which had no governmental registration of births before 1913. The Bureau of Vital Statistics microfilmed local church registers, and from those copies, certified and legal delayed birth certificates were made. Although Alaska began recording birth records in 1913, one year after becoming a territory, registration tended not to be complete until around 1945.

Marriage Records

Marriage records were first kept by the churches. As laws went into effect, the states mandated that all marriages be filed with licenses from counties, which were returned to the courthouses after the ceremonies were performed. Each statewide registration requirement is different. A typical marriage license, which generated the certificate when returned, can include at least some of the following information for both the bride and groom:

- Name of bride and groom
- Age of bride and groom
- Residence of bride and groom
- Birthplace of bride and groom
- Parents of bride and groom
- Previous marriages
- Occupations
- Consents when necessary
- Date of marriage
- Witnesses
- Who conducted the ceremony

The application for the marriage license has the most information. The certificates themselves can be basic, but, again, they vary between states and periods. When studying the online databases for marriages, understanding whether the source is the license or the certificate is important. It may be both. Once the source is determined, note who performed the marriage. If a minister or priest did so, the next step is to determine where he pastored, thereby possibly opening additional records. Also consult a church version of the marriage because it may have additional information not stated in the county records.

Often, the marriage record has only the name of the minister or priest. If initials are after his name, those will need to be explained. For example, M.G. means Minister of the Gospel, but do not always assume that to be Protestant clergy. D.D. is Doctor of Divinity, and for Roman Catholics, the initials of the order to which the priest belonged are listed. The major ones are in the chapter "Special Strategy: Catholic Religious (Priests, Brothers, and Nuns)."

The congregation for which a clergyman pastored can often be identified through an Internet search. City directories are another good source for the period the marriage took place. There is usually a section devoted to churches and the clergy who served. The church records from where the marriage occurred can be another important tool if the civil certificate or license does not have birthplaces or parents' names.

Also valuable in the marriage record are the names of the witnesses. Who are these people? They may not be anyone of interest as some parishes, for example, had couples on duty on certain days to witness all marriages. This was common in urban areas, where lots of marriages were performed. On the other hand, they might have been parents, siblings, or cousins. If they were relatives, another research strategy is potentially opened. In this case, if the birthplace in Ireland cannot be found by researching the

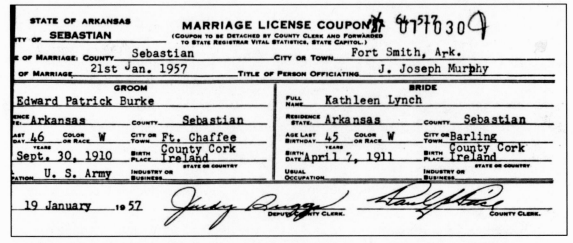

Figure 59: Edward Patrick Burke and Kathleen Lynch marriage license, 21 January 1957, Fort Smith, Sebastian County, Arkansas. Dates and counties of birth in Ireland were provided along with their current residences. Also presented was Edward's service in the U.S. Army at the time. Compare the information required for this license to that for a church marriage record, page 200. Edward and Kathleen, however, were married by a judge rather than by an ecclesiastical authority. (Image courtesy of Arkansas Department of Vital Records.)

bride or groom, look at the relative who acted as the witness. Irish origins might have been preserved in a record about his or her life. He or she likely was born in the same place as the bride or groom.

Death Records

Death records began in different years for each state. For some states, they started late and remained incomplete for decades afterward. Thus, do not be surprised if a death certificate cannot be found for an ancestor. However, even when located, be aware that it is the least reliable of all vitals for accurate information. This is because, hopefully, it was a traumatic time for the survivors who were being asked for facts when their minds were elsewhere. The crux is that the deceased did not give the information, making all of it suspect. Some families simply did not talk about the past.

While information on death certificates should be accepted with care, it can provide excellent clues, even if they are not always correct. A typical death certificate supplies some of the following:

- Name of deceased
- Residence
- Place of death
- Cause of death
- Birthplace
- Age
- Sex
- Birth date
- Age
- Parents' names
- Parents' birthplaces
- Marital status

- Funeral home
- Date of burial
- Place of burial
- Informant

It is not uncommon for the mother's maiden name to be wrong, a point needing to be considered. The birthplace of the deceased causes the most confusion for researchers. It is usual to find Belfast, Cork, Dublin, or Londonderry (Derry) as the place of birth. Those can be erroneous because they are ports from which people left, which remained in the memories of families. Nonetheless, they do indicate a section of the country where a person was born. For example, Cork is in the extreme south of the island, whereas Belfast is in the extreme north. The two are not close, and so the clue can be helpful.

The name of the informant can be important if it is not the attending physician. He or she could be a previously unknown relative. If the person was an Irish-born relative, tracing his or her records may lead to where the deceased was born.

The name of the cemetery on the certificate is usually consistent with where the burial took place. However, this is not always the case. For example, in places with multiple cemeteries, such as in urban areas, changes in burials might have occurred suddenly, after death certificates were generated. This could have been the situation if the cemetery in question has no record of a burial for that individual.

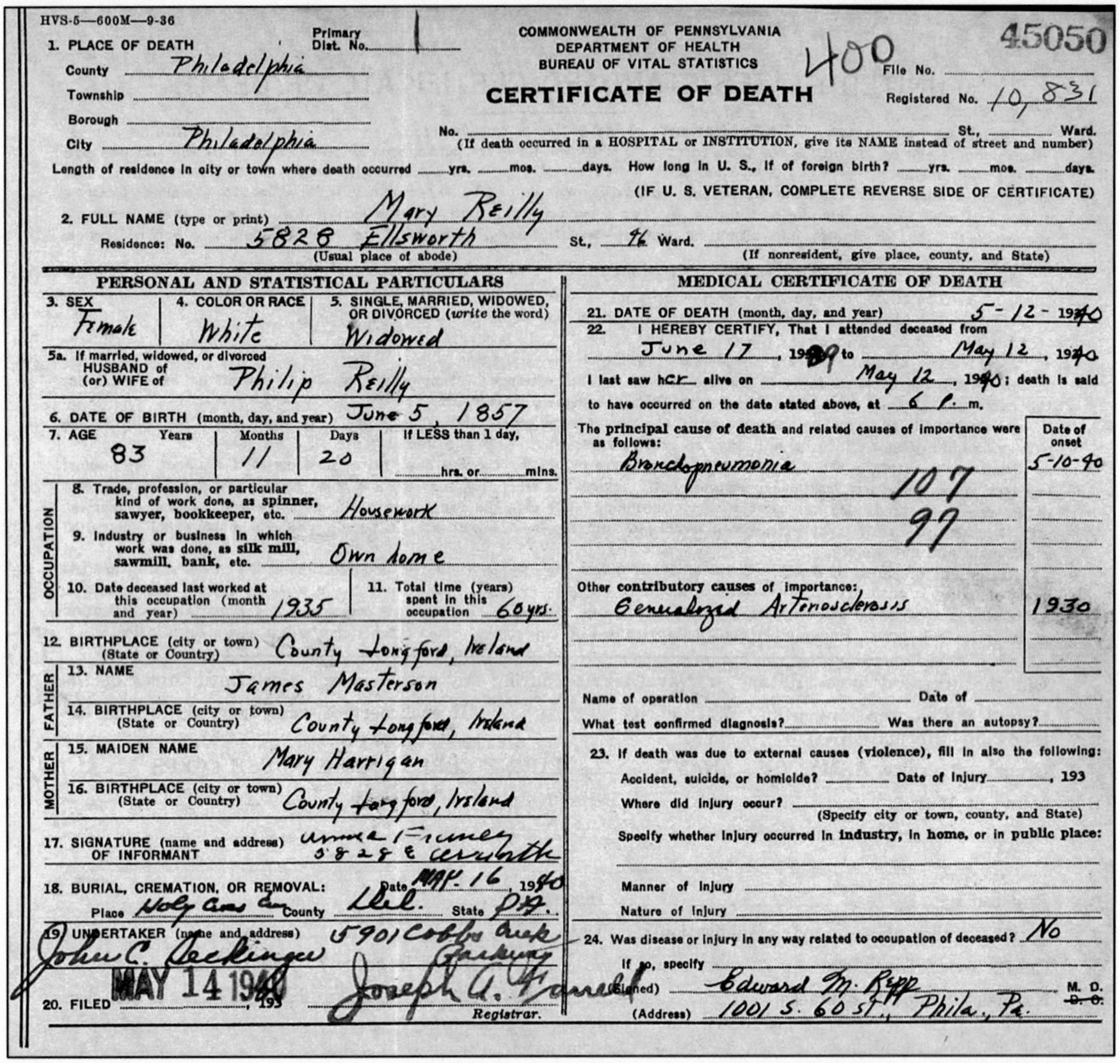

HVS-5—600M—9-36

COMMONWEALTH OF PENNSYLVANIA
DEPARTMENT OF HEALTH
BUREAU OF VITAL STATISTICS

CERTIFICATE OF DEATH

45050
400 File No.
Registered No. 10,831

1. PLACE OF DEATH — Primary Dist. No. 1
County: Philadelphia
Township:
Borough:
City: Philadelphia — No. ____ St., ____ Ward. (If death occurred in a HOSPITAL or INSTITUTION, give its NAME instead of street and number)
Length of residence in city or town where death occurred ____ yrs. ____ mos. ____ days. How long in U. S., if of foreign birth? ____ yrs. ____ mos. ____ days.
(IF U. S. VETERAN, COMPLETE REVERSE SIDE OF CERTIFICATE)

2. FULL NAME (type or print): Mary Reilly
Residence: No. 5828 Ellsworth St., 46 Ward. (Usual place of abode) (If nonresident, give place, county, and State)

PERSONAL AND STATISTICAL PARTICULARS

3. SEX: Female
4. COLOR OR RACE: White
5. SINGLE, MARRIED, WIDOWED, OR DIVORCED (write the word): Widowed
5a. If married, widowed, or divorced HUSBAND of (or) WIFE of: Philip Reilly
6. DATE OF BIRTH (month, day, and year): June 5, 1857
7. AGE: 83 Years, 11 Months, 20 Days. If LESS than 1 day, ____ hrs. or ____ mins.
OCCUPATION
8. Trade, profession, or particular kind of work done, as spinner, sawyer, bookkeeper, etc.: Housework
9. Industry or business in which work was done, as silk mill, sawmill, bank, etc.: Own home
10. Date deceased last worked at this occupation (month and year): 1935
11. Total time (years) spent in this occupation: 60 yrs.
12. BIRTHPLACE (city or town) (State or Country): County Longford, Ireland
FATHER
13. NAME: James Masterson
14. BIRTHPLACE (city or town) (State or Country): County Longford, Ireland
MOTHER
15. MAIDEN NAME: Mary Harrigan
16. BIRTHPLACE (city or town) (State or Country): County Longford, Ireland
17. SIGNATURE (name and address) OF INFORMANT: Anna Frances, 5828 Ellsworth
18. BURIAL, CREMATION, OR REMOVAL: Date May 16, 1940. Place Holy Cross Cem. County Del. State Pa.
19. UNDERTAKER (name and address): John C. Deckinger, 5901 Cobbs Creek Parkway
20. FILED MAY 14 1940, Joseph A. Farrell, Registrar.

MEDICAL CERTIFICATE OF DEATH

21. DATE OF DEATH (month, day, and year): 5-12-1940
22. I HEREBY CERTIFY, That I attended deceased from June 17, 1939 to May 12, 1940
I last saw her alive on May 12, 1940; death is said to have occurred on the date stated above, at 6 P. m.
The principal cause of death and related causes of importance were as follows: Bronchopneumonia 107 97 — Date of onset: 5-10-40
Other contributory causes of importance: Generalized Arteriosclerosis — 1930
Name of operation ____ Date of ____
What test confirmed diagnosis? ____ Was there an autopsy? ____
23. If death was due to external causes (violence), fill in also the following:
Accident, suicide, or homicide? ____ Date of injury ____, 193
Where did injury occur? ____ (Specify city or town, county, and State)
Specify whether injury occurred in industry, in home, or in public place:
Manner of injury
Nature of injury
24. Was disease or injury in any way related to occupation of deceased? No
If so, specify
(Signed) Edward M. Rupp, M. D.
(Address) 1001 S. 60 St., Phila., Pa.

Figure 60: Mary Reilly death certificate, 12 May 1940, Philadelphia, Philadelphia, Pennsylvania. It provides the name of her husband, who preceded her in death; her birth on 5 June 1857 in County Longford, Ireland; and the names of her parents. Additional strategies include examining records of Anna Frances, the informant who resided at the address where Mary Reilly died. The cemetery was also named, which allows investigation of others buried nearby or the sexton's records. (Image courtesy of Pennsylvania Department of Health.)

When a Record is Not Available

Just because a state began recording vital records in a particular year does not mean there was general compliance with the laws. In some states, observance of the laws took only a few years, while in others, it might have been a decade or so. Even when registration should have been all-inclusive, a desired birth, marriage, or death certificate cannot be found in some cases.

When viewing databases of vital records, be aware of the cutoff dates for the vitals within them. For example, if looking for a record for 1919 and one is not found, type in 1919 and leave the name and place blank. If no certificates appear for that year, they are not in the database.

Lawsuits brought against states have been successful in furnishing another source for indexes. "Reclaim the

Records" is a non-profit organization of activists comprised of genealogists, historians, and researchers who file Freedom of Information and Open Data requests to have records released by states. A state's restricting access to records and indexes that should be in the public domain is not uncommon. Reclaim the Records has filed many successful lawsuits making millions of records available to the public. Once a lawsuit is won, Reclaim the Records digitizes them and places them on Reclaimtherecords.org for free. This website should always be checked if a set of indexes or records has not been released and is not on Ancestry.com or FamilySearch.org.

Formal Dates of Earliest Vital Records

State	Births	Marriages	Deaths
Alabama	1908	1936	1908
Alaska	1913	1913	1913
Arizona	1909	1909	1909
Arkansas	1914	1917	1914
California	1905	1905	1905
Colorado	1907	1907	1907
Connecticut	1897	1897	1897
Delaware	1881	1847	1881
District of Columbia	1874	1811	1874
Florida	1899	1927	1899
Georgia	1919	1952	1919
Hawaii	1842	1842	1859
Idaho	1911	1947	1911
Illinois	1916	1962	1916
Indiana	1907	1958	1899
Iowa	1880	1880	1880
Kansas	1911	1913	1911
Kentucky	1911	1958	1911
Louisiana	1914	----	1914
Maine	1892	1892	1892
Maryland	1898	1950	1898
Massachusetts	1841	1841	1841
Michigan	1867	1867	1867
Minnesota	1900	1958	1908
Mississippi	1912	1926	1912
Missouri	1910	1881	1910
Montana	1907	1943	1907
Nebraska	1905	1909	1905
Nevada	1911	1968	1911
New Hampshire	1901	1901	1901

Formal Dates of Earliest Vital Records (cont.)

State	Births	Marriages	Deaths
New Jersey	1848	1848	1848
New Mexico	1920	1920	1920
New York	1880	1880	1880
North Carolina	1913	1962	1913
North Dakota	1907	1925	1907
Ohio	1908	1949	1908
Oklahoma	1908	1908	1908
Oregon	1903	1906	1903
Pennsylvania	1906	1885	1906
Rhode Island	1853	1853	1853
South Carolina	1915	1950	1915
South Dakota	1905	1905	1905
Tennessee	1908	1945	1908
Texas	1903	1966	1903
Utah	1905	1887	1905
Vermont	1955	1955	1955
Virginia	1912	1912	1912
Washington	1907	1968	1907
West Virginia	1917	1964	1917
Wisconsin	1907	1907	1907
Wyoming	1909	1941	1909

Marriages typically began from the establishing of each state or territory and will be found in each county's records until the start of statewide registration of vital records. Death records can sometimes also be located for a county much earlier than the dates when state records were initiated.

Chapter Fifteen

Convicts, Indentured Servants, Runaways, and the "Spirited Away" (1615-1776)

Comparable to the abominable African slave trade was white servitude, a piece of North American history encompassing all the English colonies in the Caribbean and on the mainland. Context to this disturbing topic, one that is little understood or even remembered by most Americans, is essential to research.

Bondage took many forms: convicts, desperate whites who sold themselves into servitude, the clearing of undesirables from the streets, and those who were "spirited away," that is, kidnapped from their homes. All went to the plantations, which were acquiring unimaginable wealth. This chapter concentrates on white bondage from 1615 to its discontinuance as an industry at the advent of the American Revolution. Nevertheless, the practice of bringing people from Europe to America in servitude persisted in some form into the early 1800s. It is the period from 1615 to 1776 that is the most difficult for family research.

The subject, recently emerging from obscurity, has been featured on various popular genealogy programs and has been intimately studied in academic works. Yet, books, websites, and blogs based on sensationalism and politics are attempting to counter and demean the current flowering of African American studies. These are not helpful to the family historian because they can be racist without openly appearing to be and can leave a misleading impression of the topic. Disguising no history is the contemporary, footnoted work *White Cargo: The Forgotten History of Britain's White Slavery in America* (New York, New York: NYU Press, 2008) by Don Jordan and Michael Walsh. The Irish were a chief part of this trade.

For the family historian, it is almost impossible *not* to come across whites in bondage in the colonial records for lands, courts, wills, and taxes. Their lives were linked to their masters, and all of them were intertwined with the plantation economy. The belief is that between 1620 and 1775, approximately 300,000, or two of every three, arrivals to the English colonies were in some sort of bondage. The Caribbean and mainland colonies were associated through trade, creating a natural migration pattern. For example, South Carolina was settled by families from Barbados.

Servants were of little value, bought cheap on the auction blocks and disposable. They were worth less than African slaves. Whites sold themselves into temporary slavery in hopes of better lives. Early slavery was economical, not racial. The racism came later, and with a vengeance. The financial aspect is vital to understanding this form of human trafficking and its records from the colonies.

The indentured servant had a contract usually for four to five years of work in exchange for an agreement for a given number of acres at the end of the contract. The land was held in trust by the owner, who bought the right to the indenture at the auction block. If the servant died before the contract was fulfilled, the land reverted to the owner. If a servant violated the contract by having children, marrying, or escaping, extra years were added, and the owner received the land. This system benefited few servants and presented no reason to keep them alive.

Typically, indentured servants escaping poverty were 15 to 24 years old, rarely had family and friends indentured with them, and could not select their masters or marry for the durations of their contracts. Because of the entire process of purchasing, from indentured servants to eventual freemen, this class of people did have documents, especially land and court ones. Any transgression, such as an escape, could be reported in the colonial newspapers.

Four main categories for the incoming Europeans can be found in the colonial records; however, to whom the inferences in them are being made is not always clear.

White Freeman Who Owned Property. A white male over 21 who owned real or personal property of a certain value. He was endorsed by a majority of other Freemen in the community, and he had the right to vote and pay taxes.

White Freeman. A free male over 21, not bound, was considered a white freeman. In the Southern colonies, a freeman was any freed slave or anyone who voted or paid taxes.

White Apprentice. A broad term applied to bondage, such as indentured servant, redemptioner (free-willer), and apprentice. Terms such as apprentice and servant obscured what the terms of bondage might have meant.

White Slave.   A person who was bound to a master. Chattel slavery, which was for a lifetime, grew out of the indentured servant system. Slaves could be prisoners, religious or political dissidents, orphans, or social outcasts. In the English colonies, African chattel slavery replaced the purchasing of temporary European slaves.

Whites could move up in status. An indentured servant or slave could become a freeman and eventually a landed freeman who owned slaves. Some scholars contend that the difference between a slave for life and an indentured servant is moot if the servant died before the expiration of the contract. Also, the treatment of the two groups was the same.

Laws Governing Human Bondage
Exactly who and why people were indentured servants can be somewhat blurred in the records because they could have

been convicts or those who willingly sold themselves into bondage. Convicts from Ireland were transported as early as 1620 to Virginia from the Wexford Plantation. However, care must be taken when defining what the word "convict" really means. By today's standards some of the defined crimes for which people were imprisoned and transported are appalling and mind numbing. Once convicts were on the auction blocks, they were purchased alongside the contracted indentured servants. Both groups then were indentured servants, although their terms of servitude were not alike. When speaking of colonial laws, the powerhouse colonies setting the standard were Virginia and Maryland. Both had the rich tobacco plantations and needed workers. Whatever laws these two colonies established were usually the ones the other English colonies followed.

Before 1718, the colonies were more of a "dumping ground" for convicts. Under the Transportation Act of 1718, transportation became regulated and industrialized. The government contracted ships' captains to take the transported to the colonies and the auction blocks, whereby the captains made their livings. The transported convicts became indentured servants. The buyers understood the laborers were convicts, and they were entitled to a few more years of service from them. The plantation owners were often hesitant to purchase convicts. Once freed, the convicts could settle anywhere. Over the years, the colonies tried many times to shut down the transportation of convicts, considering them undesirable as future settlers.

Indentured servitude was dissimilar to what evolved into the institution of slavery, even if the two systems were the same during the bondage period itself. However, the distinction between them is technically more about the allotted time instead of how they were treated. Indentured servants were essentially slaves for contracted periods in exchange for either passage across the ocean or for promised lands. Otherwise, a slave is a slave. A study of white bondage in England reveals the following comparisons between indentured servants, transported convicts, and free immigrants in the colonial period. *See chart on the following page.*

The America before 1776 was complex as human bondage fueled the economy. The line between who was a slave and who was not became thin. Laws defining those rights and who had them were not in place for a century.

By the 1650s, Irish Catholics were a principal commodity transported by the English government in Ireland. It included both convicts and the unwanted. This period is referred to as an ethnic cleansing of Ireland during the Cromwellian Rebellion, a true horror story.

Although the Irish had been sent to the colonies from the first decades of the 1600s, the 1641 Rebellion and the rise of Oliver Cromwell and the English Civil War (1642-1651) increased the numbers of convicts and undesirables transported from Ireland. During this time, the term "Barbadosed" entered the popular language, especially in Ireland. It meant being shipped to the Caribbean and, more

Early Immigrant Comparisons

Variable	Indentured Servants	Transported Convicts	Free Immigrants
Terms of service	4-5 years	7 or 14 years	No labor term
Emigration Reason	Escape poverty	Imposed punishment	Varies
Average age	15-24 years	20-30 years	Varies
Companions	Rarely family/friends	Rarely family/friends	Family/friends
Social status	Lower/lower middle	Lower class	Middle/upper mid.
Select master	Could not	Could not	Not applicable
Marriage	None	None	Not applicable

specifically, to Barbados by force. Thousands were sent to the English mainland and Caribbean colonies.

As the decades progressed and matters came before the courts, laws began to regulate the use and treatment of the indentured servants. The Virginia colony is an example: In a December 1662 law, women servants who became pregnant by their masters had to finish their terms and were then bound over to the local churches to be sold for another two years of servitude. An October 1670 law pronounced that all non-Christians brought by ships (by sea) were slaves for life but if brought by land (from another colony) as children, they would serve until they were 30 years old. If they were adults and brought by land, they had to serve for only 12 years. In April 1691, all whites, bonded or free, were forbidden to marry Blacks, mulattos, or Indians. The law also stated that free white women who had illegitimate children by Blacks, mulattos, or Indians would be bound out by the local parish churches for five years

and the children bound until they were 30 years old.

A series of Virginia laws passed in October 1705 defined in detail what constituted a slave. The main points, in modern English, were:

- Slaves brought into the colony by land or sea (except Turks and Moors) remained slaves regardless of converting to Christianity.

- Free people who were Christians in their own country were not to be sold as slaves.

- No Black, mulatto, Indian, Jew, Muslim, or other infidel could purchase Christian white servants.

- White men or women who married Blacks and mulattoes were to go to prison for 6 months with no bail.

- If slaves resisted the masters during correction, it was legal to kill them as part of the correction. Escaped slaves could be killed.

- Christian baptisms did not exempt persons from bondage, and the status of all children was according to the conditions of the mothers.

The laws legally separated who were indentured servants, who were slaves, and what that really meant. These laws were not present in the early decades of the industry, but over the course of a century, they defined slavery for lifetimes through color lines.

The "Spirited Away" in Bondage

One little known facet of human trafficking is those who were not convicts or indentured servants but were kidnapped and sold into the industry. The period slang is "spirited away," and the kidnappers were known as "spirits." It is a ruthless history that left communities along the coasts and navigable rivers of the United Kingdom and Ireland in fear that they would be next. The number of whites kidnapped and sold into bondage cannot be determined. However, their story is part of the narrative. This is the subject of novels and memoirs from the eighteenth and nineteenth centuries, with perhaps Robert Louis Stevenson's historical fiction *Kidnapped* (1886), set in 1751 Scotland, being among the most popular.

One fascinating example of this point is a court case in Salem, Essex County,

Massachusetts. It was published as an article by Gordon Harris as "Samuel Symonds, gentleman: complaint to Salem court against his two servants, 1661" on the Historic Ipswich website, Historicipswich.org. In the article, Harris supplied some background to the Irish in indentured servitude and the kidnapped. The story and ensuing case filed with the Quarterly Courts of Essex County is:

> "Eleven-year-old Philip Welch was kidnapped from his bed in Ireland in 1654 by Captain George Dell of Salem. He and another Irish boy, William Downing, were loaded onto the ship Goodfellow with Irish men and children destined for New England. Samuel Symonds bought William Downing and Phillip Welch from Captain Dell, who signed over William to nine years and Phillip for eleven. After working on Symonds' farm for seven years they refused to continue working and demanded their freedom. Judge Symonds had them arrested and brought to trial."

The website transcribed the court case, and part of it is in modern English. The jury found that if the covenant of Mr. Dell (the alleged kidnapper) did have a legal covenant, then they were in favor of Symonds until 10 March 1663. If it was not determined to be a legal covenant (he did kidnap them), they were in favor of Downing and Welch. The decision of the magistrates of the court was that it was a legal covenant, and they ordered the servants to complete their terms. The case was appealed, and the servants agreed to work until the next court session, which they could attend.

In the presentation of these two "spirited away" boys, the article has an epilogue. William Downing continued to live in Ipswich and appeared on and off in the court records as both plaintiff and defendant. Phillip Welch married Hannah Haggett and moved to Topsfield, where he had several children. He died in Topsfield. The owner, Samuel Symonds, served in many official capacities, including selectman, town clerk in Ipswich, and deputy assistant to the General Court from 1643 to 1673, when he became Deputy Governor until his death in 1678.

The purpose of the article was not to identify Irish origins, if that is even possible, but enough information and names are mentioned that other records and genealogies could be consulted. For example, who was Captain George Dell, and where in Ireland was his ship picking up servants? That is at least an idea to pursue. Another is whether William Downing and Philip Welch were from the same area of Ireland.

Sources for Documenting Indentured Servants

For the genealogist, the first question is whether servants, willing or unwilling, can be documented. If so, can their origins in Ireland be traced? Frankly, the chances of finding origins in Ireland are not good, but if one is discovered, it will be from a colonial, not from an Irish, source. It may be possible from a colonial record to determine who brought people over to be sold and who purchased them. Whether any of these records has a reason to state where in Ireland someone came from cannot be predicted, but none of this equates to a birth record in Ireland. Church registers in Ireland, both Catholic and Protestant, began in the late 1700s or by the early decades of the 1800s. There are a few exceptions, but for the most part, that is an accurate assessment. Irish origins, if found, are from colonial records.

Start a general search in published lists of immigrants in the *Ancestry.com* database "U.S. and Canada, Passenger and Immigration Lists Index, 1500s-1900s." It is constructed from the book series *Passenger and Immigration Lists Index* edited by P. William Filby and Mary K. Meyer. This is a massive collection of lists from published documents and includes over five million entries. In genealogy circles, it is a standard source simply known as *Filby's*. The database can be manipulated using several fields, which cannot be done with the book series. The original entries were taken from *Filby's*.

Another excellent site to explore is the "Immigrant Servant Database," which authenticates servants from any number of published sources. The goal of this project is to eventually document up to 100,000 servants for whom evidence allegedly exists. The database currently has 22,441 servants documented. The source for each entry is provided, and the database can be searched with several approaches. The "Immigrant Service

Database" cites that over half their entries cannot be found in *Filby's*.

The Periodical Source Index (PerSI), an online periodical index to article titles locked away in thousands of genealogical journals worldwide, is often the only way to find the printed material and should not be overlooked. It is the creation of the Allen County Public Library in Fort Wayne, Indiana. The database version of PerSI is available on Findmypast.com. PerSI does not index what is in the articles but only the titles and the subject matter. It is enough to access the original articles at the Allen County Public Library, which probably has the largest periodical collection for the world. Many periodicals have published articles on indentured servants, and most publications are regional.

Realize that most studies of indentured servants, especially how-to articles, are written from the English perspective because the repositories in England have the documents for some of these servants. One excellent example is Nathan W. Murphy's "Origins of Colonial Chesapeake Indentured Servants: American and English Sources," in *National Genealogical Society Quarterly*, 93 (1) March 2005, pp. 5-24. Because the situation in the Irish records differs, articles such as this can be useful from the American side of research. Those principles still apply, allowing the English-related articles to be relevant.

Newspaper articles looking for runaway white servants are valuable. Life was harsh for indentured servants, and they regularly escaped the plantations along with native and African slaves. As the plantation owners were losing their investments in them, they offered rewards for captures and returns. The ads typically stated the runaways were Irish, and although there was no reason to give birthplaces, they sometimes had indications about where the runaways were from.

General information needed for the servant to be identified and returned was a physical description, accent, and behavioral traits. While many ads do not directly assist in solving the immigrant origins' question, they can do so indirectly. For example, the ads reveal that the person was the immigrant, who the master was, and where the escape occurred. All are excellent clues. Examples of published runaway ads are in:

Boyle, Joseph Lee. *Drinks Hard, and Swears Much Given to Drinking and Whoring: White Maryland Runaways, 1763-1769*. Baltimore, Maryland: Clearfield Company, 2010-2013.

Boyle, Joseph Lee. *"Great Lovers of Drink": White New Jersey Runaways, 1720-1766*. Baltimore, Maryland: Clearfield Company, 2018.

Boyle, Joseph Lee. *White New Jersey Runaways, 1767-1783*. Baltimore, Maryland: Clearfield Company, 2019.

Boyle, Joseph Lee. *"Sly and Artful Rogues": Maryland Runaways, 1775-1781*. Baltimore, Maryland: Clearfield Company, 2014.

Boyle, Joseph Lee. *"Very Impudent When Drunk or Sober": Delaware Runaways, 1720-1783*. Baltimore, Maryland: Clearfield Company, 2014.

Boyle, Joseph Lee. *White Pennsylvania Runaways*. Baltimore, Maryland: Clearfield Company, 2015-[-].

Grubb, Farley. *Runaway Servants, Convicts, and Apprentices Advertised in the Pennsylvania Gazette, 1728-1796*. Baltimore, Maryland: Genealogical Publishing Company, 1992. (NOTE: This has been made into an Ancestry.com database.)

Numerous websites, private and academic, digitize or extract runaway ads. A particularly fascinating example of one is for two people who escaped together and is full of details and allusions that will be found nowhere else. One was for an Irishman named Thomas Macoun and a "Negro Fellow" named Robin. It appeared in the *Virginia Gazette*, published in Williamsburg, and ran from 10 August through 17 August 1739. It was reprinted on the "Geography of Slavery in Virginia" website by the University of Virginia:

> *August 17, 1739. RAN away, on the 5th of this Instant August, 1739, from the Subscriber, living in St. Mary's county, on Potowmack River, in Maryland, a Servant Man, nam'd Thomas Macoun, and with him a Negro Fellow, nam'd Robin.*
>
> *Macoun is a slender, neat made impudent Irishman, of a middle Stature, brown Complexion, very dark Eyebrows and Beard, a nimble upright Walk, and can speak broad Scotch. He professes Dancing, Fencing, Writing, Arithmetick, drawing of Pictures, and can play Legerdemain, or slight of Hand Tricks. He had on, when he went away, a large Hat, a brown Cue Wig, a dark colour'd old Cloth Coat, a German Serge Wastecoat, a Pair of short Linnen Breeches, a Pair of long Ditto, Thread Stockings, and a Pair of London Falls; he also took with him a Linnen Coat..., and it's suspected, a Silver hilted Sword, 2 ruffled Shirts, one red Cloth Wastecoat, and one blew Ditto, and several other Things.*
>
> *The Negro is a Native of Madagascar, a nimble Fellow, short and slender, has lost his Fore Teeth, and has a long Cut on one of his Shins: He had with him two dark colour'd Manx Cloth Jackets, one Ditto of Plains, fac'd with red, a red coat with Brass Buttons, and turn'd up with yellow, and an old grey Manx Cloth Great Coat. They went away in a 16 Foot Boat, with Schooner Sails, the Fore-sail very ragged, the Rudder painted red, and a Pair of red Oars.*
>
> *If they should be taken up and secured in Pennsylvania, it is requested, that Notice may be given to Mr. Franklin, Printer, in Philadelphia: If taken and secured in the southern Parts of*

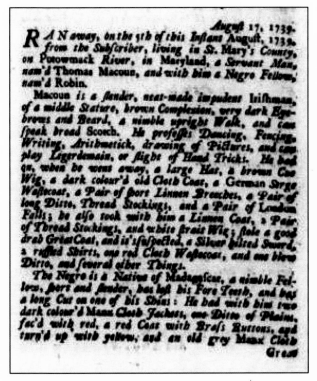

Figure 61: A runaway slave ad posted in the Virginia Gazette on 17 August 1739 for Thomas Macoun. See the full abstract on pages 216 and 217. (Image courtesy of Colonial Williamsburg. Permissions received.)

Virginia, that Notice may be given to Mr. John Taylor, Merchant in Norfolk, or to William Parks, Printer, in Williamsburg: And if they should be taken and secured in Carolina, that Notice may be given to Dr. Abraham Blackhall, at Edenton, for which Notification, a Pistole Reward shall be given by either of the Persons before-mentioned, besides what the Law allows. And Whoever will apprehend the said Servant and Slave, and bring them to me, in St. Mary's County, on Potowmack, or to Major John Waughop, in Northumberland County, Virginia, on Potowmack River, shall have 6 Pistoles Reward, and reasonable

Charges, paid by Major Waughop, aforesaid, or by me. Robert Chesley.

This runaway ad is intriguing because even though it does not state where in Ireland Thomas Macoun was from, it does note where his accomplice, Robin, was from, Madagascar! Other evidence is that Thomas could write and knew arithmetic, which denotes at least some education, even if he was self-taught; the name of his master, Robert Chesley; and that he spoke "broad Scotch," a dialect of English spoken in the Scottish Lowlands. Thus, the suggestion is that he was almost certainly Scot-Irish (Ulster Scot), born in Scotland or of Scot ancestry. The first assumption is that he was from Ulster and Protestant; therefore, his origins and religion are inferred.

The "broad Scotch" comment can possibly narrow the search to where in Ulster Thomas Macoun originated. What is most likely being indicated is Ullans, a distinct dialect or as some contend, a language known in Ulster by several names, such as Ulster Scots, Ullans, Braid Scots, or the Hamley Tongue. It is concentrated mainly in areas of Counties Antrim, Down, and Donegal. Even though it is not as common as it once was, it is still spoken by some in Ulster, with a current revival to preserve it. If "Broad Scotch" is "Braid Scots," the area of Ulster along the coast becomes the focus for further study. At that point, if a search of Irish indexes, such as those for taxes, reveals that some version of Macoun (possibly McKeon) is found in the historic Ullans speaking area, the immigrant origins' problem may indirectly be solved. For additional information on the use of Ullans in an immigration strategy, see Dwight A. Radford's chapter "Who Are the Scots-Irish" in *American Scots-Irish Research: Strategies and Sources in the Quest for Ulster-Scots Origins* (Orting, Washington: Family Roots Publishing Co., LLC, 2020).

A runaway ad dated 5 December 1751 and published in *The Pennsylvania Gazette* is for Nicholas McDaniel and is full of not only clues but also the names of relatives. This and others can be found on the web page "Runaway Servant Ads" on the website "Ireland Old News" on Irelandoldnews.com:

> *December 5, 1751*
> *The Pennsylvania Gazette*
> *Run away, from on board a sloop at Poughkeepsie, in Dutches county, an Irish Servant man, named Nicholas McDaniel aged about 20 years, came lately from Ireland with Capt. Anderson, and is about 5 feet 10 or 11 inches high; carried with him a gun, and is supposed to have gone down along the West side of Hudsonriver, to Pennsylvania; had on a brown pea jacket, a cap, and a woollen hat; he speaks but indifferent English, has a wild look, says one Henry Mulhall, in Amboy, is his uncle; he has a brother at Poughkeepsie, who is also a Servant to James Isaiah Ross, of New York, merchant, and came over in the same vessel. Whoever takes up the said Nicholas McDaniel, and*

> *secures him, so that the said James Isaiah Ross, his master, may have him again, shall have Five Pounds reward, and all reasonable charges, paid by JAMES ISAIAH ROSS.*

This most unusual ad discloses that Nicholas was born in 1731, and he came "lately from Ireland" which dates his arrival most likely in the late 1740s or at least by 1751. He came with Captain Anderson and was a servant to James Isaiah Ross, who placed the ad. Nicholas had an uncle in Amboy named Henry Mulhall and a brother in Poughkeepsie who was also a servant to James Isaiah Ross. The case is uncharacteristic because most servants did not have family connections in America. Nicholas had a brother and an uncle in New York, and his brother was bound to the same master. It could be questioned whether Nicholas McDaniel was an indentured servant in the traditional sense or more of a bound apprentice. Either way, the information is adequate for relatives to continue the research into Irish origins.

Perhaps one of the main sources for indentured servants is court records and county deeds. The court settled issues that surfaced, and recurrently, new laws were enacted that eventually defined the difference between an indentured servant and a slave for life. Recorded on the deeds is when masters purchased servants from the auctions. A traditional county deed is digitized through FamilySearch.org.

When deeds have been extracted and indexed by a local genealogy society or an individual, all the information about the named servants purchased is published. These books can be found at state archives, public libraries with genealogy collections, the Library of Congress, and the Family History Library. County deeds ordinarily reported the purchasers; people purchased; sometimes, ages; and the dates of the transactions. Tax records often have servants as taxables. Depending on the laws of the state and the years, it is not peculiar to see servants listed with the word "Irish" after their names. Even if they are not so designated, "servant" is the hint needed to access other records.

Tri-Racial Isolates

An area of fascination among historians and genealogists alike is families who have been classified by academics as "tri-racial isolates." This is a complex term for a component of America's tortured and convoluted racial history. At its core, it refers to families or isolated groups of families who, over the centuries, married or had children with Africans, Europeans, and Native Americans. Basically, they are mixed-race families. More racial groups could be added, but the tri-racial component is emphasized herein.

Because so much of this merging of cultures and peoples happened in the 1600s, it ties directly into the discussion of the Irish indentured servant. This history is not ordinarily taught in classes to students in the United States below the university level.

Researchers often discover their Irish indentured servant histories through mixed-race lineages, which then link into the Irish servant. The subject itself demonstrates the artificial nature of racial definitions in modern America. It is not uncommon for Americans who identify as white or African American or even Native American to discover their tri-racial ancestry in the 1600s. Studies of these families are well documented.

The birthplace of the Irish indentured servant will almost never be found through researching mixed-race families. Neither will it be found tracing back to the indentured servant, but in this case, it is not necessarily the point of the immigration research. The objective is to identify who the immigrant was and the circumstances of servitude, at which time the line ends. Yet, in family history of this nature, that is a legitimate goal, part of the whole picture even if it is not the entire picture. Therefore, it may be through an African American, Native American, or both lines of the family that the paper trail leads to the immigrant in bondage, and that person was Irish.

Tri-racial heritage is not uncommon, which the current DNA infusion into genealogical studies is proving. Heritage cannot be defined by color lines. Certain surnames are so strongly associated with tri-racial isolates, especially in the Mid-South, that assuredly a mixed-race lineage will be connected to those families at some stage regardless of their skin color or racial features today.

As these tri-racial families dispersed across the nation, they usually assimilated into the white, Black, or native communities, an ongoing process. However, many could not or would not assimilate. They simply intermarried among others like themselves and formed communities

Figure 62: Examples of old (prejudicial) names of tri-racial isolates used in the twentieth century. Many of these families have now reorganized and are state-acknowledged tribes, with their own legal names. For example, the colloquially known Croatans Indians of Harnett and Sampson counties, North Carolina, are now known as the Coharie Intra-Tribal Council. The colloquially known Pearson County Indians, or simply Cubans, are now organized as the Sappony Tribe, with headquarters in Pearson County, North Carolina. A South Carolina group from Orangeburg County today is known as the Beaver Creek Indians but historically were prejudicially called such terms as Brass Ankles, Croatans, Mulatto, Red Legs, and Smiling Indians.

of people who, somewhere between-white, Black, and native, became silent, isolated, invisible, and almost forgotten. Historically, it was to their advantage.

There are three *must read* articles from a genealogical perspective about mixed-race research. They will help with the context and history of this fascinating and hidden topic:

DeMarce, Virginia Easley. "Looking at Legends – Lumbee and Melungeon: Applied Genealogy and the Origins of Tri-Racial Isolates." *National Genealogical Society Quarterly,* 81, March 1993, pp. 24-45.

DeMarce, Virginia Easley. "Verry Slitly Mixt": Tri-Racial Isolate Families of the Upper South - A Genealogical Study." *National Genealogical Society Quarterly,* 80, March 1992, pp. 5-35.

Mills, Gary B. "Tracing Free People of Color in the Antebellum South: Methods, Sources, and Perspectives." *National Genealogical Society Quarterly,* 78, December 1990, pp. 262-278.

These articles have examples from a wide range of records from which to document mixed-race and "free color" families. They attempt to strip away the folklore and replace it with solid genealogical research.

Identifying Tri-Racial Isolates

The pre-1870 United States censuses list many families concentrated in specific counties as mulatto, Black, and earlier, as "free color." They can include emancipated slaves and the tri-racial isolates who might or might not have been slaves. The progenitors in bondage might have been enslaved as, for instance, an African captive man with an Irish indentured servant woman. In the early 1600s, the difference between a slave and indentured servant was unclear because slavery for a lifetime was not yet instituted regardless of the ethnicity of the servant or slave. Once parties were freed, the remainder of their lives was normally within the underclass of society.

The first suggestion of mixed-race heritage may be the censuses. If the ancestral family is listed as mulatto, Black, negro, Indian, or free color from 1790 to 1860, a research strategy may be needed to look deeper into the ethnic composition of the family. The 1870 census was the first to list everyone, including freed slaves. Sometimes, lore of a Native American in the family has passed down, and although this indubitably qualifies for further investigation, the reality may be more complex because historically, people did not talk about African ancestors. Was Indian a concealment of African?

Remember, America's racial history is tied into civil rights. In the past, civil rights were restricted to "one drop of Black blood," which in the minds of past generations meant someone was Black and not white. Thus, many people with African American and Native American ancestry "passed for white" whenever they could by marrying someone with lighter skin tones. If they could not, many in the Black community took on the identities of, for example, Moors, Turks, or descendants of African royalty, dressing as such to prove they were not African

Americans, and with success. Convoluted only begins to describe this topic.

In *Surviving Indian Groups of the Eastern United States.* (Washington: United States Government Printing Office, 1949), William Harlen Gilbert brought the subject of tri-racial isolates, before that term was coined, to a general audience. His work is still used as a source, although the names he designated for the various groups have progressed past the trite, regional, prejudicial labels given to these concentrations of households. His study preceded the tribes' reconstructing and discarding those derogatory descriptions. In South Carolina alone, Gilbert noted communities known as Brass Ankles, Buckheads, Croatans, Marlboro Blues, Red Bones, Red Legs, and Turks. This significant work can be found on several websites.

The subject of mixed race cannot be separated from the free-color population of the South. As Gary B. Mills states in his article "Tracing Free People of Color in the Antebellum South: Methods, Sources, and Perspectives," by 1800 there were over 100,000 free people of color, 61,000 of whom lived in the Southern states. He also notes that the number climbed to 488,000 at the outbreak of the Civil War, with the majority, about 262,000, in the South.

Many family historians think that these families cannot be traced. This simply is not true, although because of the interweaving of free color into the white and native populations in general, genealogical research has to be tailored to reflect records generated about them. If a mixed-race family married into an incoming Scot-Irish family in the 1700s, obviously the Irish line descends through that line as well as it does for the older Irish indentured servant in the 1600s. Dissimilar research methods, though, have to be utilized for a 1700s Scot-Irish immigrant than for a 1600s Irish servant.

Any older published family history may hold keys to mixed-race lineages. However, because of attitudes in the past, it was not to the author's advantage to claim Black or native ancestry. In Jim Crow America, doing so was not prudent. Therefore, with many older published family histories, all the ancestors may be presented as white, but the surnames in the pedigree almost always supply the proper indications of the truth. Today, books, databases, and funded historical projects can emphasize any or all the aspects of mixed-race lineages.

One noteworthy series of research in selected states underscores the African portion of the lineages. The subject is the same in most cases as that for bi-racial and tri-racial heritage. Paul Heinegg's website *Freeafricanamericans.com* is an indispensable source for classifying all these free-color lineages no matter where the recognizable color line eventually falls. Many white and native researchers tie into this work to the same extent as African Americans do. The website, which is updated periodically, is based upon Heinegg's award-winning books on the subject, tracing each family line from about 1810 or 1820 to as far back as possible, often to the Irish indentured servant. His studies currently include free-color families in Delaware,

Maryland, North Carolina, South Carolina, and Virginia. He also delves into free-color households in Tennessee and Indiana. One of his groundbreaking explorations is how the "East India Indians" from the Indo-Pak Subcontinent merged into the colonial mixture, which potentially brings in a fourth ethnic line.

In the free-Black populations of North Carolina, Heinegg determined that of 298 families, most were the descendants of white servant women who had children by slaves or free Blacks. Only about 1% of them were descended from white owners who had children by their servants and slaves. He also found that the free African American colonial families were landowners and generally accepted by their white neighbors. During this earliest period, he noted the free Native Americans tended to blend with the free-Black communities. In the first settlements, these mixed-race families were not in separate communities but intermarried. Heinegg contends that only later did the light-skinned descendants of free Africans form the tri-racial isolates of Virginia, North Carolina, South Carolina, Tennessee, Kentucky, Ohio, and Louisiana. His introduction to the topic is creditable as background into colonial slavery and the intermixing of the races.

An example from Heinegg's work from his Maryland and Delaware research is about the indentured servant Christian Collins:

> *Christian Collins, born say 1697, had three years remaining on her indenture to William Smith on 24 March 1718/9 when she confessed in Prince George's County court that she had an illegitimate child. The court adjudged that the child was "begot by a Negroe man" and ordered her master William Smith to deliver her up to the court to be sold when her indenture was completed and ordered that the child serve Smith until the age of thirty-one [Court Record 1715-20, 809].*

In his writings about North Carolina, South Carolina, and Virginia, he specifies:

> *Polly Fletcher, born say 1745, was an Irish servant who was indentured to Matthew Whiting, Esq., of Prince William County, Virginia. Whiting's executor, E. Brooke, Sr., certified in the Court of the District of Columbia in Alexandria that Polly was the mother of Betsy, Mary, and Alice Fletcher, "Mullato" women [Arlington County Register of Free Negroes, 1797-1861, nos. 57, 59, 61, 62, pp. 51-3].*

The supposition is that Christian Collins was the immigrant from Ireland because she was the indentured servant. Stated is that Polly Fletcher was an Irish servant, and the assumption is she was also the immigrant and not simply of Irish heritage.

Whether they were indentured servants, convicts, or "spirited away" kidnapped, all intermixed with others in bondage, and thus the tri-racial isolates were born.

Reconstructing Tribes

In the racially charged culture of the United States, these mixed-race families had to account for who they were, especially if they could not "pass for white." They used terms such as Portuguese or Turks to describe themselves, possibly because it was to their advantage to not be classified as having African heritage in their geographical areas, eras, and societies. This is not unlike Cherokee and Chickasaw mixed-race families who used the term "Black Dutch" or "Shanty Irish" to account for their non-white physical features. Regardless of the reason, the truth is that the Portuguese and Turkish mariners can also be documented in the colonial records.

The current trend is for tri-racial isolates to embrace the native parts of their lineages, compile genealogies, and reconstruct tribes. In reclaiming the native heritage, the long and tedious process of supplying paperwork and applying for state and federal acknowledgments are submitted. Some tribes can generate the proper documentation and are granted the status of a legal tribe. Others are so integrated into the white or Black communities that distinct native links cannot be documented, and the tribes are denied state or federal recognition.

One group of mixed-race families who successfully gained legal status is the Lumbee Tribe of North Carolina, headquartered in Pembroke. Today, it is the largest tribe east of the Mississippi River and is state recognized. Centered in Robeson County, the members' skin tones appear to be African American or Native American or European or everything in between. The Lumbees are an excellent example of how color as a definition of race is artificial and meaningless. Instead, tribal heritage is culture and identity, and the Lumbees have fought hard to maintain that identity.

The Lumbees have gained the interest and attention of academics as well as historians. Some of the standard books on the market demonstrating this include:

Blu, Karen I. *The Lumbee Problem: The Making of an American Indian People*. Cambridge and New York: Cambridge University Press, 1980.

Dial, Adolph L. and David K. Eliades. *The Only Land I Know: A History of the Lumbee Indians*. San Francisco: Indian Historian Press, 1975.

Lowery, Malinda Maynor. *The Lumbee Indians: An American Struggle*. Chapel Hill, North Carolina: University of North Carolina Press, 2010.

Lowery, Malinda Maynor. *Lumbee Indians in the Jim Crow South: Race, Identity, and the Making of a Nation*. Chapel Hill, North Carolina: University of North Carolina Press, 2010.

When studying the Lumbee Indian core surnames, it is apparent that many of them can be traced to Heinegg's *Freeafricanamericans.com*, which in turn, has the potential to take them back into the indentured white servant in the 1600s.

Surnames associated with the Lumbee Nation are:

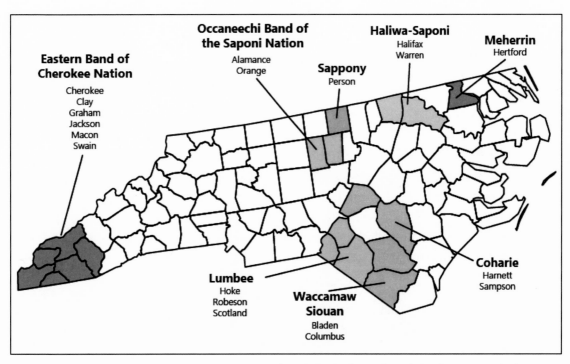

Figure 63: Presently, North Carolina has seven state-acknowledged tribes and one federally recognized tribe. It is common for enrolled tribal members to have some combination of Indigenous, European, and African American ancestry. This map reflects the counties where enrolled tribal members can be found today and in the past. The one federally recognized tribe is the Eastern Band of Cherokee whose home is on the 56,000-acre Qualla Boundary, adjacent to the Great Smoky Mountains National Park.

Adkins (Atkins), Allen, Bell, Bennett, Berry, Black, Blanks, Blu, Braboy (Braveboy, Braceboy), Brewington, Bridger, Brooks, Brown, Bullard, Burnett, Butler, Callins, Chapman, Chavis, Chooms, Cooper, Cumbo (Cumba, Comboes), Cummings, Dial, Dees, Emanuel (Manuel), Fields, Freeman, Godwin, Graham, Hammonds, Harding, Harris, Howard, Huggins, Hunt, Jackson, Jacobs, Johnson, Jones, Lambert, Locklear, Lowrie, Lucas, Mainor, Martin, Mitchel, Moore, Morgan, Oxendine, Paine, Porter, Peavy, Ransom, Revels, Sampson, Sanderson, Scott, Sealy, Smith, Spaulding, Stuart, Sweat, Sweet, Strickland, Taylor, Tadlock, Thomas, Thompson, Warriax, Weatherly, Wilkins, Wilkinson, Williams, Williamson, Wood, Wooddell, Wright, Winn and Young.

Specific surnames are consistently found within one group of tri-racial isolates or shared between several. For those such as the Lumbees, who were inclined to stay in a local community, the process of documenting the group has produced the rebirth of the tribe itself.

Others have widely dispersed and have not reestablished a tribe. One important example is the Melungeons, who had a clear-cut Scots-Irish link, settling among them as they dispersed. The Lumbees, on the other hand, have a stronger African connection because they remained in

Robeson County, North Carolina. However, both have tri-racial lineages as they progress further back.

The old, prejudicial name Melungeons was popular even though no such tribe existed. Nonetheless, because it is such a common term for the subject, it has to be used to access the almost unlimited websites, books, and articles on these families. The Melungeon families historically have been concentrated along the North Carolina-Virginia border, East Tennessee, and Eastern Kentucky.

Through these families, many modern Americans first come across their own mixed-race history. As families spread out from the Mid-South on the migration trails, they settled in areas such as Highland County, Ohio, where they were known locally as the Carmel Indians. Other similar communities are identifiable once the surnames are known. One well-known and documented community is in Vardy, Hancock County, Tennessee, and an entire collection of Melungeon-related materials has been preserved as the "William P. Grosche Collection," digitized at FamilySearch.org. The community still lives on Newman's Ridge. These families have been the subject of many books and documentaries. The many academic works on the market about the Melungeons include:

Hashaw, Tim. *Children of Perdition: Melungeons and the Struggle of Mixed America*. Macon, Georgia: Mercer University Press, 2006.

Hirchman, Elizabeth C. *Melungeons: The Last Lost Tribe in America*. Macon, Georgia: Mercer University Press, 2004.

Winkler, Wayne. *Walking Toward the Sunset: The Melungeons of Appalachia*. Macon, Georgia: Mercer University Press, 2005.

A great deal of Melungeon research has come from organizations such as the Melungeon Historical Society and the Melungeon Heritage Association. The latter advertises itself as "One People, All Colors." Organizations such as these are noteworthy because they explore the diverse views on Melungeon origins, from the academic to the mythological. Taken as a whole, all the studies contribute to a unique and growing field of study by preserving genealogies, genetic data, and folklore memories.

Common Melungeon surnames found in Kentucky, North Carolina, Tennessee, and Virginia have been adapted from Virginia Easley DeMarce's article "'Verry Slitly Mixt': Tri-Racial Isolate Families of the Upper South - A Genealogical Study" and N. Brent Kennedy and Robyn Vaughan Kennedy's work *The Melungeons: The Resurrection of a Proud People* (Macon, Georgia: Mercer University Press, 1994):

Adams, Adkins, Barker, Barners, Bean, Beckler, Bell, Bennett, Berry, Biggs, Boland, Bolen, Bolton, Bowlin, Bowling, Bowman, Branham, Bullion, Bunch, Burton, Byrd, Campbell, Carrico, Carter, Casteel, Caudill, Chavis, Clark, Clounts, Coal, Coffey, Cole, Coleman, Coles, Colley, Collier, Collins, Collinsworth, Colyer, Cox, Coxe, Crow, Cumba, Cumbo, Cumbow, Curry, Davis, Denham,

Dorton, Dye, Ely, Evans, Fields, Freeman, French, Gann, Garland, Gibson, Gipson, Goen, Going, Goins, Goodman, Gorvens, Gowen, Gowing, Graham, Gwinn, Hale, Hall, Hammond, Hendricks, Hendrix, Hill, Hillman, Hopkins, Ivey, Jackson, Keith, Kennedy, Kiser, Lawson, Lopes, Lucas, Maggard, Maloney, Martin, Melons, Minear, Miner, Minor, Mize, Mizer, Moore, Morley, Mullins, Nash, Niccans, Nichols, Noel, Orr, Osborn, Osborne, Perry, Phelps, Phipps, Piniore, Polly, Powers, Pruitt, Ramey, Rasnick, Reaves, Reeves, Roberson, Robertson, Robinson, Sexton, Shephard, Short, Sizemore, Stallard, Stanley, Steel, Sweat, Sweats, Sweet, Swett, Swindall, Tolliver, Turner, Vanover, Watts, White, Whited, Williams, Willis, Wright, Wyatt.

East India Indians

No discussion of tri-racial research is complete without adding a fourth element, the East India Indians, indentured servants and slaves from the Indo-Pak Subcontinent. They have been documented in Heinegg's website Freeafricanamericans.com. His research proves these people from British India were brought over from England. They were referred to by the English as "East Indians." Heinegg provides evidence for East Indians from the court records of Maryland, Virginia, and North Carolina of the 1600s and 1700s. He notes that although they married into the free-color community, they also intermixed with the indentured white community. The court records are the source of the term "East India Indians."

One very interesting case from the Spotsylvania County Order Books (1735-1738) showed the distinction between the East Indians and African slaves (page 440):

> *"Zachary Lewis, Churchwarden of St. George Parish, presents Ann Jones, a servant belonging to John West, who declared that Pompey an East Indian (slave) belonging to William Woodford, Gent., was the father of sd child which was adjudged of by the Court that she was not under the law having a Mullato child, that only relates to Negroes and Mullatoes and being Silent as to Indians, carry sd. Ann Jones to the whipping post."*

Ann Jones, presumably a white indentured servant, had a child by Pompey, an East Indian slave. The laws had already restricted white indentured servants from having children with African slaves, but they had not caught up with the East Indian issue. In the end, Ann's sentence was the whipping post!

Another illustration from Heinegg's database for Maryland and Delaware, replete with all kinds of clues, is for Thomas Mayhew. Here, when the word Indian is used, it does not mean Native American but East India Indians:

> *Thomas Mayhew, born say 1708, may have been identical to "1 Indian Man Named Tom" who was valued at 32 pounds and listed*

among the slaves of the Honorable Thomas Addison, Esquire, deceased, on 10 August 1727 when his widow Eleanor Addison brought the estate to an appraisement in Prince George's County, Maryland [Prerogative Court Inventories 1727-9, 12:295-313]. Thomas India petitioned the Prince George's County court in March 1729 stating that he was free born, baptized in England, and imported with his mother into Maryland under indenture. However, he was detained as a slave by Madam Eleanor Addison [Court Record 1728-9, 413]. He was probably the father of Thomas, born say 1735.

The son Thomas escaped from the Prince George's County jail, according to the *Maryland Gazette* published 29 May 1760, and he was described as "of a very dark complexion, his father being an East-India Indian . . . ." He was also referred to in a court record as Thomas India.

The East India Indians were apt to intermarry with the free-color community, and so the free-color people are then tied back into the white indentured servants, making this ethnic group of consequence in potentially connecting to the original Irish servant.

Bondage Dictionary

The world of historic slavery and bondage is foreign to the modern mind. Although it still exists, it is not on the developed scale it was for centuries. Because researchers are removed from the topic, terms or phrases in old books and documents pertaining to it can seem baffling and otherworldly. Whether they are found in classic nineteenth-century literature or court records from the seventeenth and eighteenth centuries, a dictionary is needed to explain what they meant at the time. This "Bondage Dictionary" focuses on words associated with African, European, East Indian, and Native American bondage. It is not exhaustive, but, rather, it is an introduction to old English terms.

Remember how huge and lucrative the trafficking in human bondage was in the New World. The Dutch, English, French, Portuguese, and Spanish colonial powers were involved. England began honing the business by originally placing people from the British Isles into the system. It eventually caught up with the other nations and perfected the industry with Africans.

Abandonment: When a slaveholder deserts his or her slaves.

Absentee Owner: A plantation or estate owner who did not live on and manage the property directly.

Bondage Dictionary (cont.)

Absolute Slave: A slave for life; not a term slave.

Adults: African men and women generally older than 13 or 14 years of age or taller than four feet, four inches. Specific age ratios differ by time and place.

Agent: In the indentured servant trade, an agent recruited the servants and redemptioners. They set up recruitment centers in port towns and inland market towns to convince people to emigrate to the Americas as servants. The agents commonly sold or assigned their rights to the servants to labor-starved American colonists. Many colonists made trips back to the British Isles to recruit their own servants, bypassing the agents altogether.

Agricultural Laborer: After men completed several years as agricultural servants, married, and established households, they became agricultural laborers.

Agricultural Servant: Young, single men who lived in rural areas were commonly contracted to serve farmers for one-year periods, during which they were trained in agriculture. Factors of this practice evolved into the indentured servant industry.

Apprentice: An individual contracted to serve a master for a specific number of years to learn a trade, usually for a low wage. Parts of this practice evolved into the indentured servant tradition. Often, in an indenture contract, the word apprentice signals that a child is being indentured, not necessarily that the child would be learning a trade.

Apprenticeship: The period an individual was bound under contract as an apprentice, usually until the age of 21.

Barbadosed: A seventeenth-century term for white dissidents who were shipped into slavery in the Americas for political resistance. Originally used for dissidents transported to Barbados.

Boys: Immature male slaves. Generally, slaving traders classified boys as shorter than four feet, four inches or younger than 13 to 14 years of age. On most slaving vessels, captains confined and, depending on their ages, chained boys to specific below-deck compartments toward the centers and sterns of the vessels.

Branded: A permanent mark made with a hot iron to identify property. Cattle and some slaves were branded to designate ownership.

Breeding of Slaves: The economic decision through deliberate planning to ensure the increase of slave property over and beyond natural reproduction. The subject is used when the value of a female slave is expressed relative to her breeding ability.

Chattel Slavery: A form of slavery introduced by Europeans in which the slave is treated as a property belonging to the owner and with no rights. The children of chattel slaves were also slaves.

Bondage Dictionary (cont.)

Child Ratio: The proportion of enslaved African children shipped into the trans-Atlantic slave trade. Approximately 26% of all slaves carried to the Americas were classified as children.

Children: Immature slaves, defined in the British slave trade as being shorter than four feet, four inches or younger than 13 to 14 years.

Commodity: An article of trade, especially a raw material or product. Chattel slaves were also treated as commodities.

Contract: Also called an indenture, the emigrant agreed to work as a servant without pay for a fixed number of years in return for passage to the New World.

Convict Servant: Criminals in the British Isles who accepted exile were given mandatory labor from seven to fourteen years as an alternative to execution or prison. They were transported to the American colonies from 1615 to 1776 and to Australia from 1787 through 1868.

Court of Mixed Commission: In 1817, a British-sponsored international treaty created a Court of Mixed Commission to hear cases concerning captured slaving ships. The Court included officials from an assortment of countries to ensure impartiality.

Domestic Servant: A man or woman who worked for hire in a person's home for pay. Domestic servants were different than indentured servants.

Domestic Slave: A slave who worked in a household instead of in the fields.

Driver: An overseer of slaves. The driver was another slave or a European.

Duty Boy: A seventeenth-century term for white child slaves, orphans, and those taken from parents and shipped into slavery in the Americas. Duty Boys were considered the living dead because their enslavements in Virginia and the West Indies were basically death sentences.

East India Indians: A Colonial American term for people from the Indo-Pak Subcontinent; especially in Maryland and Virginia. They arrived as indentured servants or slaves from England and intermarried with the free Blacks or white indentured servants.

Elderly Free Black: A free person of color sixty years of age or over.

Elderly Slaves: A slave sixty years of age and over.

Emancipation: Being set free or granted rights equal to others who already enjoy them. It is the freeing of a people from slavery.

Enslavement: To make a slave of a person or to hold in captivity or servitude.

Bondage Dictionary (cont.)

Enticers: Whites who urged white slaves to flee or who assisted fugitive white slaves. Enticers could be flogged with thirty lashes.

Enticing Slaves: The act of encouraging slaves to engage in disobedient behavior or to run away. Slaves could be enticed by whites, free color, or other slaves.

Estimated Value of Slaves: The estimation of the value of a slave or group of slaves provided by individuals, including appraisers appointed by courts.

Exile: An individual expelled from his or her native country for opposing the government's views.

Fate: The documented outcome of a slaving voyage. Slavers hoped to complete their voyages by returning to their home ports having purchased and sold slaves. Because of the risks of the sea, captures, and rebellions, one in four slaving vessels failed to return to their home ports.

Fear of Enslavement: Used whenever free persons of color expressed a fear they might have been enslaved or re-enslaved. It was also used when slaves who had been promised freedom expressed fear that they would be kept in slavery for the remainders of their lives.

Field Slave: A slave who planted, tended, and harvested crops on a plantation.

Fine: A common term for a man imprisoned for any offense. It also referred to a fine of 84 months or transportation for seven years.

Free Black: Sometimes called free persons of color or free color, these were free slaves, African Americans who were born free, or mixed-race who were bi-racial or tri-racial.

Free Color: see Free Black

Free Man/Woman: Someone not enslaved.

Free Person of Color: see Free Black

Free-willers: see Redemptioners.

Freedom Dues: Payment of articles of clothing, food, or lands by masters or the colonial governments to satisfy terminated contracts of indentured servants. Convict servants did not receive freedom dues.

Freedom Papers: Legal documents verifying the freedom status of a person of color. It can also appear on documents as a certificate of freedom.

Bondage Dictionary (cont.)

Freedom Suit: The process of a slave going to court to petition for his or her freedom.

Girls: Immature female slaves. Generally, slaving traders classified girls as shorter than four feet, four inches or younger than 13 to 14 years of age. On most slaving vessels, captains confined girls to specific below-deck compartments toward the sterns of the vessels.

Guineaman: A sailing ship refitted for the slave trade.

Half Freedom: A limited form of freedom offered by the Dutch to some of the early slaves. Half Free slaves enjoyed new liberties, but they were required to remain in Manhattan, to pay a yearly tax, and to return to service when needed. The children of Half Free remained enslaved.

Headright: A grant of land to individuals responsible for transporting their families and immigrants to Colonial America. The headright was usually 50 acres and motivated investors to transport servants to the colonies.

Held as a Slave: A term that referred to free people of color held in slavery who asked the court to release them from bondages or to affirm their free statuses.

Hired Servant: A servant who received wages for his or her labor and had power to select his or her own master and period of service. They were not always immigrants, although many immigrant servants after their freedom did become hired servants.

Hiring Value of Slaves: The estimated or actual hiring value of a slave or group of slaves given at a monthly or annual rate.

Homeward Passage: The voyage leg returning a vessel to its home port.

Human Agency: The actions of individuals that influenced the outcomes of voyages. By resisting their shipboard confinements, Africans raised the costs of slaving voyages. Some gained control and scuttled ships, some escaped to shore, and some committed suicide. A few sailors also mutinied. Captains' experiences and abilities helped to determine coastal transactions and health care on board ships.

Immigrant Servant: A general term used to describe all immigrants who came to the colonies as servants, including convict servants, indentured servants, and redemptioners.

Imported Servant: A modern term for immigrant servant.

Imported Slaves: The number of enslaved Africans disembarked in the Western Hemisphere or if captured by anti-slaving patrols, in Africa.

Bondage Dictionary (cont.)

Impress (impressment): The forcible recruitment of sailors into the Navy. The Royal Navy relied almost exclusively on impressments to man the fleets throughout the age of sailing. Slaving vessels were particularly susceptible to impressments because of the large crews, which became redundant in the Americas.

Indented Servant: A contemporary term for an indentured servant.

Indenture: A contract between a master and an indentured servant specifying the length of time required to serve in order to pay for the trans-Atlantic passage. The indenture often would promise free land or money when the contract was terminated.

Indenture Servants: Indentured servants were Europeans, mostly between 18 and 25 years old, who contracted themselves to employers in the New World for between four and seven years, after which time they were free to work for themselves. The term is also used to describe the practice in other circumstances, such as Africans sent to Jamaica in the nineteenth century and Indians exported to South Africa in the nineteenth century.

Indian Servant: A Native American employed by a European as a servant.

Insubordination: The actual or alleged behavior of slaves or apprentices who refused to submit to the authority of their masters.

Intended: Slaving vessels loaded trading goods to exchange for an intended number of slaves. Captains usually fell short of purchasing their proposed number of enslaved Africans. Captains also sailed for intended ports of call in Africa, the Americas, and Europe, at which most traded.

Interloper: Slave traders operating in violation of monopoly company privileges. During the Iberian dominance of the slave trade (1450 to 1650), the English, Dutch, and French were seen as interlopers into a trade to which the Spanish and Portuguese had been granted a monopoly by the papacy. Individual traders also acted as interlopers when trading in Africa, in defiance of monopoly companies. Frequently, interlopers and African merchants opened new trading outlets for enslaved Africans, thus preceding company ships in many markets.

Invoice Date: The date on a bill of sale.

Jumper: Constable responsible for inflicting punishments on slaves.

Kidnapped: The forcible seizure of a free person with the intent of selling him or her into slavery. This term usually applies to the African slave trade as well as to the white kidnapping rings along the coasts of the British Isles. It applies to whenever people are taken by force and sold.

King's Passengers: A term for convict servants.

Bondage Dictionary (cont.)

Labor Term: A contract between an immigrant servant and a master for a period of service, during which the servant labored without wages in exchange for passage to the colonies.

Laid Up: The situation of a ship when unrigged because of winter, for want of employment, or when unfit for service. Because the slave trade was seasonable, ships laid up in port.

Landless Slave Owners: Individuals who own slaves but no land on which they could work.

Likely: A term used to describe a slave as valuable.

Maid Servant: A female indentured servant that eventually meant an unmarried female servant.

Male Ratio: The number of male slaves relative to the number of female slaves. The ratio was skewed toward males because plantation owners desired "prime male slaves" above others and African societies wanted to retain female slaves. As a result, slaving ships embarked more male than female slaves.

Manumission: A legal process by which slaves could buy their freedom or be freed by the masters.

Master: In European bondage, a man who owned the labor of an immigrant servant for a number of years. In African bondage, a man who owned a slave. For an apprentice, the master was the person who trained him or her.

Men: Adult male Africans sold into the trans-Atlantic slave trade. Generally, slaving traders classified men as taller than four feet, four inches and older than 13 to 14 years. On most slaving vessels, captains confined and chained men to specific below-deck compartments toward the centers and bows of the vessels.

Merchant: An individual who purchased immigrant servants in Europe and assigned or sold their contracts to the colonists when the servants arrived in the colonies.

Meritorious Service: Extreme acts of devotion or loyalty that served as grounds for freeing a slave.

Mistress: A female master.

Mortality: The number of Africans or crewmen who died on board the ships, whether while anchored off the coast of Africa, on the Middle Passage, or in American harbors.

Mortgage Value of Slaves: The collateral value of a slave or group of slaves used to secure a debt.

Bondage Dictionary (cont.)

Organization (of Slave Voyages): Organizing slave voyages required outfitters to purchase trading goods in demand in regional African markets. Captains also needed to hire requisite numbers of crewmen to work as sailors, craftsmen, and guards. Over time, slave prices rose, and African merchants demanded greater quantities of high-quality trading goods; only ports with sufficient infrastructures could organize large numbers of slaving ventures.

Outward Passage: The first leg of a slaving voyage, from the port of departure to Africa. Crewmen worked on the outward passage, preparing the vessel to receive human cargo by configuring below-deck prisons.

Overseer: The person on the plantation who was paid to organize and manage the work of slaves.

Pawns: see Slave Purchase

Plantation: A large estate or farm on which cash crops and provisions were grown, usually by slave workers. Plantations constituted the destinations of most enslaved Africans.

Political Rebel: A person whose political views were in opposition to the government. Political Rebels were often transported to the colonies as punishments.

Price/Standardized Price: Price of slaves at a port of sale in the Americas, standardized in English pounds sterling.

Prime Slaves: Healthy slaves between the ages of 18 and 30. Slave traders desired prime slaves above others and paid premiums for them.

Privateers: A ship privately owned and manned but authorized by a government during wartime to attack and capture enemy vessels. Armed slaving vessels often purchased letters of marque during wars to capture enemies shipping on their own volition.

Privilege Slave: An enslaved African given to the ship's officer by the slave ship owner as a special honor or privilege.

Purchase of Freedom: Money paid to a slave owner in return for the owner emancipating the slave. The price could have been paid by a third party, a family member, or by the slave.

Redemptioner: An individual who traveled from Europe to the American colonies without paying. In theory, upon arrival on the docks, he or she would be redeemed by someone for payment. The passage cost was usually paid by friends or relatives in the colonies. If the funds were not available, the redemptioner was sold as an indentured servant. He or she was also known as a free-willer.

Bondage Dictionary (cont.)

Resistance: Acts by slaves or crewmen to gain freedom or improve their shipboard conditions. Most Africans resisted their slave statuses and shipboard confinements; some sailors resisted the power of tyrannical officers.

Return Passage: See Homeward Passage.

Runaway Servant: Immigrant servants often ran away from their masters to escape their contracts. If caught, they were punished, often whipped, and extra years were attached to their original contracts.

Sailing Orders: Merchants' orders to slaving captains, usually specifying the voyage patterns to Africa, the captains' monthly wages and commissions, and chains of command should captains and officers die on the voyages.

Seasoning: People seasoned to new climates, disease environments, and work routines. Captains preferred to hire seasoned sailors, those men with experience in the slave trade and who had survived the seasoning period. Similarly, enslaved Africans who survived their first few years in the Americas were seasoned to the new disease environment and had learned work routines. The principle was the same in the white immigrant servant trade, where a seasoning period was expected and the servant either lived or died.

Servant: A term with multiple meanings. In bondage, it can be any person who serves a master, as in an immigrant servant.

Seven Year Servant: A contemporary term for a transported convict servant.

Skilled Slaves: A slave identified as possessing or practicing a particular skill.

Slave: Bondage that applied to kidnapped Africans, European immigrant servants, and Indian servants. Slaves were the property of another person, whether by capture, purchase, or birth. Originally, the difference between a slave and a servant was uncertain.

Slave Auctions: Public selling of slaves to the highest bidder. Other terms are "cried off," "vendue," and "public outcry."

Slave Colony: A settlement on plantations based on the labor of slaves.

Slave Execution: The legally sanctioned act of putting a slave to death as punishment for an alleged crime.

Slave Hunter: A person who made a living, or bounty, by capturing runaway slaves and returning them to their masters.

Slave Insurance: An insurance policy on a slave.

Bondage Dictionary (cont.)

Slave Labor: Work carried out by the slaves for the profit of others.

Slave Purchase: Captains often purchased more slaves than they later transported from the African coast. In some cases, they transshipped slaves to auxiliary vessels; in other cases, they re-landed slaves who might not have survived the Middle Passage. Some captains advanced trading goods on credit to African merchants, receiving pawns (human collateral or commercial hostages) in return. Captains redeemed pawns once slaves were delivered. Lengths of time to complete a slave purchase were variable, from several weeks to sometimes more than 18 months.

Slave Ship: A sailing ship refitted for the slave trade, known also as a Guineaman. Most slaving ships were second-hand vessels that frequented other trades. Owners sought to purchase fast sailing vessels and/or ones that could be retooled below the main decks to maximize the number of Africans who would be imprisoned.

Slavers: Individuals who earned their living by capturing, trading, and transporting slaves. The term is also applied to the ships engaged in the transporting of the slaves.

Slavery: The institution that kept people as property.

Soul Driver: A slang term for an individual in the colonial period who purchased immigrant servants in bulk and transported them inland in chains to be sold in frontier settlements.

Spirit(s): A person who kidnapped white men, women, and children and forced them onto slave ships bound for the colonies, where they would be sold as servants.

Spirit Away: A term for kidnapping used commonly in the British Isles in the white slavery rings.

Swapping Slaves: The trading of one slave for one or more slaves in lieu of money.

Term Slaves: Slaves who would become free after serving a specified term or at a set date in the future or upon arriving at a designated age.

Trafficking: The illegal or improper transport of slaves. Trafficking and smuggling of slaves existed throughout the legal and illegal periods of the slave trade.

Transportation: Also termed transported, a British person was carried away involuntarily to another country by order of the government. After 1776, Australia became the new British destination for felons.

Transported Felon: Another term for a convict servant.

Travel Passes: A permit that allowed a slave the right to leave and circulate freely beyond the limits of the plantation.

Bondage Dictionary (cont.)

Triangular Trade: The name often given to the trans-Atlantic slave trade. It describes the three parts of the routes the slave ships took, from Europe to West Africa, then to the Caribbean and the Americas, and finally back to Europe. The routes are also known as the Outward Passage, the Middle Passage, and the Homeward Passage.

Vagrant: A wandering individual found guilty of an offense such as begging. He or she was frequently sent to the colonies as a worker.

Venture: Slaving voyages are often described as ventures because, as in any business, one ventured one's capital.

Vessel: The sailing craft used to transport enslaved Africans to market.

Virtually Free Slaves: Slaves who openly lived as if they were free and engaged in the activities of free people. They were generally treated and acknowledged by their neighbors as quasi free.

Voyage: The trans-Atlantic journey between two or more ports.

Voyage Dates: Dates when slaving vessels departed from and arrived at markets in the Atlantic world. Dates of departure are generally the days on which the vessels cleared customs.

Voyage Itinerary: The ports visited as part of a slaving voyage. Before the voyages, slaving captains received itineraries from the ship owners, instructing them about which ports to visit.

Voyage Length: The time taken to complete a slaving voyage.

Warranty on Slaves: The act of a seller to assure the buyer that he had a valid title to the slave and the slave was free from physical, mental, and moral defects. It was primarily associated with a suit filed by a buyer for breach of contract when a seller allegedly misrepresented the slave.

Wench: A term for a female African slave. It was also used in common English for white women.

West Indies: Islands in the Caribbean Sea.

White Slave: Another term for an immigrant servant.

Women: Adult female Africans sold into the trans-Atlantic slave trade. Generally, slaving traders classified women as taller than four feet, four inches or older than 13 to 14 years. On most slaving vessels, captains confined women to specific below-deck compartments toward the sterns of the vessels. Women, often not shackled, occasionally broke into arms' chests located in or near the captains' cabins and helped instigate insurrections.

Chapter Sixteen

African Americans and the Irish Slave Holder

It is not uncommon for African Americans descended from slaves to potentially have ancestors from Ireland. The slaves' last owners might not have been those ancestors but could have owned one or more generations of their families. The African American researcher must first identify the Irish slave holder for that line to be pursued to immigrant origins. Even if the last slave owner before emancipation was not the Irish ancestor or even an ancestor, he or she still has to be found to trace the Irish ancestor. The process is similar to following land ownership to the original grantee or grantor. This chapter centers on the slavery period through the end of Reconstruction in 1877 in the quest for family history and includes the 1870 United States census as a key document.

The common myth that locating an ancestor of a slave is impossible is not true. It may be difficult, but it is not unachievable. The stage delaying researchers is identifying the last owners of families and the last plantations on which the families lived. Once that is done, everything potentially unwraps layer by layer. Excellent instruction books and chapters in books can help build a solid foundation for research. Among these are:

Burroughs, Tony. "African American Research." *The Source: A Guidebook to American Genealogy*. 3rd ed., Loretto Dennis Szucs and Sandra Hargreaves Luebking. Provo, Utah: Ancestry, Inc., 2006, pp. 651-676.

Burroughs, Tony. *Black Roots: A Beginner's Guide to Tracing the African American Family Tree*. New York: Fireside, 2001.

Fears, Mary L. *Slave Ancestral Research: It's Something Else*. Westminster, Maryland: Heritage Books, 1995.

Howard, Barbara Thompson. *How to Trace Your African-American Roots*. New York, New York: Citadel Press, Kensington Publishing Corp., 1998.

Rose, James and Alice Eichholz. *Black Genesis; A Resource Book for African-American Genealogy*. 2nd ed., Baltimore, Maryland: Genealogical Publishing Co., 2003.

Smith, Franklin Carter and Emily Anne Croom. *A Genealogist's Guide to Discovering Your African American Ancestors: How to find and record your unique heritage*. Baltimore, Maryland: Genealogical Publishing Co., 2003.

Taylor, Frazine. *Researching African American Genealogy in Alabama: A Resource Guide*. Montgomery, Alabama: New South Books, 2008.

Walton-Raji, Angela Y. *Black Indians Genealogy: African-American Ancestors Among the Five Civilized Tribes*. Westminster, Maryland: Heritage Books, 2007.

Woodtor, Dee Parmer. *Finding a Place Called Home: A Guide to African-American Genealogy and Historical Identity*. Rev. ed., New York: Random House Reference, 1999.

Quality books and websites from historical and genealogical perspectives are plentiful, and an impressive and amazing selection of records for African Americans is online. Primary websites for resources in this research include Ancestry.com and FamilySearch.org.

African Americans and Surnames

How African American families acquired their surnames is often misunderstood. The popular notion is that the slaves took the ones of their last masters at emancipation. In some cases, this may be correct, but this accepted idea if followed too rigorously may lead research in the wrong direction. An Irish surname among African Americans may or may not reflect direct Irish ancestry.

Clear thinking about how a family arrived at its last name is imperative. It could well be that it is not a "slave name" at all but

that it was with a family for generations. The 1870 census is the first federal schedule with full names of former slaves. This is a pivotal record for examining surnames from geographical areas.

In some African American families, surnames came into use just like they did with any other ethnic group, from the fathers or the mothers. If the father was white or the mother already had a surname from her side, one or the other might have been carried forward, the common situation for many generations in free families. In slave families, surnames were often used, although not publicly because there was little purpose for them. Furthermore, owners had no reason to know or to even care about slaves' last names. Slaves were property, not individuals and self-aware people.

The surnames of slaves might have denoted a significant event or person in the family history. For instance, a surname possibly was from a favorite master or possibly the first master. Some owners were benevolent, even paternal, in which circumstances the surnames were status symbols of respect and honor, reflecting those master-slave relationships. On the other hand, families did not choose the names of brutal, cruel, and sadistic slave holders.

Often, surnames were selected for other reasons, perhaps relating to political figures (Washington, Lincoln), first names (David, John, George), colors (Black, Brown, White), principles (Freeman, Love, Pride), occupations (Carpenter, Mason, Smith, Turner, Weaver), or places, a sentimental way of forging an identity as a family unit apart from the brutalities of slavery. Even these can be complex. For example, Pride is a principle but is also a European surname. The same is true of the surname Jordan. It is symbolic of the River Jordan from the Bible stories, but it is also a European surname.

Sometimes, if a family was separated through a slave sale, a surname became a psychological connection to a parent or grandparent who feasibly was never seen again. The name might have been the master's at the time and thus kept the original family bond alive, even if in a disjointed way.

Not all siblings necessarily adopted the same last name after emancipation, especially if they were separated through slavery and if they did choose a surname. Conversely, a family that already used a surname could have continued doing so. Remember, a family could have had an unofficial surname for generations, but the first recorded evidence of it might have been in the 1870 census.

The slave insurance records demonstrate how, even during slavery, some of the masters knew the slaves' surnames, which were not the same as those of the owners. Many slaves were insured against damage or death with only a first name listed, although surnames are listed more than would be expected. Ancestry.com has a searchable feature linked to the original databases not on its website.

An example from the Ancestry.com database "California, Slave Era Insurance Policies Index, 1847-1860" has links to the original database on the California Department of Insurance website, Insurance.ca.gov. It shows that Abraham Fox was a slave living in Henderson County, Kentucky. The slave owner was William Nunn, who was living in the same place. The insurance company, licensed in California yet insuring a Kentucky slave, was New York Life Insurance Company.

The insurance company operating in Illinois, from the Ancestry.com database "U.S., Slave Era Insurance Policies Index," has a record for the slave Tom Wood. He lived in Fayette County, Kentucky, which was the residence of the slave owners Hunter & Bruce. According to the policy, Tom Wood died on 28 August 1846, but the name of the insurance company in Illinois insuring a Kentucky slave was not reported.

It is essential to ascertain how both Abraham Fox and Tom Wood were obtained by their owners. Were they the original owners, and if not, from whom did they buy the slaves? Tom Wood is an interesting illustration because his owners were Hunter & Bruce, probably a company. If so, what type of company? What industry or operation in Fayette County, Kentucky, in the 1840s required a slave to be insured? Fayette County is where the city of Lexington is located, and so either tobacco or horses is a logical assumption.

In addition, why were the Fox and Wood surnames known to the owners? Another series of questions is thereafter raised about those slaves only listed by first names. Did they have surnames? Logically, the answer in some cases is yes.

Slave Schedules and the 1870 United States Census

The 1870 United States census is the launching point for documenting African Americans and perhaps their former slave owners. This key evidence ties back into one of the last records of the slave period, the 1860 United States Slave Schedule.

The 1870 census, taken just five years after the Civil War ended, was the first with the names, ages, and birthplaces of *everybody*. By then, the newly freed slaves were establishing their lives, with many planning to move on. Nevertheless, most still lived close to or even on the old plantations. In 1870, it was common for freed slaves to work on the plantations under a share-cropping system, which for many freed slaves, was little better than slavery. Yet with all its faults and abuses, the system kept both white and Black mouths fed. Former slaves and owners had to work together, allowing a few years of transition for everybody. Consequently, the whites living in the neighborhoods of former slaves in 1870 could have been their owners originally.

Always start with the theory that the slave-owning family can be found in the ancestor's neighborhood. This may not always be the case, but it is logical. With a few assumptions, research can explore the slave schedules that accompanied the 1860 United States census. Slave schedules also supplemented the 1850 United States census, but only the 1860 slave schedules are discussed here.

The slave schedules do not list the first or last names of the slaves. There are some exceptions, such as a slave of 100 or more years old or the census enumerator not following the instructions on the form. The standard form has the names of the *owners* and the slaves by statistics. The categories for the statistics are males, females, ages, and color.

After studying the 1870 neighborhood where the ancestors lived and compiling a list of possible white owners, examine the 1860 slave schedule. Did the potential owners have slaves in the same age categories as those in the 1870 census? Study the 1860 slave schedule closely for how the statistics were written. Did the census taker place family units together? If so, correlating the statistics between the 1860 slave schedules and the 1870 census is much easier.

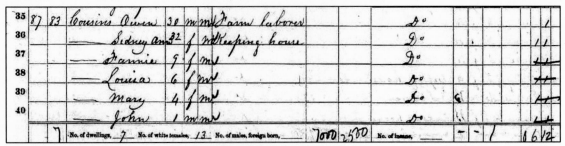

Figure 64: 1870 census for Bald Knob, Franklin County, Kentucky. The presumed husband and wife were indexed as "m" for "mulatto." However, when the image is inspected closely, the wife could be interpreted as "w" for white. For the period, many interesting possibilities are thus raised. (Image courtesy of the National Archives and Records Administration.)

If finding the family in the 1870 census is troublesome, utilize what has been discovered about first names and ages from the 1880 census and examine the 1870 enumeration again. In the latter search, study first names, not surnames. If it is determined the family was going by a different surname between the 1870 and 1880 enumerations, research can continue to move back to the 1860 slave schedules. There, the owner may be found.

When working to identify potential owners, keep in mind that *some* slaves did have the surnames of their last owners. Some slaves were the children of the masters, and they kept the owners' surnames after emancipation. Therefore, whites with the ancestors' surnames may be research targets, an especially valued clue if the 1870 census shows the ancestors as mulatto.

The Reconstruction Era (1865-1877)

After the Civil War ended and all slaves were emancipated in 1865 (1866 in Indian Territory), there was at least a twelve-year period in which the country attempted to integrate again, referred to as the Reconstruction Era. During this complex adjustment, both Southern Black and white societies had to redefine who they were.

Reconstruction policies were instituted to rebuild the South. Reconstruction began in the southern states while most of them were occupied by Union troops. Not until the end of the war was the entire South under its policies. Even though much good resulted from the Reconstruction of the South, there was also much bitterness, corruption, and injustice. The repercussions of the Reconstruction era have been felt to this day. In many ways, the Reconstruction policies failed the very people they were intended to assist. However, a treasury of documents about the former slaves and their lives was generated from the programs instituted.

In March 1865, the government established the Freedmen's Bureau, a program providing food, clothing, and fuel to destitute former slaves and white refugees. It assisted in negotiating labor contracts and establishing new relationships between freedmen and former owners. There were abuses under its policies. Abandoned and confiscated Southern lands were often returned to the former white owners instead of being redistributed to the freedmen.

The Freedmen's Bureau's process of forcing plantation owners to bargain and contract work from Black laborers eventually led to the infamous sharecropping system. What was intended to assure economic independence for the Black laborers trapped them in another form of slavery because of the debts they incurred.

The Reconstruction Era yielded some noteworthy records for family historians. Its programs aimed to redistribute lands, install loyal governments, and take care of the destitute freed slaves and indigent whites. Reconstruction policies and their documents mainly, but not exclusively, concerned the former Confederate states. If the family had already migrated northward or westward, not all the records apply to research. In the South, if ancestors are named in Reconstruction papers, the location of the old plantations might be as well. Documents include marriages, censuses, banking accounts, and murders.

The Freedmen's Bureau and the Freedman's Savings and Trust Company are prime examples of how Reconstruction records can take lineages one step back toward identifying the plantations, last owners, or even parents' names. Many of the records are online at Ancestry.com, FamilySearch.org, or the website "Freedmen's Bureau Online," Freedmensbureau.com.

The Freedmen's Bureau program, officially called the Bureau of Refugees, Freedmen, and Abandoned Lands, was established by the War Department by an Act of 3 March 1865. The Bureau supervised all relief and educational activities relating to refugees and freedmen, including issuing rations, clothing, and medicine. It assumed custody of confiscated lands and property in the former Confederate States, Border States, District of Columbia, and Indian Territory. It also documented crimes and white violence against freedmen and other whites. The Bureau records constitute the richest and most extensive documentary source available for investigating the Black experience in the Reconstruction Era. Many of these records discuss the last owners of families.

The labor contract is another Bureau record type that may have clues to the last owner of the family. The Bureau assisted in drawing up labor contracts between freedmen laborers and planters stating terms of employment and the pay, clothing, and medical care the freedmen were owed. It also outlined the portions of the crops to be retained by both parties. The contracts also dealt with apprenticeships and the legal obligations of each party. Often, contract laborers moved across state lines. An example is W. A. Barner of Cabarras County, North Carolina, contracting freedmen from Anson County, North Carolina, in December 1866 to work on his farm in Tennessee. The term was 1 January 1868. An additional example is:

> *December 15, 1866. State of North Carolina, Anson County. Toney Richardson, wife Mary, and two children, Ann and Calvin, indentured to W. A. Barner to work farm in Tennessee until January 1, 1868.*

The marriage records are another fascinating series of Bureau records that might reconstruct a family unit. The Bureau acted to legally marry couples who were living together under slavery. Some of the records supply parents' names, race, and mentions of the masters. Two such certificates issued in November 1866 from the Bureau office in Washington, D.C., are:

> *William Duvall to Margaret Johnson. Joined by a note from their masters. December 18, 1855 in Annarundell [sic] County, Maryland. Friendship Village their residence. Ceremony by Rev. McCauley (Methodist).*

James Williams to Nelly Brooks. Joined by a note from their master by an Episcopalian minister in Prince George County, Maryland (their residence). Time, 1846. Three children.

The Tennessee Bureau mainly documented marriages from Gibson and Shelby Counties. The forms asked for dissimilar information than did the ones from the Washington, D.C., Bureau. Notice the race descriptions in this sample list that are clues to the white ancestries of the former slaves:

Charles M. Sanders m. Hannah Jones, both of Memphis, TN
Date: July 26, 1865 Place: Memphis, TN
*Man: 31 yrs old; color: **yellow**; father: **white**; mother: unknown; lived with another woman 3 years, separated from her by master. Woman: 25 yrs old; color: **yellow**; father: **yellow**; mother: **yellow**. They, unitedly had 1 child; the man by previous connection had 2; the woman by previous connection had 0.*

Arter Sandow m. Margaret Galmon, both of Memphis, TN
Date: November 25, 1865 Place: Memphis, TN
*Man: 78 yrs old; color: **black**; father: **black**; mother: **black**; lived with another woman 35 years, separated from her by death. Woman: 55 yrs old; color: **griff**; father: **mulatto**; mother: **mulatto**; lived with another man 16 years, separated from him by*

death. They, unitedly had 0 children; the man by previous connection had 0; the woman by previous connection had 5.

Harry Sandrich of Co. E 59th US Col'd Inf. m. Caroline Tate of Memphis, TN
Date: January 29, 1865 Place: Memphis, TN
*Man: 24 yrs old; color: **black**; father: **black**; mother: **black**. Woman: 27 yrs old; color: **yellow**; father: **white**; mother: **brown**; lived with another man 6 years, separated from him by slavery. They, unitedly had 3 children; the man by previous connection had 0; the woman by previous connection had 3.*

While color is certainly subjective, in a society conscious of it, the designations at least are indications about ancestries. In these examples, the terms black, brown, griff, mulatto, yellow, and white are used. Two of these require further examination. Griff is usually an old Louisiana term. It can be interpreted as a child of a Black and a mulatto, a person of mixed Black and Native American ancestry, or simply a mulatto, especially a woman. In the case of Margaret Galmon, who married Arter Sandow, both her parents were listed as mulatto. The Bureau performing their marriage in Memphis is significant and may reveal she was originally from downriver in Louisiana. It could also mean the clerk or minister conducting the ceremony was from Louisiana. Although it is not stated, a consideration is that Margaret might have been from there. Both her parents were mulatto, and thus white ancestry was on both sides, possibly her grandparents' generation. Margaret was 55 years old (born in 1810).

The term yellow is subjective but does connote a person of fair skin, almost yellow in appearance. One historical label, although crude, for a very light-skinned person was "high yellow" or "high yeller," a person who most likely had a white parent or both parents who themselves had a white parent. In a racially charged culture, this might have been the first step of an African American "passing for white," which is another historically crude term. Charles M. Sanders was yellow, and his father was white, the clue sought. His mother was African American, but nothing was known about her. His wife, Hannah Jones, was yellow, as were both her parents. It is through any of this assortment of white and yellow lines that Irish ancestry for either Charles or Hannah is possible.

Harry Sandrich, from the above example, was identified in his Memphis marriage record of 1865 as a veteran who served in Company E, 59th United States Colored Infantry. He was Black, as were his parents, which by default removes him a few generations from any white line. His wife, Caroline Tate, was yellow, her father was white, and her mother, brown. Caroline was born in 1838, and at 27 years old in 1865, she had three children by another man. As the marriage record stated, she and the father of her children were together for six years before being separated by slavery. The indication that she was a slave makes the fact her father was white and her mother brown noteworthy.

The reasonable question is whether the white father of Caroline, who was born into slavery, was also the slave owner. Her mother being brown also suggests mixed race on her mother's side, but how remains to be explored and might account in part for why Caroline was listed as yellow. Her mother might have had Native American ancestry. Additional good evidence is that Harry Sandrich fought for the Union, which left another set of records. Whether he was from the North or had been a slave was not divulged in the marriage record.

The other Reconstruction source of extreme value is the Freedman's Savings and Trust Company. The United States government set up banks in urban areas called the Freedman's Savings and Trust Company to guide the economic development of African American veterans, former slaves, and their families. It functioned from 1865 to 1874. It had 37 offices in 16 states and the District of Columbia, with 70,000 depositors and $57,000,000 in deposits. Current research into the bank and its place in African American history can be found on the website Freedmansbank.org.

The bank's account books often have personal details about its clients and their histories. Former owners and plantation life are constant themes in the freedmen's applications. The 70,000 account records contain about 480,000 names. The program was originally successful, but it began to be ruined in 1870. At that time, bank management started to make risky investments in the stock market and in real estate. The United

States Treasury found it impossible for the bank to survive the severe depression of 1873, and so it was closed in 1874. Under law, clients could recover 62% of their accounts, but most repossessed nothing at all.

The records are housed at the National Archives. They are indexed and digitized on Ancestry.com as "U.S., Freedman's Bank Records, 1865-1871" and on FamilySearch.org in the searchable database "United States, Freedman's Bank Records, 1865-1874." The FamilySearch.org database is one of the largest databases linked to African Americans because it connects the depositors with the names of their parents, which are also in the bank records. The bank branches represented were in the following states and cities:

- Alabama: Huntsville, Mobile
- Arkansas: Little Rock
- Florida: Tallahassee
- Georgia: Atlanta, Augusta, Savannah
- Kentucky: Lexington, Louisville
- Louisiana: New Orleans, Shreveport
- Maryland: Baltimore
- Mississippi: Columbus, Natchez, Vicksburg
- Missouri: St. Louis
- New York: New York

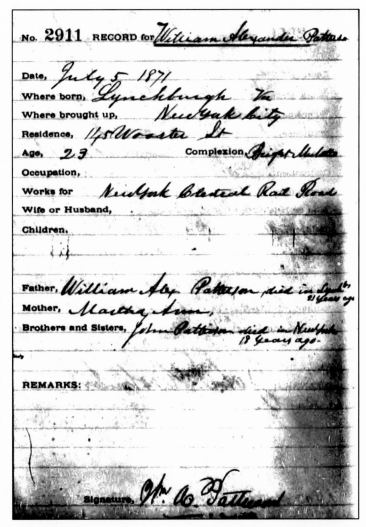

Figure 65: Freedman's Bank record for William Alexander Patterson. He was born in Lynchburgh, Virginia; raised in New York City; and claimed the same name as his father, who, as William stated, died 21 years earlier in Lynchburg. Also, a brother was identified. Most importantly, William's complexion was recorded as "bright mulatto." This man's descendants might have been noted as "white" in future censuses and other documents. (Image courtesy of the National Archives and Records Administration.)

- North Carolina: New Bern, Raleigh, Wilmington
- Pennsylvania: Philadelphia
- South Carolina: Beaufort, Charleston
- Tennessee: Memphis, Nashville
- Virginia: Lynchburg, Norfolk, Richmond
- Washington, D.C.

The bank records are more accurate than some other documents because the depositors were supplying the answers to questions. FamilySearch.org, as the pioneer in indexing these books, has studied the depositors' records and found the following information could be part of them:

- Account number
- Name of depositor
- Date of application
- Birthplace
- Place brought up
- Residence
- Age
- Complexion
- Occupation
- Name of employer
- Spouses name
- Children's names
- Father's name
- Mother's name
- Brothers' and sisters' names
- Name of former master or mistress
- Name of plantation
- Regiment and company served in during the Civil War
- Wife's maiden name or the name of a former spouse
- Names of nieces, nephews, aunts, uncles, grandparents, and in-laws
- Residence of these individuals and whether they were living or dead
- Death certificate copies

Such details can be successful in linking a former slave to the plantation, slave owner, birthplace, and relatives.

The Civil War (1861-1865)

The vast majority of African Americans who fought in the Civil War did so for the Union. Some slaves did fight for the Confederate States of America or were impressed into a service roll for the troops. This discussion is limited to the Union side of the war.

African Americans made a vital contribution to the Union forces. The segregated units known as Colored Troops consisted of some 186,097 soldiers. This number included 7,122 officers and 178,975 troops in 163 units. The troops included both free and escaped slaves. In other words, roughly 10% of the Union soldiers were African American.

On 17 July 1862, Congress passed two acts allowing the enlistment of African Americans, but official enrollment occurred only after the Emancipation Proclamation_took effect 1 January 1863. However, state and local militia units had already begun enlisting Blacks. The Colored Troops fought and lost their lives just as their white counterparts did, but not at the same rates. The Colored Troop casualty rate was about 20% by the war's end. The death rate among white soldiers stood at about 8.9%.

Many records exist from which to document a soldier in the United States Colored Troops. The value of this topic should not be underestimated. Jeannette Braxton's *Guide to Tracing Your African Ameripean Civil War Ancestor* (Westminster, Maryland: Heritage Books, 1997, 2019) states that almost all African Americans have a family member who fought with the Colored

Troops. This is a reasonable assumption since the Great Migration to the northern cities brought massive numbers of Southern families in contact with families from the North.

When using the Civil War records for Colored Troops, remember that most are similar to the documents for white soldiers, but the information gleaned from them can be quite different. For example, the pension application for a veteran or his widow should contain the same biographical facts as a pension for a white veteran would, such as birthplace, name of spouse, and date and place of marriage. However, it may also include plantation names and former masters, making these pension files comparable to no other documents.

Slaves and the Plantation (pre-1865)

Slavery, as an economic enterprise, was not originally developed along color lines, and so anybody with colonial ancestry (pre-1776) may have an ancestor who was in a form of bondage. He or she could have been Black, white, or native. To the early colonials, the word slavery implied economic exploitation, not a race. It became racial later.

Bondage, where one person was owned by another, potentially for life, was known as chattel slavery. *(See also Bondage Dictionary in the previous chapter, pp. 226-236).* The first African slaves arrived in Virginia in 1619. Chattel slavery of one kind or another became legal in the American colonies in 1654 and continued until 1865. Black chattel slavery can be thought of in two periods, the Middle Passage and the Second Middle

Passage. The original Middle Passage is a term used to describe the slave trade portion of a larger "triangular trade" that developed between the European powers, Africa, and the New World. The kidnapping and shipment of slaves from Africa is this first Middle Passage.

During this period, between 9 and 12 million slaves were sent to the New World. Brazil obtained the largest amount, about 3 million or roughly 35% of all those enslaved during the Middle Passage. It was the time, from 1440 to 1640, that Portugal, the colonial power of Brazil, had a monopoly on the slave trade. By the 1700s, Great Britain became a foremost player and was responsible for enslaving 2,500,000 Africans out of the estimated 6 million during that century. What became the United States received about 645,000 of the Middle Passage slaves. This number helps to place the family histories of slave descendants into perspective. All African Americans who descended from slaves are from those 645,000.

By 1860, the number of descendants had grown to over four million. Many African American and white lines interconnected through the centuries so that descendants of those 645,000 original Africans almost always have one or several European ancestors. This happened through several methods, including rape, relationships with indentured white servants, mutual relationships, casual encounters, and slave prostitutes. Regardless, it is not uncommon for African American DNA test results to display an expected percentage of European ancestry, including Irish.

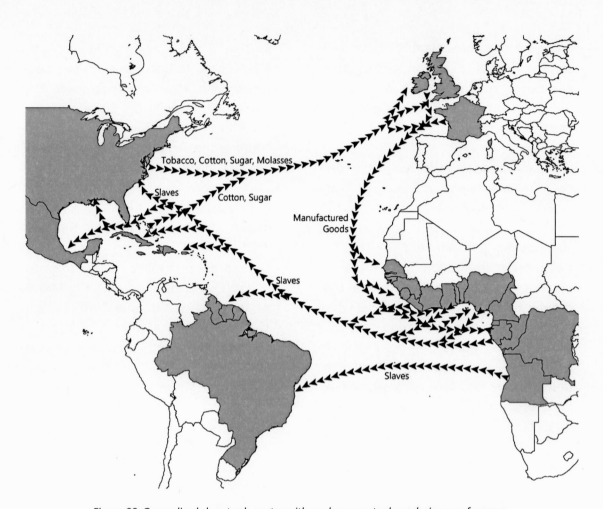

Figure 66: Generalized slave trade routes with modern country boundaries as references.

In trying to connect back into the white line, the Second Middle Passage from 1776 to 1850 is most crucial but is where a context is needed. As the nation expanded westward, so did the institution of slavery. This passage was not across the Atlantic but across land. Families were torn apart and sold just as they were during the original Middle Passage. With the acquisition of Native American lands, new westward lands were opened for planting cotton and other crops. Laborers were required, resulting in a massive migration of not only white families but also their slaves. Furthermore, the market for newly purchased slaves from the East was launched. Some historians

view the Second Middle Passage as *the* central event in American slave history between the Revolutionary War and the Civil War.

Nobody knows exactly how many slaves moved from the Old South (Maryland, North Carolina, South Carolina, and Virginia) to the Deep South (Alabama, Georgia, Louisiana, Mississippi, and Texas). As whites acquired larger tracts of property in the new lands, they needed slaves.

Some historians estimate that up to 1,000,000 slaves were transported to the plantations being established on the frontier lands in the Deep South, which attracted business-oriented white families. The effect on the African American population was traumatizing. Both slaves and free Blacks lived in fear of their families being taken away. Historians judge that approximately 60 to 70% of the slaves transported as part of the Second Middle Passage were sold by their owners, which transfers are necessary to track so that a lineage can move back from the Deep South into the Old South.

Most of the slave sales during this period were through slave traders. In this industry, the traders acted as brokers between the sellers and the buyers. Slave traders had no interest in selling intact families. The profit was in the stock for breeding that could be used by the new owner to increase a future work force, and so equal numbers of men and women were bought and then sold. The slave trade became the largest industry in the South except for that of the plantations' products. Not only did the slave business help to develop modern transportation but it also revolutionized the financial markets by enriching the economy during the time. The scale of this accepted and sanctioned human trafficking was so immense by the end of the Second Middle Passage that slavery was ingrained and integrated into every aspect of Southern culture. Hardly anybody, Black or white, was untouched by it.

The records for this industrial-scale slave traffic are those always sought for pre-1865 African American family history. It is through the plantation experience that so many white lines intersect with the African lineages, but it is not the only way.

Female slaves were exploited as prostitutes for white men in the cities, and Black women were house servants, nannies, and domestics in white households. Slaves were loaned and rented under contracts for various purposes. To assume a plantation owner was the father of a woman's children may be incorrect. DNA tests are answering many of these questions.

Plantation Records

Plantation records from which to trace a slave ancestor might have survived. If the owner has been identified, efforts can proceed to explore his or her plantation records. These were business records because the plantations were large-scale family enterprises as well as family homes, and thus the lives of plantation owners and slaves were interconnected. The safety and well-being of the slaves and the control of the slave work force were always concerns since healthy and compliant slaves equated to income for the communities and the plantations. There was little way to separate them.

Several methods can determine whether the plantation records exist or where they are kept. One is to contact public libraries or county historical societies. The reference staffs may know exactly where they were deposited because others have inquired previously. Plantation records are usually at regional and university libraries, state archives, or with the descendants of the plantation owners.

Because the historical value of these records is obvious, many were placed at research libraries for safekeeping. The records can include ones for business, accounts, slave lists, contracts, overseers' reports, slave births and deaths, diaries, and private letters. As private businesses, keeping records was not uniform, and what is in them cannot be known without a previously compiled inventory for each plantation. Plantation records illustrate almost every aspect of plantation life. Gleaned from them can be day-to-day business operations, family affairs, the roles of women, racial attitudes, the slave-master relationships, social and cultural life, the treatment of the slaves, and master-slave tensions.

The plantations' birth records are those most desired. In this culture, children were the property of their mothers' masters, the reason the births were recorded. Some states, such as Kentucky (1852-1862), required the slave owners to register slave births with county officials, and so the plantation records became county records. For slave births, the names of children and the mothers are listed but not those of the fathers. Kentucky is an odd example. Commonly, a plantation owner registered the births of his slaves and failed to register the births of his own children by his wife. Kentucky, as a border state and technically a Union state, did not eliminate slavery during the Civil War. It was not until 1865 that slavery was abolished, and by that time, most of the slaves were already free or had left Kentucky for states farther north.

Records of Ante-Bellum Southern Plantations from the Revolution Through the Civil War by University Publications of America is an enormous collection spanning the South. Inventories of it, which bring together plantation records from the state archives and libraries, universities, and historical societies, can be found online through a general Internet search. Documentation for the larger plantations can be extant from at least the War of 1812 through the Civil War. The records in this collection are widely available on microfilm, which is also at the Family History Library.

Slave Sales in County Land Deeds

Since slaves were considered properties of their owners, deeds were registered at the courthouses when slaves were bought or sold. County land deeds are a primary source from which to document the series of owners for slaves. It may seem odd to think of the sale of a slave as a "deed," but the slave was the transaction of property.

Some families even used the county (parish or district) deeds as a means of distributing estates before death. Old folks often gave the farms and slaves to one of their children. Usually, the parents continued to live in the family homes until their deaths and were cared for by the children who took over the farms, situations identified by phrases like "for my natural love" in the deeds' introductions or everything being sold for $1.00, which was the legal filing fee. The sales of slaves were included. County land deed books are perhaps among the most important sources to consult in moving a slave line back in time to a former owner.

Because of the intense interest in slavery in American history, some amazing databases are being compiled. One, sponsored by the University of North Carolina, Greensboro, is "People Not Property

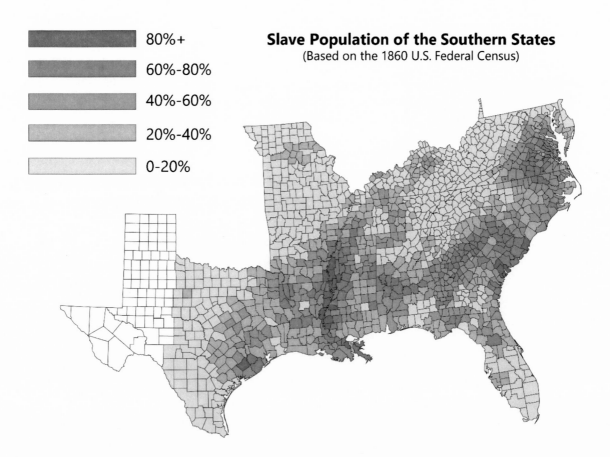

80%+
60%-80%
40%-60%
20%-40%
0-20%

Slave Population of the Southern States
(Based on the 1860 U.S. Federal Census)

Figure 67: African American slave demographics entering the Civil War era, imposed on modern-day counties.

- Slave Deeds of North Carolina." The library.uncg.edu website aspires to index and digitize all known slave transactions in the state.

The land deed books for most of the eastern United States and former slave states have been microfilmed or digitized. These can usually be found at a state archive or on FamilySearch.org. The original books are sometimes still at the courthouses. Once a county, district, or parish is known, some key concepts for using them are:

Slaves are not listed by name in the manuscript deed indexes. To use the original indexes, the name of the last owner has to be known. In this case, it is deeds for the owner (buyer or seller) that are being sought. It is within them that slave transactions are mentioned. If the owner is not known, the 1860 Slave Schedules will help. The first step is the indexes, not the deeds themselves.

Once the owner is identified, the manuscript index has the volume and page number so that the manuscript deed can be consulted. The hope is that through the buying and selling of an ancestor as property, the original owner, who is perhaps the father, will be identified. Ancestors were reported by first names, ages, and sometimes descriptions or with families if the sales were for mothers and their children. In the index, a buyer (grantee) and the seller (grantor) are listed.

In researching the buyer and seller, be aware of where everybody lived. A transaction might have occurred in one county, but the parties involved might have been from another county. These are clues to where the slave ancestor was originally from.

Sometimes, the deed books have been transcribed, indexed, and published by individuals or genealogical societies. A well-done compilation generally includes: A) a slave index by first name; B) a buyers' and sellers' index; C) a list of everybody mentioned in the deed, such as neighbors; and D) a geographical index of land and water features mentioned in the deeds. For some places, such as South Carolina and Virginia, these published works can save hours of research in the digitized manuscript editions. They are not substitutes for the original records, but they can be of great assistance, especially the slave indexes.

The format of a deed is usually standard. This is not set in stone but is a guide only. Deeds may vary in their content, but the legal content is standardized. Although

the subject herein is the transactions of buying and selling, do not always assume that an ancestor was being sold. Through a careful reading of the deed, it may be found that an ancestor was collateral in some legal matter in much the same way that real estate was. Or perhaps an ancestor was being leased for a certain sum to another plantation. In these cases, the ownership never changed. Always read the legal language carefully. Principal parts of a deed include: 1) Date of transaction; 2) Name and residence of buyer/grantee; 3) Name and residence of seller/grantor; 4) Name of slave; 5) Age of slave; 6) Color of slave; 7) Relationship of slave to others; 8) Additional miscellaneous information; 9) Witnesses to the transaction; and 10) Date the deed was registered.

Keep in mind when studying land deeds that the focus of research has to be shifted from the ancestor to the owner. Think in terms of two goals layered together that cannot be separated.

With each deed found, new bits of knowledge are gained. The deeds are a foremost step in identifying the slave master, but whether he was the owner or the actual father of the slaves he sold is always the next step. A DNA test may support the paper trail that has been gathered. The concept of slaves as property is complex. Remember, if a mother and child were sold separately, it may indicate that the master was the father of the child and he was disposing of evidence. Plantation wives, once they became aware of the situations, often demanded that their husbands sell female slaves because their mixed-race children were hard to hide. Such a possibility requires an open mind and some reading between the lines.

Slave Transactions and Probate Records

Probate refers to a court action dealing with the distribution of an estate. If the deceased died with a will that the court finds to be valid, the estate is said to be testate and the court generally follows the instructions outlined in the will. If the deceased died without a valid will, the person is said to have died intestate and the court disposes of the estate according to the inheritance laws of the time and place. Probate proceedings created many different records. These may include the determinations about the validity of wills, assignments of executors in cases of testate estates or administrators in cases of intestate estates, postings of bonds, appraisals and inventories, dispositions of estates, and decisions such as final decrees. Counties often filed testate records separately from intestate records.

In reading these records, whether testate or intestate, the concern is what happened to the slaves of a family after the deaths of the owners. The key here is that slaves were someone's property and part of the estate.

Testate estates are relatively straightforward. A person dies leaving a written will of his or her wishes, and the estate is distributed accordingly. Courts intervene less often with testate probate matters than with intestate ones. The passing of slaves in a written will can identify them by first names. An ownership history can be valuable. As with all wills, if the estate

is small, the possibility of the slaves being named is good. If the estate is huge, with hundreds of slaves, the will giving the names of the slaves is not as probable. One custom was that slaves often went to the daughters and the lands, to the sons.

An aspect to consider about wills and slaves as property is that like land, the same slave can be named in several wills depending on the deaths of the owners. The majority of wills for the slave-holding states are at the Family History Library. Ancestry.com has been compiling large collections of wills and estates based on the state instead of the county level. In the Ancestry.com indexes, the search can be limited to a county within the collection. Otherwise, probate material can be at a county courthouse or state archive.

If the slave-holding family is known, looking for the owners' wills is not a problem. These are usually indexed in published books, at the beginnings of the manuscript will books, or on online databases. Even though slave names are not mentioned in a manuscript index to an original record or in an online index, they may be included in a published index created by an individual or through the efforts of a genealogical society.

For small estates with no personal plantation records, the wills (and the deeds) may be the only documents available with slaves' names. The information varies from will to will, from freeing the slaves to supporting them with the estate funds. Details of a will cannot be known until it is examined.

If an owner died without leaving a will but had property, the county courts became involved. Probate cases sometimes dragged on for years with many court hearings, but they did produce miscellaneous records not found in testate cases. If estates had debts, even more reports were generated, which are typically county court or probate ones. Large collections of these, like the testate material, can be found at the Family History Library, Ancestry.com databases, state archives, or county courthouses.

Black Biographical Dictionaries

"Black Biographical Dictionaries, 1790-1950" is a major gathering of old biographical dictionaries containing more than 30,000 references. The entries record individuals famous in history as well as average people. The 297 volumes, on 1,070 microfiche, range from listings of national activists, state and local personalities, women, professionals, fraternal order members, and church leaders and missionaries, among others. The collection is widely available, especially at academic and university libraries. The titles are from more than 100 public and private repositories across the United States and Great Britain. The compilers of this library include Randall K. Burkett, Nancy Hall Burkett, and Henry Louis Gates, Jr.

If the name of a former slave ancestor is in these works, the owner or series of owners may also be mentioned. For example, volumes 181-183 are Abigail Field Mott's *Biographical Sketches and Interesting Anecdotes of Persons of Color* published in 1826, 1837, and 1839.

These are descriptions of freed slaves or people from free families. The sketches frequently disclose birthplaces, parents' names, and former slave owners.

For identifying owners, a biographical sketch about a person of the era has information not usually found in many places. A three-volume index to this collection is titled *Black Biography, 1790-1950: A Cumulative Index*. The first two volumes index biographies alphabetically, with volume three functioning as an index by place of birth, occupation, religion, and sex.

A second series has supplemented the dictionaries as new books are being identified. These are also indexed. Both the supplements and the indexes can be found at numerous university and academic archives. Any university with an active program of African American studies has these index books or the microfiche editions of historic books.

Figure 68: The slave market in Atlanta, Georgia, 1864. (Image courtesy of Library of Congress. Copyright expired.)

Chapter Seventeen

Catholic Religious (Priests, Brothers, and Nuns)

One markedly overlooked area in genealogical research is family members who joined Catholic religious orders. They are usually disregarded because they never married or had children, and, therefore, the assumption is that their value in family history research is limited. The opposite is true. Within the records about these persons, some families each having several members who served, are the locations of Irish origins, and so exploring their documents is essential.

Understandably, the religious in a family were educated, well-traveled, and intellectual, traits leading to records they left, such as journals, books, and personal memoirs. As they were accepted into orders and pursued their studies, they were

asked questions, certainly one of which was about birthplace.

Why a man or woman joined a specific order is always asked in family history. Among the number of reasons, a practical one is that the parish to which the family belonged or the church school the children attended was served by that order. In consequence, it was promoted by the priests and nuns. Historically, the religious were looked upon with awe and mystery. Their words were heeded, and they were trusted, valued, and distinguished figures in their parishes and communities in the same way Protestant ministers were respected in their districts.

Exceptions do exist, and in this respect, the Catholic Church is no different from any other denomination. People are people, the religious also. It is not uncommon for Catholic families to harbor horror stories about priests or nuns, and these can offer research clues as well. The tales of nuns "from hell" who were teachers in parochial schools can be epic and entertaining. Repeatedly, the relationships parishioners had with the religious in their parishes defined generations of attitudes toward the Church. It can help explain why an otherwise Irish Catholic family joined, for example, the Methodist Church.

From a genealogical perspective, the article "Researching Catholic Nuns, Brothers and Priests in the U.S. for Place of Origin" in *The Irish At Home and Abroad,* 4, #3 (1997), pp. 121-125), by Kyle J. Betit

DEATH OF BISHOP MULLEN.

Erie's Aged Prelate Passes Away After Three Years' Illness.

Rt. Rev. Tobias Mullen, D. D., Bishop of Erie, Pa., died at his Episcopal residence on the night of April 22, after suffering nearly three years from a stroke of paralysis. Bishop Mullen was the youngest of six sons, was a native of County Tyrone, Ireland, and was born in the parish of Urney, March 4, 1818. His parents were Thomas Mullen and Mary

Travers. From early youth he manifested a desire for a religious life.

In 1840 Bishop Laughlin held an examination of the students preparing for the priesthood, and such was young Tobias Mullen's proficiency that he was selected among others to be sent to the Irish College at Paris. But while he was making the preparations for his departure for Paris he stood another and more rigid general examination and competition with all the students of the diocese; and such was the distinction he won in this ordeal that he was selected by the Bishop for immediate entrance into the college of Maynooth.

Ordained in Erie.

In 1843, in the month of October, the first Bishop of Erie, Right Rev. Michael O'Connor, visited Maynooth on his way from Rome, soon after his consecration, with a view of providing priests and religious for his diocese. Bishop O'Connor made an appeal for volunteers for the American mission, and among the five young Levites who responded was the Rev. Tobias Mullen. He was ordained to the priesthood by the Right Rev. Bishop O'Connor on the 1st of September, 1844, in the Cathedral in Erie.

His first Mass was celebrated in St. Philomena's Church, assisted by the venerable Rev. J. N. Neumann, C. SS. R., afterward Bishop of Philadelphia, and whose cause for beatification is now being forwarded at Rome.

The young priest was first employed in the holy ministry of the Cathedral of St. Paul. For the purpose of providing for a higher education for boys in the city of Pittsburg, the Bishop in 1846 established a high school, and named the young priest as its principal.

After two years the Bishop sent him to take charge of the Church of St. John Gualbert, Johnstown, with the additional mission of Wilmore. This was about the close of the year 1846. In this laborious mission he spent nine years, and he was then appointed pastor of St. Peter's Church, Alleghany, succeeding Rev. James Kearney, Oct. 24, 1854.

Thirteen years were devoted to faithful service in Allegheny, several of which saw him add the additional duties of Vicar-General under the Right Rev. Michael Domenec. His services at Allegheny were eminently successful.

Beat the Knownothings.

As pastor of St. Peter's he had charge of the Catholic inmates of the Western Penitentiary. Prior to the organization of St. Andrew's parish he performed the same office of mercy to the unfortunate proteges of the House of Refuge, when bigotry would condescend to permit. The fanatical opposition of the officers of the institution to the visits of the priest occasioned quite a spirited public correspondence between Father Mullen and John J. Logan, president of the Refuge in 1862. Through the influence of Father Mullen, a supplement to the act of incorporation of the institution was introduced into the Legislature, by which the inmates were permitted in time of sickness to confer with a minister of their choice, in sight, but, if desired, not in hearing of the officers of the institution, as the rules previously required. The act was approved March 31st of that year, and the unfortunate children felt their condition somewhat ameliorated by being able to make their confession, a privilege from which they had before been debarred.

On the death of Right Rev. Josue M. Young, Bishop of Erie, September 16, 1866, Fr. Mullen was appointed the third Bishop of that see.

Two years intervened between the death of Bishop Young and the appointment of his successor; the Very Rev. John D. Coady serving as the administrator of the diocese.

On Sunday, the 2d of August, 1868, Fr. Mullen was solemnly consecrated Bishop in the Cathedral at Pittsburg. Right Rev. Bishop Domenec was the consecrator. There were present at the solemn rite as assistant Bishops, Right Rev. Dr. Rappe, of Cleveland, and Right Rev. Dr. Wood, of Philadelphia. Right Rev. Bishop Luers, of Fort Wayne, Ind., and the late Bishop Shanahan, of Harrisburg, Pa.

Three weeks after his arrival he had assisted in establishing St. Vincent's Hospital, one of the most noted institutions of its kind in the State. It is in charge of the Sisters of St. Joseph. He built an orphan asylum at a cost of $60,000, which gives shelter, board and education to about two hundred homeless children; this institution is also in charge of the Sisters of St. Joseph.

No sooner had he paid off every cent of this indebtedness than he began to build the magnificent structure known as St. Peter's Cathedral, which cost in round numbers $300,000. The site was purchased in 1868, ground was broken for the foundation in 1873. The building was completed and dedicated in October, 1893,

> without one penny of debt hanging over it.
>
> Bishop Mullen was a profound student and deep thinker. He wrote an erudite treatise on the "Canon of the Sacred Scriptures," issued from the press about nine years ago. It is an invaluable book to students and clergy.
>
> He attended the Vatican Council at Rome in 1869, at which there were in attendance over one thousand Bishops from all parts of the world. He had journeyed to Rome three times since. Owing to his illness he resigned his office in 1899, when the Right Rev. John E. Fitzmaurice was consecrated coadjutor Bishop with the right of succession.

Figure 69: (Continued from previous page) Descriptive obituary of Rt. Reverend Tobias Mullen, posted 28 April 1900 in Irish World, New York City. (Image courtesy of GenealogyBank.)

is valuable. It is dated, but the strategies are current.

Records of the Religious

Some assumptions need to be corrected so that records being studied can make sense. The stereotype is that priests, brothers, and nuns never married or had children. Even though this is accurate for most young men and women entering an order, keep in mind that not all were young. Many widows entered the convent after their husbands died and their children were grown. It was no different with men and the priesthood. Whether the persons were young or old, the religious life is considered a vocation and is taken seriously. Upon entering, the men and women are theoretically celibate, in which state they serve their communities.

When developing an immigrant origins' strategy, realize that each order keeps records, and after the death of one of its members, his or her personal papers customarily become part of the order's archive. Information such as birthplace, parents' names, and marriage information about the parents is routine. This is exactly where theology creates records.

Historically, priests, for instance, had to provide evidence of their baptisms and parents' marriages. An illegitimate son could not become a priest, being born in sin out of wedlock. Because of this documentation process, an American-born priest of Irish-born parents could be just as important to research as an Irish-born priest. The hope is that the places of the parents' births and marriage have been preserved in the records about that religious.

When engaging in this angle of research, fundamental pieces of information should be sought, the foremost being which order the priest, brother, or nun joined. Many researchers first come across the name in a newspaper obituary, which the religious ordinarily had because of their positions in the communities. If OFM is after a priest's name, he was with the Order of Friars Minor, the Franciscans. If it is OP, he was from the Order of Preachers, the Dominicans.

For women religious, the research procedure and logic are no different. If an obituary has BVM after her name, she was a Sister of Charity of the Blessed Virgin Mary, not to be confused with the letters PBVM, the Sisters of the Presentation of the Blessed Virgin Mary, called Presentation Sisters.

An extended list of abbreviations can be found on the Internet. One website page is "Abbreviations of Religious Orders and Priestly Fraternities" on Fisheaters.com. Another one is Catholicdoors.com. The initials are also commonplace in the obituaries for the siblings of the religious. Wherever they are discovered, it may be easier to begin researching the religious in the family instead of the direct ancestor.

Once the order is identified, search for the order itself. *The Official Catholic Directory* has the contact numbers, but it may be as easy as an Internet search. If the priest served a diocese, contact that diocese, which again is a simple Internet search for current contact information. The records, whether they are in an order or a diocese, are private and do not have to be released. Privacy rules apply as they do for any other denomination. However, most orders are accustomed to genealogical requests because many priests and nuns are avid genealogists themselves!

Men Religious

Men religious can be priests or brothers. A man can serve in several ways. For example, he can bond himself to a diocesan bishop and is thus a "diocesan priest." If he is in an order and serves wherever the order assigns him, he is a "religious priest." Religious priests can serve anywhere, far from their homes and families.

Brothers are dissimilar to priests and are referred to as Brother rather than Father. These men choose to join religious orders and have consented to obey their rules. Some orders have both priests and brothers, but ones such as the Irish Christian Brothers are totally composed of brothers.

A matter of pride for many Irish immigrants was having priests in their families. The priests in most communities acted as advocates for the parishioners, many of whom were often unskilled and illiterate. As literate and educated men, the priests were more than qualified to write articles and petitions to address the injustices so common in the nineteenth-

Religious Orders and Their Abbreviations (Men)

Abbreviations	Religious Orders for Men
CFC	Congregation of Christian Brothers (of Ireland)
CM	Congregation of the Missions (Vincentians)
OFM	Order of Friars Minor (Franciscans)
OFM.Cap	Franciscans (Capuchins)
OFM.Conv	Franciscans (Conventual)
OP	Order of Preachers (Dominicans)
OSA	Order of St. Augustine (Augustinians)
OSB	Order of St. Benedict (Benedictines)
SJ	Society of Jesus (Jesuits)

Figure 70: Franciscan Monastery. Cardinal Gibbons: Episcopal Jubilee, February 1919. (Image by Harris & Ewing, photographers. Courtesy of the Library of Congress. Copyright expired.)

century American labor arena. Such men naturally created records during their lifetimes. Likely, they also had informative obituaries when they died, with, hopefully, all the biographical details any family historian could ever want.

The selected orders on the previous page, especially attractive for Irish men, were operating in the United States. The abbreviations for them are in documents and listed in obituaries. These are not the only orders, but they are examples of them.

Women Religious

Religious women, like priests, were educated and regularly served as instructors or in the medical field. Because of their education and skills, they left records. The goal, of course, is to find the records of the order at the motherhouse and determine whether the papers about acceptance into the order, education, and training for service reveal where in Ireland parents were born. Obituaries could have the rest of the details.

Religious orders for women were popular among the Irish in Ireland and in the United States. At times, it seems as though one girl in every Irish Catholic family joined a religious order and, occasionally, more than one in one family. For some girls, choices in Ireland were limited to marriage or the convent. If neither was wanted and the money was

Religious Orders and Their Abbreviations (Women)

Abbreviations	Religious Orders for Women
BVM	Sisters of Charity of the Blessed Virgin Mary
CSJ	Congregation of the Sisters of St. Joseph
CSC	Congregation of the Sisters of the Holy Cross
OCD	Order of Discalced Carmelite Nuns
OSB	Sisters of the Order of St. Benedict (Benedictine Sisters)
OSF	Sisters of St. Francis (Franciscans)
OSU	Order of St. Ursula (Ursuline Nuns)
RSM	Religious Sisters of Mercy
SGM	Sisters of Charity (Grey Nuns of Montreal)
SND	Sisters of Notre Dame de Namur
PBVM	Sisters of the Presentation of the Blessed Virgin Mary (Presentation Sisters)

available, emigration became a third option. Otherwise, many single Irish girls went to the convent.

When researching, religious might have had other names normally adopted by new members to signify their commitment and service. Mary, of course, was popular, but, certainly, others were as well. An internal logic and process inspired how a sister chose or was assigned a new name, although the underlying customs are specific to each religious order.

In some orders, new sisters suggest a name they would like to have, but the acceptance or rejection of it is left to the leaders. Names are typically after saints, Christ, or, naturally, Mary. If an order is named after Mary, it may be common for all the sisters to receive Mary as part of their new names. Also, names of favorite saints or saints of their home parishes may be in their religious names. A parent

with a saint's name can account for part of the nun's name. Some orders simply assigned names, and a sister could receive the one of a deceased member. Although it has been traditional to change women's names to reflect their new lives as religious, some orders allow them to keep their baptismal names, explaining that the religious vocation is ultimately linked to the baptismal call.

If the order a young woman might have joined is not known, find her home parish. What order served it or the school she might have attended? The answer can be located therein.

Selected orders operating in the United States that were especially attractive for Irish women are above. The key to identifying a nun's order and accessing her records is the initials after her name. The list is not complete but demonstrates the intention of this subject.

Chapter Eighteen

The Irish and American Spiritualism

To many family historians, neither Spiritualism nor its connection to the Irish is familiar. The religion is not addressed in genealogy instruction books even though its records are now being gathered and digitized online. Accordingly, the understanding of it is essential to research and, subsequently, needs to be fully developed as a valid genealogical topic.

Irish and Scots-Irish immigrants throughout the history of the United States commonly believed in some form of esoteric or folk practices, as seen in the Scots-Irish in the 1700s as they settled in the Appalachian Mountains. They contributed to the development of Hoodoo (also known as Conjure), a merger of Germanic (Pennsylvania Dutch), Native American, African, and Scots-Irish folk magic, folk religion, and folk medicine. In an isolated rural community, the Hoodoo Doctor, with his or her herbs, salves, amulets, and incantations, often was the only doctor.

In Conjure, the legendary High John the Conqueror is the most powerful and magical root in the Hoodoo mojo bag and was revered by blacks and whites. Some Hoodoo expressions can still be heard today, such as those surrounding the birth of a child in "veil witch" (birth caul) or "seventh son of a seventh son." Hoodoo is not to be confused with Haitian Voodoo (Vodou) or New Orleans Voodoo, and it is not confined to history since it still is practiced today.

Excellent works on this made-in-America, abstruse, magical, blended version have been published. Most recent ones focus on the African American contribution to the subject. These books remain of assistance for understanding the history of Hoodoo and American Spiritualism because the line between them is thin, with the power and guidance of the spirits being an emphasis in both. Fascinating volumes include:

Casas, Starr. *Old Style Conjure: Hoodoo, Rootwork & Folk Magic.* Newburyport, Massachusetts: Red Wheel/Weiser, 2017.

Hazzard-Donald, Katrina. *Mojo Workin': The Old African American Hoodoo System.* Urbana, Illinois: University of Illinois Press, 2013.

Leslie, Paul J. *Low Country Shamanism: An Exploration of the Magical and Healing Practices of the Coastal Carolinas*

SPIRITUALISTIC MEETINGS.

SPIRITUALISTIC PHENOMENA ASSOCIATION, Berkeley Hall, Sunday, at 2.30 p. m., address, etc., by the guides of Mr. A. E. Tisdale, the noted Spiritualist orator. Exquisite music; J. Aldrich Libby, Miss Wakefield, Mrs. Harding, Mrs. Edwards, Prof. Milligan and others. D. J. Ricker, president.

BOSTON SPIRITUAL LYCEUM, Paine Hall, Sunday at 11 a. m. Dr. Fred Crockett will give psychometric readings. Reading, recitations, vocal and instrumental music. Seats all free. Services every evening this week at Ladies' Parlors, 1031 Washington st.

MISS JENNIE K. D. CONANT of Scotland will hold in her parlors a circle for trance and psychometric tests, Sunday and Wednesday evenings at 7.30 o'clock; also, Saturday afternoon at 2.30 o'clock, and private sittings at 20 Bennett st., Boston, Mass.

AT 127 DIVISION ST., CHELSEA, seances for tests and psychometric readings are held every Sunday and Wednesday evenings at 8. Private sittings after 2 p. m.

BOSTON SPIRITUAL TEMPLE SOCIETY, at Berkeley Hall, 4 Berkeley st., Odd Fellow's Building—Lectures Sunday at 10.30 a. m. and 7.30 p. m. by Mrs. A. H. Colby.

CHELSEA SPIRITUALIST MEETING—Pilgrim Hall, Odd Fellows' building. Sunday conference at 3 p. m.; at 7.30 A. A. Tisdale will occupy the rostrum.

FIRST SPIRITUAL TEMPLE, cor. Exeter and Newbury sts.—Services Sunday, at 2.45 and 7.30 p. m. Miss M. T. Shelhamer, trance speaker. Seats free.

SPIRITUALIST LADIES' AID PARLORS, 1031 Washington st., Sunday evening at 7.30. Test seance by Mrs. J. F. Dillingham and Mrs. Sue Fales.

FRED CROCKETT CIRCLE—For study and test of "spirit gifts." Sunday evening, 7.30 p. m. 254 Shawmut avenue, corner of Bradford street, Boston.

MRS. A. E. CUNNINGHAM will hold a test seance at her rooms, 459 Tremont st., suite 1, Sunday evening at 7.30.

MRS. W. H. RICH will hold a seance every Sunday and Thursday evening, at 8 o'clock, 277 Shawmut av.

Figure 71: A list of Spiritualistic meetings as displayed in the Boston Daily Globe on 11 December 1886.

and Georgia. San Bernardino, California: Path Notes Books, 2014.

Smith, Theophus H. *Conjuring Culture: Biblical Formations of Black America.* New York: Oxford University Press, 1994.

Ireland is known for its rich folk practices and beliefs. Today's generally dismissed superstitions were at one time serious considerations in searches for meanings, answers, and guidance. It is no wonder that the Irish immigrants were attracted to the new religion of Spiritualism after

its birth in 1848. They thought of it as a continuation of older folk beliefs. It is not unusual to hear someone talk about an ancestor who "had the gift" or "could see things." Sometimes, the lore is blunter with "She talked to the dead."

In the nineteenth century, hundreds of thousands, if not millions, of average Americans became involved to some degree with groups, philosophies, or practices that had roots in the idea that communication with the dead was possible. For the modern reader, the concept of communion with the dead or spirit entities can be confusing because of its relationship to the occult, whose basic terminology keeps evolving. For instance, the word paranormal was not added to the dictionary until 1920. Words pertaining to paranormal phenomena need to be explained to comprehend them more fully:

Occult. The word in the nineteenth century meant hidden as opposed to *apocalypse,* which meant revealed. Occult knowledge was obtained through hidden sources, such as communication with the dead. The word is Latin and can be found from 1520 to 1530. Originally, it had nothing to do with evil or Satanism.

Medium. Occult information is given through a medium, who acts as a conduit between the world of the living and the world of the dead. Mediums can convey messages while in a trance or normal state. The title for them can be traced back to 1837.

THE

YEAR-BOOK OF SPIRITUALISM

FOR

1871.

PRESENTING THE STATUS OF SPIRITUALISM FOR THE CURRENT YEAR
THROUGHOUT THE WORLD; PHILOSOPHICAL, SCIENTIFIC, AND RE-
LIGIOUS ESSAYS; REVIEW OF ITS LITERATURE; HISTORY OF
AMERICAN ASSOCIATIONS; STATE AND LOCAL SOCIETIES;
PROGRESSIVE LYCEUMS; LECTURERS; MEDIUMS;
AND OTHER MATTERS RELATING TO
THE MOMENTOUS SUBJECT.

BY

HUDSON TUTTLE AND J. M.

BOSTON:
WILLIAM WHITE AND COMPANY,
BANNER OF LIGHT OFFICE,
158 WASHINGTON STREET.
LONDON: JAMES BURNS, 15 SOUTHAMPTON ROW.
1871.

Figure 72: Confirming the widespread nature of Spiritualism in the 19th century, this "Year-Book of Spiritu-alism" dated 1871 is one of many such publications. Within its pages can be found lists of Spiritualist lectur-ers representing almost every walk of life.

Psychic. A psychic is different than a medium or a channeler. A psychic imparts readings of information that do not necessarily involve a trance state or communication with the spirit world. Psychics' sensing abilities relay information they find in clients' auras or "etheric fields." The field, which is believed to be around each person, contains data on a person's past, present, and future. Psychic readings are regarded as gifts and involve intuition. All mediums are psychics, but not all psychics are mediums, with the difference blurred. The word was first used between 1855 and 1860. The most documented psychic of the twentieth century remains the former Kentucky Christian Church Sunday School teacher, Edgar Cayce (1877-1945).

Clairvoyance. All these terms overlap in clairvoyance, the ability to perceive objects, events, or people that may not be discerned through the normal senses. It is a frequent psychic experience within the paranormal realm. Clairvoyance may express itself as an internal or external vision. At its simplest level, it is an internal vision of symbolic images that must be interpreted more deeply. At higher planes, clairvoyance is the perception of nonphysical reality. Mediums and psychics claim to experience clairvoyance in the forms of healings, spirit travels (remote viewings), visions out of space and time (shamanistic experiences), dreams, communications with spirit entities, and astral travels (astral projections, or out-of-body experiences). From French, the word was introduced about 1840 to 1850.

The related topics of channeling and channeled literature are required for this discussion. Channeling is the revelatory process in which the medium or other intermediary is the open conduit, standing between the physical and spiritual worlds so that information can flow between the two. The word is defined as a "channel of conveyance for truth" and dates to 1748; however, its popular usage began in the 1960s. Before the word channeling became prevalent, the medium was often described as a "spiritual telegraph" and later a "spiritual telephone." Entire bodies of channeled literature were prompted through this practice. Key ones remain, and others have been long forgotten.

Some works are so culturally and historically significant and influential that others to this day continue to revise and build upon them. Madame Helen Petrovna Blavatsky's pivotal, controversial, classic, and esoteric *Isis Unveiled* (1877) and *The Secret Doctrine* (1888) reached far beyond her Theosophical Society. Messages from her "spiritual masters" transformed the Western occult tradition. The Theosophical Society in India helped to set the stage for Indian Independence from the British. John B. Newbrough's *Oahspe: A New Bible* (1882) was one of the first books composed on a typewriter, and it was received through automatic writing. The famous Shalam Colony (Land of Shalam) was a commune founded near Las Cruces, New Mexico, in 1884, built upon *Oahspe* teachings. Levi H. Dowling's *Aquarian Gospel of Jesus Christ* (1908) was created through automatic writing. He was a Disciples of Christ minister. This work remains renowned and is presently a source for the explosion of "Jesus in India" books.

The Great Depression also saw its share of channeled works. Written anonymously, *The Urantia Book* (1925-1935) was delivered through apparitions of celestial beings. Guy Ballard (a.k.a. Godfré Ray King), founder of I AM Activity, and his timeless and extremely prominent *Unveiled Mysteries* (1934) and *The Magic Presence* (1935) were the channeling of St. Germain. Ballard's writings brought notoriety to Mount Shasta, California, as a pilgrimage spot where many believe

mystical portals exist between dimensions. Betty White, a medium, received *The Betty Book* (1937) while in a trance, and it was recorded by her husband, Stewart E. White. It was the first in a trilogy.

Even with a historic body of channeled literature, the great age for this genre began in the 1960s and peaked in the 1980s with the explosion of otherworldly and interdimensional voices, said to be the voices of Abraham, Emmanuel, Lazarus, Ramtha, Seth, and the reappearance of St. Germain. One of the most culturally powerful contemporary works was thought to be from Jesus, as the

Figure 73: Mount Shasta, California, popularized by "I Am" Activity (founded by Guy Ballard) as a place where portals between dimensions exist. Elevation 14,179 feet, or 4,322 meters. (Photograph by Dwight A. Radford, October 2019.)

channeled inner voice of Helen Cohen Schucman in *A Course in Miracles* (1976). An extremely popular series is the automatic writings of Neale Donald Walsch in his three-volume *Conversations with God: An Uncommon Dialogue* (1996-1998), which have all been *New York Times Best Sellers*. These are just a few eminent ones in an astounding array of literature ranging from introductory texts to deeply profound metaphysical tomes.

Perhaps a contemporary account of this entire discussion concerning the evolution of metaphysical thought can be summed up in the modern parable adventure books of James Redfield. The original of his four-volume *Celestine Prophecy* series (1993-2011) about spiritual awakening spent 165 weeks on the *New York Times Best Sellers'* list.

In post-modern America, the fascination with paranormal phenomena is greater than ever, reinforced with sensationalized television shows featuring ghost hunters and professional mediums. In its prevailing stage, Spiritualism has been remodeled by the New Age movement emerging in the 1960s that infused Buddhism, Christian Mysticism, Hinduism, Sufism, and Taoism with already modified Swedenborgian, Theosophical, New Thought, and Spiritualist ideas. Although it has been altered and is sometimes even unrecognizable, Spiritualism remains.

The records generated by a rising interest in Spiritualism since 1848 may hold the keys to identifying where an immigrant was from in Ireland. Yet, they typically pertain to the categories of people who appear in those records, such as mediums, lecturers, healers, social reformers, and authors. Spiritualism, with all its quirky personalities, has caught the attention of scholars, who have sought to understand its impact on American religious history. It is a diverse and complex topic by any standard. The following works provide considerable background, although they are not the only ones that do:

Braude, Ann. *Radical Spirits: Spiritualism and Women's Rights in Nineteenth-Century America*. Boston, Massachusetts: Beacon Press, 1989, 2001.

Brown, Michael F. *The Channeling Zone: American Spirituality in an Anxious Age*. Cambridge: Harvard University Press, 1997.

Buescher, John B. *The Other Side of Salvation: Spiritualism and the Nineteenth-Century Religious Experience*. Boston, Massachusetts: Skinner House Books, 2004.

Carroll, Bret E. *Spiritualism in Antebellum America*. Bloomington, Indiana: Indiana University Press, 1997.

Cox, Robert S. *Body and Soul: A Sympathetic History of American Spiritualism*. Charlottesville, Virginia: University of Virginia Press, 2003.

Goldsmith, Barbara. *Other Powers: The Age of Suffrage, Spiritualism, and the Scandalous Victoria Woodhull*. New York, New York: Alfred Knopf, 1998.

Horowitz, Mitch. *Occult America: The Secret History of How Mysticism Shaped Our Nation.* New York, New York: Bantam Book, 2009.

Natale, Simone. *Supernatural Entertainments: Victorian Spiritualism and the Rise of Modern Media Culture.* University Park, Pennsylvania: Penn State University Press, 2016.

Stuart, Nancy Rubin. *The Reluctant Spiritualist: The Life of Maggie Fox.* Orlando, Florida: Harcourt Inc., 2005.

Weisberg, Barbara. *Talking to the Dead: Kate and Maggie Fox and the Rise of Spiritualism.* San Francisco, California: Harper San Francisco, 2004.

Roots of Modern American Spiritualism

Spirit communication as a philosophical system in the nineteenth century has been termed by scholars as harmonialism, stretching from Swedenborgianism through Mesmerism, Spiritualism, Christian Science, and New Thought. Some historians delete Christian Science. Harmonialism as it appeared in religion teaches that God is a positive healing force with whom people must harmonize. This harmonialism also extended into the awakening sciences and reform movements of the nineteenth century.

Harmonialism, whether found in religious, scientific, or social ideologies, draws on the ideas and experiences of Emanuel Swedenborg (1688-1772). In harmonialism, religion is approached as demonstrable, thus it was scientific. Religion was in harmony with science, not in opposition. Swedenborg himself was an accomplished scientist of his day, and when he described his understanding of the afterlife in his classic *Heaven and Its Wonders and Hell* (1758), he did so in a matter-of-fact, scientific style. The assumption that spirit communication could be scientific flowered in America.

The merger of three currents of thought into a definable harmonialism was the first step that created the American phenomenon of Spiritualism. The three were Swedenborgianism, Mesmerism, and Fourierism. When combined in the mid-1840s, harmonialism was born. It attracted small numbers of mostly men in the Northeast and Midwest who were educated, middle class, and white. Swedenborg's writings were an essential element in the possibility of spirit communication, but they had a limited audience through the Church of the New Jerusalem. His writings also reached the educated elite through the liberal social reformers who founded the New England Transcendental Movement in 1836. Transcendentalism arose out of American Unitarianism, which was a radical wing of New England Congregationalism. *For more about Swedenborg, see pp. 94-99.*

The second notable stream consisting of harmonialism was the popular 1830s fad of Mesmerism that swept through America by storm. Mesmerism was a philosophy promoted by the Austrian physician Franz Anton Mesmer (1734-1815).

Mesmer became famous in Europe by claiming that healing could be accomplished through fluid dispersed throughout the universe. This fluid within the human body could produce cures and what became known as a mesmeric trance. The mind-cure aspects of mesmerist philosophy went on to profoundly affect Christian Science and its sister movement, New Thought. Mesmerism began during a time when Americans were seeking non-scriptural sources for spiritual edification.

Figure 74: Franz Anton Mesmer (1734-1815). (Image too widely used to determine provenance...)

The mesmeric trance is now known as a hypnotic state or as an altered state of consciousness. While in these trances, mesmerists claimed communications with the dead. Mesmerism affected the birth of modern psychology by the twentieth century as Mesmerism was translated into various mind-cure philosophies through which the potential of the mind was seriously investigated. Mesmerism instilled the idea into the American mainstream that the human experience extended beyond the physical senses.

The third current of thought of harmonialism was the communitarian philosophy of French socialist reformer Charles Fourier (1772-1837). Fourier taught that social and spiritual harmony required the reorganization of human society into small communities and that human and economic relationships were based on "natural forces of attraction." In the 1840s and 1850s, communities, called phalanxes, were founded in the Northeast and Midwest. Most did not last, disappearing by the mid-1850s. Greeley, Colorado, was founded as one such community.

Fourier's ideas profoundly affected reformers such as Andrew Jackson Davis (1826-1910), whose *The Principles of Nature, Her Divine Revelations, and a Voice to Mankind* (1847) merged Swedenborgianism, Mesmerism, and Fourierism into an American harmonialist philosophy. This established the foundation for Spiritualism as a religion. As Swedenborgianism held the door open for Mesmerism, the transition from Mesmerism to Spiritualism is the story of America. Many social, political, economic, religious, and cultural forces that encouraged new religious movements were operating at the same time.

In New York, all the forces came together in 1825 as the Erie Canal linked the Atlantic Ocean and the cities of the East with the newly settled areas west to the Great Lakes. Rapid growth revolutionized the region. From this fast cultural change came intense revivalism that emphasized a personal religious experience accompanied with reform of both the individual and society. Overall, the general feeling in the country produced three independent movements in Upstate New York: Mormonism (1830), Adventism (1844), and Spiritualism (1848). Of these three, only Adventism denied that communication with the dead was possible. Although Mormonism has its spiritualistic nuances, it cannot be defined as a spiritualist religion because communication with the dead is not a tenet of faith.

What is American Spiritualism?

The rise and decline of Spiritualism in America along with its subsequent revivals shaped one of the most colorful episodes in American religious history while offering an alternative to white American Protestantism. Spiritualism took root throughout America with its strength in the Northeast and the Midwest. Boston, Buffalo, Cincinnati, Cleveland, New York City, Providence, Rochester, and St. Louis became centers.

Modern Spiritualism began on 31 March 1848 at the Fox home in Hydesville, New York, some twenty miles from Rochester. On that date, the teenage sisters Margaret Fox (1833-1893) and Kate Fox (1836-1892) announced that they were communicating with spirits via rappings on a bedroom wall. The rappings were said to be from a man who had been murdered in the house years before and who was contacting the sisters to let them know that he was buried on the premises. Their communications were noticed by local dissident Quakers, who believed the rappings were indeed from the spirit world. As news of the "Rochester Rappings" spread, the Fox sisters began to demonstrate their abilities on stage, reaching celebrity status.

Figure 75: Andrew Jackson Davis (1826-1910). (Image too widely used to determine provenance...)

An alphabet was devised by investigators so that the rappings could be translated into words. The Fox sisters caught the interest of Spiritualist proponents such as Andrew Jackson Davis, who was laying the groundwork for his own harmonional philosophy. In 1843, he began to experience trance visions and spirit messages, earning him the title in American history of the "Poughkeepsie Seer." His writings over 30 years exerted a profound influence on Spiritualism, but in the early years, the "Rochester Rappings" attracted more attention to his goals than did his writings on harmonialism. For this reason, he explained harmonialism in terms of the Fox sisters in his 1850 *The Philosophy of Spiritual Intercourse*.

The tragedy of the Fox sisters is that they found themselves trapped in other people's agendas and the center of something bigger than they were. Although the Fox sisters remained a fixture in Spiritualism, it took only a few years for them to be joined by thousands of trance mediums who delivered the spirit messages through speech and made the cumbersome alphabetic rappings obsolete. In 1888, the sisters confessed and demonstrated how they invented the rappings. Margaret retracted her confession the next year. The Fox sisters are credited as the founders of American Spiritualism; however, they were only teenagers in 1848.

Spiritualism remained popular and controversial through the 1870s, when it crested. It experienced revivals in the 1880s, during World War I, and with the "Great Age of the Mediums," the 1920s, arising during periods when death and disease were everywhere and people were looking for proof of life after death instead of faith. Many found their evidence of life after death through Spiritualism because people felt it could be demonstrated.

Spiritualism crossed racial, religious, and economic boundaries. There are Christian Spiritualists and non-Christian Spiritualists. The two have much in common, although they differ about the status of Christianity. The Christian Spiritualists look for proof of Christian claims. Christian and non-Christian Spiritualists see Jesus as one of the greatest mediums.

African-American Christians did not have the need to be identified as Spiritualists until the twentieth century because spirit communication has been a part of their culture from the slave period. It was not seen as dangerous or contradictory to Christianity. White evangelical Christians have always been the most hostile toward Spiritualism. Southern white Spiritualists were more likely to identify themselves as Christians than were Northern white Spiritualists.

The effect of Spiritualism in American history and culture is often obscured today, yet it produced leaders for the Suffrage Movement and for health reform. Some historians state that one of Spiritualism's most substantial contributions, along with the rise of Liberal Protestantism, helped to dismantle the strict Calvinist culture embedded in American life.

Spiritualism as a Social and Religious Reform Movement

The Antebellum and Victorian attitudes about women contributed to the spread of Spiritualism and mediumship. Popular attitudes were that women were weak minded, emotional, and sick as well as keepers of virtues and values, the guardians of the homes, and more spiritual than men. Thus, they were receptive to spiritual matters. These same stereotypes prohibited women from public speaking, and the vast majority were denied a religious voice. Women were also forbidden access to higher education, the right to vote, control over childbearing, the legal right to their children, and were required to wear restrictive clothes.

Figure 76: "Spiritualism originated Mar. 31st, 1848, in this House, Newark, N.Y." (Postcard image in possession of and courtesy of E. Wade Hone. Postmarked 27 July 1908. Copyright expired.)

In 1848, when news of the Fox sisters began to disseminate, the first women's rights convention was being held in Upstate New York. Some of the earliest proponents of women's rights were dissident Quakers. The earliest investigators and converts to Spiritualism were some of these Quakers. While not all feminists were Spiritualists, all Spiritualists were feminists. Spiritualism taught that women were equal to men and that the individual was the ultimate vehicle for truth, offering a powerful example to radical, reform-minded Americans.

Through Spiritualism, women in America began to break many of the social barriers imposed upon them, accomplished through the rise of the medium as a profession. Nineteenth-century mediums were not professionally trained because their abilities were thought of as gifts. Paid mediums were vehicles for upward mobility.

The trance of the medium was generally understood as an elevated state in which the medium had access to the spirits and their knowledge. It was understood that this knowledge was beyond human consciousness without the trance state.

As trance mediums, women for the first time found a public arena from which they could deliver religious and reform messages to a mixed audience of men and women. Even though they were still denied a church voice, they could pack halls with thousands in the 1850s and 1860s, and they became public speakers for a variety of causes, such as health reform, dress reform, marriage law reform, abolitionist causes, the temperance movement, and, specifically, suffrage.

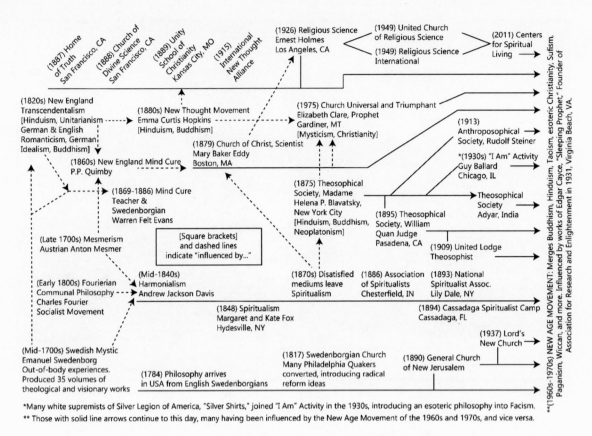

Figure 77: Metaphysical America: Its Select Development.

The spirits brought reform messages to receptive audiences.

With newly found speaking skills, trance mediums lectured at women's suffrage conventions nationwide. So prominent were they in the arena of women's rights that in the popular imagination, the two became linked, blurring the difference. It was often while attending a lecture by a trance medium that the audience became acquainted with ideas specific to women's issues. During this period, a woman speaking on social causes from her own conscious ideas was unacceptable, but a woman in a trance being unconscious and with the voice of a spirit could speak on the same subject and enthrall audiences.

Stereotypes about women led to the spread of Spiritualism in the home. There, a woman was expected to host activities. The home environment was conducive to the formation of the Spiritualist Circle, also known as the Sacred Circle, a small, intimate gathering of close friends and investigators. They could study Spiritualist writings or simply sit around the séance table seeking spirit messages. The medium who headed the circle was often the woman of the house. As an oracle of truth, her messages were taken seriously.

During the ritual of the séance, the medium was at the head of a table with the participants sitting close together touching fingers. The ideal séance setting was with every other seat occupied by a member of the opposite sex. The table served as an altar where the participants formed a battery to make spirit communication possible. It created a cosmic harmony.

The introduction of the planchette (forerunner of the modern Ouija board) in America allowed the home to also be a place where family members could investigate their own mediumships, further spreading Spiritualism and mediumship at a grassroots level. The planchette originated in France and was brought to America in the 1850s, although it was not mass-produced until the 1860s. It was believed to respond to the magnetic forces passing through the bodies of those who placed their fingers on it, thus communicating messages from the spirits. The planchette clouded the difference between a parlor game and serious religious inquiry.

Within a decade, the female trance mediums were no longer a novelty in American life. As the uniqueness wore off, the next generation of American women was allowed to find their own voices without acknowledging spirits as they lectured on any number of social topics.

The female trance mediums had a huge impact on health reform. In the nineteenth century, medicine in America was still in its infancy, if not dangerous. Male doctors ordinarily prescribed treatments of alcohol, narcotics (opium and morphine being a favorite), and mercury. From this national distrust of the medical establishment, trance mediums arose as medical mediums. Through the physically benign healing they offered, the public found hope for an alternative to medical practices of the day.

The Fall of American Spiritualism as a Social Force

Several factors led to the decline of the mediumship, the largest being its own success. As mediumship became widespread, so did fraud. An internal struggle developed as physical mediums began to replace the trance mediums in the 1870s. At that point, the public's awareness of the medium became associated with entertainment more than with an oracle for truth. When mediumship turned to the display of physical manifestation instead of trance, it lost its internal empowerment for women. The American Society for Psychical Research, created in 1885 in Boston, investigated the claims of mediums through scientific methods and publicly exposed frauds, further damaging the reputation of mediums.

With the disclosures of so much deceit, two well-organized belief systems began attracting waves of disgruntled Spiritualists. The rise of both the Theosophical Society and Christian Science in the 1870s caught the attention of Spiritualists, who saw the physical mediums as not representing their vision. The new movements were founded by women and offered their own platforms for creating societal change.

A factor that saw the decline of Spiritualism as an instrument for social change was the introduction of Liberal Theology in American Protestantism. Liberal Theology was the inspiration for Christians to be involved in some of the same reform causes that were originally championed by Spiritualists. This brought reform into the mainstream.

The Spiritualist Camp

As the lecturing trance medium began to decline, many Spiritualists shifted their interests and activities to the Spiritualist camp. The camps were places where thousands of people could gather, share in entertainment, hear reform speeches, socialize, privately consult mediums (some famous), hear Spiritualist lectures, and generally be involved in Spiritualist activities at lakes, beaches, or in mountain environments. It was not rare for camps to host 5,000 to 10,000 people at a time. Some camps lasted only weeks out of the year. Others became permanent communities. In these towns, the populations were from a few hundred in off season to thousands in the peak seasons. The oldest and most historic ones are:

Lily Dale in Chautauqua County, New York, has roots back to 1855 and is the headquarters of the National Association of Spiritualist Churches. It remains a New Age mecca. *See image on the next page.*

Cassadaga Spiritualist Camp in Volusia County, Florida, was founded in 1894, but its roots go back to 1875. It is today an independent Spiritualist community unaffiliated with any larger Spiritualist organization. It remains a New Age mecca.

The New England Spiritualist Camp-meeting Association (NESCA) was formed in Lake Pleasant, Franklin County, Massachusetts, in 1874. It is historical only, but it was one of the largest camps by the late nineteenth century. It was a long-time member of the NESCA that founded the National Spiritualist Alliance (TNSA) in 1913. The NESCA was disbanded in the 1970s, but the TNSA is present.

Camp Chesterfield in Chesterfield, Madison County, Indiana, is home to the Hett Memorial Art Gallery and Museum, which houses artifacts of Spiritualism. Camp Chesterfield was founded in 1886 and is home to the Indiana Association of Spiritualists. It remains a place of pilgrimage. *See image on p. 278.*

Spiritualist Records

Efforts are currently in progress to identify and preserve what is left of Spiritualist records. One website seeking to safeguard Spiritualism's disappearing history is "Ephemera" at Lapsop.com/spirithistory. It hosts almanacs, directories, newspapers, and essays and is an ongoing project. Digitized material can also be found on the website of the "International Association for the Preservation of Spiritualist and Occult Periodicals." The published records, such as newspapers and directories, of Spiritualism can be deceiving. The foremost principle is that not all Spiritualists are listed in them, the premise being that people's information to be published required reasons to do so. A lecturer, medium, or healer qualified.

the courage of his opinions, and

Figure 78: The Maplewood, Lily Dale Assembly, Lily Dale, New York. (Postcard image in possession of and courtesy of E. Wade Hone. Postmark illegible. Copyright expired.)

Male, Irish-born medium Dr. W. M. Forster is an example. He was in an occupation whose majority of members were women. An extensive biography of Dr. W. M. Forster was published in the 1896 book *Workers in the Vineyard: A Review of the Progress of Spiritualism, Biographical Sketches, Lectures, Essays and Poems* (San Francisco, California: Julia Schlesinger, 1896), pp. 191-192, by Julia Schlesinger. He was never referenced by his full name, only Dr. Forster or Dr. W. M. Forster. In works such as this, the purpose was not to trace his origins but to expound upon his joining Spiritualism and his contributions to the movement. Clues were given about his birthplace:

> *Born and raised in "blue" Presbyterianism, he nevertheless had*

at the early age of fifteen years seceded to the Methodist denomination, of which he was a lay preacher and propagandist at the age of eighteen years. His desires and tendencies being toward the medical course, he was apprenticed to a firm of apothecaries in Ireland, and after graduating in the various schools necessary for the practice of his adopted profession, commenced a tour of the world, which a few years ago ended, for the time being, in San Francisco, Cal. Here his success has been phenomenal.

The term "blue Presbyterian" or "true blue Presbyterian" has a definition from the Genevaninstitute.org website: "A 'True-blue Presbyterian' is an enlightened, true-hearted son of a church that aims at pursuing the chief end of man: to glorify God and to enjoy Him forever." This, at first glance, speaks of an Ulster and Scots-Irish connection.

In another part of the sketch are more hints about his origins, although they are not specifically stated:

Figure 79: Chesterfield Chapel, Chesterfield, Indiana. A Spiritualist church. (Photograph courtesy of Dwight A. Radford, August 2015.)

Dr. Forster is a descendant of an illustrious English family, whose name is contemporaneous with advanced politics in the middle and later portions of the nineteenth century. We have much pleasure in saying, however, that although his paternal ancestry was derived from the eastern side of St. George's Channel, his maternal ancestry were raised and bred on the green sod of "old Ireland" – a combination which should go to make an ideal American citizen.

This section adds some fascinating details and raises possibilities. The indication is that the Forsters were of English descent, although there is no suggestion that Dr. Forster's father was born there, implying the family was Anglican. His mother's history is murkier. His maternal side is described as "raised and bred on the green sod of 'old Ireland.'" Whether she was of Scots-Irish ancestry or of native Gaelic Catholic ancestry has some possibilities. Was the Forster family Anglo-Irish, at least in part?

Spiritualism as the focus of the biographical sketch ties Dr. Forster's life into his conversion and to the religion:

Dr. Forster, some fifteen years ago (although from an early age aware of his occult powers), became convinced of the reality of "physical phenomena" through the mediumship of his infant son and his own powers; latent powers were developed, and automatic writing, independent slate writing, levitation of heavy bodies, spirit lights, etherealization, and that much-disputed phase of spiritual phenomena – spirit photography – were developed. Of late years Dr. Forster has confined his mediumship to that phase known as "medical clairvoyance"; the utility of this will be seen when it is remembered that he has been a very extensive traveler, a keen observer of men and things, and an educated gentleman, one whose first thoughts and aspirations were for the benefit of humanity. It is rarely we meet so many good things combined.

For a well-known medium, such as Dr. Forster, little doubt is left that this biographical sketch was the only document about him. He was a professional, as were his female counterparts, which generated additional period sources likely scattered throughout the Spiritualist newspapers, periodicals, and books.

Only a fraction of those who practiced the religion were as famous as Dr. Forster. The major difficulty with Spiritualism for the family historian is that it is hard to determine who was a Spiritualist since so many practiced in private or remained in the Christian congregations in their areas. Spiritualists could range from professional mediums to those who quietly attended séances or privately consulted the planchette (forerunner of the Ouija board). Some clues exist which may identify someone as a Spiritualist:

- If an ancestor had an interest in Swedenborgianism, Shakers, Transcendentalism, Universalism, dissident Quakerism, Theosophy, Christian Science, or New Thought, he or she might have also been involved in Spiritualism. The first five contributed the earliest members to Spiritualism (1848-1870s) while the latter three drew their earliest members from a declining Spiritualism (1870s-1880s). This point can transition an ancestor between movements and interests, and all kept records.

- By the 1860s, many Universalist congregations and a large percentage of dissident Quakers had merged completely into Spiritualism. In the case of the Universalist Church, Spiritualism was allowed to operate within the denomination. Generally, if ancestors were of a more liberal nature, they were receptive to Spiritualism. The Universalists are now part of the Unitarian-Universalist Church.

- Post-Millerite Adventists, when Christ did not physically come in the clouds on 22 October 1844, spiritualized the message. First, hundreds of spiritualizers sought stability in the Shaker communities after the "Great

Disappointment." They moved on to Spiritualism after 1848. Many of these went to live in the famous Mountain Cove, [West] Virginia, Spiritualist colony. Finally, these religious seekers transitioned from Spiritualism and merged into the rising Sabbatarian Adventism (Seventh-day Adventist Church). This can lead to Adventist Church records.

- If an ancestor was among the members of the budding women's rights movement, especially from 1848 until the 1870s, because Spiritualism and women's rights were intertwined. Always consider a female ancestor involved in these social issues as a possible Spiritualist. This can also instigate a search of suffrage-related records.

- Spiritualists' tombstones often have, instead of dates of deaths, the dates the deceased "entered the Summerland," the Spiritualist heaven. Other tombstone terminology includes "awakened to the newness of life in the Spirit World," "Passed to the Spirit Land," or "Translated." Another clue on tombstones is that to this day, many Spiritualists still observe Spiritualist Time, which dates the calendar year from 1848. To many Spiritualists, the beginning of Modern Spiritualism was with the Fox sisters and the Rochester rappings, hence the year being the Spiritual Era.

- If an ancestor can be documented residing part time, full time, or visiting a community known to have a connection with Spiritualism. This includes Spiritualist towns built around a seasonal camp, former Fourierist commune, and other experimental communities such as Hopedale in Worcester County, Massachusetts, and Modern Times on Long Island, New York. Many experimental communities became hotbeds of Spiritualism along with other American towns such as Auburn in Cayuga County, New York. The United States censuses can disclose this point.

Several repositories have noteworthy collections of Spiritualist material, usually in the forms of periodicals and directories. The American Antiquarian Society and the Library of Congress have the largest, with other considerable ones at Andover-Harvard University Theological Library; New York Public Library; Boston Public Library; Van Pelt Library at the University of Pennsylvania; Bancroft Library, University of California, Berkeley; Cecil H. Green Library at Stanford University; and the State Historical Society of Wisconsin. Many of the old periodicals and directories can be found at websites such as HathiTrust.org and Archive.org. A general Internet search will bring up these publications in the public domain. The Marion H. Skidmore Library in Lily Dale, New York, has the largest private collection of Spiritualist and occult books in the world.

The activities of nineteenth-century Spiritualists, such as those of lecturers, mediums, and Spiritualist missionaries, can be traced easily in various directories. Some of these directories also list people involved in the anti-slavery and temperance movements as well as spiritual healers. Foremost directories are found below:

Select Spiritualist Directories

Year	Name
1857	Uriah and Eliza Clark, *The Spiritualist Register with a Counting House & Speaker's Almanac; Containing Facts and Statistics of Spiritualism, for 1857.* Auburn, New York: Y. U. Clark, 1857.
1858 to 1859	Uriah Clark, *The Spiritualist Register, May 1858, May 1859: Facts, Philosophy, Statistics of Spiritualism.* Auburn, New York: U. Clark, Spiritual Clarion Office, 1859.
1859	Uriah Clark, *The Spiritualist Register for 1859: Facts, Philosophy, Statistics of Spiritualism.* Auburn, New York: U. Clark, Spiritual Clarion Office, 1859.
1860	Uriah Clark, *Fourth Annual Spiritual Register, with a Calendar and Speakers' Almanac, for 1860: Facts, Philosophy, Statistics of Spiritualism.* Auburn, New York: U. Clark, Spiritual Clarion Office, 1860.
1861	Uriah Clark, *A Spiritualist Register; with a Calendar and Speakers' Almanac, for 1861 Facts, Philosophy, Statistics of Spiritualism.* Auburn, New York: U. Clark, Spiritual Clarion Office, 1861.
1862	Andrew Jackson Davis, *The Progressive Annual for 1862: Comprising an Almanac, a Spiritualist Register, and a General Calendar of Reform.* New York, New York: A. J. Davis & Co, 1862.
1863	Andrew Jackson Davis, *The Progressive Annual for 1863: Comprising an Almanac, a Spiritualist Register, and a General Calendar of Reform.* New York, New York: A. J. Davis & Co., 1863.
1864	Andrew Jackson Davis, *The Progressive Annual for 1864: Containing an Almanac, a Spiritualist Register, and a General Calendar of Reform.* New York, New York: A. J. Davis & Co., 1864.
1871	James M. Peebles and Hudson Tuttle, *The Year-Book of Spiritualism for 1871: Presenting the Status of Spiritualism for the Current Year throughout the World; Philosophical, Scientific, and Religious Essays; Review of Its Literature; History of American Associations; State and Local Societies; Progressive Lyceums; Lecturers; Mediums; and Other Matters Relating to the Momentous Subject.* Boston, Massachusetts: William White and Company, 1871.
1925	William C. Hartmann, *Who's Who in Occult, Psychic and Spiritual Realms in the United States and Foreign Countries.* Jamaica, New York: Occult Press, 1925.
1927	William C. Hartmann, *Who's Who in Occultism, New Thought, Psychism and Spiritualism.* Jamaica, New York: Occult Press, 1927.
1930	William C. Hartmann, *Hartmann's International Directory of Psychic Science and Spiritualism.* Jamaica, New York: Occult Press, 1930.

Select Spiritualist Publications

Publication	Name	Place Published
1849 to 1856	Buchanan's Journal of Man	Cincinnati, OH
1852 to 1857	Spiritual Telegraph	New York, NY
1857 to 1907	Banner of Light	Boston, MA
1860 to 1865	Rising Tide	Independence, IA
1865 to 1907	Religio to Philosophical Journal	Chicago, IL and San Francisco, CA
1867 to 1872	Lyceum Banner	Chicago, IL
1871 to 1877	Hull's Crucible	Boston, MA
1876 to 1889	Olive Branch	Utica, NY
1876 to 1887	Voice of Angels	Somerville, MA
1876 to 1918	World's Advance Thought	Salem, Portland, OR
1878 to 1883	Mind and Matter	Philadelphia, PA
1880 to 1887	Spiritual Offering	Ottumwa, Iowa
1880 to 1891	Watchman	Chicago, IL
1882 to 1887	Facts	Boston, MA
1883 to 1907	Lucifer	Valley Falls, Topeka, KS and Chicago, IL
1884 to 1893	Carrier Dove	Oakland, CA
1884 to 1921	Star	San Francisco, CA
1885 to 1890	Golden Gate	San Francisco, CA
1886 to 1892	Better Way	Cincinnati, OH
1889 to 1912	Progressive Thinker	Chicago, IL
1890 to 1909	Sunflower	Lily Dale, NY
1892 to 1906	New Thought	Chicago, IL

Spiritualist newspapers had advertisements, convention news, directories, local news, and letters. Ann Braude's *News From the Spirit World: A Checklist of American Spiritualist Periodicals, 1848-1900* (Worcester, Massachusetts: American Antiquarian Society, 1989) lists 214 periodicals, including newspapers and directories, by name, period, geographical area, and publisher. Of the 214 periodicals identified in Braude's inventory, only 15% lasted five years or longer. The newspapers offer the longest range of study for an individual's involvement in Spiritualism. Those that have survived for at least five years are found above.

Because of the independent nature of Spiritualism, its ability to become organized and thus to generate institutional records was a long and difficult process. Since it had no orthodox doctrines, official leaders, or memberships, it wasn't until 1893 that the National Spiritualist Association of Churches (NSAC) was founded. The NSAC, as the first successful organization, bound together a variety of Spiritualist congregations. By the early twentieth century, the NSAC helped to influence and bring Spiritualism from the home circles and stage demonstrations of the nineteenth century into a modern, organized system based upon the Protestant model of churches.

Two organizations, each representing different aspects of the paranormal, can be resources in the search for a Spiritualist ancestor, the American Society for Psychical Research and the Morris Pratt Institute. The American Society for Psychical Research (ASPR) operated as an independent investigative organization from 1885 to 1889 and again from 1906 to the present. In between, it functioned as a branch of the Society for Psychical Research in England. The ASPR is an investigative organization into the paranormal. Its studies have analyzed the fraud of mediums as well as investigated what it deems to be legitimate claims. It has been publishing the quarterly *The Journal of the American Society for Psychical Research* since 1885, which is available at many major libraries nationwide and on websites such as Archive.org and HathiTrust.org. This journal also has lists of members.

Although many mediums and paranormal phenomena were investigated by the ASPR, only a fraction of the investigations were reported in the *Journal*. In the ASPR library, located in New York City, are the correspondences and case files for all investigations, whether they were published or not. The ASPR houses an extensive parapsychology library containing over 10,000 volumes and over 300 periodical titles, including information on nineteenth-century Spiritualism. The Society's archives incorporate rare photographs, case records, trance drawings, spirit photographs, automatic writings, original letters, film footage, spontaneous cases, and other material spanning more than a hundred years. The library is open by appointment.

The Morris Pratt Institute, founded in 1901, is the Spiritualist school employed by the NSAC. It is in Milwaukee, Wisconsin. Founded in 1901, it was originally a residential school where men and women from all over the country boarded during its school term. In 1935, it became a correspondence school. The Institute's records are scattered, and an effort has been made to gather and catalog them. The earliest student registers that have been found began in 1913 and include the names of the students, courses taken, instructors, and ages. When the Morris Pratt Institute became a correspondence school, records were kept in a card file, which is intact. The card file has the names of the students, addresses, Spiritualist congregations, and courses.

The records of Spiritualist congregations are evolving as researchers seek to identify what has survived. Spiritualist congregations are free to develop their own rituals and record-keeping procedures. Currently, no study has been done about what is typically generated by the individual congregations. Some have a consecration ceremony performed on infants of members or adult converts. This "baptism" of sorts, though, is not a washing away of sins but a blessing. Traditional Christianity sees original sin, but the Spiritualists see an original blessing.

Infants often have naming ceremonies that welcome the children into the communities. Some congregations may retain membership records, church minutes, marriages, and deaths. Congregations can be contacted individually or through organizations such as the NSAC.

Mediums and Mediumship

In the nineteenth century and into the early twentieth, several types of mediums provided services for clients or audiences. All are present to this day, with the most popular mediums involved in healing and in trance work. A reliable reference booklet for the background of mediumship and paranormal phenomena was written in 1938 by Mark A. Barwise, *A Preface to Spiritualism* (Cassadaga, Florida: National Spiritualist Association of Churches, 1973).

Medical Medium. The mediums can see a patient's internal body, and they prescribe non-invasive healing. Medical mediums were extremely popular before the rise of Christian Science and New Thought. Whereas orthodox religion and medicine considered the human body to be flawed from birth and in need of assistance, the medical mediums thought the opposite. They viewed the human body as the image of God and the laws of nature, and so health was a natural condition. Spiritualist cures involved restoring patients to their lost harmony with God and the laws of nature. Mediums also authored books that were widely read and distributed in America, such as Lucina Tuttle's *The Clairvoyant's Family Physician* (New York, New York: Partridge & Brittan, 1855) and Andrew Jackson Davis's *Harbinger of Health* (New York: New York: Andrew Jackson Davis & Co., 1862). Both contributed to the health reform movements already operating in the country.

Most medical mediums were women, and so untrained, female medical mediums were pitted against the professionally trained, male medical establishment that regarded these women with antagonism. Medical mediums, nonetheless, were not necessarily hostile toward the medical profession. Medical mediums were well represented among the first women in America to be trained in the medical profession when the sex barrier was broken.

Mental Mediumship. The sensitivity of the medium's spirit body to things in the Spirit World enables these mediums' spirit eyes and spirit ears to see and hear things clairvoyantly. Through clairaudience, music from the Spirit World is heard, and through clairsentience, a spirit may be sensed as it approaches the medium's aura. All the powers are through the mediums' abilities to be attuned to "vibrations from the Spirit World."

Normal Mediumship. During the 1850s and 1860s, male mediums presided over small meetings and gatherings that could easily reach into the thousands, and the men traveled the lecture circuit addressing their audiences in "normal" states outside the trance states. In normal speaking, they expressed their beliefs about Spiritualism as well as about a wide

Continued on next page

Mediums and Mediumship (cont.)

range of reform causes. They reflected the American social values of the time, which assumed men were *conscious* on the stage while women had to be *unconscious* in trance states to address audiences. However, many female trance mediums did become active in reform movements, learning to employ their "normal" voices on the reform platform.

Physical Mediumship. The theory behind the physical phenomena demonstrated by mediums is that the spirits work though the physical as well as the mental energies of the mediums. Physical mediumship can be demonstrated in phenomena such as spirit rappings, table tipping, slate writings on chalk boards (also called independent writing), direct voice sounds, flashes or balls of light, the materialization and dematerialization of objects, levitation, transfiguration (the medium's face or form is transformed into that of the controlling spirit), spirit photography, spirit painting, spirit cabinets, spirit music, and even the actual materialization of a spirit being. These phenomena take place apart from the body of the medium.

Physical mediumship made fraud easier to detect, causing some Spiritualist camps to ban its practice. A physical medium could have a private practice or work for crowds of hundreds and thousands. Not all physical mediums were involved in controversy or accused of deceit. Devoted mediums and Spiritualists consider physical phenomena as simply a starting point of belief and not a substitute for the knowledge that can be gained through spirit communication.

Trance medium. The trance mediums entered alternative states of consciousness wherein they had access to the spirits and their knowledge. They were viewed as oracles of spiritual truth, and the only test that could be applied to them was whether some of their messages were incorrect. Their explanations were that they were channels, with the messages still coming from human beings. Consequently, a certain amount of error was expected.

Test Medium. In physical mediumship, test conditions were often implemented to assure that the mediums were not creating the phenomena. These test mediums could be blindfolded, gagged, tied up, or locked inside cabinets while the spirit manifestations occurred around them. Test mediumship simplified proving deception.

Index